The Media in American Politics

Contents and Consequences

David L. Paletz
Duke University

LONGMAN

An imprint of Addison Wesley Longman, Inc.

New York • Reading, Massachusetts • Menlo Park, California • Harlow, England
Don Mills, Ontario • Sydney • Mexico City • Madrid • Amsterdam

Associate Editor	Jessica Bayne
Marketing Manager	Megan Galvin
Supplements Editor	Jennie Errickson
Project Coordination and Text Design	York Production Services
Cover Designer/Manager	Nancy Danahy
Cover Photos	PhotoDisc, Inc.
Photo Researcher	Mira Schachne
Full Service Production Manager	Richard Ausburn
Senior Print Buyer	Hugh Crawford
Electronic Page Makeup	York Production Services
Printer and Binder	The Maple-Vail Book Manufacturing Group
Cover Printer	Coral Graphic Services, Inc.

Library of Congress Cataloging-in-Publication Data

Paletz, David L., 1934-
    The media in American politics: contents and consequences/David L. Paletz
        p.   cm.
    Includes bibliographical references and index.
    ISBN 0-321-02991-7
    ISBN 0-321-04496-7
    1. Mass media—Political aspects.   2. United States—Politics and government—20th century.
    I. Title.
    HE8689.7.P6P35   1998
    302.23'0973—dc21
                                                                            98-35082
                                                                            CIP

Please visit our website at http://longman.awl.com

ISBN 0-321-02991-7 (paperback)

ISBN 0-321-04496-7 (case)

3 4 5 6 7 8 9 10 — MA— 0 1 0 0 9 9

For
Gabriel Michael Paletz
and
Susannah Batyah Felicity Paletz

Contents

Chapter 16   Conclusions and Change   330

Appendix A   Commentary   351

Appendix B   Movies on Congress   363

Preface

This book describes the mass media's political contents, and analyzes and explains the consequences they have for American democracy.

In so doing, it goes beyond textbooks on the subject in two ways. First, while covering all the usual subjects, it adds several topics, such as the media's depictions of gender and race, pornography, the police, and terrorism; plus the media's effects on public policy, and the repercussions of new technology on political life. Second, the book incorporates popular culture—humor, movies, music, and much more— making the study of media and politics releveant to student's lives.

The opening chapter introduces the subject, sets forth the book's themes, and presents the media's four types of political content. It then reports research on movies to show that specifying the meaning of this political content can be complex, and follows with an original study of political humor, illustrating how meaning can be extracted and likely consequences identified.

The rest of the first part of this book details the media. Chapter 2 on media modes covers advertising, television, radio, the music industry, newspapers, magazines, book publishing, and the movie business, as well as the issues of globalization and concentration. The third chapter is devoted to news, explaining how it is defined, gathered, selected, and presented. Chapter 4 describes the formal laws and regulations and the informal influences that restrain (and sometimes sustain) the media's freedom.

The second part of the book focuses on the consequences of the media's contents for the public. Differing in their backgrounds, socio-economic positions, and political interests, people respond in various ways to those contents. Thus, chapter 5 considers the research about how people receive and react to media material. Political socialization and public opinion are the subjects of the next two chapters, followed in chapter 8 by the media's depictions of and influences on political participation.

The book's third part deals with the consequences of media contents for the intermediary organizations and processes that link the public and government. This means interest groups and political parties in chapter 9; and campaigns and elections in chapter 10.

Government is the subject of the fourth part. It considers authority-holders' situations and techniques for dealing with the media and for trying to obtain favorable coverage. The chapters in this part focus sequentially on Congress and its members (chapter 11); the presidency (chapter 12); bureaucratic agencies, including the police and the military (chapter 13); and the judiciary (chapter 14). These analyses and accounts are followed by an attempt to specify the consequences of media contents for the policy-making process and public policies (chapter 15).

The final chapter summarizes the book's findings for American democracy and then examines how new technologies (whose uses are alluded to throughout the book) may be changing these consequences.

There are two appendices. The first discusses commentary, categorizing the voices and range of political opinion in the media. The second surveys movie depictions of Congress and its members.

Neither tome nor tract, the book contains ideas, arguments, even a few opinions. It includes and occasionally critiques research from academic journals, scholarly and popular books, and magazines. Identifying a cornucopia of research gaps and therefore possibilities, the book should stimulate research.

Without detracting from its scholarly mien, I have also aspired to make the book pleasurable to read, suffusing it with anecdotes, examples, cartoons, and photographs.

My ambivalent attitude toward the media is manifest in the book. I am a fervent moviegoer, avid skimmer of television fare, devoted listener to radio and music, devout reader of newspapers, peruser of magazines, and wedded to books. Some of my best friends are journalists or involved in making media content. I am particularly indebted to the *New York Times* (national edition) as a fount of information included herein. However, I often treat media material skeptically and am prone to analyze and dissect rather than accept it.

This book's intended audience consists of students in courses on political communication, media and politics, politicians and journalists, and related topics in departments of political science, sociology, communications, journalism, and speech in the United States and abroad. It could well be assigned in the introductory American government and politics courses whose texts underemphasize the media. The book should also appeal to scholars and teachers and to people who want to understand how the media interact with and influence the public, politics and government, and public policies.

Acknowledgments

My acknowledgments increase exponentially with age. Over the years, I have gathered, read, sometimes nurtured into print, and benefitted from the research and writing of an array of talented individuals from around the world. Many have favored me with their friendship. In addition to my co-editors on other books, Lance Bennett, Karol Jakubowicz, Pavao Novosel, and Alex Schmid, they include the ineffable Jay Blumler, Akiba Cohen, José-Luis Dader, Wolfgang Donsbach, Tatiana Galvan, Peter Gross, Barrie Gunter, Jim Halloran, Cees Hamelink, Ito Youichi, Karen Kedrowski, Hans Mathias Kepplinger, Chie-Woon Kim, Ildiko Kovats, James Lemert, Tamar Liebes, Philippe Maarek, Oleg Manaev, Paolo Mancini, Gianpietro Mazzoleni, Dennis McQuail, Annie Méar, Marian Meyers, Harvey Molotch, Ralph Negrine, Manuel Pares I Maicas, Javier Protzel, René-Jean Ravault, Gertrude J. Robinson, Susan Smith Reilly, Josep Rota, Robert Sahr, Victor Sampedro Blanco, Philip Schlesinger, Klaus Schoenbach, Jan Servaes, Colin Seymour-Ure, K. M. Shrivastava, Annabelle Sreberny-Mohammadi, Sermin Tekinalp, Oya Tokgoz, Teun van Dijk, Liesbet van Zoonen, France Vreg, and Gadi Wolfsfeld.

As the field of political communication flourishes, with its own journal, and sections in the American Political Science Association and in the International Communication Association, the contributions of U.S. researchers to this area ever grow in significance. We are all indebted to Bob Boynton, Dick Brody, Steven Chaffee, Bernard Cohen, Timothy Cook, Ann Crigler, Richard Davis, William Dorman, Herbert Gans, the duo of George Gerbner and Marsha Siefert who so ably edited the *Journal of Communication,* Todd Gitlin, Doris Graber, Dan Hallin, Rod Hart, Stephen Hess, Shanto Iyengar, Kathleen Hall Jamieson, Marion Just, Lynda Lee Kaid, Montague Kern, Sidney Kraus, our pioneers Gladys Engel Lang and Kurt Lang, Steven Livingston, John Maltese, Jarol Manheim, Maxwell McCombs, John Mueller, Diana Mutz, Russell Neuman, Patrick O'Heffernan, Diana Owen, Ben Page, Tom Patterson, the late Ithiel de Sola Pool, Michael Robinson, Everett Rogers, Holli Semetko, Bob Stevenson, Mary Stuckey, David Swanson, David Weaver, Darrell West, Cleveland Wilhoit, Lewis Wolfson, and John Zaller, to name just a few. This book's footnotes display my debt to these and many others scholars and researchers.

The Gannett-funded Freedom Forum Media Studies Center; the Joan Shorenstein Barone Center on the Press, Politics, and Public Policy at Harvard University, led by Marvin Kalb and Pippa Norris; the Twentieth-Century Fund, and the Markle Foundation have all at one time or another supported political communication research.

All researchers owe gratitude to the Vanderbilt Television Archive for preserving, compiling, and making available tapes of the television networks' evening newscasts and other programs. The Archive's costly and time-consuming work is indispensable. Similarly worthy is the Political Communication Archive housed at the University of Oklahoma. I also benefitted from receiving copies of their polls from CBS News/The New York Times and from the Pew Research Center for the People and the Press.

A semester researching and teaching at The Annenberg School for Communication at the University of Southern California immeasurably facilitated my thinking about the topics covered in this book. I am indebted to then-Dean Peter Clarke for inviting me, to his colleagues Sandra Ball-Rokeach, Bill Dutton, Janet Fulk and Peter Monge, Sheila Murphy, and Michael Noll, for conversation and hospitality; and to Sheila Braslau, Jean Campbell, Bill Darst, and Robert Wang for administrative, secretarial, and technical assistance way beyond the call of duty.

At Annenberg, I benefitted from three graduate students as my research assistants. Their work is reflected herein: Shari Erlichman on restraint (chapter 4); Deneen Nethercutt on public policy (chapter 15); and especially Jane Stokes on reception (chapter 5).

While in Los Angeles and thereafter, my life was enlivened by the ministrations and hospitality of special friends Larry Dietz, Karen Stabiner, and their Sarah Ivria, dear Billie Ruth Galef, Helene and Lou Galen, Selma Holo and Fred Croton, Carrie Menkel-Meadow and Bob Meadow (an Academy Award), and satirist Harry Shearer, without whose help there would be no cartoons from Matt Groening in the book.

Several Duke University undergraduates had the pleasure and pain of co-authoring publications or papers with me. They have almost all gone on to better things. Notable among them are John Ayanian, Robert Dunn, Martha Elson, Rocco Femia, Peter Fozzard, Susan Herbst, Dennis LaFiura, Barbara McIntyre, Peggy Reichert, John Short, Clay Steinman, Laura Tawney, Richard J. Vinegar, Donald Willis, and especially K. Kendall Guthrie and William H. Harris.

Other Duke students have also contributed to this book. Notable among them are storyteller Milbre Burch; crime novelist Taffy Cannon, who brought the Nixon envelope to my attention; Sony's Rob Cohen; Kathleen DeLaski, most recently of the Defense Department; my man in Tinseltown Karl Kurlander; Joanna Shelton, formerly at the State Department; Gail Slocum, sometime mayor of Menlo Park; journalist and biographer Susan Tifft; and CNN's Judy Woodruff.

Duke undergraduates Colin Brown, Christina Chou, the unbelievably industrious Catherine Jhee, Lauren Porcaro, Chris Pressley, and Tyler Thorson invaluably rounded up cartoons, strips, and photographs for possible inclusion in the book. The results of their work delight and instruct herein.

John Boiney and C. Danielle Vinson both served as invaluable graduate research assistants, in the process metamorphosing into co-authors and friends. I am also appreciative of the research assistance of Duke graduate students Dan Lipinski, John Ratliff, David Spence, Katina Stapleton, and Krista E. Wiegand.

It was my former student and subsequent colleague Robert Entman who first cajoled-convinced me to set down my ideas about political communication in book form. I cherish our jointly written work, *Media Power Politics* (Free Press, 1981), and in a few instances have drawn upon it for this volume.

This book was written during the humid summers, monsoon winters, and dulcet springs and autumns of Durham, North Carolina, the home of Duke University, where I have taught off and on since 1967. Appreciation is due to the students in my various media and politics courses for tolerating my abundant reading and writing requirements, stringent grading, and allegedly mercurial temperament. I particularly acknowledge those who responded to this book in manuscript and to my fall 1997 class, especially Kristen Bellstrom, who suggested the idea for the cover.

Thanks, too, to my colleagues in Political Science at Duke, particularly sometime chairmen John Aldrich, James David Barber (and Amanda Smith), Allan Kornberg, and Peter Lange, for tolerating my wayward ways, offbeat courses ("Politics and the Libido"), and idiosyncratic humor. A bow to Jay Hamilton, Ellen Mickiewicz, and Joel Smith, sharers of my passion for studying the media. Appreciation to the Duke University Research Council for occasionally providing modest but essential financial support for my research.

I give thanks once more to the Political Science department's ever-tolerant Lillian Fennell, helpful Susan Emery, buoyant Marisa Law, and considerate Juli Rowland. Appreciation and derring-do to Duke reference librarians Helene Bauman, Ken Berger, Margaret Brill, Laura Cousineau, Steve Cramer, Joline Ezzell, Rebecca Gomez, Ashley Jackson, Kelley Lawton, John Sharpe, Eric Smith, and Alice Tucker for successfully answering my arcane questions, most of the time. And to Susan Sauls of the library staff for determined book retrieval. Hail to

Duke's Bob Bliwise, John Burness, and Geoffrey Mock for convincing me by example that integrity and drollery can be compatible with public relations.

Others who have contributed to this book in ways they may not all have fully comprehended at the time are Bob and Everett Bacon; John Moriarty and Ed Canoy; Phyllis Greer; Ruth Murphy; Judith Olney; Dennis Patterson of the Associated Press's Raleigh, North Carolina, office; cartoonist Dennis Renault, founder of the Center for the Study of the Satirically Challenged; Debbie Selinsky and Melinda Stubbee of the Duke News Service; Taylor Sisk, who facilitated the search for cartoon reprint permissions; angel of mercy Shadra Smith; Nick Tanna of Morse Computers; and Carlene Ward of American Airlines.

My editor Lauren Silverman understandingly resolved my concerns and demands and persuaded me to sign the contract. Her successors—Maria Hartwell, the estimable Leo Wiegman, and Peter Glovin—displayed essential and almost unlimited patience. The heymish Mira Schachne diligently rounded up copyrights and permissions. Jennie Errickson was unfailingly responsive. Thanks too to Megan Galvin, Nancy Danahy, Kevin Bradley, and Lawrence Rosenthal.

Maudy Benz, Peter Clarke, Susan Evans, Marjorie Ferguson, Terry Pristin, Cassie Pyle, Deanna Robinson, and my lunch-mate Marianna De Marco Torgovnick all combine critical acumen and creative scholarship with friendship in remarkable and quite distinctive ways.

Gratitude (and sympathy) to Mary Kay Blakely, Adrienne Fox, and Helen Schwiesow for reading, commenting on, and correcting various chapters; and to Paula Grant for copyediting.

Thanks and acknowledgment for commenting on this work in manuscript, and thereby immensely improving the final version, to Tami Buhr, formerly of Harvard University; Stephen Frantzich of the U.S. Naval Academy; Michael G. Hagen of Harvard University; John C. Pitney, Jr. of Claremont McKenna College; Mary Stuckey of the University of Mississippi; Darrell West of Brown University.

Appreciation and affection to Ibby Nathans for invaluable and timely nurturence; Jack Nessel and Ginger Curwen for friendship, accommodation, and psychic drollery; Nancy Buirski and Ken Friedlein for helping with the title; Pepper Fluke and Monte Moses for making the Carolina Theater even more memorable to me and my family; Sue and John Leonard for support when most needed; the *ne plus ultra* Roberta Pearson; Eleanor Cartwright, my companion in sorrow; and Harry Rochlin. Long may they all prevail.

Sydney Nathans (abetted by Judith White) is the most treasured of friends; a sharer of sadness and joy, supportive in all things, a caring, guiding soul.

This book is dedicated to my children, occasional co-authors and researchers, Gabriel Michael Paletz and Susannah Batyah Felicity Paletz. In their individuality and style, by their accomplishments, and with their love, they remind me daily of their mother, Darcy, their grandmother, Hetty, and of the compensations and blessings that life can provide.

David L. Paletz

Part I
The Media

◆ ◆ ◆

Chapter 1

Introduction

◆ ◆ ◆

The media are indispensable to democracy, a political system predicated on the consent of the governed. To be meaningful and effective, that consent should be informed: based on truth, not falsehood; knowledge, not ignorance. As Thomas Jefferson wrote:

> The basis of our government being the opinion of the people, the very first object should be to keep that right; and were it left to me to decide whether we should have a government without newspapers or newspapers without a government, I should not hesitate a moment to prefer the latter.[1]

Note, however, that Jefferson appreciated the media significantly less as president than he did when making this statement.[2]

Ideally, the media should inform people about the issues confronting their society and the world and about the policy alternatives for trying to resolve those issues. Disseminating a wide range of views, the media should stimulate robust public discussion and political participation. They should inform the rulers about the beliefs and opinions, preferences, needs, and desires of the public. And they should assiduously report the relevant behavior, decisions and nondecisions, the actions and inactions, of those in power, thereby holding them accountable.[3]

The purpose of this book is to describe the media, analyze their contents, and explain the consequences they have for American democracy—its people, politics, government, and policies. In so doing, it will reveal the differences between the democratic ideal and actual media performance and explain why they occur.

This book is not, however, a jeremiad damning the American media for failing to live up to unrealistic, perhaps impossible, standards. Explanation and understanding are its intent, not condemnation.

APPROACH

In pursuing this intent, this book articulates and documents the following five themes. First, the media are pervasive, permeating American life. Second, their contents are rife with explicit and implicit political meaning, which, although often complex, can be identified. Third, people in public life deploy an arsenal of techniques to try to influence media contents in their interests.[4] Fourth, the successes and failures can be traced and explained. And fifth, media contents have significant and discernible effects on the public, politics, and government and its policies.[5]

In pursuing these themes, this book takes a broad perspective on politics. It covers people's socialization: how they acquire politically relevant values, beliefs, and knowledge, and how these are expressed as public opinion. It also encompasses the range of people's participation in politics (including terrorism), as well as the activities of the social movements and interest groups they join.

Special attention is devoted to elections, so vital for democracy, and to the panoply of techniques candidates use to promote themselves and to denigrate their opponents in the media.

Governmental institutions and the decisions and actions of public officials and their attempts to control or influence media contents are discussed in detail. For the book's ambit extends beyond the institutions of Congress, the presidency, and the judiciary to include governmental bureaucracy and such agencies as the police and military. It takes in governmental policy-making and policies, as well.

The view of media in this book is also generous. Media are defined as organizations of communication that take different forms, such as broadcasting and print, and create and transmit a vast array of content.[6] This definition goes way beyond the news, opinions, and commentary conventionally viewed as politically relevant content to embrace popular culture in all its aspects.

Consider postage stamps. They are not normally viewed as possessing political content.[7] Yet they display American symbols, most prominently the flag. They feature past presidents, George Washington above all, but also those recently deceased, such as Richard Nixon. They commemorate events in the nation's history; celebrate the American landscape and comic strips; extol individuals who have contributed to the national heritage, such as film comedians, and jazz greats. They promote such values as liberty, education, conservation, and the fight against such diseases as breast cancer and AIDS. As a consequence, they likely reinforce patriotism and legitimize the American political system (see photo on page 5).

Of course there are no stamps recording American public officials' embarrassing moments or depicting notorious villains or "evil" foreign leaders, such as Saddam Hussein.[8]

Political Contents in the Media

By including popular culture in our ambit, it becomes clear that the media express political content in four different, although occasionally overlapping, ways.

Explicit and Intentional Content   The most familiar political content is explicit and intentionally aimed at influencing people's political views and behavior. Clear examples are "get-out-the-vote" advertisements, candidates' debates, and a lot of commentary about politics and public affairs.

David Scull/NYT Pictures

© *Nicole Hollander*

Some popular culture also comes under this category. For example, the scripts for the widely seen and ever-popular teenage sitcom "Saved by the Bell" are submitted to a consultant working for NBC. She ensures that the scripts contain educational and informational content. About one script she wrote: "The message is voting gives you the power to have your voice represented in some of the most important decisions that will affect your life. This is the essence of democracy."

Explicit and Unintentional Content   The second type of political content in the media is explicit but not usually intended by its makers to influence the views or behavior of the audience. Much news is in this category. When journalists report that a politician is being investigated for unethical behavior, they are not consciously trying to diminish his or her reputation and support even though their story is liable to do just that. Of course, undermining the politician may be the intention of the sources who provide reporters with some of the information for the story, but their motive is not usually shared by the reporters. Humor explicitly about politicians and public affairs is also in this second category.

Implicit and Intentional Content   The third type of political content is implicit and intentional. It is mainly expressed in entertainment programs by depictions of the protagonists (individuals or groups), the values they espouse (e.g., liberty, equality, justice), their means of achieving these values (e.g., competition, negotiation, violence), and the resolution of the situation (e.g., love, wealth, survival). On "The Simpsons," Bart hates school and breaks its rules; Lisa fights gender stereotyping; and Grandpa demands his senior-citizen rights.

To what extent the makers of such shows intend to influence the audience is not always easy to ascertain or verify. Sherwood Schwarz may have been speaking tongue-in-cheek when he said that "Gilligan's Island" represented a "'socialistic community.'"[9] Nor was this socialism obvious to most of the show's many viewers.

Implicit and Unintentional Content   The fourth kind of media political content is implicit and any political effects are unintentional. "Wheel of Fortune" embodies individualism, capitalism, the consumer society, and wealth. But it is not intentionally designed to get people to espouse these values.

Complexity   For certain authors, it is clear and simple: The mass media propagate and perpetuate "images and themes that support militarism, imperialism, racism, sexism, authoritarianism, and other undemocratic values."[10]

What such attacks miss is the complexity of the media's political content. It is diverse even within one mode (e.g., movies) and certainly between modes (e.g., newspapers and music). It also changes over time.[11] Even the same character can appear in different incarnations: Batman was grim in 1940s' comic books, patriotic in 1940s' movie serials, campy in 1960s' television, and postmodernistically somber in the 1980s' comic art series and the 1989 blockbuster movie.[12]

One reason for the complexity of content is that mass culture can be polysemic; that is, contain a multiplicity of meanings.[13] The same content can also communicate contradictory messages: promoting consumer capitalism, but also reflecting social struggles and changes, conflict and upheaval.[14] Consider Beavis and Butt-head. Capitalizing on the characters' MTV popularity, their owners, the Viacom conglomerate, put them in a Paramount movie and in Simon & Schuster books. B and B mindlessly accept the political status quo, but they are also nihilists: At a high school assembly, Butt-head asks President Clinton why he doesn't "'invent some country and light it on fire.'"[15]

Political Contents in Movies

So, trying to specify the meaning of the media's political content can be daunting and treacherous. Understanding is further complicated by a dearth of research in some areas, a lack of convincing evidence in others, and contradictory arguments and findings.[16] These problems are graphically illustrated by the academic literature on the political contents of movies.[17]

Terry Christensen looked at some two hundred Hollywood movies with messages about politics and social problems. He concluded that even the most progressive "are suffused with conservative themes, mirroring and reinforcing traditional American values such as individual solutions to public problems, mistrust of politicians and of power, and faith that the political system works as it should."[18]

Another study was far more critical, contending that Hollywood films have historically displayed and therefore legitimated an ideology of "capitalism (with its values of competition, upward mobility, and the survival of the fittest), patriarchy (with its privileging of men and its positioning of women in a secondary social role), and racism."[19]

Complicating this kind of overall conclusion, depictions of American government and politics in Hollywood films have changed over time. After all, film-makers do not operate in a commercial and political void. Oversimplifying, one can find specific motifs highlighting different periods. It was one man who could make a difference in the 1930s (*Mr. Smith Goes to Washington, Gabriel Over the White House*); media-bred demagogues in the 1940s and 1950s (*All the King's Men, A Lion in the Streets*); and cold war paranoia in the 1960s, best exemplified by the audacious and riveting *The Manchurian Candidate*, which skewered Communists, anti-Communists, liberals, moderates, and conservatives alike. The 1970s and 1980s saw political murders and right wing conspiracies (*The Parallax View*); and the 1990s have brought untrustworthy, packaged political candidates (*Bob Roberts*).[20]

But scholars still differ about the meanings of the political contents of movies. Michael Ryan and Douglas Kellner assert that some popular Hollywood movies of the late 1960s and early 1970s registered the social issues and critical perspectives of the civil rights movement, feminism, the sexual revolution, antimilitarism, and environmentalism of the time. Thereafter, however, reflecting the failure of liberalism in the 1970s, "conservative themes, characters, and styles began to dominate Hollywood film once again."[21] They became predominant during the Reagan presidency of the 1980s.

In contrast, other researchers argue that the old, self-censoring, mainstream film industry has been replaced by a "new, more liberal, and decidedly antiestablishment Hollywood."[22] The members of this film-making elite express such perspectives in their movies: bureaucratic heartlessness in *E.T.*, military incompetence and dishonesty in *Rambo: First Blood, Part II*, and "the sinister complicity of government, the police, and business with organized crime in *The Godfather* movies."[23] Curiously, despite providing content analyses of numerous films, the authors of this quote offer no data about depictions of specifically political institutions. Nor do they explain the appearance of such films, as *Apollo 13*, which contradict their thesis.[24]

POLITICAL HUMOR

This discussion of movies shows that they are full of identifiable political content but that researchers do not always agree about its meaning. Acknowledging that meaning can be complex, this book is nonetheless based on the tenet that it can be plausibly elucidated.

The following study of political humor is provided to substantiate this view. Although it draws on the extant scholarly literature, much of the analysis is original, even speculative. For there is little research on humor's political consequences.[25]

Yet, humor is pervasive in life and in the media.[26] It is featured throughout this book in the form of cartoons and comic strips.[27]

Much humor is directly political. "'The Republican convention started this past weekend,'" said Jay Leno, "'so don't forget to turn your clocks back 400 years.'" About vice presidential candidate Jack Kemp, he observed: "'He's known . . . as a compassionate conservative. . . . That means he'll help an old lady across the street, but when she gets there, he'll cancel her Medicare.'" Not to be outdone, David Letterman pointed out that "'during the convention, the speeches are limited to 10 minutes, or 50 lies, whichever comes first.'"[28]

The Leno and Letterman jokes should be taken seriously not least because 40 percent of young American adults are supposed to take their information on politics from late-night television comedy.[29]

The jokes also reveal that political authority is a perpetual source of humor, offering abundant targets to laugh at and about. Witness the bumper sticker "Diapers and politicians need to be changed often—usually for the same reason." Some of the subjects are perennial: the foibles, self-importance, chicanery, corruption, scandals, and blunders of rulers; as well as their policies that may be inept from the start, or be made so through incompetent execution. All offer the opportunity for a raft of witticisms.[30]

Democracies, by their nature, would seem to invite humor publicly directed at their rulers. After all, elected authority-holders are chosen from the people and can expect, eventually, to be returned to them either by electoral defeat or because of term limits. Besides, in contrast to autocrats, whose vengeance can be swift and sure, rulers in democracies are usually unable summarily to punish the people who devise and direct humor at them. Most important in the United States is the tradition and practice of free speech famously asserted by the First Amendment to the U.S. Constitution.

The obvious question is whether this humor directed at authority-holders matters.[31] The conventional view takes its inspiration from Sigmund Freud in arguing that the expression of humor releases "the tensions of repressing the impulse to be aggressive."[32] It enables us to elude external and internal censors. This makes it particularly suitable for attacks on authority-holders, who are often otherwise protected against direct disparagement.

Sublimating aggression and relieving tension, humor is thus therapeutic for humorists and their audiences. Its effects on its targeted rulers, one surmises, would be to perpetuate their rule by dissipating the intensity with which they are

© Doug Marlette

opposed.[33] Even more beneficial to authority-wielders, it may be that viewing "something humorously is generally to cease to regard it as an enemy. . . . To laugh at someone in political humor is a step toward community with him."[34]

There is a contrary view: humor as anarchic and subversive because it heaps scorn and abuse on respected figures or cherished institutions, and does so in a way that, were it not presented as humor, would be unacceptable.[35] Surely, authority-holders who feel threatened by humor and contrive to repress it are simply being sensitive to their power stakes, to the vulnerability of their authority. For humor can enable people to confront authority, to diminish it, to reduce its distance and majesty, thereby revealing authority-holders as imperfect mortals, error-prone humans, ordinary people unworthy of special respect, deference, and continuation in office.

These arguments are not mutually exclusive. Humor ranges along a spectrum in its relationships with authority from supportive to subversive. In between, it can be benign or undermining.[36]

The approach taken in this book is to suggest some criteria for distinguishing and categorizing the different types of political humor and summarily apply them to the political humor of Bob Hope, Washington D.C.'s Gridiron dinner, Harry Shearer, and Lenny Bruce.

Criteria for Categorizing Political Humor

Humor directed against authority can range from supporting to subverting depending on its actual targets, focus, social acceptability, and presentation.

Targets   Political authority exists on five levels: the individual occupying an authority position; the policies that person espouses and promotes or takes responsibility for; the authority position itself (e.g., a particular congressional seat); the institution housing the position (e.g., the U.S. House of Representatives); and the political system as a whole, including its dominating ideas and assumptions (e.g., democracy and the notion that people possess the capacity for self-government). Individual politicians may not like it, but in democracies they are the most obvious target. As Joseph Boskin observes, the primary focus of political humor in America is "on the political official as the flaw in the system while the system itself and its underlying theory remain unexamined."[37]

Humor that attacks the political system itself usually includes other levels of authority. The results can be dramatic and drastic, generating system change.

Focus   The focus of political humor relates to the particular aspect or element of the authority level the humor emphasizes. In the case of individual authority-seekers or -holders, the foci are their appearances, foibles and proclivities, hollow rhetoric, crass pieties, and, much rarer, betrayal of principles.

Richard Nixon was a prime example. More than perhaps any other post-World War II political figure, he attracted the shafts of humorists: stand-up comics, cartoonists, television comedians, film-makers, and even other politicians.[38] Sometimes the humor focused on a physical characteristic, poking fun at his ski nose, jowls, or saturnine appearance. On occasion it highlighted his alleged lack of integrity and scruples: "'Nixon is the kind of politician who would cut down a redwood tree, then mount the stump for a speech on conservation.'"[39] Of Nixon's tendency to be less than truthful during the Watergate saga, television talk show host Johnny Carson observed that "'whenever anyone in the White House tells a lie, Nixon gets a royalty.'"[40]

Nixon was even the butt of humor after his death. Some wag designed an envelope so that when the Nixon postage stamp was placed on it, he appeared to be facing the viewer from behind prison bars.

Richard Nixon

USA
32

© Copyright The Santa Cruz Comic News 1995

The point is that some foci are more damaging, more devastating, than others.
Even at the level of individual authority, a focus can be debilitating. Similarly, the
focus of humor at a different level of authority will often do no more than echo
conventional complaints; for example, about the law's delay and the insolence of
office. Humor directed at stereotypes soothes, comforts, is usually benign.

But a new or unexpected focus can alert and challenge the audience, bringing to its members truths about authority that they might rather not know or actively avoid. Consider the illuminating insights Finley Peter Dunne offered in his newspaper column through his fictional creation Mr. Dooley: on the vice presidency, "'It isn't a crime exactly'"; and on the U.S. Supreme Court, it "'follows th' iliction returns.'"[41]

Ambrose Bierce in his *Devil's Dictionary* defined the vote as: "'The instrument and symbol of a freeman's power to make a fool of himself and a wreck of his country.'"[42] Having derided voting, Bierce went on to mock American politics as "'a strife of interests masquerading as a contest of principles. The conduct of public affairs for private advantage.'"[43]

Acceptability   With rare exceptions, the more acceptable a piece of humor, the less subversive it is. Conversely, daring and outrageous humor tends to be spurned, rejected, or just ignored.

Authority-holders themselves are particularly constrained. They can joke about their rivals, and certainly about themselves: Self-deprecating comments display their common humanity with the electorate and are especially appealing coming from such patrician-appearing presidents as Franklin D. Roosevelt and John F. Kennedy.[44]

Defeated politicians with no further ambition for office can reveal their wit freely. Appearing on the "David Letterman Show" after the 1996 presidential election, Bob Dole responded to the host's comment that Mr. Clinton was fat with, "'I never tried to lift him, I just tried to beat him.'" Dole noted that since he was heading for Florida, he would change his campaign slogan from "'A better man for a better America' to 'A better tan for a better America.'"[45]

But incumbent public officials are usually cautious. Uttering subversive witticisms would be polluting the political trough from which they feed. They also want to avoid antagonizing any sizable segment of the electorate.

For many politicians, this is no problem; they lack a sense of humor. Those endowed with one tend to resist temptation, but not always successfully. Ronald Reagan recited an ethnic joke during the 1980 primary election season. To wit: "How do you tell the Italians at a cockfight? They're the ones who bet on the duck. How do you know the Mafia's involved? The duck wins."

Reagan survived the gaffe, although not without arousing concern among his advisors. Indeed, in part because of his ability to joke under intense physical pain and duress (at least as reported by his aides and doctors), he seems to have made display of a ready wit an asset as long as it consists of noncontroversial observations confined to acceptable subjects.

Professional humorists are obviously less restricted. After all, comedy is their business. But even they have to reckon with the acceptability of their targets and foci. As just one example, the comedian Will Durst said on the "Letterman" show: "My idea of a joke is to give Hinckley a bigger gun." The remark, referring to the 1981 attempt on President Reagan's life by John W. Hinckley, is believed to have hurt Durst's career. It certainly curtailed his appearances on the show.

Something more seems to be at work here than choice of target and foci. It may have to do with humor as tension relief. Humor that is supportive of, or benign toward, authority can relieve tension in several ways: with a punch line, a reassuring conclusion, and, most commonly, through laughter. Subversive humor, on the other hand, frequently lacks resolution.[46] Or, worse for the audience's psychological security, it offers a conclusion that is widely believed to be both undesirable and painful—in the Durst example, the assassination of the incumbent American president—with the result that it often worsens the problem by failing to provoke the other mode of tension relief, laughter.

Presentation The final criterion helping determine the placement of humor along the authority-supporting, authority-subverting spectrum is the mode of presentation. This combines not only the medium (i.e., the setting in which the humor is presented) and the show's production values, but also the humorists' delivery and body language, the extent to which they communicate a sense of complicity with the audience, the amount of hostility they express, and how openly. These elements conduce to a presentation that is "slick" at one extreme, "raw" at the other. In general, "slick" is supportive of political authority, "raw" subverts it.

With the inevitable procrustean effects, the four criteria will now be applied to representative examples of humor directed at authority. These examples are suggestive rather than definitive and have been chosen from abundant possibilities.

Supportive Humor

The quintessential comedian of authority-supporting jokes has been Bob Hope. Throughout his long career on the stage, on radio, in films, and on television, Hope's targets were presidents' foibles and idiosyncrasies. The day after one of his performances, the president and Hope would play golf together, attesting to the inoffensiveness and acceptability of the humor. As Hillary Clinton affirmed on the last of his 284 television specials: "He can get away with the things he says because we all know he respects the presidency."[47]

When Hope's targets were other aspects of government, his choices were obvious, his focus on stereotypes. His opening monologue on one of his television specials is typical. "How about that marvelous flight of the space shuttle *Challenger!* Everything went well but there was a slight delay before the blast off: The astronauts forgot to pass through the metal detector." And, "Did you read where the astronauts' space suits cost $2 million each? When did NASA hire Gucci?"[48] The shuttle is celebrated, as are the astronauts themselves, who are also humanized but not demeaned by the metal detector reference. The foci of the comedian's remarks are the hardy perennials: bureaucratic procedures and waste.

Even when Hope turned to a different governmental institution, his target and focus were predictable: "Well, like everybody else I've paid my income taxes, and I'd like to congratulate our cameramen for their trick photography. You'd never know I'm not wearing a shirt; and the IRS took my pants too." Telling, here, is the assertion that this law-abiding and loyal citizen paid his taxes, followed by the highly optimistic claim that everybody else has done likewise. As to his avowal of penury, Hope was one of America's wealthiest men. On the very same comedy special he could be seen serving as the spokesman for Texaco in that company's commercials.

The Hope comedy special—with its roster of comedic notables (all of whom were either as supportive of authority as Hope or apolitical) with its expensive production costs, and with its use of state-of-the-art technology—was eminently slick. It was presented in a spirit of inoffensive fun.

Bob Hope was dedicated to an America whose economic and political systems served him well. His loyalty and commitment to his country were reflected in his numerous and celebrated trips to entertain American servicemen and -women abroad. He would not knowingly damage political authority in America. As he said during a television interview, "I never go deep, I just prick 'em a little; I never draw blood."[49]

Benign Humor

One of Washington, D.C.'s strangest events is the annual Gridiron dinner. Washington reporters and their bosses, editors, and publishers dine with and entertain, by dressing up in silly costumes and performing in satirical skits, the people in government and politics they write about the rest of the year.

At first impression, the Gridiron is a kind of love feast, or at least a mutual admiration society. The press jibes at political authority-holders and, in so doing, pokes fun at itself. Then, before the night is over, the public officials have their opportunity to respond. Their responses are sometimes quite droll. "Please withhold subpoenas until all the jokes are told," quipped President Clinton at one dinner. He later read a list of jokes allegedly approved by his lawyers, including: "Knock-knock: Don't answer that."[50]

The Gridiron dinner is not entirely supportive of political authority. The targets are individuals and policies, but the foci are diverse, ranging from the familiar to the arcane, the trivial to the vital. The ritualization of the event renders the humor acceptable, but it is not always appreciated let alone welcomed by its subjects in attendance. The presentation is an odd combination of slick and raw. The press performers are amateurish, the setting relatively makeshift. On the other hand, the white-tie event is prestigious; the president, vice president, their spouses, several U.S. Supreme Court justices, congressional leaders, governors, and diplomats attend.

So, the Gridiron dinner is benign rather than supportive. What this means in terms of its relationship to political authority is best summed up in the words of the Gridiron president welcoming President Reagan: "'We think you . . . know, as we do, that it is a precious thing that we can kid each other and have good fun together.'"

Undermining Humor

Writer, actor, and director Harry Shearer is perhaps most recognized for his performance in the fake rockumentary film *This Is Spinal Tap*. But it is his long-running program on National Public Radio, "Le Show," that best expresses his satire.[51]

During the Reagan presidency, it featured a segment entitled "Hellcats of the White House." This segment purported—as the sonorously voiced announcer intoned to the accompaniment of triumphal music—to present tapes from "the Holmes Tuttle Collection, the West's Leading Active Archive of Historic Storylines." These tapes, we were told, contained "tales of action, adventure, and romance in our nation's executive mansion."[52]

What listeners heard were the apparent voices of President Reagan, his trusted aides, his wife, and an occasional show business hack, as they went about their affairs at the White House, on *Air Force One,* at the president's ranch, and abroad. An aide tells the president of his forthcoming speaking assignments. The president reads the list: "SDI Forum," "Citizens for a Drug-Free Nicaragua," "Americans United for Mining in National Parks." In another episode, the president speaks to the nation following his return from the Geneva summit. Addressing the issue of disarmament negotiations with the Soviet Union, he comments:

> We'll be doing our utmost to convince them to trust us when we say that we would never use our strategic defense initiative to launch a first strike against them. But we'll also be underlining our concern for sound verification procedures for any agreement we do reach. Because, unfortunately, we can't trust the Russians even if they would trust us. If there's one game show the Russians could never be on, it's "To Tell the Truth."

In fact, the entire show is Shearer's invention and creation. He writes the script to represent and reflect the president's activities of the past week. An extraordinary mimic, he does all the voices, capturing timbre, breathing, intonation, pauses, and speed.

This humor undermines political authority. Certainly President Reagan was an unexceptional target. Moreover, the focus appeared to be conventional: the president's unself-conscious capacity for (public) self-delusion. The mimicry implied a certain grudging respect, almost affection, for the president. But Shearer went beyond the obvious alleged sins of the incumbent to far more disturbing aspects of the presidency: the vagaries of the president's decision-making process, the internecine power struggles among his aides, the endemic media manipulation, and the contradiction (some might call it a chasm after listening to Shearer's programs) between the behind-the-scenes reality of the behavior of the denizens of the White House and the sanitized (dry cleaned) version provided to the public.

The two other criteria (presentation and acceptability) also contribute to the authority-undermining quality of Shearer's work. The presentation and use of technology are sophisticated, but essentially Shearer is a one-man operation, relying on his ingenuity and extensive radio experience to compensate for a meager budget. Since it is broadcast on radio, Shearer's show has some acceptability, but it airs on Sunday mornings from a public radio station in Southern California. Moreover, in the examples of Shearer's humor directed at President Reagan discussed in this section, rather than appealing to the mass audience by reducing tension, Shearer's humor increased tension through its open-ended format, by having the protagonists ask questions that were never answered, and by ending with a series of soap operatic suspenseful questions from the announcer. Like messy life, nothing was resolved; the saga continued on for week after week.

Understanding "Hellcats," moreover, required a certain familiarity with Ronald Reagan's past: Holmes Tuttle was the name of a Ford automobile dealer in Los Angeles who helped bankroll Reagan's political career; *Hellcats of the Navy* was a film in which the future president appeared with his future wife, Nancy. Appreciation of the program's humor was also enhanced by knowledge of recent national events.

So, although its following keeps growing, the show remains for the cognoscenti in comparison to the audience for the Bob Hope special.

Subversive Humor

Lenny Bruce died in 1965. During the last years of his life, he was beset by the law enforcement, legal, and judicial systems. He was arrested on three occasions for obscenity. The verdicts were, respectively: innocent; guilty but reversed on appeal; and guilty, affirmed on appeal.[53]

In August 1965, a few days before his death, Bruce appeared in a nightclub in San Francisco, one of the few cities in which he could legally perform without being subject to arrest and where his performance would not incur the wrath of local public officials, including prosecuting attorneys and the police. His work that night was filmed in 16 mm and, under the title *Lenny Bruce Performance Film,* offers a rare glimpse of the untrammeled, albeit somewhat weary, Bruce doing his act.

With the transcript of his most recent obscenity trial close at hand, sometimes in his hand, he contrasts and compares his actual nightclub performance with the version of it reported by the police for which he was indicted by the grand jury and found guilty by the judge. Bruce's litany of complaints about the "peace officer's" inadequate and thoroughly misleading version of his act is dismaying, convincing, and funny in a gallows-humor way. Bruce points out that he had to go to court not to vindicate his act as it really was, but to defend the policeman's misbegotten version of it.

He then chronicles, with increasing ferocity and despair, his frustrating clashes with the legal system. A typical example is his encounter with Federal Appeals Court Judge Thurgood Marshall, an African-American whom President Lyndon B. Johnson would later elevate to the U.S. Supreme Court:

> So Thurgood Marshall says to me, "What are you doing here? You didn't exhaust your remedies in state court." So he's a Negro. I figure I'll grab him and he will understand my problems in the state court. I said, "What's it like is I'm a Negro in Alabama [during segregation] and I'm looking to use the toilet and by the time I get the relief it's going to be too late." He says, "You're no Nigger." I say, "It's an analogy." Appeal denied.

For Bruce, Marshall represented an American judicial system that—through its structure, processes, and personnel—is uncaring, incompetent, and unjust. Thus, by his worn physical presence, by recounting what actually happened to him, and through the content of his act, Bruce destroys illusions about American justice. He dissects it by showing how it dissected him.

Bruce's presentation was raw: He was wont to introduce his act with the phrase: "Dirty Lenny is going on soon." His language was uninhibited, employing notorious four-letter words. This enabled him to reveal a prurient malevolence within authority, to portray the wielders of authority as con men, but it significantly reduced the acceptability of his humor. His act was eventually limited to a few nightclubs and concert appearances, although a much larger audience was to emerge after his death.

Combine these facts with the relatively high authority level of Bruce's targets, his disturbing foci, and the way his humorous bits usually exacerbated tension in the audience by their lack of satisfactory resolution. Lenny Bruce becomes, then, the quintessential authority-subverting comedian.

This discussion has neglected the performance forum. For example, different forums are variously hospitable or hostile to subversive humor, with nightclubs, advertiser-free (*Mad*) or desk-top published magazines (*Hillary Clinton Quarterly, The Flush Rush Quarterly, Slick Times*) at one extreme and, at least in the United States, network television at the other. Commercial concerns, allied to formal, informal, and self-censorship, serve to limit the availability of corrosive political humor in the mass media. As a CBS television network censor pronounced: "'It's ok to satirize the President, as long as you do so with respect.'"[54] The main exceptions were some of the shows on the cable channel Comedy Central, particularly its instant comedy analysis of live events, such as the parties' National Conventions, presidential inaugurations and State-of-the-Union messages.

Forums are also intimately related to changes in comedians' targets and foci. Richard Pryor is one example. His early nightclub monologues ("diatribes" is a more accurate word) were bitter excoriations of American life, politics, and race relations. Speaking in 1971 of the Reverend Martin Luther King, Jr., he said: "I been to the mountaintop too, and what did I see? Mo' white folks with guns." Later on, as he graduated from seedy nightclubs to video specials to feature films, he mellowed into tolerance, although always retaining a critical edge.[55]

But times and attitudes change. So-called dirty words are an example. They still may not frequent most daily newspapers or be bandied about on radio and network television, but they are staples in many humorists' lexicons, including those who eschew politics in their acts. Most authority-holders are no longer enraged enough to threaten or undertake punitive action against the users of "dirty words."[56] "'Words that Lenny Bruce got arrested for in 1962 you can see being said by women on the big screen.'"[57]

The middle-to-late 1990s have seen more outspoken political humor in the mainstream media. The appealingly (or appallingly) irreverent "Politically Incorrect" has moved from Comedy Central to late night on the ABC network. On NBC's "Saturday Night Live," the fake news "Weekend Update" has gotten away with the kind of statement so damaging to Will Durst: saying about a possible pardon for alleged Whitewater co-conspirators, "Clinton may pardon them if they can't be killed."

Above all, there is shock-jock humorist Don Imus. His political commentary is scathing, his parodies deflating; and he makes merciless fun of his guests. Yet politicians flock to be on his radio show, attracted by its huge audience consisting mostly of white males aged between twenty-five and forty.

Imus was even invited to be the main speaker at the Radio and Television Correspondents' annual dinner attended by the Clintons.[58] There, he lambasted those attending with "in your face" humor. Much of it focused on their appearances, but some was more substantial. The president was referred to as "a pot-smoking weasel" and as sexually obsessed; and the first lady as possessing criminal tendencies. Other Washington politicians and their families were tarred as hypocrites and opportunists. Clinton's cabinet was described as "like the bar scene out of *Star Wars.*" News anchors, correspondents, commentators, and pundits were portrayed as egocentric, vacuous, and violence-prone.

To its regret, the White House had approved the invitation. Indeed, Imus had run many of the jokes about the president past a Clinton advisor, who convinced him to remove or tame down some of the material (e.g., that the president could combat womanizing charges by becoming a Mormon and having several wives).

The speech aroused predictable outrage. Cokie Roberts of ABC News and National Public Radio said, "'You can't [meaning shouldn't] make fun of the President in that manner when he is sitting right there.'"[59] The chairman of the Correspondents' Association wrote a letter of apology to the Clintons. The president's press secretary sought unavailingly to persuade C-SPAN not to rebroadcast the speech.

Showing how much times have changed, Imus benefitted rather than suffered for his appearance. His radio program picked up more stations and began to be simulcasted on the cable channel MSNBC.

CONCLUSION

This chapter has laid out the purpose of this book as describing the media, analyzing their contents, and explaining their consequences for the American people, politics and government, and democracy.

It specified the book's five themes: the media are pervasive; their contents are rife with detectable political meaning; people involved in public life have developed an armory of weapons to try to influence media contents in their interests; their successes and failures can be documented and explained; and media contents have widespread, significant, and discernible political effects.

After defining politics and the media broadly, the chapter identified four types of political content in the media. It used research on movies to show the complexity of specifying the meaning of political content. It followed this with an original study of political humor, illustrating how content can be dissected, meaning extracted, and likely consequences identified.

Notes

1. Jefferson, Letter to Edward Carrington, 16 January 1787, *The Writings of Thomas Jefferson*, ed. Paul Leicester Ford (New York: G. P. Putnam's Sons, 1894), 359–60.

2. This was pointed out to me by Professor Mary Stuckey.

3. See Michael Gurevitch and Jay G. Blumler, "Political Communication Systems and Democratic Values," in *Democracy and the Mass Media*, ed. Judith Lichtenberg (Cambridge: Cambridge University Press, 1990), 270, for a set of eight normative standards for appraising mass-media systems in democratic societies; also relevant is their *The Crisis of Public Communication* (London: Routledge, 1995).

4. Documented by Jarol B. Manheim in *All of the People All the Time* (Armonk, N.Y.: M. E. Sharpe, 1991).

5. John Zaller, "The Myth of Massive Media Impact Revisited," in *Political Persuasion and Attitude Change,* ed. Diana C. Mutz, Paul M. Sniderman, and Richard A. Brody (Ann Arbor: University of Michigan Press, 1996), 17–78.

6. See David L. Altheide and Robert P. Snow, *Media World in the Postjournalism Era* (New York: Aldine de Gruyter, 1991), for the argument that media forms and formats can determine, even become, content.

7. Appreciation and acknowledgment to Cathy Collins and Beth Cohen for their 1983 paper "Are You Getting Your Twenty Cents Worth?" written for my undergraduate "Media and Politics" course at Duke University. It provided historical and content analysis data, and furthered my thoughts about the politics of postage stamps.

8. For the stamp selection process, see *Domestic Mail Manual,* vol. 47 (Pittsburgh, Pa.: Government Printing Office, 10 April 1994), sec. G900, subsec. 1.2, p. G–21.

9. Cited in Darrell Y. Hamamoto, *Nervous Laughter* (New York: Praeger, 1989), 81–82.

10. E.g., Michael Parenti, *Make-Believe Media* (New York: St. Martin's Press, 1992), vii.

11. For changes in television content, see Ella Taylor, *Prime-Time Families* (Berkeley: University of California Press, 1989).

12. Roberta E. Pearson and William Uricchio, eds., *The Many Lives of Batman* (New York: Routledge, 1991).

13. John Fiske, *Television Culture* (London: Routledge, 1987), 84. Also relevant are Elayne Rapping, *The Movie of the Week* (Minneapolis: University of Minnesota Press, 1992); Peter Stead, *Film and the Working Class* (New York: Routledge, 1989); and John Tulloch, *Television Drama* (New York: Routledge, 1990).

14. Douglas Kellner, *Television and the Crisis of Democracy* (Boulder, Colo.: Westview, 1990).

15. Quoted in Elizabeth Kolbert, "Keeping Beavis and Butt-head Just Stupid Enough," *New York Times,* 17 November 1993, H44.

16. For a thoughtful collection, see Mary E. Stuckey, ed., *The Theory and Practice of Political Communication Research* (Albany: State University of New York Press, 1996).

17. Brian Neve, *Film and Politics in America* (New York: Routledge, 1992). For additional background, see James Combs, *American Political Movies: A Filmography* (New York: Garland, 1992); James Combs, ed., *Movies and Politics* (New York: Garland, 1993); and James E. Combs and Sara T. Combs, *Film Propaganda and American Politics* (New York: Garland, 1994). For an original approach, see Jonathan Rosenbaum, *Movies as Politics* (Berkeley: University of California Press, 1997).

18. Terry Christensen, *Reel Politics* (New York: Basil Blackwell, 1987), cover. For a potted, international history, see Leif Furhammar and Folke Isaksson, *Politics and Film,* trans. Kersti French (New York: Praeger, 1971).

19. Summarized by Michael Ryan and Douglas Kellner in *Camera Politica* (Bloomington: Indiana University Press, 1988), 1.

20. Jim Koch, "Hollywood on the Potomac," *New York Times,* 25 October 1992, H29.

21. Ryan and Kellner, *Camera Politica,* 9.

22. Stephen Powers, David J. Rothman, and Stanley Rothman, "Hollywood History and the Politics of Motion Pictures," in *The Mass Media in Liberal Democratic Societies,* ed. Stanley Rothman (New York: Paragon House, 1992), 270. This argument is extensively elaborated in their *Hollywood's America* (Boulder, Colo.: Westview, 1996).

23. Powers et al., "Hollywood History and the Politics of Motion Pictures," 298.

24. For these two criticisms, see Richard M. Merelman's review in the *American Political Science Review* 91:3 (September 1997): 753–54.

25. This discussion is based on my "Political Humor and Authority: From Support to Subversion," *International Political Science Review* 11:4 (October 1990): 483–93, an article written with assistance from Mike Adlin and Gabriel Michael Paletz. This material is used here with permission of Sage Publications Ltd.

26. Paul E. McGhee, *Humor: Its Origin and Development* (San Francisco: W. H. Freeman, 1979); and Jeffrey H. Goldstein and Paul E. McGhee, eds., *The Psychology of Humor* (New York: Academic Press, 1992). For a synthesis of theories of humor, see Murray S. Davis, *What's So Funny?* (Chicago: University of Chicago Press, 1993).

27. On the history of American political cartoons, see Stephen Hess and Milton Kaplan, *The Ungentlemanly Art* (New York: Macmillan, 1968).

28. All quoted in Caryn James, "Coverage That's Most Unconventional," *New York Times,* 15 August 1996, A14.

29. Farai Chideya, "Tune Out, Turn Off, Zone Out?" *Time,* 21 October 1996, 64.

30. For a droll collection of political jokes, see Itzhak Galnoor and Steven Lukes, *No Laughing Matter* (London: Routledge & Kegan Paul, 1985).

31. For a play portraying the political effects of different types of humor, see Trevor Griffiths, *Comedians* (New York: Grove Press, 1976); see also the interview with him, "Transforming the Husk of Capitalism," *Theatre Quarterly (TQ),* 6:22 (Summer 1976): 25–46.

32. Sigmund Freud, *Jokes and Their Relation to the Unconscious* (New York: Norton, 1960, first published in German in 1905). The quote comes from Charles E. Schutz, *Political Humor* (Rutherford, N.J.: Fairleigh Dickinson University Press, 1977), 31.

33. Gregor Benton, "The Origins of the Political Joke," in *Humor in Society,* ed. Chris Powell and George E. C. Paton (New York: St. Martin's Press, 1988), 33, 54.

34. Schutz, *Political Humor,* 331.

35. George E. C. Paton, "The Comedian as Portrayer of Social Morality," in *Humor in Society,* ed. Chris Powell and George E. C. Paton (New York: St. Martin's Press, 1988), 207–08.

36. For an illuminating discussion of the difference between conservative and subversive humor, see Ronald G. Webb, "Political Uses of Humor," *ETC* 38:1 (Spring 1981): 35–50.

37. Joseph Boskin, "American Political Humor: Touchables and Taboos," *International Political Science Review* 11:4 (October 1990): 473.

38. Stephen J. Whitfield, "Richard Nixon as a Comic Figure," *American Quarterly* 37:1 (Spring 1985): 114–32.

39. Adlai Stevenson, quoted in Arthur Power Dudden, ed., *American Humor* (New York: Oxford University Press, 1987), 153.

40. Quoted in ibid., 153.

41. Finley Peter Dunne, *Mr. Dooley on Ivrything and Ivrybody,* selected and introduced by Robert Hutchinson (New York: Dover, 1963), 160, 216.

42. Quoted in Schutz, *Political Humor,* 287.

43. Quoted in Dudden, *American Humor,* 58.

44. On the power of presidential humor, see Gerald C. Gardner, *All the Presidents' Wits* (New York: Morrow, 1986).

45. Both quotes are from Katharine Q. Seelye, "Dole Gets a Few Laughs, and $200, on a Talk Show," *New York Times,* 9 November 1996, 10Y.

46. See Glenn D. Wilson, "Ideology and Humor Preferences," *International Political Science Review* 11:4 (October 1990): 461, for the finding that "conservatives were intolerant of jokes that failed to provide resolution of incongruous elements."

47. *Bob Hope . . . Laughing With the Presidents',* NBC, 23 November, 1996.

48. *Comedy Special,* NBC, 20 April 1983.

49. "CBS Morning Show," 15 January 1987.

50. Taking His Knocks, Clinton Delivers a Knock-Knock," *New York Times,* 22 March 1998, A1 1.

51. For background, see Andy Meisler, "He'd Rather Satirize a Star Than Be One," *New York Times,* 6 March 1994, H39, H42.

52. All quotes are from tapes provided by Shearer, copyrighted by Century of Progress Productions.

53. See Albert Goldman's book, based on the journalism of Lawrence Schiller, *Ladies and Gentlemen Lenny Bruce!!* (New York: Ballantine Books, 1974), for the details of Bruce's life and a meditation on the meaning of his career.

54. Quoted in Doug Hill and Jeff Weingrad, *Saturday Night* (New York: Vintage Books, 1987), 22.

55. On African-American humor, see Mel Watkins, *On the Real Side* (New York: Simon & Schuster, 1994).

56. On the issue of such words as threats to authority, see David L. Paletz and William F. Harris, "Four-Letter Threats to Authority," *Journal of Politics* 37:4 (November 1975): 955–79.

57. Paul Krassner, quoted in Casey McCabe, "Beyond Stupid Pet Tricks," *Mother Jones* 11:5 (July–August 1986), 18.

58. I have drawn on Paul McCreath's paper, "The Don Imus Address to the 1996 Radio-Television Correspondents Association Dinner" (written for my "Politics and Media" seminar, November 1996).

59. Cited in Dusty Saunders, "Good Taste in Broadcasting Appears to be Taking a Vacation," *Rocky Mountain News,* 26 March 1996, 8D.

Chapter 2

Media Modes

◆　◆　◆

This chapter provides basic information about the mass media.[1] Its purpose is to identify and discuss the factors that determine their contents (aside from news). Thus, as applicable, it covers the media's organization, ownership, funding, and processes of production, distribution, promotion, and sales.

Advertising is discussed first because it is the significant source of most media's funding and contents. The broadcasting industries of television and radio and the related music business are next. The print businesses of newspapers, magazines, and books follow. Because the output of the film industry (like the book publishing industry) is not *overtly* funded by advertising, it is treated last.

This chapter includes brief suggestive discussions of the political contents and consequences of product advertising, music, and books, not covered elsewhere in the book. It concludes with the fundamental issues of globalization and concentration.

ADVERTISING

Most television and radio stations, newspapers, and magazines rely on advertisements to stay profitably in existence. No wonder advertising is a multibillion-dollars-a-year business.

Despite the consolidation of several large agencies into global superagencies which threaten to dominate the industry, advertising companies are relatively easy to form and are highly competitive. The advertising industry unites, sometimes uneasily, three main parties: sponsors, advertising agencies, and media sales personnel.

Major advertising sponsors are the long-distance telephone companies, food and patent-medicine firms, automobile manufacturers, airlines, tobacco companies, and department stores. Their ads are designed to sell specific products or services and/or to promote the image of the sponsoring corporation or institution.

Sponsors often desire more than (simply!) increasing sales. Toshiba, for example, wanted advertising to establish it "as the preeminent manufacturer of portable computers, and in the process, convince customers that the desktop computer was a dinosaur, and the laptop, the full-service computer of the future."[2]

Sponsors hire advertising agencies and their three types of personnel: creative developers of the ads; planners responsible for strategy, market research, and media placement; and account managers who link client and agency. The sponsor-agency relationship is often, "either an active flirtation or a soured romance."[3]

Production and Placement

Karen Stabiner spent a year observing at Chiat/Day, one of the most innovative agencies (devisers of the Energizer Bunny). She found that because many goods are no different from those of the competition, "the foundation of an ad was often nothing more than an imaginary distinction. . . . It was incumbent upon the advertising agency to skew the consumer's perception, to communicate an advantage that was based on style, not content."[4] Advertising agencies use "focus groups, telephone tracking studies, demographic and psychographic research, creative teams and media experts to bend public loyalty toward the client's brand."[5] This entails, in John Updike's words, "the search for the arresting phrase and image, on the edge of the indecent, that incites people to buy—that gives them permission from the mythic world of fabricated symbols, to spend."[6] Thus, many advertisements make untestable, even unjustifiable, claims and may well mislead, if not deceive, members of their audience.[7]

Millions of dollars are spent to devise and produce advertising, as chronicled in Michael Arlen's drolly deadpan account of the meticulous making of just one television commercial, albeit with five situations and ten scenes, for AT&T's "Reach Out" campaign. It employed a roster of participants from the client and advertising agency, and a panoply of songwriters, performers, film-crew members, stylists, actors, editors, and others.[8]

The largest share of advertising expenditure (about 25 percent) goes to newspapers, closely followed in decreasing percentages by television, then direct mail, radio, magazines, and outdoor ads.

The criteria for placing ads are the size of the audience (*reach*); how often the ad will be received (*frequency*); whether the medium reaches potential customers (*selectivity*); and the costs to reach a specific number of people (*efficiency*).[9] The objective is to expose the ads to the desired number and demographics of the audience, segments based on age, gender, income, and race. And to do so often, on the assumption that repeating the same claim in an ad and repeating the ad will imprint the message on people's consciousness (and unconsciousness).

For fear of offending consumers, most advertisers avoid associating their products with provocative programs or controversial modes of behavior (see the "Television" section later in this chapter for examples). Some also try to influence nonadvertising media content, often news, by threatening to or actually withdrawing ads. They may also engage in censorship and corruption of the editorial process. Censorship can be direct, dictating what people shall or shall

not hear; or it can be indirect, with someone in the media hushing or distorting a story to placate an advertiser without actually being asked to do so. Corruption of the editorial process also occurs when a commercial is disguised as a news story.[10]

Some programs consist entirely of advertisements. Many programs shown on Music Television (MTV) are obvious examples, although not so obvious to many viewers. But the most flagrant instance is the billion-dollars-a-year business of televised "infomercials."[11] Often guised as talk shows or news reports, these programs are lengthy sales pitches for psychics, make-over makeup, car polish, juicers, and exercise machines; and for tapes and books that will give you "personal power," make you rich through real estate, enable you to diet easily, and transform your relationship. The pitches are accompanied, variously, by a rapturous, applauding audience, featuring (has-been) celebrities, before-and-after split-screen transformations, personal testimonials, and, almost invariably, a money-back guarantee.

A handful of companies produce the most prominent infomercials, make them available by satellite twenty-four hours a day, and pay television stations a fee, sometimes quite high, to show them, usually late at night, early in the morning, and on weekends.

Political Contents and Consequences

Naturally, advertisers are disinclined to sponsor content that is critical of corporations and capitalism. Moreover, because advertising benefits from being associated with media content designed to encourage a buying mood, it tends to support and perpetuate homogeneous upbeat material.[12]

Advertisements tend to portray an idealized world, particularly on television. They depict romance, friendship, supportive (often family) relationships that involve relatively attractive, usually youngish, happy, basically healthy people. The primary problems presented are personal (e.g., bad breath, colds, dandruff, headaches, hemorrhoids) and the need for clean bathrooms, dishes, floors, kitchens, and people.[13]

For some observers, therefore, advertising is seen as a purveyor of false messages and empty values. Its political impact is to "repetitively suggest that social and personal problems are best solved through the purchase of consumer goods or services."[14] When it presents nonconformity and rebellion, advertising is accused of channelling them into acquiring the sponsors' products.[15] It thereby neutralizes alternative ways of thinking about the world and political and social issues.

Katherine Hale and Michael Mansfield go further, contending that advertising trivializes politics. It reduces conflict to differing preferences and choosing among products. The social contract and civility are associated with a four-wheel drive. Advertising's trivialization of politics "encourages divisiveness and disunity through its failure to treat conflict and its resolution seriously."[16]

Commercial advertisements wield societal and political influence through the products they sell, the corporate images they promote, and the values and beliefs they embody.[17] But advertising comes in other noncommercial forms that try to influence politics directly. These forms will be discussed in subsequent chapters: public service advertisements (chapter 8), ads advocating policy positions (chapter 9), and candidates' commercials (chapter 10).

TELEVISION

There are approximately 1,160 commercial (advertising-based) television stations scattered across the United States.[18] About 85 percent are affiliated with one or other of the networks, which provide the bulk of their programming. The main networks are ABC, CBS, and NBC, plus the rapidly catching up Fox Broadcasting. These networks also own and operate very profitable stations in the largest markets.[19] Paramount and Warner Brothers are newly developing networks created to exhibit programs their owners produce.

In Section 307(b) of the Communications Act of 1934, Congress established the Federal Communications Commission (FCC) to serve and protect "the public convenience, interest, or necessity" in licensing radio, and later television, stations.

Depending on the political views of its members, the FCC has tried to pursue this objective in two ways, with more or less enthusiasm at various times. First is through localism, by requiring stations to be responsive to their local communities. Second is through encouraging diversity, by preventing control of broadcasting by a few entities and encouraging minority and small business ownership.[20]

The FCC has justified its actions on the basis of spectrum scarcity. The advent of cable would appear to weaken if not obviate this argument, and the commission has essentially permitted consolidation of ownership interests by media conglomerates by permitting a company to own all the stations it wants to own as long as those stations do not reach more than 35 percent of all American households.[21]

Advertisements

The cost of advertising on television ranges from over one million dollars for thirty seconds for the Super Bowl's national audience to a few dollars to reach local viewers on a cable channel.

Most advertisers shun controversial content. For example, predictably absent from the "coming out" episode of "Ellen" were the "fast-food, beverage and car advertisements which usually fill prime time."[22] Some companies are conspicuously wary: Kraft General Foods kept its commercials out of "Roseanne" when the eponymous star was kissed by an actress portraying a lesbian, from an episode of the show dealing with masturbation, and out of a "Law and Order" show involving racism.[23]

Sometimes advertisers are in a bind. Especially during daytime, most rely for their programming on the syndicates, which mainly offer talk shows that are inexpensive to produce, specialize "in salacious subjects and emotional confrontations," draw large audiences, and reap huge profits.[24] So advertisers are tempted to use these shows to reach their desired viewers, and often succumb.[25]

Responding to widespread complaints, Congress in 1990 limited the air-time of commercials on children's television to ten and a half minutes per hour on weekends and twelve minutes on weekdays. The legislation also requires the FCC to evaluate the quality and quantity of the programs shown on a station when a broadcaster's license comes up for renewal.

Contents

The networks produce mainly news, public affairs, sports shows, and some soap operas. The bulk of their programming for their affiliates they commission and finance in part from production companies, often divisions of film studios, located mainly in Los Angeles.[26] But for every thousand pilot shows proposed, only about thirty become series, and most of these last less than one season. Being aired guarantees neither quality nor success.

The other programs on the networks' affiliates and most of those on independent stations come from two main sources: from the stations' few productions, basically local news and public affairs; and from the owners-syndicators with which they contract for currently produced shows (e.g., "Oprah," "Jeopardy"), for reruns of ones (e.g., "I Love Lucy"), and for packages of old movies.

The networks' and stations' objective is to attract the largest possible demographically desirable audience for advertisers: people between the ages of eighteen and thirty-four, sometimes expanded to forty-nine, who disproportionately buy most products. The more successfully a show appeals to this segment, the higher the rates sponsors will pay to air their commercials on it.

The basic way to success is with familiar genres, conventional formulas, and upbeat content comfortable for the audience.[27] For many shows, this entails "the same actors returning week after week, star popularity being their main route to ratings."[28] Also desirable are a propitious time slot, an effective promotion campaign, and counter programming so that the show is not competing for the same audience with similar shows being aired at the same time.

Uncommon on network television, therefore, are presentations of painting, sculpture, architecture; performances of original drama and dance; and discussions of books.

Innovations Unusual and risky programming is usually undertaken when competition is aggressive, technology is changing, demands by distributors are in flux, and government policies are altering.[29] When initiated by the networks, it often comes from the one doing worst in the ratings. Programmers at this network commission new shows from those producers and writers with an imaginative bent and a track record of success. Thus, executives at the underdog Fox network commissioned "The Simpsons." Ultimately wildly popular, this program revealed the potential audience for the new and unusual on television.

The makers of such commercially successful shows become relatively free to experiment and explore basic subjects, such as race, gender, and class, and to do so over the several years the show lasts.[30]

Ratings Programs' popularity is revealed by their ratings. If we believe what people tell the ratings services, television sets are on an average of approximately seven hours each day, with each household member watching (whatever that means in practice) more than three hours.

The largest audience is at prime time, from 8 p.m. to 11 p.m. (from 7 p.m. on Sundays). Ratings services, the A. C. Nielsen Co. most prominently, periodically "measure" each show's audience size. They report two basic figures: the percentage of homes watching television that are tuned in to the show (its rating); and a lower figure, the percentage of all households, whether or not watching television, tuned in to the show (its share).

The ratings services exclude people outside the familial home, such as those in college dormitories, bars, summer camps, prisons, hotels, hospitals, military bases, and homes for the elderly. Nor do they detail the audience's actual reactions to the shows.[31] Nonetheless, it is clear that networks' share of the audience is declining as more and more channels become available on satellite and cable.

Cable

In an eloquent polemic some years ago, Jerry Mander presented several arguments for why people would be better off with the elimination of television.[32] Instead, spurred by the advent of cable, television spreads its tentacles ever wider.

A cable system has five sources of programming: local origination, including public-access channels; local stations; superstations (a local station carried on many systems); special cable networks, such as MTV; and pay services, usually commercial-free, such as HBO.

Cable operators have two sources of income: subscription fees and local advertising. Some 70 percent of American homes now subscribe. For various prices, they can purchase channels in tiers as defined by the companies: basic, nonbasic (HBO, Cinemax, etc.). This brings them channels featuring the arts, comedy, courts, ethnicity, government and politics, music, religion, retail products, the weather, and much more. But the cable programs attracting the largest audiences are Hollywood movies, sports, news, syndicated reruns of network-derived fare and, above all, professional wrestling.

Cable sometimes presents new and original, or at least unusual, programming. HBO commissions films on topics the networks eschew, ventures into satire, and nudges back the boundaries of acceptability with some of its *risqué* programs. Comedy Central is consistently innovative (e.g., its animated show "South Park" and its takeoff on the news "The Daily Show"), when it isn't relying on reruns. C-SPAN and C-SPAN2 provide floor debates of the House of Representatives and the Senate, respectively, as well as other material dealing with government, politics, and public affairs.[33]

Community-access channels show local government, school boards, and other public groups in action, offering a diversity of opinion (including hate material), and community-oriented programs. But too often public-access is starved for production and promotion funds, neglected, and censored. Which brings us to public television.

Public Television

The Corporation for Public Broadcasting (CPB) was created by Congress in 1967 as a private, nonprofit corporation to oversee the development of public television and radio.[34]

© 1981, *Washington Post Writers Group. Reprinted with permission.*

The CPB receives an annual allocation from Congress, most of which is funneled to 363 public television and 629 public radio stations to pay for their operations and for their acquisition and production of programs. CPB also funds the creation of programs by issuing calls for proposals and giving awards of seed money.

Congress also created the Public Broadcasting Service (PBS) to underwrite and commission programs for sale to PBS member television stations. Because these programs are produced by a few major suppliers and large stations, this system penalizes independent producers.

CPB's board members are appointed by the president, making them responsive and vulnerable to the dictates of the administration in office. Marilyn Lashley documents how the divergent policy preferences and executive turnover imposed on public broadcasting by the Johnson, Nixon, Carter, and Reagan administrations mired it in budgetary crises and transformed its programming content.[35] Congress got into the act in 1992, charging CPB to review programs after transmission for objectivity and lack of balance or fairness and, if necessary, to correct the imbalance by funding additional programs.[36]

Public broadcasting stations receive about 14 percent of their funding from the federal government; 30 percent from local and state governments and from state colleges and universities which house many of the stations; and varying amounts from viewers, usually responding to on-air appeals and annual or more frequent funding drives.

The largest source of funding for national programming (almost 30 percent) comes from corporate underwriters, which receive acknowledgments ("This program was brought to you by . . .") that are sometimes quite close to actual advertisements for the sponsor's image and products. These advertisers are disinclined to support challenging, provocative programs.

By the mid-1990s, public broadcasting was under assault from members of the Republican congressional majority determined to cut, if not eliminate entirely, its federal funding. They objected to the principle of spending government money on a television channel, argued that the abundance of cable channels could take over or duplicate most of its content, and complained about supposed liberal documentary and other programs.

Other critics have noted that public television is unnecessarily costly because of stations with overlapping signals and duplicative schedules, because the bulk of funds are spent on station operations rather than programs, and because the quality of locally produced programs is mediocre and the quantity is declining.

Liberals complain that public television has increasingly catered to its conservative critics; that it offers no weekly programs with the perspectives of working people or consumers or environmentalists, or weekly talk shows with progressive hosts; and that many of its programs (conspicuously those about cooking, crafts, and travel) are innocuous, boring, or better suited for commercial channels.[37]

In response, the system's defenders point out that it is torn by the mandate to produce and provide original, challenging programs versus the need to broaden its appeal beyond the educated elite; that it delivers and disseminates instructional programs to schools; that many of its programs, in particular those such as "Sesame Street" for children, would never have been developed by commercial television, nor could be in the future; and that many Americans cannot afford to subscribe to cable or are not in a location to receive it.

RADIO

There are approximately ten thousand commercial radio stations in the United States.[38] Dependent on advertising revenue to survive, they periodically suffer economic vicissitudes: In 1990, half of the stations lost money and 300 licensees left the air.[39]

Radio is particularly popular in states such as California, New York, and Texas where people spend a lot of time in their cars driving or in traffic jams. Thus, driving time (6 a.m. to 10 a.m. and 3 p.m. to 7 p.m.) is radio's equivalent of television's prime time.

Large-market radio is dominated by a few big companies that have stations in New York, Los Angeles, Chicago, and other big cities. Nonetheless, the majority of stations have been independently owned, although many of them are affiliated with one or other of the twenty plus national networks reaching millions of listeners.[40]

In 1992, however, the FCC allowed a single owner to have eighteen AM and eighteen FM stations, including two of each in a single market. The result was to reduce the number of station owners by 25 percent or more.[41]

Then, in 1996, Congress enacted and the FCC promulgated revised telecommunications regulations. The new rules permit companies to own eight stations in major cities. They also remove any limits on the number of stations a company can own overall unless they reach more than 35 percent of all American households.[42]

This has led to a frenzy of mergers and acquisitions. For example, Westinghouse, owner of the CBS radio and television networks, acquired Infinity, the nation's largest independent broadcaster. This created a radio giant of 83 stations, many of them in the top ten markets.

Contents

Some stations offer varied programming, including automobile advice and psychic counseling.[43] Most stations specialize in particular programs aimed at a distinct audience based on musical preference, racial or ethnic background and language, and interests (e.g., sports).

Music dominates. Between them, radio stations play roughly forty kinds. Country music is the most common, heard on about a quarter of the commercial outlets, followed by, in percentages, adult contemporary (16.6), religious (8.7), oldies (7.5), top 40 (5.6), jazz/alternative rock and classical (with .5 percent each).[44]

Religious programming is also a common radio format. According to the trade group National Religious Broadcasters, there are approximately 800 AM and 400 FM Christian stations in the country. Aside from their obviously religious (often inspirational) content and Christian music, they offer programs on marriage and family issues, and advice for the troubled. Much of their content is politically relevant, especially their espousal of conservative values and views. Their major problem is the reluctance of national advertisers to sponsor their programs, supposedly because they do not reach large audiences.[45]

News on radio usually consists of headlines, even on all-news stations. Talk radio, however, can be important in reaching large audiences and in influencing people's political views (see Appendix A).

There are also low-wattage community broadcasters operating beyond the limits of FCC regulation. (The FCC refuses to license stations under 100 watts.) Dubbed "pirate radio" or, more favorably, "free radio," they usually assert views and play material unheard on regular stations. These "stations" are usually beset by FCC legal challenges and lawsuits and police harassment.[46]

Public Radio

There are over 1,700 "educational," thus noncommercial, FM radio stations.[47] Funded by contributions from listeners; in some cases, by the federal and state governments; and like public television, increasingly underwritten by corporations and foundations, they cater to a small (6 percent) but select audience: white, predominantly male, over age thirty, and relatively affluent.[48]

National Public Radio (NPR) was established in 1970. It provides its entire program service for one price to its network of 377 affiliated stations. NPR produces some fifty hours of original programming weekly. It is best known for its national news and public affairs programs, especially "All Things Considered" and "Morning Edition" and their weekend equivalents. Many NPR stations also occasionally produce news about and other programs for their local communities.

American Public Radio (APR) is a second national program service. More a commercial business than an organization of members, it offers news, music, comedy, and variety programs that stations select as they want.[49] In contrast to NPR, which produces most of its programs in-house, APR acquires its shows from radio stations and independent producers.

The Pacifica network provides an alternative, somewhat radical, perspective on news and public affairs. Other networks (Sheridan and the National Black Network) are owned by and oriented to African-Americans or (*Caballero*) Latinos. There are also several American Indian radio stations.

MUSIC

Music recording is big business: Annual revenues from the sales of recorded music are more than $9 billion.[50] And it is immensely and consistently profitable. In 1994, Time Warner's film group made $565 million in pretax operating income, but its music labels (Warner Brothers, Elektra, Atlantic, and others) achieved $720 million.[51]

There are six major recording companies. They generate most of their revenues from big-name American performers who sell at home and in the increasingly important international market. They also search for new talent (singers, musicians, songwriters, arrangers, lyricists) and sounds that will be successful in the marketplace. They find them through demonstration records usually submitted by agents, in performances at clubs, and through recommendations of established performers. As a result, thirty to forty bands break through to achieve recognition each year. A few survive more or less successfully, most decline into obscurity after one hit.

Consequently, a tiny number of stars command multi-million-dollar contracts and are paid vast sums in the expectation, not always realized, of continuing popularity and sales. These performers can earn lavish incomes from the sales of their records, from personal appearances, and from the merchandising of buttons, T-shirts, posters, linens and towels, lunchboxes, keychains, etc.

Production and Sales

The record companies are mainly responsible for producing recordings (roughly 5,000 singles and 2,500 albums each year); then packaging, publicizing, advertising, promoting, and merchandising them. Key is getting the record played on influential radio stations and the music video on television—assuming one is made, for they can cost $50,000 and up.

Jobbers, who service the record racks in variety and large department stores, account for 65 percent of record sales. Record stores are next, with 15 to 20 percent; these are mainly chain stores controlled by a few companies.[52] Records are also sold directly to consumers by record clubs and through television ads for collections.

People buy around 12 million compact discs and albums every week. Rock music dominates sales. Country and rhythm and blues come next, with 10 percent each; followed in decreasing percentages by rap, gospel, jazz, and classical.[53]

Political Contents and Consequences

Music can be politically challenging especially when it speaks (sings) to and for the young. For music often displays the rebellious attitudes of successive generations of American youth. Mark Crispin Miller called 1960s' rock "a cry of revolt underwritten by major corporations."[54] Rap may be a contemporary equivalent. Earlier, folk music was often explicitly political. Its most famous exponents have been Woody Guthrie and his songs of the dust-bowl migrants of the 1930s, and the still-going-strong Pete Seeger, with his union songs of the 1940s and 1950s.[55] Guthrie's "This Land Is Your Land" would make a fitting radical national anthem.

Political content in music is more often implicit than explicit. Country is an example, with its songs of love-sick yearnings, domestic life and strife, and despair. Its most popular songs portray fierce individualism, economic class consciousness, exploitation of the poor, "unsatisfactory working conditions and the fatalistic lack of faith in ever fulfilling the American Dream."[56]

Music Videos   The most visible form of popular music are music videos. A key to musical groups' success, they are program-long commercials mass marketing popular songs.

Music videos are full of implicit political contents that is often reactionary. Sexism, racism, and violence abound. A typical story line is boy meets-loses-wins girl. "Male images include sailors, thugs, gang members, and gangsters. Female images include prostitutes, nightclub performers, goddesses, temptresses, and servants."[57]

Yet, MTV is "committed to the promotion of an 'alternative' culture (however cynically or self-servingly), it has an investment in risk taking."[58] It thus occasionally opens up the political agenda both in its music content and news programs. As Andrew Goodwin observes, the music videos' "use of news and documentary footage can render the pop song more socially specific and . . . articulate political positions that might otherwise be absent."[59]

Indeed, looking specifically at the political messages in music videos, Anne Johnston Wadsworth and Lynda Lee Kaid found that, despite "some hope that world peace might be achieved through a grassroots effort," the videos were filled with "threats of oppression and the inevitability of nuclear disaster," with people's future "manipulated and controlled by powerful (and sometimes inept or comical) political . . . figures."[60]

NEWSPAPERS

There are over 1,600 daily newspapers in the United States with an estimated combined circulation of 63 million.

Ownership

Some 130 group owners control about 70 percent of them, accounting for more than 80 percent of circulation. The largest chains are Gannett (close to 100 dailies, over 6 million circulation) and Knight-Ridder.[61] There are about 7,000 weekly newspapers, some free, with an estimated combined circulation of 39 million. Also weekly are the supermarket tabloids, most prominently the *National Enquirer.*

A few newspapers—notably *USA Today,* the *Wall Street Journal,* and the national edition of the *New York Times*—are available nationwide. But most newspapers aim for a general readership in specific areas: large cities (e.g., Los Angeles), or suburban communities (e.g., Long Island), or medium-sized towns (Durham, N.C.). Consequently, 85 percent have circulations lower than 50,000.

For several decades, the number of cities with competitive dailies has decreased; now, over 90 percent have only one daily newspaper. Circulation has also declined in relation to the number of potential readers: from 111 per 100 households in 1960, to 67 now. Contributory factors are television and its news, "the weakening of urban culture; the lost sense of identification with the central city; the growth of the underclass; changed family structure . . . and the time pressures that followed entry of women into the workforce."[62]

Funding

A. J. Liebling put it best: "The function of the press in society is to inform, but its role is to make money."[63] And, despite occasional recessions and increases in costs (as in the price of newsprint), make money it does for its proprietors and chief executives.[64] Chains seek and obtain profits of roughly one third of revenue.

Comments one critic: "These bloated margins, to a large extent, come out of the hides and labor of the 'underclass' of small-town journalism and at the expense of millions of American readers who are poorly served by shoestring news budgets."[65] Corroborating this argument in part, the amount of a newspaper's revenue that some companies spent on news-gathering declined from 15 to 20 percent in the 1960s to 9 percent by 1990.[66]

Another reason daily newspapers can be so profitable is that they are monopolies in their cities. Even where they ostensibly compete, as in New York, they attract somewhat different clientele—upscale for the *New York Times*, blue-collar for the *Daily News.* So advertisers seeking to reach these newspapers' readers have nowhere else to go.

Indeed, advertisers contribute from 70 to 90 percent of newspapers' gross revenues; the remainder comes from circulation (subscriptions and single-copy sales).

There are four sorts of advertising: national (e.g., cigarette), preprints (e.g., the inserts in Sunday editions), local, and classified. Local retail advertising (60 percent) comes from department stores, supermarkets, drugstores, movie theaters, and the like. Classified (about 25 percent) consists of announcements about jobs available, cars for sale, services offered, and such.

Catering to advertisers helps to explain the prevalence in newspapers of food, automotive, travel, and similar sections that are more promotional than hard news.

However, because department stores account for a significant part of all retail advertising, a decline in their fortunes reduces advertising. Since the usual ratio of advertising to newscopy is 65 to 35 percent, this leads to thinner newspapers with less news.

Contents

Still, newspapers do contain a plethora of news, advertising, and other contents. There are cartoons, comics, editorials, columns of all sorts (medical, humor, advice, opinion), astrology, reviews (of movies, records, restaurants), recipes, stock market data, and lots more.

Most of this content is generated by the newspaper's staff or purchased from syndicators, such as King Features and United Media. Practically every newspaper buys syndicated material: mainly columns (e.g., "Ann Landers," Ellen Goodman), comics (e.g., "Bloom County," "Peanuts").

Syndicates usually go with features that are safe. Newspaper editors, moreover, are inclined to stick with their current roster. Readers object to losing familiar content, so there is little incentive to change. But at the same time syndicates and newspapers are looking for new material that will appeal to an audience between college age and forty, for the next "Doonesbury" and George Will. So occasionally innovation occurs; new strips and columnists break through.

Since it is young people and women who lack the habit of regular readership, many mass-circulation dailies have also introduced elements that are supposed to appeal to them (e.g., color, more photos, shorter stories, more features, and fluff); but without obvious success.

Catering directly to special audiences are the African-American press (three dailies, the rest weeklies) with a circulation of around 5 million in some thirty-three states and Washington, D.C., and the Spanish-language press of seven dailies and forty-eight weeklies. There are also Asian-language newspapers, and ones for American Indians. Indeed, the ethnic press consists of several hundred newspapers in at least forty languages.[67]

MAGAZINES

Scrutinize magazine racks and it becomes clear that magazine publishing executives keep track of the public's interests. They react speedily to economic, demographic, and sociological trends by creating new magazines, relaunching or redesigning old ones.[68]

Contents

There is a mind-boggling variety of magazine fare, from the obvious (*People*), to the arcane (*Soap Opera Hair*). There are ones on travel, physical activities, and sports; a positive panoply of magazines directed at women and their asserted interests, presumptively romance, fashion, and beauty; ones for men, many featuring sex; some for children and adolescents. There is a cornucopia of magazines about food and drink; several on health; a buzz of magazines on music and equipment for playing it; an assemblage of magazines on computers, crafts, games, hobbies (including guns and automobiles); a mystique of psychic and horoscope magazines; sober periodicals about business, medicine, law, religion, and the military; magazines galore about entertainment, entertainers, and celebrities; flesh magazines for all preferences; the news weeklies and ones that are explicitly political.

Given roughly 4,000 general magazines widely available, distribution is essential: Titles not picked up by a national distributor never reach the 140,000 retail outlets that sell magazines. Accounting for 45 percent of sales, supermarkets are "so important that publishers pay the stores a premium of about $20 per checkout rack to have their titles prominently displayed."[69]

The total magazine annual circulation (paid subscriptions plus newsstand purchases) is around 400 million copies. But only *Reader's Digest, TV Guide*, and *National Geographic* sell more than 10 million copies each.

Ownership

Although magazine publishing is less concentrated than the newspaper industry, the top five publishers account for approximately a third of the total revenue generated. And while the business is less foreign-owned than other media, three of the top ten magazine publishers are headquartered outside the United States.[70]

Magazine publishing has traditionally been easy to enter: "Hugh Hefner reportedly assembled the first issue of *Playboy*, appropriately enough, from his bedroom, while *Rolling Stone* began in a loft."[71] *Utne Reader*, which analyzes, summarizes, quotes from, and reprints material from alternative publications, began as a 25,000-circulation newsletter; it is now bimonthly with a circulation of around 300,000.[72] Most recently, *Wired* became a circulation success.

The relatively cheap economics of desktop publishing also facilitate the appearance of publications outside the magazine mainstream, witness "zines" such as *Hip Mama*.

Nonetheless, starting a magazine aimed at a mass audience usually requires such a large capital outlay, followed by so much more to promote it to advertisers and potential subscribers, that new magazines usually go for several years before making a profit. That is, if their owners don't kill them first: Of the eight hundred or so magazines started in 1994, no more than 25 percent are likely to survive.[73] Those that do are often acquired by large publishers: Advance Publications, publishers of *GQ*, the *New Yorker, Vanity Fair, Vogue*, and many others, bought *Wired* in 1998 for close to $80 million.[74]

Funding

Most magazines rely on advertising—supplemented by subscriptions (postal rate increases are thus costly) and newsstand sales—for their income or, at least, to survive. Exceptions to breaking even are many of the opinion magazines which often lose money and depend on subsidies, usually from foundations and a few wealthy individuals.

Magazine advertising is increasingly based on studies designed to measure a magazine's readership, how long readers look at its ads, and how much it costs per ad to reach a target audience. The number of advertising pages indicates—often accounts for—a magazine's success.

This produces two somewhat contradictory results. On the one hand, advertisers want to reach young, middle- and upper-class people with money to spend and years to spend it; which explains why magazines such as *Premiere, Vanity Fair, GQ,* and *Esquire* often seem to run interchangeable articles. On the other hand, the more a magazine can occupy a specialized niche unchallenged, the greater its appeal to its advertisers: There is a magazine for young lawyers, another for Southern brides. *Out,* a national magazine directed at affluent gay men and lesbians, attracts advertising from American Express, Apple Computer, Banana Republic, Calvin Klein, and Sony Electronics.[75]

Lack of advertiser support can be deadly. It was blamed for the fate of three magazines aimed at intelligent, fashion-conscious, young women interested in substantive articles. *New York Woman* and *Lear's* ceased publication; and *Mirabella,* after six years of losses estimated at $15 million annually, was sold.[76]

Magazines are therefore even more responsive to advertisers than the other media. When *MS* emulated *Mad* and some consumer magazines by becoming ad-free (thereby having to increase its newsstand price substantially) after years of failing to attract enough advertising to break even, Gloria Steinem wrote that advertisers had such control over women's magazines that their demands were dictated to ad salespeople as official policy. For example, Procter & Gamble products were not to be placed in any issue containing *any* material on gun control, abortion, the occult, cults, or the disparagement of religion. Picking random issues of women's magazines *Glamour, Vogue, Redbook, Family Circle* and others, Steinem found that the overwhelming majority of their pages consisted of advertisements or content complementary or related to ads.[77]

Magazine integrity is also compromised by the importance of celebrity covers in boosting newsstand sales.[78] The editors of magazines such as *Vanity Fair, GQ, Vogue, Entertainment Weekly,* and *Premiere* often have to negotiate with publicists representing the stars "about the cover photograph, the photographer, the cover concept, the timing of the story, the writer, the access that the writer has to the star and to other sources, and the questions that the writer may ask the star."[79]

Comics

A few words are necessary about comics, a type of magazine that unites illustrations and words in often deft combination. They range from Disney cartoon characters, to *Richie Rich* and the like, on to superheroes, and culminating with the dark protagonists of *Youngblood.* They can be quite daring, as in *Tales of the Closet* about gay and bisexual teenagers and their problems.

Given their readership among preteens, adolescents, and many adults, comic books have been a perennial object of assault, variously accused of corrupting young minds, of propagating imperialist ideology, and much more.[80]

BOOKS

Each year sees the publication of more than fifty thousand new books covering every imaginable subject.[81] The largest sales categories are trade books for general readers (28 percent); college, elementary, and high school texts (25 percent); professional books for academics and those whose work requires them (18 percent); mass-market paperbacks that sell any place other than bookstores (8 percent, almost half of them romance novels); and religious books (4 percent).[82]

Foreign ownership and consolidation are the recent trends in book publishing. A few companies now dominate the business. Their preferred way to receive trade book proposals and manuscripts is through literary agents. Unsolicited submissions, disparagingly called "slush," are mostly rejected with a form letter. Editors themselves sometimes generate ideas for books and seek out the appropriate authors to write them.

Funding

Publishers' main income comes from book (and audio book) sales (retail price minus discounts for wholesalers and booksellers) and subsidiary rights (book clubs, foreign and paperback rights, and reprint permissions). Aside from manufacturing and operating costs, their primary expenses are royalties; a few famous authors command multi-million-dollar advances, which they retain even if royalties from their book's sales fall short of the cost of publishing it.

The profit motive increasingly prevails in publishing as conglomerates dominate the business. Thus, many books of little merit are published because of their sales potential. Notorious are quickie, sensationalist books about mass murderers and slain celebrities. In the same vein are trash biographies, typified by Kitty Kelley's (gossip presented as fact) assault on Nancy Reagan, for which Simon & Schuster paid the author an advance of $3.5 million. Even more millions were paid out by publishers to those involved with and some people barely peripheral to the O. J. Simpson trial.

Indeed, a few big titles often subsidize the rest. Books published by Random House's adult trade division that were listed as "notable books" of 1993 in the *New York Times' Book Review* collectively lost $698,000. Most of them achieved glowing reviews, considerable attention, and much promotion from the publisher. They were paid for by two titles that, enjoying far fewer accolades, made $1.4 million profit: *Wouldn't Take Nothing for My Journey Now* by Maya Angelou, and *A Woman's Worth* by Marianne Williamson.[83]

Still, many books (of poetry, for example) are published on artistic, intellectual, or cultural grounds. There are several reasons: publishing is a profession that attracts some individuals who love books more than money; depending on how much is paid to the author as an advance, books do not have to sell widely to make money or to at least break even; and authors can be nurtured in the hope that they will achieve artistic and popular success.

Book publishing, moreover, is rife with uncertainty. Certainly, there are some sure-fire authors, like the prolific Stephen King whose works usually sell widely (and are often made into forgettable movies), but, like movies, books for which publishers have high expectations flop, and unlikely ones are best sellers.

Besides, there are literally hundreds of publishers. Many of them are more willing to take risks than the large companies. University presses, by definition nonprofit, aim at the professional market and a literate and concerned public, with a nodding hope that some of their books will be chosen as texts for college courses. Some publishers specialize in particular areas. A few people publish their own work. Others even pay to be published by so-called vanity presses.

Incidentally, not all books are actually written by the authors to whom they are attributed. Celebrities, sports figures, politicians, and others may record or tell their stories to ghostwriters hired by publishers, who then try to make the material literate and coherent. The collaboration may or may not be acknowledged. In extreme cases, the putative author may be quite unfamiliar with the contents of his or her book.

Promotion and Sales

Authors want their books to be promoted and sold. Many are neither. The favored receive some combination of author tour, national print and television advertising, excerpts printed in magazines prior to or simultaneously with publication, and a floor display for bookstores.

Beneficial for several sorts of books (e.g., advice, diet, how-to, polemics, pop psychology, psycho-babble) are their authors' appearances and interviews on television, radio, and in print. Appearing on "Oprah" can be a sales bonanza.

Reviews help book sales, especially if a book is reviewed in the *New York Times Book Review,* and if the review is favorable. But many trade books and mass-market paperbacks are ignored: The *Times* reviews 10 to 15 percent of the 12,000 to 15,000 books it receives annually.[84] Its editors' decisions are often erratic: Meritorious works are slighted or overlooked; mediocre ones reviewed, often favorably. The *New York Review* is also important, but it reviews few books.

Books are ubiquitously available: at college and university bookstores; on newsstands; in supermarkets, drugstores, and airports; via mail order; through book clubs; and in libraries. Large chain bookstores, especially Barnes and Noble and its subsidiaries, account for about 40 percent of all books sold in the United States. They emphasize best sellers, rarely keeping copies of other books longer than a few weeks.

Fortunately, a significant number of individually owned bookstores still exist, sometimes with knowledgeable, book-loving staffs, stocking diverse titles and, less common, an ample supply of used books.

Political Contents and Consequences

Books are portable, require neither electricity nor batteries to operate, are usually uninterrupted by advertising, can be opened (and closed) at any time and place, and are amenable to being marked up, underlined, torn apart. Their readers are often opinion-makers and leaders. Perennially, certain books stir the public conscience and influence public policy, as Betty Friedan did for feminism, Michael Harrington for the poor, and Rachel Carson for the environment.[85] Books also influence the rest of the media. They are turned into movies (also the reverse), television miniseries and programs, and excerpted in magazines and newspapers.

FILMS

Overwhelmingly, the hundreds of movies released annually are commodities made to make money. The business is dominated by the major studios, which finance and distribute about a third of the feature films produced and, because of their power and connections, distribute many of the movies made by independent producers.

Production

The studios annually receive some ten thousand screenplays, books, treatments, or oral pitches.[86] They make around two hundred of these into movies for release each year.

The most desirable screenplays "are sufficiently original that the audience will not feel it has already seen the movie, yet similar enough to past hits to reassure executives wary of anything too far out."[87] Which helps explain the making of sequels to successful films about aliens, dinosaurs, and the like. Common ingredients are a likable star as the hero to root for, sex (with female topless nudity), action and violence, special effects, and a happy ending; all are designed to appeal to an audience at home and abroad, a majority of whose members are under age thirty and male.

Other films, more character driven and with compelling narratives, are made to appeal to women aged between thirty and fifty who, although tougher to get into theater, influence their husbands and boyfriends about what to see.[88]

Talent agencies, such as Creative Artists Agency (CAA) and International Creative Management (ICM), are particularly powerful in the film industry, often putting together movie deals (stars, director, writer) for the studios. A few prominent producers, usually those with close relations with studios, have similar clout.

Beyond their standard fare, the studios offer a few original movies. These usually originate with successful artists who have the clout from their previous box-office suc-

FEIFFER®

Feiffer © 1991 Jules Feiffer. Reprinted with permission of Universal Press Syndicate. All rights reserved.

cesses to obtain the funds to make, within limits, whatever film they want, as Steven Spielberg accomplished with *Schindler's List.* But a few failures can limit this leeway.

Other unconventional movies emanate from production and distribution companies that are independent from or relatively autonomous subsidiaries of the major studios.

Unusual or offbeat movies also arise from individuals unconnected with the Hollywood studios who use various wiles (charging their credit cards to the limit) to fund their films. Most of their movies are little noticed, but a distinctive few (e.g., *Slackers*) receive acclaim and wide distribution. Ever eager for lucrative new talent, the studios can then fund their makers' next films, which are more or less adventurous in form and content.

Nonfiction films are an aesthetically thriving form embraced by independent film-makers and disdained by Hollywood. At their best, as in the work of Frederick Wiseman, they capture authentic experience and emotion, and reveal American institutions in action (and inaction).[89]

Funding

Hollywood movies often incur colossal production and advertising costs (averaging $60 million in 1996); audience preferences are sometimes quite unpredictable; and creative accounting inflates the costs of production, prints, advertising, interest, distribution, and overhead fees.[90]

Nonetheless, by combining all possible sources of income, it is possible to increase a film's probability of financial success even before it is released. These sources include guaranteed theatrical play dates, presales to the overseas market, and advance sales to television in the United States and abroad.

Sales by video stores are particularly important, generating twice as much revenue for the studios as movie theaters. They can be a bonanza: *The Lion King* video sold 20 million copies on its first day of availability.[91] There is also the possibility of ancillary sales and rentals of merchandise (e.g., posters, T-shirts, toys, watches, candy) related to the movie. If a film is a box-office hit, these income sources can be a huge boon: *The Lion King* earned around $1 billion in retail merchandising sales.[92]

The industry practice of product placement, an indirect form of advertising, can add substantially to a film's income. *The Goonies* contained Baby Ruth, Hi-C fruit drink, Budweiser beer, Peter Pan peanut butter, Baskin-Robbins ice cream, Jiffy Pop popcorn, and Nature Valley granola bars; each paid "either to be in the film or to share in its promotion."[93] One cigarette company spent a million dollars over four years to put images of its products into movies.[94]

Consequently, in a good year, around 60 percent of studio films make a profit or break even. In a bad year, fewer than a third are profitable.[95]

Distribution and Promotion

The United States has approximately 30,000 movie screens, most of them in multiplexes with several screens clustered around a central concession stand. Major chains, some of them owned by movie studios, account for some 80 percent of all box-office revenue. The heaviest theater-going periods are summer, Christmas, and Easter.

Theater owners pay distributors, and through them the film-makers, a percentage of the income generated by ticket sales. The more popular the movie, the higher the percentage; the longer the movie remains, the lower the percentage drops. Theater owners often make most of their profits not on the movies they exhibit but on concession sales.

The studios dominate the distribution business, dispatching to theaters their films and some of the independently produced movies they have financed in part or picked up as marketable. Other independently made and foreign films are distributed by smaller companies.

A movie expected to be popular, and also having met with audience approval at screenings, will be preceded by an advertising blitz of coming-attraction trailers and posters in theaters and advertising on television. There will be an orchestrated publicity campaign of favorable stories with promotional appearances and interviews by the director and stars (but rarely the writers), with clips from the movie on news and talk shows. Sound tracks or hit songs may be broadcast, ideally as music videos. The movie will then be released to one thousand or more first-run theaters simultaneously.[96]

More obscure movies depend on public relations ingenuity to attract media and public attention. Thus, Miramax reaped reams of publicity when its scheduling of a film about a gay priest for release on Good Friday aroused bitter objections from Catholic prelates.

Most movies, unless their distributors believe them to be awful, will be shown in advance to reviewers. Some blockbusters enjoy so much free publicity and promotion as to be reviewer proof. Other movies can be hurt by negative and helped by positive reviews, especially if there is agreement among the reviewers. Favorable reviews in prominent newspapers or magazines can make successes out of independent or foreign movies by bringing them to the attention of other media, emboldening their distributors to spend more money on their promotion campaign and broaden their release patterns, and encouraging exhibitors throughout the country to play them.

After theatrical exhibition or even without it, many movies continue to be available. They are shown on pay and free television stations, offered for sale and rental in video stores, taught in schools. American masterpieces, such as Buster Keaton's *The General* and Orson Welles' *Citizen Kane,* continue to inspire and delight.

GLOBALIZATION AND DOMINATION

This chapter's account of the media's organization, funding, production, contents, distribution, and promotion and sales leads to and concludes with two basic issues: globalization and domination of ownership. (The book's final chapter is devoted to a third issue: the changing media environment caused by the Internet and other technologies.)

A few large multinational corporations are global media empires. Rupert Murdoch owns the movie studio Twentieth-Century Fox; the Fox television network; television stations reaching much of the country; video production companies; newspapers, such as the *New York Post;* several magazines; HarperCollins publishers; and bookstores. He has even moved into cable, buying from religious broadcaster Pat Robertson the Family Channel, which is carried on almost every cable system in the country. Murdoch's overseas holdings include major newspapers in Great Britain and other countries, and satellite broadcasters that beam programming over much of the world.[97]

Relatedly, starting in the 1980s, many of the new owners of U.S. media were not American. The movie studios Columbia and Tri-Star were purchased by Japan's Sony, and MGM by a French bank. The British and Germans acquired U.S. publishing houses. In 1998, the German media giant, Bertelsmann, bought the book publisher Random House, to go with Bantam Doubleday Dell it already owned, to become the world's largest publisher of English-language trade books. Five of the six largest producers of records are conglomerates headquartered outside the United States.[98]

This globalization raises significant questions about the control, financing, regulation, and production of media content, including what is not produced. As Joseph Turow points out, the largest media corporations, by defining audiences globally and by seeking crossover projects (i.e., same company owns and promotes the book, movie, and music), narrow their range of cultural products.[99] A company can use the various media at its command to transmit the same images, ideas, and personalities to the international and national audience in different forms.

Tied to globalization is the growing domination of the media industry by big business. Certainly ownership is increasingly the province of the few. Rupert Murdoch is part of a coterie including Gerald M. Levin of Time Warner and Michael D. Eisner of Disney Capital Cities/ABC.

After merging with Turner Broadcasting System, Time Warner controls the Warner Brothers and other movie studios, film libraries, the Cable News Network (CNN) and related channels, HBO, Cinemax, and TNT, and the Cartoon Network, and it has part ownership of other cable channels, including Court TV and Comedy Central. It is one of the largest owners of cable systems, with 11.5 million subscribers. It owns around fifty record companies, the book publishers Little Brown and Warner Books, as well as the Book of the Month Club; and it publishes such magazines as *Fortune, People, Sports Illustrated,* and *Time.*

After merging with Capital Cities/ABC, the Disney conglomerate consists of several film and television production studios and distributors; newspapers, record companies, and publishers; a television network and television and radio stations; as well as the Disney cable channel. It also has stakes in ESPN, "A&E," and Lifetime.

Other powerful media conglomerates are Viacom, Inc., Seagram, CBS-Westinghouse, and Newhouse. Thus, Viacom, Inc. controls the Paramount movie studio and television production companies; several cable networks, including MTV, VH1, and Nickelodeon; film libraries; and several publishers, including the Free Press, Macmillan, Pocket Books, and Prentice-Hall. It owns movie theaters, Blockbuster, and television stations.

This domination by the few is compounded by vertical and horizontal integration. Vertical because each of the conglomerates owns programming and the means to distribute it. Horizontal because the companies have joint ventures with one or more of the others. Symbolic of these interconnections, the six executives of another conglomerate, Tele-Communications, Inc.'s (TCI) company Liberty Media, which owns all or parts of dozens of cable and broadcast organizations, sit on more than forty executive boards. Among their main objectives: "'create strengthened alliances, new businesses, and shared economics.'"[100]

This raises the following issues of entry, competition, availability, and content.

Entry The cost of capital and the amount required for operations are formidable obstacles to entry into the media industries by new competitors, although it is no problem for the conglomerates that have access to vast funds.

Competition A few firms, such as TCI and Time Warner, operate cable television systems enrolling the bulk of subscribers. Obviously, they carry the channels they own or control. Conversely, by refusing to carry a channel, they can undermine its prospects for survival.

Availability Many people live in cities or towns that have one newspaper, one cable system owner, a limited range of radio stations, and a few bookstores featuring mainly best sellers. Access to media content is further reduced as more and more programs are available only at a price—on cable TV for example.

Contents Prominent among those sounding the alarm over media domination by a few corporations is Ben Bagdikian. In *The Media Monopoly,* he charts what he contends is the antidemocratic potential of corporate control: news weighted in favor of business values; censorship; retaliation against journalists who violate the solicitude with which media regard the depredations of their large advertisers; and neglect of the interests and activities of Americans who are poor or over age fifty.[101] It is easy to add to this litany: For example, Rupert Murdoch has been accused of using newspapers under his control to support political figures he favors.[102]

In fact, the situation is more complex than the doomsayers allow: There are at least three different forms of media ownership and control: monopoly, oligopoly, and monopolistic competition.

In a monopoly, one firm dominates each area. Examples are the cable television franchise and the single community daily newspaper. Consumers have no alternatives to choose from within each area.

In an oligopoly, a few companies dominate. The movie and recording industries, as well as the television networks, are all oligopolies. Most of the movies and records available to people are produced and distributed by just a few firms.

In monopolistic competition, there is a marketplace of many sellers, but limited competition in any one area. This describes the radio and magazine businesses: several radio stations in a community but only one classical; lots of magazines but only a few covering rock music.[103]

Clearly, these ownership-control situations vary in the opportunities they offer consumers. But when one considers the different media modes, the diversity among and within each type, and the competition among all of them, it could be argued that most people have a lot of media content from which to choose.

In addition, "there is considerable freedom for the entrepreneurial spirit to thrive."[104] For the actual content of the media is produced by individuals working alone or in small groups. Their motives are complex: some combination of job survival, lucre, responsibility and pride, serve the public, and desire to win awards (Emmy, Grammy, Pulitzer, Oscar). Creativity and innovation do exist within the mass media, even thriving on occasion. Besides, these makers of media content cater to a diversity of particular (but not necessarily mutually exclusive) audiences: listeners to gangsta rap, viewers of *Hard Copy,* readers of the *Nation,* purchasers of this book.

It is not clear, moreover, how much globalization and corporate domination it takes seriously to threaten access to and diversity of ownership. Nor whether a greater spread of ownership necessarily produces increases in the quantity, quality, and diversity of media content. Certainly economic competition and competition in the marketplace of ideas are not synonymous.

We can tentatively conclude for the time being "that the underlying structure of the system is able to encourage a robust exchange and competitive flow of ideas, entertainment, information and commerce throughout the media."[105]

CONCLUSION

The media are ubiquitous; their contents pervade public and private life. This chapter explained the causes of these contents (news excepted), showing the similarities and differences by mode. It accomplished this by describing each mode's organization, ownership, funding, and processes of production, distribution, and promotion and sales.

In sum, the media are overwhelmingly based on the profit motive, reduced in some cases to making enough money to survive. Advertising and audiences supply the main sources of funds. The need to attract them explains why much media content, for example on commercial television, is inoffensive, undemanding, and upbeat.

Exceptions to conventional content come occasionally from nonprofit organizations, such as NPR, despite funding limitations and politically motivated interference. Freer are media forms appealing to special segments of the population: music for the youth market, cable television's Comedy Central for the hip, talk radio for people interested in politics. Magazines and books offer the most diversity.

Global conglomerates may be on the way to dominating the media industries. Whether they will decide media content to the detriment of diversity and originality is an open question.

Notes

1. For an extensive discussion of the media industries, including many details omitted in this chapter, see Joseph Turow, *Media Systems in Society* (New York: Longman, 1992); and Joseph R. Dominick, *The Dynamics of Mass Communication* (New York: McGraw-Hill, 1994).

2. Karen Stabiner, *Inventing Desire* (New York: Simon & Schuster, 1993), 282.

3. Ibid., 44.

4. Ibid., 46.

5. Ibid., 81.

6. John Updike, *The Afterlife* (New York: Knopf, 1994), 112.

7. Ivan L. Preston, *The Tangled Web They Weave* (Madison: University of Wisconsin Press, 1994).

8. Michael J. Arlen, *Thirty Seconds* (New York: Farrar, Straus & Giroux, 1980).

9. Dominick, *Dynamics of Mass Communication*, 384.

10. For these categories and anecdotal examples, see Ronald K. L. Collins, *Dictating Content* (Washington, D.C.: Center for the Study of Commercialism, 1992).

11. David Barboza, "The Media Business," *New York Times,* 7 December 1995, C5.

12. William Gamson et al., "Media Images and the Social Construction of Reality," *Annual Review of Sociology* 18 (1992): 377–78.

13. Leo Bogart, *Commercial Culture* (New York: Oxford University Press), 80–85.

14. Stuart Ewen, "Capitalist Realism," *Journal of Communication* 35:2 (Spring 1985): 192; see also Sut Jhally, *The Codes of Advertising* (New York: St. Martin's Press, 1987).

15. Leslie Savan, *The Sponsored Life* (Philadelphia, Pa.: Temple University Press, 1995).

16. Katherine Hale and Michael W. Mansfield, "Politics: Tastes Great or Less Filling," in *Politics in Familiar Contexts,* ed. Robert L. Savage and Dan Nimmo (Norwood, N.J.: Ablex, 1990), 94.

17. On advertising's societal impact, see Michael Schudson, *Advertising, The Uneasy Persuasion* (New York: Basic Books, 1984).

18. Federal Communications Commission release 51785, 24 January 1995.

19. For background, see George Comstock, *The Evolution of American Television* (Newbury Park, Calif.: Sage, 1989). For an exhaustively detailed description of the takeovers by business people, subsequent cutbacks, cost-cutting, and personal conflicts, as well as programmers' decisions about which shows reach the air, see Ken Auletta, *Three Blind Mice* (New York: Random House, 1991).

20. Andrew C. Barrett, "Public Policy and Radio—A Regulator's View," *Media Studies Journal* 7:3 (Summer 1993): 147.

21. "Rules of Ownership Changing for Media," *New York Times,* 9 March 1996, 24Y.

22. Courtney Kane, "Only Real Surprise on 'Ellen' Was Lineup of Advertisers," *New York Times,* 2 May 1997, C2.

23. Stuart Elliott, "Homosexuality Is an Issue Sharply Dividing Marketers," *New York Times,* 23 February 1994, C1.

24. For this quote and observations, see Bill Carter, "After Killing, Hard Questions for Talk Shows," *New York Times,* 14 March 1995, A1, A8.

25. Bill Carter, "Television," *New York Times,* 20 March 1995, C5.

26. Pioneering background books on the production of television content are Muriel G. Cantor, *The Hollywood TV Producer* (New York: Basic Books, 1971); and Muriel G. Cantor and Joel M. Cantor, *Prime-Time Television,* 2nd ed. (Newbury Park, Calif.: Sage, 1992). Also relevant are Todd Gitlin, *Inside Prime Time* (New York: Pantheon, 1983); and Horace Newcomb and Robert S. Alley, eds., *The Producer's Medium* (New York: Oxford University Press, 1983).

27. For analyses and critiques of television content, see Richard Adler and Douglass Cater, eds., *Television as a Cultural Force* (New York: Praeger, 1976); Leah R. Van de Berg and Lawrence A. Wenner, eds., *Television Criticism* (White Plains, N.Y.: Longman, 1991); and Horace Newcomb, ed., *Television: The Critical View,* 5th ed. (New York: Oxford University Press, 1994).

28. Gitlin, *Inside Prime Time,* 320. For an amusing real-life novel depicting the production of a television sitcom, see Charlie Hauck, *Artistic Differences* (New York: Morrow, 1993).

29. Joseph Turow, "Unconventional Programs on Commercial Television: An Organizational Perspective," in *Mass Communications,* ed. D. Charles Whitney and James Ettema (Newbury Park, Calif.: Sage, 1982), 107–29.

30. Bernard Weinraub, "In Sheer Quality, TV Is Elbowing Hollywood Aside," *New York Times,* 14 February 1995, B1.

31. For a thoughtful discussion of the conceptual, empirical, and measurement problems entailed in the notion of a television audience, see Ien Ang, *Desperately Seeking the Audience* (London: Routledge, 1991). For a trenchant criticism of ratings, see Eileen R. Meehan, "Why We Don't Count," in *Logics of Television,* ed. Patricia Mellencamp (Bloomington: Indiana University Press, 1990), 117–37.

32. Jerry Mander, *Four Arguments for the Elimination of Television* (New York: Morrow, 1978).

33. For an exhaustive study, see Stephen Frantzich and John Sullivan, *The C-SPAN Revolution* (Norman: University of Oklahoma Press, 1996).

34. For thoughtful overviews, see William Hoynes, *Public Television for Sale* (Boulder, Colo.: Westview, 1994); and Marilyn Lashley, *Public Television* (New York: Greenwood, 1992).

35. Marilyn E. Lashley, "Even in Public Television, Ownership Changes Matter," *Communication Research* 19:6 (December 1992): 770–86.

36. The Twentieth-Century Fund Task Force on Public Television, *Quality Time* (New York: Twentieth-Century Fund Press, 1993), 36.

37. Janine Jackson, "If PBS Can't Be Reformed, It Should Be Replaced," *EXTRA!* 7:5 (September/October 1994): 25.

38. Federal Communications Commission release 51785, 24 January 1995.

39. Andrew C. Barrett, "Public Policy and Radio—A Regulator's View," *Media Studies Journal* 7:3 (Summer 1993): 141.

40. For useful background material, see Michael X. Delli Carpini, "Radio's Political Past," *Media Studies Journal* 7:3 (Summer 1993): 23–35.

41. Andrea Adelson, "Radio Station Consolidation Threatens Small Operators," *New York Times,* 19 April 1993, C1.

42. "Rules of Ownership Changing for Media," *New York Times,* 9 March 1996, 24Y.

43. Al Stavitsky, "Ear on America," *Media Studies Journal* 7:3 (Summer 1993): 77, 90.

44. Sean Ross, "Music Radio—The Fickleness of Fragmentation," *Media Studies Journal* 7:3 (Summer 1993): 98, citing the industry newsletter, *M Street Journal,* February 1993.

45. James B. Kelleher, "Christian Radio Stations, Riding a Wave of Change, Keep Their Popularity," *New York Times,* 10 January 1994, C6.

46. This information comes from Jesse Drew, "Micro Radio," *EXTRA!* 6:7 (November/December 1993): 27.

47. Federal Communications Commission release 51785, 24 January 1995.

48. Karen De Witt, "New Chief Wants to Widen NPR's Financial Base," *New York Times,* 28 March 1994, C6.

49. Stephen L. Salyer, "Monopoly to Marketplace—Competition Comes to Public Radio," *Media Studies Journal* 7:3 (Summer 1993): 178–79.

50. Dominick, *Dynamics of Mass Communication,* 235.

51. James Sterngold, "Seagram Deal Buys Glamour and a Cash Cow Called Music," *New York Times,* 10 April 1955, A1, C8.

52. Dominick, *Dynamics of Mass Communications,* 226.

53. Ibid., 224–25.

54. Mark Crispin Miller, *Boxed In* (Evanston, Ill.: Northwestern University Press, 1988), 180.

55. R. Serge Denisoff, *Great Day Coming* (Baltimore, Md.: Penguin, 1973); and David King Dunaway, "Music as Political Communication in the United States," in *Popular Music and Communication,* ed. James Lull (Newbury Park, Calif.: Sage, 1987), 36–52.

56. Stephen A. Smith and Jimmie N. Rogers, "Popular Culture and the Rhetoric of Country Music: A Revisionist Interpretation," in *Politics in Familiar Contexts,* ed. Robert L. Savage and Dan Nimmo (Norwood, N.J.: Ablex, 1990), 195; see also Cecelia Tichi, *High Lonesome* (Chapel Hill: University of North Carolina Press, 1994).

57. Pat Aufderheide, "Music Videos," in *Watching Television,* ed. Todd Gitlin (New York: Pantheon, 1986), 125.

58. Andrew Goodwin, *Dancing in the Distraction Factory* (Minneapolis: University of Minnesota Press, 1992), 178.

59. Ibid., 165.

60. Anne Johnston Wadsworth and Lynda Lee Kaid, "Political Themes and Images in Music Videos," in *Politics in Familiar Contexts,* ed. Robert L. Savage and Dan Nimmo (Norwood, N.J.: Ablex, 1990), 169.

61. Stephen Lacy and Todd F. Simon, *The Economics and Regulation of United States Newspapers* (Norwood, N.J.: Ablex, 1993); see also Dominick, *Dynamics of Mass Communication,* 122.

62. Leo Bogart, *Preserving the Press* (New York: Columbia University Press, 1991), 156.

63. A. J. Liebling, *The Press* (New York: Ballantine, 1964), 7.

64. See Doug Underwood, *When MBAs Rule the Newsroom* (New York: Columbia University Press, 1993).

65. Richard Harwood, "Journalism's Underclass," in *Messages,* ed. *Washington Post* Writer's Group (Boston: Allyn & Bacon, 1991), 64.

66. William Glaberson, "Departures at Paper Ignite Debate on Owners' Priorities," *New York Times,* 15 February 1995, C16.

67. Sreenath Sreenivasan, "As Mainstream Papers Struggle, the Ethnic Press Is Thriving," *New York Times,* 22 July 1996, C7.

68. I am indebted to my friend, magazine editor Jack Nessel, who taught a summer course at New York University on the subject, for sharing his insights on the magazine business with me; see also Dominick, *Dynamics of Mass Communication,* 136–37.

69. Dominick, *Dynamics of Mass Communication,* 143.

70. Ibid., 143–44.

71. Benjamin M. Compaine et al., *Who Owns the Media?* 2nd ed. rev. (White Plains, N.Y.: Knowledge Industry Publications, 1982), 149.

72. Deirdre Carmody, "From Some 2,000 Alternative Magazines, a Digest," *New York Times,* 4 January 1993, C17.

73. Deirdre Carmody, "On the Annual Scoreboard of New Magazines, It's Sports 67, Sex 44," *New York Times,* 12 June 1995, C5; see also Turow, *Media Systems in Society,* 83.

74. Amy Harmon, "Digital Culture Pioneer Sold to Condé Nast," *New York Times,* 11 May 1998, C2.

75. Jay E. Rosen, "*Out* Magazine's National Reach," *New York Times,* 7 March 1994, C6.

76. Deirdre Carmody, "Sale Planned for *Mirabella* After 6 Years of Losses," *New York Times,* 23 March 1995, C6.

77. Gloria Steinem, "Sex, Lies and Advertising," *MS* 1:1 (July/August 1990): 18–28.

78. An illuminating discussion of celebrity in contemporary America is Joshua Gamson, *Claims to Fame* (Berkeley: University of California Press, 1994).

79. John Seabrook, "Annals of Showtown," *New Yorker* 70:5 (21 March, 1994): 221.

80. Fredric Wertham, *Seduction of the Innocents* (New York: Rinehart, 1954); and Ariel Dorfman and Armand Mattelart, *How to Read Donald Duck* (New York: International General, 1975).

81. For a useful survey of the publishing business, see *Media Studies Journal* 6:3 (Summer 1992).

82. Dominick, *Dynamics of Mass Communication,* 157.

83. Sarah Lyall, "Book Notes," *New York Times,* 2 March 1994, 20.

84. Dominick, *Dynamics of Mass Communications,* 162.

85. Betty Friedan, *The Feminine Mystique* (New York: Norton, 1963); Michael Harrington, *The Other America* (New York: Macmillan, 1962); and Rachel Carson, *Silent Spring* (Boston: Houghton Mifflin, 1962).

86. Mark Litwak, *Reel Power* (New York: Morrow, 1986), 68. This book recounts the Hollywood movie-making process in revealing, painful, sometimes gruesome detail.

87. Ibid., 74.

88. Bernard Weinraub, "What Do Women Want? Movies," *New York Times,* 10 February 1997, B1.

89. Worthwhile reading on nonfiction film is Bill Nichols, *Representing Reality* (Bloomington: Indiana University Press, 1991).

90. Litwak, *Reel Power,* 289.

91. Bernard Weinraub and Geraldine Fabrikant, "Turmoil at Disney: The Sequel," *New York Times,* 13 March 1995, C6.

92. Bernard Weinraub, "Clouds Over Disney," *New York Times,* 9 April 1995, F12.

93. Litwak, *Reel Power,* 244.

94. Philip J. Hilts, "$1 Million Spent to Put Cigarettes in Movies, Memos Show," *New York Times,* 20 May 1994, A8.

95. Bernard Weinraub, "Shaken Hollywood Is Relieved to See 1994 Reel to 'The End,'" *New York Times,* 29 December 1994, B1.

96. For a mock but close-to-reality discussion of how to market movies, see "The New Auteurs," *Harper's Magazine* 286:1717 (June 1993): 33–45. This drollery was brought to my attention by Terry Pristin.

97. Richard W. Stevenson, "Mondo Murdoch," *New York Times,* 29 May 1994, E1ff.

98. Paul M. Hirsch, "Globalization of Mass Media Ownership," *Communication Research* 19:6 (December 1992): 677–78.

99. Joseph Turow, "The Organizational Underpinnings of Contemporary Media Conglomerates," *Communication Research* 19:6 (December 1992): 682–704.

100. Ken Auletta, "American Keiretsu," *New Yorker* 20–27 October 1997: 226.

101. Ben H. Bagdikian, *The Media Monopoly,* 4th ed. (Boston: Beacon Press, 1992); see also Leo Bogart, *Commercial Culture* (New York: Oxford University Press, 1995).

102. Ken Auletta, "The Pirate," *New Yorker* 71:36 (13 November 1995): 90.

103. For these distinctions, see Douglas Gomery, "The Centrality of Media Economics," *Journal of Communication* 43:3 (Summer 1993): 190–98.

104. Harold L. Vogel, *Entertainment Industry Economics* (New York: Cambridge University Press, 1990), 287.

105. Compaine et al., *Who Owns the Media?,* 465.

Chapter 3

News

◆　◆　◆

This chapter is devoted to news. News is composed of reports and accounts by journalists of what is going on in the world. These stories often include the reactions of those involved or affected, and the observations and interpretations of supposedly knowledgeable experts.

A lot of media content consists of news, and much of that news contains stories about politics and government. This material reaches a significant portion of the American people: 65 percent of adults polled say they watch local television news, 50 percent claim to have read a newspaper the previous day, and 42 percent regularly watch one of the three nightly network news programs.[1]

This chapter covers the criteria, acquisition, conversion, presentation, and purveyors of news. It focuses on the beliefs and attitudes of individual journalists, the routines they follow, and the norms of the organizations for which they work.[2] Later chapters will look in detail at the techniques of politicians and public officials to influence the news, tracing their successes and failures, and explaining why they occur.

JOURNALISTS

Journalists' backgrounds and beliefs can influence their decisions about which stories to cover and even how to report them.[3] So it matters that a majority of journalists are white, middle class, middle-aged (give or take a few years), and male.[4] And that, at around 10 percent, there is a dearth of minorities employed by U.S. dailies.[5]

Women have had to wage a long and sometimes lonely struggle to establish a place in the profession.[6] By the 1970s and 1980s, they were filing charges of discrimination in hiring and promotion against the AP Wire Service, and instituting law suits against the *New York Times* and other media organizations.[7] They now compose about one third of all U.S. journalists.[8] One consequence has been the expansion of the definition of news to include issues particularly relevant to women, such as child care.[9]

For S. Robert Lichter, Linda Lichter, and Stanley Rothman, it is not race and gender but journalists' liberal or left attitudes that impose a bias on the news.[10] While there is little evidence of intentional distortion in news reporting, note that 89 percent of Washington reporters responding to a survey voted for Clinton in 1992.[11] Such uniformity of views might have some impact on professional behavior, however indirect and unintentional. (See the study of Common Cause and the *New York Times* in chapter 9.) Thus, the Lichters and Rothman "document" their bias argument with content analyses of three long-running stories: nuclear power plant safety, school busing for racial integration, and the oil industry's role in the energy crisis.

Critics, notably Herbert Gans, have trenchantly assailed their methodology and conclusions on the grounds that the authors highlight the data supporting their argument, "report findings about journalists which do not accurately reflect the answers they gave to the survey questions they were asked," treat "their answers as strongly felt opinions in a way that makes the journalists appear militant and radical," and, most important, present "a mass of data on the personal backgrounds and alleged political opinions and values of the journalists without any evidence that these are relevant to how the journalists report the news."[12]

Certainly, journalists' opinions can influence their coverage, but they probably do so less than the criteria of news and the processes they follow to acquire, convert, and present it. Irrespective of their original opinions, journalists are hired and work at organizations (newspapers, television stations, magazines, etc.). They are socialized to the organizational and professional norms of their occupation. They are subject to the budgetary requirements of their corporate employers. Their autonomy is limited. Those who disagree with the news orientation of their newspapers or television stations do not stay there long.[13]

For celebrity journalists—many of them earning lavish incomes (e.g., Sam Donaldson's $2 million annually)—fees of up to $30,000 for speaking engagements may pose more of an ethical problem than charges of ideological bias.[14] These payments compromise their credibility, give at least the appearance of conflict of interest, and may encourage them to indulge in controversy as a means of maintaining their appeal. They are certainly incompatible with Theodore White's definition of a good reporter as "a cross between a beggar and a detective, a wheedler and a prosecutor."[15]

CRITERIA

Journalists have in their heads some notion, often inchoate and unexpressed, of what news is and where it comes from. A regular viewer of television or a reader of the press can quickly discern most of the defining criteria. Violence (especially wars, revolutions, and coups); disasters wreaked by humans and nature; conflict, crises, controversy, scandals, and outrages; and occasional reassurance about actions being taken to alleviate or repair the damage—all are news.[16]

'In accordance with network policy, we are warning our viewers the following program will feature unimaginable violence to adults and children alike, scenes of sexual depravity and behavior which could lead impressionable viewers to lose faith in established social values Now for the nightly news.'

Dennis Renault, Sacramento Bee

Government and politics expressed by the decisions and actions of the president, key members of Congress, the U.S. Supreme Court, and some governmental departments are all grist for news. But some things are more newsworthy than others. As then-President Richard M. Nixon heartfully (and hurtfully) observed, based on his many years in public life: "'For the press, progress is not news—trouble is news.'"[17]

Exceptions are dramatic interruptions of routine that celebrate reconciliation, such as the signing of a peace treaty and the pomp and circumstance of presidential inaugurations and funerals. These events are deemed historic, transmitted in real time.[18]

When ordinary people become newsworthy, it is usually in one of five categories: as actual or alleged law breakers and violators; as visible disrupters of the social order (e.g., protesters, strikers, or rioters); as participants in unusual activities; as victims; and as voters, survey respondents, and other aggregates.[19]

But news is more than doom and gloom, the activities of elites and celebrities, and, less frequently, the disruptive or uncommon activities of unknown people. There is also a catch-all category dubbed "human interest," consisting of novel, upbeat tales. Common in newspapers, they often conclude national and local television news shows.

Two other determinants of news are timeliness and proximity. News is timely, something that just happened (e.g., an assassination attempt on a president) or that is newly exposed (e.g., a presidential candidate's suddenly revealed extramarital affair, even if it happened in the past).

Timeliness also means that some fresh information or details are usually necessary for a story to stay in the news. Stories with a powerful emotional impact are an exception; they remain newsworthy until they are resolved. The most famous and extreme example was the American embassy personnel held hostage for a year in Iran. Although nothing much transpired publicly after the hostages' initial incarceration, aside from the abortive rescue attempt, the story was kept in the news until their 1980 release.

Proximity also matters. Nearby events are generally more newsworthy than similar ones far away. A local murder is given more prominence than many deaths in a distant country. Notice in this respect, however, that while events outside the United States can be newsworthy, many of the international stories on the television networks' news and even in the *New York Times* emanate from the United States, present the perspectives of American officials, and are datelined Washington or New York.

ACQUISITION

Journalists acquire the news in three somewhat overlapping ways: They originate, receive, and gather it. In the process, they follow work routines and observe the practices of their profession.[20]

Note, however, that acquiring news can be difficult if not impossible. Events often occur in far-off places. Governments, intent on preventing the release of bad news, refuse entry to foreign journalists, stop them from reporting if they get in, censor their dispatches when written, expel them, and sue and ban their publications. Journalists are persecuted, imprisoned, kidnapped, and murdered.[21]

This helps to explain why some of the worst horrors of the later part of the twentieth century were barely reported at the time (e.g., the slaughter in Cambodia by the Khmer Rouge). Even the most open of governments has been known to restrict access to some of its undertakings and censor coverage, as the United States did during the Gulf War.

Originate

Reporters often witness news or its aftermath. They report from the scenes of wars, earthquakes, crimes, fires, press conferences, and elsewhere. On occasion, news may actually happen to them.

Sometimes journalists develop news. The most time-consuming and expensive way is by investigative reporting with its in-depth searching into a subject.[22] Corruption and incompetence by government and individuals are common subjects of investigations. Examples are the dogged pursuit of the involvement of President Nixon and his aides in the Watergate break-in by Carl Bernstein and Bob Woodward of the *Washington Post*.[23]

Investigative reporting is not limited to the lavishly financed press. The *Washington* (North Carolina) *Daily News,* with a circulation of 10,700, won journalism's most prestigious award, the Pulitzer Prize, in 1990 for "its series of articles . . . uncovering contamination of the city water system by cancer-causing chemicals."[24]

Most investigative stories consist of "follow-ups or advances of leaked or published government reports."[25] Investigations of the more-difficult-to-expose malfeasance of business are particularly uncommon. Morton Mintz, a former investigative reporter at the *Washington Post,* attributes this difficulty to

> bias, boosterism, careerism, cowardice, libel risks, economic imperatives, friendships, ignorance, lack of resources, laziness, protection of news sources, retreats from investigative reporting, stupidity, suppression, survival instincts, and the pro-business orientation of owners and of the managers they hire.[26]

Receive

It has been estimated that roughly one third of the news content of many newspapers, especially the less prestigious ones, is spurred by press releases. In other words, a lot of news is supplied to reporters. One important reason is that their news-gathering time and tools are limited: They cannot compel people to talk to them or to reveal useful information. So reporters often depend on others: Legislative committees, regulatory agencies, and governmental departments and commissions conduct investigations, hold hearings, and issue reports that journalists can turn into or make part of their news stories.

In addition, there are a lot of people desirous of having their views and perspectives transmitted by, even appearing in and on, the media. The careers and fortunes of many public officials, entertainers, businessmen and -women, and many other sorts of people can be helped by favorable or hindered by unfavorable coverage. Some communicate directly with journalists (see discussion of sources later in this chapter). Others are abetted by aides, press agents, personal representatives, and other hirelings. Methods include use of press releases, press conferences, more-or-less exclusive interviews, video releases, and ways of devising what they hope is newsworthy behavior to encourage attention.

Reporters also draw on the relatively reliable work of academic researchers by summarizing soon-to-be or just published research (prestigious medical journals are particularly favored) on health, psychological (personal relations), social, and media subjects.

Less reliable are many of the polls, studies, statistics, and research reported as news but supplied by self-interested organizations. Too often, these are reported straight-faced; the sponsors' interpretations and spin of the data accepted with little question.

Gather

Reporters' stories are often based on second-hand accounts (i.e., what people tell them happened) or third-hand retelling (i.e., what people tell them others told them happened). They thus gather the news and reconstruct events through legwork and on the telephone. One can learn a great deal about reporters' ability, experience, and effectiveness from the number of names and range of contacts listed on their Rolodexes.

Reporters increasingly make use of computerized data bases. They are sometimes able to obtain confidential government, business, and personal documents this way. More common, through LEXIS, NEXIS and other systems, they can locate what has been previously written on a topic by reporters and researchers. And through Profnet, should they be so inclined, they can find academic experts on virtually any subject.[27] Indeed, more and more reporters are using new technology, particularly LEXIS and NEXIS, as a substitute for reporting rather than as a supplement to it.

News-gathering is facilitated by events that are scheduled in advance, recurring, or at least predictable (e.g., elections, trials, legislative activities, U.S. Supreme Court decisions, the president's State of the Union address, and press conferences).

Beats   Routinizing this news-gathering, all the major news organizations assign reporters to beats. They are responsible for covering particular institutions, usually governmental, and their occupants, or certain subjects (e.g., environmental policy). The White House is one such beat, as are, to mention a few, Congress, the U.S. Supreme Court, the State Department, and the Defense Department.

The actions of low prestige or unpopular beats, such as those dealing with economic issues and regulatory agencies (e.g., the Securities and Exchange Commission), have to be striking to earn prominent coverage. Institutions, organizations, and subjects off the beat(en) track generate even fewer stories.

Most beats have their complement of press secretaries, spokespersons, and information offices to deal with the press as effectively as possible in the interests of the organization and its leaders. As is documented throughout this book, they try to control and shape the information flow, structure the news, and coordinate responses.

Sources   In gathering news and working their beats, reporters necessarily interact with and often rely extensively on sources to provide them with information.[28] Whether the sources do so eagerly, willingly, reluctantly, or under extreme duress depends on their motivation. These motives include some combination of self-promotion, keeping channels open, building credit, revealing a wrong that cannot be corrected through regular government channels, revenge, and the desire to advance or obstruct a person, policy, or course of action.[29] Motives may be the most interesting aspect of a story, but they are rarely included in it because they cannot be clearly identified, and reporters want to avoid speculating about them or disrupting their relationship with the source.

Sources may provide information openly and unrestrictedly or anonymously, subject to various conditions: such as the information cannot be used in any form (off-the-record); it can be used but not quoted or attributed to the source (deep background); or it can be used as background attributed other than by the source's name (e.g., not to the Secretary of State but to a senior State Department official). These distinctions are usually confined to the higher levels of the U.S. national government (e.g., the White House, State Department, Defense Department). Generally, sources and what they say can be identified unless there is prior agreement not to do so.

Leaking by a source (i.e., passing messages to journalists outside channels) is an art form. Some leaks are actually authorized; for example, the trial balloon floated by the White House to test the appeal of and opposition to an appointment or proposal under consideration. Others are unauthorized.[30] Some are quite complicated: "The daring reverse leak of information apparently for one reason but actually accomplishing the opposite."[31]

The reporter-source relationship is often symbiotic: They need each other. Howsoever and by whomever provided, information is the vital currency of news. When reported early and exclusively, it can result in approbation from editors and enhanced professional reputation. The reverse happens to reporters denied cooperation from or, worse, access to sources.

Strategies   Reporters have devised several strategies to elicit or con or pry information from their sometime reluctant, even recalcitrant, sources. Former President Richard Nixon, familiar with them all, has left us some translations.[32] "I really want to write a positive story" means that a knife is about to be stuck in the source's back. "If you don't talk to me, your side of the story won't be represented" can mislead because many reporters know their story angle before they interview you. "You should hear what this other guy said about you" is designed to provoke a source into responding negatively about the other person, a response which is likely to appear in the story without the initial critical comment. "I'm going to write the story whether you talk to me or not" often means that the reporter has no story unless the source talks. And about "Oh, and just one more question," Nixon writes: "Forget the other ten he asked; this is what he really came for."

Experts   There is a second sort of source eager to talk to the media: "experts" who are called on to provide background to, comments on, interpretations of, and predictions about the news. Journalists, especially those in Washington, D.C., tend to rely on a limited number of these sources. Some are former politicians and government officials. Others are academics, such as Kathleen Hall Jamieson, dean of the Annenberg School for Communication at the University of Pennsylvania. Yet others are associated with putative think tanks, such as Tom Mann, director of governmental studies at the Brookings Institution, and "King of Quotes" Norman Ornstein of the American Enterprise Institute.[33]

According to an extensive survey of the scene, "news shapers used by Washington reporters come from pro-status quo institutions; experts from anti-status quo institutions are never interviewed." And "the most frequently used 'experts' are often wrong, say little of consequence, represent a very narrow range of views, and have political axes to grind."[34]

Quotes   Reporters solicit and deploy quotes to give their stories sustenance and support and to insulate them from accusations of imposing their own points of view on the material. It is not unknown, however, for reporters to "try to get you to say what they want you to say, not what you've got to say."[35] Or to quote out of context, thereby changing or distorting the original meaning.

In general, though, quotes do reflect their makers' perspectives. Powerful people in particular exercise considerable control over their quotes. Entrepreneur Carl Icahn "talks to reporters only on the condition that any quote be read back to him in context, and he goes over and over the quotes, listening for each nuance, demanding a word change here, a phrase deleted there." He allows his employees to speak to reporters "on the condition that their quotes too be checked—not with them but with him."[36] Other people record their interviews with reporters so that they can challenge any "erroneous" quote. Reporters may also record so that they can verify a quote in case it is challenged.

Scoops   Howsoever they obtain the news, most journalists lust to scoop the competition; that is, report a story first and exclusively. Being visibly scooped is embarrassing. To avoid it, reporters—for example, at the *Washington Post*—watch the television evening news and scramble to match any scoops. Similarly, news organizations across Washington await the *Post*'s first edition and "'borrow' . . . from any exclusive stories that appear."[37] An unfortunate consequence is that, usually due to lack of time for checking, any error in the original story is perpetuated.

Indexing

U.S. policy-makers' perspectives, especially on foreign policy issues, often dominate governmental stories. Lance Bennett contends that these views are often "indexed:" The range of voices reporters include in these stories reflects the debate among powerful decision-makers. Sometimes this approximates the diversity of views on a topic in the society. But it can be less than representative when, for various reasons, the debate among policy-makers is limited: Congressional Democrats downplaying for political reasons their opposition to President Bush's impending decision to undertake the Gulf War would be an example.[38]

Of course, "indexing" can explain only some content. But it is a useful way of thinking about the news. (See the discussion of foreign policy in chapter 15.)

CONVERSION

Information may be lacking, facts unclear, details partial, yet reporters must take their material and convert it into news stories: writing it up in some logical and coherent order for the newspaper, arranging the pictures and connecting them to their voice-over for television. And do so in a relatively brief period, often working under a tight deadline. In the process, they encounter other influences: owners and editors, objectivity, framing, facts, language, and pictures.

Owners and Editors

Based on his interviews of a small sample of newspaper publishers, Frederick Schiff concludes that they perceive the opinions of their readers in terms of their own business and upper-class interests. They "establish organizational policies and taken-for-granted practices in their newsrooms that influence what kind of news content is produced for whom."[39] That news enhances or at least is consistent or rarely clashes with their interests.

Corroborating evidence comes from J. H. Snider and Benjamin Page's finding that "media owners used their control of the airwaves to enhance their efforts at lobbying elected officials" for the successful passage of a provision of the Telecommunications Act of 1996 giving "existing TV broadcasters free usage of spectrum valued at between $11 billion and $70 billion."[40]

Top management also sometimes intervenes to block or change stories for business (e.g., to placate a major advertiser), personal, or political reasons. This may be done overtly: Reporter Richard Manning resigned from the (Montana) *Missoulian* after his editors stalled for six months before publishing his exposé of corporate logging deforestation of vast stretches of the Rocky Mountains, and then removed him from the environmental beat.[41]

Because stories are available on the computer screen in advance of publication, intervention by higher-ups can be expressed subtly and taken indirectly—a suggestion or word to the relevant section editor will suffice. Thus, the prevalence of owner-publisher-management actual interference for nonjournalistic reasons is difficult to determine.

In any event, whether assigned to a story or when pursuing it of their own volition, reporters usually consult with their editors (assignment editors, producers, and executive editors in television) before they begin, while collecting material, and when converting it into stories. For, although their relationship with reporters is usually cooperative, involving negotiation and compromise of any disagreements, editors "exercise an absolute right to assign stories and to run, kill, edit, package, and place the texts that result."[42]

Objectivity

Journalists are guided by the canons of their occupation. They usually strive in their news stories to be impartial and fair, to exclude their personal opinions, to achieve balance by including different sides, and to avoid intentional bias.[43] In other words, they try to be objective. They are sometimes successful. Inclusion of the reporter's perspective (subjectivity) is allowed for feature and interpretive stories, and for editorials that explicitly assert arguments and points of view.

Facilitating objectivity, much reporting is descriptive, based on what is assumed to be reality, oriented around questions of who, what, where, when and, if possible, the problematic "why." These questions are usually addressed early in the story.

In fact, objectivity is undermined by several elements of the conversion process: particularly framing, facts, language, and pictures.

Framing   Applying a central idea to give meaning to the events reported is the essence of framing. Reporters often approach news-gathering with some notion of the way the story will turn out and how the material will be organized and structured, in a word, how it will be *framed*. They may even begin with the frame and collect material to fit it. Sometimes, a story may have a few frames, but one usually predominates.

Little understood by the news audience, framing is crucial; for it is through their frames that news stories depict events in particular ways, bring a perspective to bear, emphasize some aspects at the expense of others.[44] It is difficult to identify social actors and name an action without also presenting an attitude toward them. This is inherent in the very process of selecting, editing, organizing, and presenting stories.

Journalists tend to operate with a relatively small repertoire of familiar frames, a reliance increased by the way they cover stories in groups or packs. For many years, international news was fitted—sometimes shoe-horned—into a United States vs. Soviet Union cold war frame. Japan is often framed as an unfair trading partner, except when overwhelmed by an earthquake.

Many frames are underlined by cynicism: "a prejudice against the face-value explanation bordering on disbelief, accompanied by a ready willingness to ascribe base motives."[45] Thus, frames recurring in stories about government and politics are bureaucratic incompetence, inefficiency and waste, corruption, politicians motivated mainly by vote-seeking, elections as horse races, policy-making as strategy and tactics rather than substance, and relations within and between the branches of government as conflictual.

At the same time, public officials, candidates, and others involved in government and politics provide journalists with self-serving (although not necessarily inaccurate) and thus favorable story frames: bureaucratic competence, politicians motivated by the public interest, congressional achievements; and cooperation between the branches of government in the benefit of all.

In general, the media are likely to accept governmental frames on foreign policy issues that have bi-partisan support among policy-makers in the country, but not on domestic issues rife with disagreement and conflict over policies.

Facts   Reporters are sometimes able to identify the facts (something that occurred, exists, is true) from the morass of rumor, gossip, and hearsay; of errors and misinformation; of partial perceptions and lies. But even when they can, they must still decide which facts to include and exclude, how prominently, and from which sources. These decisions inevitably impinge on objectivity.

Further complicating objectivity, facts often require interpretation. When a Soviet military aircraft tracked a Korean airliner for roughly two and a half hours before shooting it down, President Reagan said this showed that the Russians must have known it was a civilian plane and wantonly destroyed it; but for the Soviet government, the tracking displayed patience and civilized restraint.[46]

Language   Communicating exactly or even clearly is not easy; the words, phrases, and sentences we use are often freighted with more or less meaning, even a different meaning, than we intend. So language can be a trap.[47] Consider the apparently innocuous phrase: "Columbus discovered America." From a Eurocentric point of view, it is reasonable and accurate. From the point of view of the native inhabitants of the "discovered" continent, the phrase should be "Americans discovered Columbus."

Journalists are sensitive to and wrestle with this problem; words are, after all, the currency of their profession. They know that there are different effects of using the words "says," "states," "contends," "claims," "acknowledges," or "admits." They are aware that headlines in particular, brief and pithy, which they rarely write, can frame and structure stories in particular ways.

A related problem is journalists' heavy and often unthinking reliance on shorthand catchwords, stereotypes, and labels, which can legitimize or stigmatize an individual, group, organization, and even institution.

This is exacerbated by "modes of pseudo-reportage" common to journalism, wittily identified and labeled by the Australian scholar John D. May.[48] In "ghostliness," thoughts, expectations, beliefs, and understandings are imputed to nobody, everybody, or just the atmosphere, as in: It is claimed, understood, expected, or seen. In "anthropomorphism," groups and institutions (e.g., the Pentagon) are endowed with human qualities: They seek, push, warn, or think. In "wingery," political parties and other movements are endowed with left, right, and extreme wings, even though the meaning of such terms is often unclear.

In recent years, as a way of avoiding stale language and "pseudo-reportage," some reporters in the conventional news media have been given leeway to indulge in subjective, impressionistic, and even expressive language. Describing a trip by President Clinton, Maureen Dowd of the *New York Times* wrote that he had returned "for a sentimental journey to the university where he didn't inhale, didn't get drafted, and didn't get a degree."[49] The compatibility of such language with objectivity is problematic. Compare it to the more straightforward words of Ann Devroy of the *Washington Post:* "President Clinton ended his D-Day anniversary tour of Europe today with a nostalgic stop at Oxford University, defying the ghosts of his youth to revisit the campus where he struggled to avoid military service in Vietnam."[50] Yet even some of Devroy's language ("defying . . . struggled to avoid") can be seen as subjective.

Pictures   Television news is picture-driven: Stories with appealing or even available pictures are more likely than those without to be played prominently. This partly explains why for many years the U.S. savings and loan scandal was virtually uncovered and unreported on television news.

The centrality of visual news compounds the objectivity problem: A picture may be worth a thousand words, but it is more prone to mislead, even deceive (especially if it has been retouched or altered by digital technology). Viewers don't usually know what is not shown, what happened before or after, the extent to which those pictured are behaving for the camera. Camera angles, distance from the subject (especially close-ups), length of shot, camera movement, and editing all influence viewers' impressions. As watching television with the sound off reveals, visuals often are unclear or ambiguous without the anchor person's introduction and the reporter's words to give them meaning.[51] (These observations also apply to photographs in the print media.)

Wire and Other News Services

Thus far, this chapter has focused on the acquisition and conversion of news by individual reporters. But almost all news media rely on the wire services, primarily the Associated Press (AP) and, if they subscribe, the United Press International (UPI), Reuters, and others. These agencies transmit stories from their own staff and from reporters who work for newspapers and other organizations that are members of the services.

The wire services' day-to-day reporting from part of the developing world and the smaller industrialized nations comes from part-time local correspondents called stringers. Former AP Paris bureau chief Mort Rosenblum, after praising some of them as "highly competent and dedicated professionals," comments that "others are untrained in Western press traditions and unwilling to risk unemployment, jail terms or worse for the sake of a few dollars paid by some faceless editor in New York."[52] He notes that "local authorities often pressure them to report what the government wants." Adding that "even if there is no pressure, many are reluctant to reveal hard truths about their own cultures and societies."

The stories flow from the news services' main (trunk) wires, to the regional wires serving smaller media, to the newspapers, television, and radio stations. The selection process at each level tends to winnow a relatively rich mixture of news "to a sparse, violent, and conflict-laden portrait of the world, especially for the Third World."[53]

For the less prestigious and less wealthy, or more profit-oriented American newspapers—meaning the overwhelming bulk of them—the wire services provide the international and most of the national news stories they publish. They may also subscribe to and thus print material from other news services such as that of the *New York Times.*

As a result of this dependence on services, the international and national news of many newspapers throughout the United States is quite similar.

News on television also often relies on the wire services for stories. These are easily recognizable to the discerning viewer as items, usually brief and accompanied by a still photo or unmoving graphic, read by the anchor person. The reliance on the wire services is even more dominant on radio.

The main television equivalent of the wire services are the London-based international television agencies Worldwide Television News (WTN) and Associated Press Television (APTV), both owned by the Associated Press; and Reuters

Television, owned mainly by Reuters and NBC. They supply their subscribers with narrationless, natural sound video and brief printed informational scripts. These come from their staffs and stringers, freelancers, and other services, and occasionally from private organizations that have their own video units, such as the environmental activist group Greenpeace.[54]

As a consequence, news, particularly from the Third World, is determined by the Anglo-American perspective of these London-based agencies.[55]

Some news outlets seek a more in-depth, knowledgeable, and different perspective on relatively neglected regions of the world than provided by the major print and picture wire services. They obtain material from such organizations as the Africa News Service, the Pacific News Service, and other independent providers known to produce ground-breaking journalism and original stories on shoestring budgets.

PRESENTATION

The distinguished journalist David Broder describes newspapers as "a partial, hasty, incomplete, inevitably somewhat flawed and inaccurate rendering of some of the things we have heard about in the past 24 hours."[56] His description applies also to television news. Sources may be unreliable, their motives suspect, facts confused and disputed. Yet the news is presented with a straight-forward assurance that belies its construction and uncertainty, the frailty of objectivity, and the ambiguity of words and pictures. As a consequence, even though people can still be suspicious of individual stories or the news media in general, the credibility of the newspaper they are reading and of the television news program they are watching is sustained.

Several conventions and techniques contribute deliberately or unintentionally to this impression of credibility. In newspapers, they include headlines, sectioning, the pyramid style, and personalization; on television, the use of anchors and correspondents, narratives, and clusters.

Newspapers

Headlines enhance credibility by giving the impression of encapsulating the essence of the story. Some headlines are definitive: "Headless Body in Topless Bar" front-paged the *New York Post*. But most are actually interpretations of the news: The end of the world would likely be "World Ends Today" with a subhead "See Details, Page 8" in the *New York Times*. Compare this to "World Ends! Stock Market Closes for Good" in the *Wall Street Journal,* and "World Comes to an End! Women and the Poor Hurt Most!" in the *Washington Post*. Most people, reading only one of these newspapers, would be unaware of the different interpretations.

Sectioning involves the division of newspapers into different parts based on subjects (e.g., international, national, local news) and approaches. The division is consistent and predictable. Readers come to know and feel comfortable with the placements. Regularity enhances credibility.

The inverted pyramid, with the essential facts at the beginning and less important information following, is the basic way of writing stories in newspapers. This enhances credibility by giving the impression that importance is obvious and that reporters are able to identify the facts that signify it.

Reporters tend to personalize many of their stories; that is, to emphasize individuals and the human interest angles of the events and topics they report.[57] Thus, stories about unemployment begin by routing the fate of one of its victims. This focus on real people rather than on abstract economic and social forces lends reality and therefore credibility to the account.

Television

News on television is heralded by music, displays an official-looking set, and is interlaced with teasers ("coming up next . . .") and admonitions to stay tuned. It is hosted by anchors who, on the networks, seemingly abide forever, providing continuity and stability in the inferno of news. They appear to possess common sense, rationality, and sanity; seem knowledgeable, informed, and impartial. If male, they are authoritative; if female, likable (as measured in surveys). They present, summarize, frame, seem to summon forth images at will, and control what is seen.

Adding to anchors' credibility are the formal way they are announced, accompanying music, their dress, the camera's respectful distance, and the (often scripted) dialogue they sometimes conduct with correspondents at the conclusion of a report.

Similarly, the correspondents are apparently trustworthy, their demeanor unemotional, uninvolved, dispassionate. They authenticate their presentations by reporting from the scene of an event (in front of the White House, the Capitol, the Supreme Court building), or from a studio simulation. They, too, are shown at an appropriate distance from the camera—no revealing close-ups for them.

Television news has a few basic modes of presenting stories. The briefest has the anchor reading, usually from a wire service report, against a relevant background graphic, such as a map. Or narrating over a piece of film showing, for example, the destructive effects of an exploded car bomb. A single segment is longer: It consists of an anchor's introduction, followed by a correspondent's locational report, often with various visuals and sound bites (a sentence or two from someone relevant to the story) inserted. The lengthiest are multisegments involving more than one reporter and location.

Even though they rarely last more than a few minutes, single and multisegment stories are told as narratives, with beginnings, middles, and ends, bookended by the anchor's introduction and the correspondent's conclusion. Events are presented as plotted stories "involving all the drama of filmed confrontation . . . and the portrayal of complex matters in terms of simple conflict."[58] This takes place even though they are usually much more complicated and the material (some of it on the cutting or editing room floor) may lend itself to other frames and meanings.

Beyond segments are clusters, the grouping together of supposedly related stories. Clusters, too, sustain credibility by giving the impression that the stories are logically linked. But connections within a cluster may be forced: Sometimes quite disparate stories of innocence and guilt are tied together under such rubrics as trials and criminality; or conflicts in different parts of the world's grouped under violence.

PURVEYORS

As the discussion of presentation suggests, despite similarities in their criteria of news, ways of acquiring it, and conversion processes, the U.S. news media are far from identical. In fact, there is a spectrum of purveyors. It is based on the audience aimed at and concomitant differences in the treatment of events, placement, and language of stories. I dub these purveyors elite, prestige, popular, and tabloid.

In giving the main examples of each one, it must be acknowledged that some placements can be challenged and others are inexact. Thus, local commercial radio and weekly newspapers are clearly too diverse to occupy any one category, and the networks' news magazines fall uneasily between popular and tabloid.

Elite

The elite press tends to emphasize government and politics, employs or uses foreign correspondents and reports their stories, strives to delve into issues and trends, and indulges in investigative journalism. Its news stories include background and explanations, often containing more than one perspective and source. It treats the news with relative sobriety, downplays flamboyant material, and eschews hyperbolic (but not evocative) language.

The elite press is represented by the *New York Times,* as well as the *Washington Post, Los Angeles Times,* the *Wall Street Journal,* National Public Radio's "All Things Considered" and "Morning Edition," and weekend equivalents, and Public Television's "The NewsHour with Jim Lehrer."

The *New York Times* especially serves as a guide, even guru, for the rest of the press: Its news stories set the agenda; its frames are frequently adopted and adapted by other news outlets.

Prestige

The news magazines *Newsweek, Time,* and *U.S. News* fall into this category, and the paradigmatic examples are the networks' evening news programs. Traditionally, these shows have observed most of the canons of the "elite" press. The size of their audiences, the massive resources they can deploy to cover a story if so inspired, and the influence of their coverage (which can vastly amplify the stories of the elite media) all conduce to their prestige. As, in some perverse way, do the vast sums they pay their anchors and star reporters.

In recent years, though, the networks have cut back on their acquisition of news.[59] They have always been handicapped by lack of time to report all the news in their half-hour-minus-time-for-commercials newscasts: Announces the anchorman, "Moses just came down from Mt. Sinai with the Ten Commandments; here's

Sam Donaldson with the top three." Now, they have in essence gone from news-gathering to news-production organizations. ABC, CBS, and NBC have closed many of their bureaus around the world, leaving them with fewer than ten each, thus slashing their foreign coverage.

When especially newsworthy events occur in one of the many places where they have no correspondents, the networks "parachute" one in. This reactive expedient is inadequate when the reporters "end up in places they have never seen before, with no knowledge of the language, the customs or the background to the story they are covering."[60]

Domestic cutbacks have also taken place: NBC, for example, has dropped its New York and Miami bureaus, reducing its number to seven. Consequently, much more of the news on the networks now comes from outside organizations, such as those they own and operate and their affiliate stations across the United States. Many of their visuals from abroad are provided by news services.

In contrast, CNN has expanded its coverage of world news as the networks have contracted theirs, thus joining the "prestige" group. Moreover, it can go to breaking events while the networks continue with their regular fodder. This means that CNN is often a primary source for other news organizations, even setting or at least adding to their agenda of what to cover.

But CNN too has its limitations. International and national stories are often short and superficial; fluff abounds.

Also problematic, some of CNN's coverage—live or on a just-received tape—is transmitted directly and instantaneously. This eliminates much of the processing of material by reporters in the field and by editors at CNN. The benefits are speed, immediacy, and vividness. But the footage is often raw: It has not been structured and organized, or given clear coherence and meaning by journalists at CNN. The network is thus vulnerable to the charge of being a conduit for those whose activities it transmits in this way.

Relatedly, CNN's "World Report" shows news stories provided by various national broadcast organizations from around the world. These stories reflect the suppliers' views, that of their governments in state-controlled systems, thus providing a diversity of perspectives otherwise virtually unseen on television and absent from the press.

Popular

Purveyors in this category emphasize "drama, action, entertainment, simplicity, brevity, immediacy, and personalization."[61] They unite news with show business.[62]

The most visible example is *USA Today*. With its simple layout, striking graphics, abundant color, brief stories, and excessive attention to celebrities, it is designed to be simple to read. But it usually gives more space to its colorful weather map than to foreign news. So short are its stories that some staffers have suggested in jest that a new Pulitzer Prize category be created "for best investigative paragraph."[63]

Because of its innovations and supposed reader appeal (which took several years to translate into actual profit), at a time when newspaper circulation has been declining, *USA Today* is being emulated by the local press across the country.

Doonesbury © 1987 G. B. Trudeau. Reprinted with permission of Universal Press Syndicate. All rights reserved.

Presided over by "happy talk" anchors engaging in jovial chatter, most local television news also falls into the popular category. It attracts an overwhelming percentage of the American public.[64] This news relies on the quartet of crash, casualty, crime, and corpse stories from the police and fire departments, and emphasizes human-interest pieces that evoke audience sympathy, pity, or admiration. Lots of time is given to weather and sports. The objective is for high ratings even at the expense of information: If it bleeds it leads, if it doesn't it may not air at all.

Well-paid consultants tell station executives what appeals to their audiences. The results are sometimes quite provocative, especially in the competitive market of Los Angeles. "Real Live Sex Slaves and Their Captors" was one news headline;

Chris Britt/Copley News Service

viewers were polled on such subjects as the sexiest woman and man in Holly-wood. In covering storms, reporters were ordered not to carry umbrellas. As the news director told them: "'Action news is not umbrellas . . . action news is wet in the rain.'"[65] Ratings increased as the station trivialized the significant and inflated the trivial.

Tabloid

Syndicated television shows such as "American Journal," "A Current Affair," "Hard Copy," and "Inside Edition" and weekly "newspapers" such as the *National Enquirer* and the *Star* fall into this category. They emphasize sexy crime, celebri-ties, and scandal; use hyperbolic language; and re-stage events as they may or may not have occurred. They are willing to skirt journalistic ethics by using long-lens cameras, engaging in high-speed chases, paying for interviews and exclusive rights to information (known as checkbook journalism). Their stories are often fanciful, if not invented.[66]

The tabloids are notorious for such stories as Gennifer Flowers' claim (accu-sation) of her alleged affair with then-presidential candidate Bill Clinton. Origi-nally published in the *Star,* which paid her a lot of money for it, her story was also featured in the February 7, 1992 exclusive of "A Current Affair." She was more celebrated than interviewed, fed questions she seemed prepped to answer. Adroit editing made her responses seem fluent and convincing. The program served as her forum, a conduit for her assertions; she was never challenged. Quite different treatment is accorded someone the show is out to get.

Yet, the tabloids do sometimes produce serious stories, as in the January 23, 1995, "Hard Copy" piece on prominent women's reactions and responses to Speaker of the House of Representatives' Newt Gingrich's comments on women in the military. And they have been known to undertake detailed investigative stories that produce useful revelations.

One could argue, too, that the tabloids are implicitly defending family, moral standards, and the so-called traditional American values, even as they display them being breached. In this sense, they uphold traditional values.[67]

CONCLUSION

The news media are beset by public hostility, second-guessing from academics, and persistent criticism by self-appointed press watchers. They are a whipping post of choice for politicians, who blame the messenger for the bad news message. Yet, journalists combine intelligence, industry, integrity, and expertise to report the truth, or at least reality as they perceive it. They tell us much about national and international events. To do so, they often struggle against obstruction, obfuscation, evasion, deceit, and reprisal from authority-holders.[68]

But the news media must be found wanting against democracy's need for deliberation. Episodic, lacking historical perspective, elite-oriented, and person-centered at the expense of broad social issues, news fails to provide the public with as wide a diversity of perspectives as desirable, or even necessary. Instead, the news media often fail to comprehend the range of alternative views available, infrequently explain and amplify the positions and arguments they do convey, and rarely effectively show the likely effects of ideas.[69]

The reasons for these failures (in addition to profit-making and attracting advertising discussed in the previous chapter) are limited criteria of news, the restraints imposed by objectivity, and the processes of acquiring, conversion, and presentation of news.[70]

It is usually up to newspaper editorialists and columnists, radio and television talk show hosts and their pundits, as well as politically oriented magazines to express the opinions and analyses and to provide much of the public discussion of issues and ideas essential for democracy. Appendix A presents the most prominent of these individuals and their outlets.

Notes

1. Pew Research Center for the People and the Press, "TV News Viewership Declines," 13 May 1996, 1–3 (news release).

2. For a review and evaluation of the factors that influence the content of news, see Pamela J. Shoemaker and Stephen D. Reese, *Mediating the Message* (New York: Longman, 1991). For discussions of news content, see Robert Karl Manoff and Michael Schudson, eds., *Reading the News* (New York: Pantheon, 1987).

3. See Thomas E. Patterson, "News Decisions: Journalists as Partisan Actors" (paper presented at the annual meeting of the American Political Science Association, Chicago, September 1995); also documented for foreign affairs by John Crothers Pollock, *The Politics of Crisis Reporting* (New York: Praeger, 1981).

4. For journalists' backgrounds, see David H. Weaver and G. Cleveland Wilhoit, *The American Journalist in the 1990s* (Hillsdale, N.J.: Lawrence Erlbaum, 1996).

5. For a critical account by an African-American journalist, see Jill Nelson, *Voluntary Slavery* (Chicago: Noble Press, 1993). For a more positive perspective, see Patrice Gains, *Laughing in the Dark* (New York: Crown, 1994); and Jake Lamar, *Bourgeois Blues* (New York: Plume, 1991); see also Jorge Quiroga, *Hispanic Voices: Is the Press Listening?* (Cambridge, Mass.: Harvard University, The Joan Shorenstein Center, Discussion Paper D-18, January 1995).

6. Maurine H. Beasley and Sheila J. Gibbons, eds., *Taking Their Place: A Documentary History of Women and Journalism* (Washington, D.C.: American University Press, 1993); Nan Robertson, *The Girls in the Balcony* (New York: Random House, 1992); and Judy Woodruff, "Covering Politics—Is There a Female Difference?" *Media Studies Journal* 11:2 (Spring 1997): 155–58.

7. Kay Mills, *A Place in the News* (New York: Dodd, Mead, 1988), chap. 10.

8. David Weaver, "Women as Journalists," in *Women, Media, and Politics,* ed. Pippa Norris (New York: Oxford University Press, 1997), 21–40.

9. Kay Mills, "What Difference Do Women Journalists Make?" in *Women, Media, and Politics,* ed. Pippa Norris (New York: Oxford University Press, 1997), 41–55.

10. S. Robert Lichter, Stanley Rothman, and Linda S. Lichter, *The Media Elite* (Bethesda, Md.: Adler & Adler, 1986).

11. Elaine S. Povich, *Partners and Adversaries* (Arlington, Va.: Freedom Forum, 1996), 174.

12. Herbert J. Gans, "Are U.S. Journalists Dangerously Liberal? *Columbia Journalism Review* 24:4 (November/December 1985): 29–33, from which these quotes are taken. See also Albert E. Gollin, "Plumbing the 'Uncharted Recesses of the Media Mind,'" *Columbia Journalism Review* 25:6 (March-April 1987): 59–64.

13. Stephen D. Reese, "The News Paradigm and the Ideology of Objectivity: A Socialist at the *Wall Street Journal,*" *Critical Studies in Mass Communication* 7 (1990): 390–409.

14. For the facts and a thoughtful discussion, see Alicia C. Shepard, "Talk Is Expensive," *American Journalism Review* 16:4 (May 1994): 21–27, 42.

15. Quoted in Edward T. Thompson, ed., *Theodore White at Large* (New York: Pantheon, 1992), 550.

16. Akiba A. Cohen, Hanna Adoni, and Charles R. Bantz, in *Social Conflict and Television News* (Newbury Park, Calif.: Sage, 1990), trace the prevalence of conflict in the television news of five countries, including the United States. For the appeal of scandals and the like, see Suzanne Garment, *Scandal* (New York: Anchor Books, 1992); and Larry J. Sabato, *Feeding Frenzy* (New York: Free Press, 1991).

17. Quoted in William Safire, "The Press is the Enemy: Nixon and the Media," *New York* 8 (27 January 1975): 44.

18. Daniel Dayan and Elihu Katz, *Media Events* (Cambridge, Mass.: Harvard University Press, 1992).

19. Herbert J. Gans, *Deciding What's News* (New York: Pantheon, 1979), 13.

20. Important books on these elements of news-making are Leon V. Sigal, *Reporters and Officials* (Lexington, Mass.: D. C. Heath, 1973); Edward Jay Epstein, *News From Nowhere* (New York: Vintage Books, 1974); Herbert J. Gans, *Deciding What's News* (New York: Vintage Books, 1980); Gaye Tuchman, *Making News* (New York: Free Press, 1978); Mark Fishman, *Manufacturing the News* (Austin: University of Texas Press, 1980); Richard V. Ericson, Patricia M. Baranek, and Janet B. L. Chan, *Visualizing Deviance* (Toronto: University of Toronto Press, 1987); and Phyllis Kaniss, *Making Local News* (Chicago: University of Chicago Press, 1991). On television news in Sweden, Ireland, and Nigeria, see Peter Golding and Philip Elliott, *Making the News* (New York: Longman, 1979).

21. See the annual *Attacks on the Press* reports of the New York–based Committee to Protect Journalists.

22. David L. Protess et al., *The Journalism of Outrage* (New York: Guilford Press, 1991); see also Harvey Molotch, David L. Protess, and Margaret T. Gordon, "The Media-Policy Connection: Ecologies of News," in David L. Paletz, ed., *Political Communication Research* (Norwood, N.J.: Ablex, 1987), 26–48.

23. Recounted in their *All the President's Men* (New York: Simon & Schuster, 1974).

24. "Pulitzer on the Pamlico!" *Washington Daily News,* 13 April 1990, 1. Ashley B. (Brownie) Futrell, Jr., the newspaper's president and publisher, was an undergraduate student at Duke University during the 1970s.

25. Christopher Georges, "Confessions of an Investigative Reporter," *Washington Monthly* 24:3 (March 1992): 38.

26. Morton Mintz, "A Reporter Looks Back in Anger," *The Progressive* 55:12 (December 1991): 29.

27. Jonathan Rabinovitz, "Computer Network Helps Journalists Find Academic Experts," *New York Times,* 23 May 1994, C9.

28. For a thoughtful discussion of the relations between reporters and sources, see Philip Schlesinger, "Rethinking the Sociology of Journalism: Source Strategies and the Limits of Media-Centrism," in *Public Communication,* ed. Marjorie Ferguson (Newbury Park, Calif.: Sage, 1990), 61–83; and Richard V. Ericson, Patricia M. Baranek, and Janet B. L. Chan, *Negotiating Control* (Toronto: University of Toronto Press, 1989).

29. Stephen Hess, *The Government/Press Connection* (Washington, D.C.: Brookings Institution, 1984), chap. 7.

30. See Elie Abel, *Leaking* (New York: Priority Press, 1987).

31. Hugh Heclo, *A Government of Strangers* (Washington, D.C.: Brookings Institution, 1977), 226.

32. The following quotes are from Richard Nixon, *In the Arena* (New York: Simon & Schuster, 1990), 256–57.

33. Steven Waldman, "The King of Quotes: Why the Press Is Addicted to Norman Ornstein," *Washington Monthly* 18:11 (December 1986): 33–39.

34. Lawrence C. Soley, *The News Shapers* (New York: Praeger, 1992), 146, 149.

35. Mary Matalin and James Carville with Peter Knobler, *All's Fair* (New York: Random House, 1994), 186.

36. Connie Bruck, *The Predators' Ball* (New York: American Lawyer/Simon & Schuster, 1988), 149.

37. Richard Harwood, "The Problem with Sources," in *Washington Post* Writer's Group, *Messages* (Boston, Mass.: Allyn & Bacon, 1991), 80.

38. W. Lance Bennett, "An Introduction to Journalism Norms and Representations of Politics," *Political Communication* 13:4 (October-December 1996): 373–84. This issue of the journal contains several articles testing and amplifying the indexing theory.

39. Frederick Schiff, "How 'Public Opinion' Is Perceived and Produced by U.S. Newspaper Publishers," *Javnost The Public* 4:2 (1997): 88.

40. J. H. Snider and Benjamin I. Page, "The Political Power of TV Broadcasters" (paper presented at the annual meeting of the American Political Science Association, Washington, D.C., August 1997).

41. Richard Manning, *Last Stand* (Salt Lake City: Peregrine Smith Books, 1991).

42. Paul H. Weaver, *News and the Culture of Lying* (New York: Free Press, 1994), 110. For the relationship of editors and reporters at the *New York Times,* see Edwin Diamond, *Behind the Times* (New York: Villard Books, 1994), 242–47.

43. On objectivity, see Denis McQuail, *Media Performance* (London: Sage, 1992), pt. 4. For the argument that bias is unavoidable in political reporting, see Michael L. Geis, *The Language of Politics* (New York: Springer-Verlag, 1991), esp. chap. 4.

44. See William A. Gamson, *Talking Politics* (New York: Cambridge University Press, 1992); Robert M. Entman, "Framing: Toward Clarification of a Fractured Paradigm," *Journal of Communication* 43:4 (Autumn 1993): 51–58; and Michael B. Cornfield, "The Press and Political Controversy: The Case for Narrative Analysis," *Political Communication* 9 (1992): 47–59.

45. Paul Starobin, "A Generation of Vipers," *Columbia Journalism Review* 33:6 (March-April 1995), 26.

46. David L. Paletz and C. Danielle Vinson, "Constructing Content and Delimiting Choice," *Argumentation* 8 (1994): 357–66.

47. For a sophisticated discussion of the construction, content, and effects of news language, see Teun A. van Dijk, *News as Discourse* (Hillsdale, N.J.: Lawrence Erlbaum, 1988); and his *News Analysis* (Hillsdale, N.J.: Lawrence Erlbaum, 1988); see also Roger Fowler, *Language in the News* (London: Routledge, 1991).

48. John D. May, "The Malpractice of Australian Journalism: Four Insidious Convention," *Politics* 12:1 (May 1977): 141–42.

49. Maureen Dowd, "Oxford Journal: Whereas, He Is an Old Boy, If a Young Chief, Honor Him," *New York Times,* 9 June 1994, A1.

50. Ann Devroy, "Clinton Urges Unity in Cause of Peace," *Washington Post,* 9 June 1991, A19.

51. For a thoughtful discussion of pictures, see Paul Messaris, *Visual 'Literacy'* (Boulder, Colo.: Westview, 1994).

52. Mort Rosenblum, *Coups and Earthquakes* (New York: Harper Colophon, 1979), 10. On the reporting of news from abroad, see Stephen Hess, *International News & Foreign Correspondents* (Washington, D.C.: Brookings Institution, 1996).

53. G. Cleveland Wilhoit and David Weaver, "Foreign News Coverage in Two U.S. Wire Services: An Update," *Journal of Communication* 33:2 (Spring 1983): 132–48.

54. Most of this information comes from a 10 August 1992 discussion with Lowndes Lipscomb, managing editor of WTN, profiled in Michael Goldstein, "On the Media Front Line," *Duke Magazine* 82:1 (November-December 1995): 35–38; and Jeremy Tunstall, "Europe as World News Leader," *Journal of Communication* 42:3 (Summer 1992): 88.

55. Christopher Paterson, "Wholesalers or Agenda Setters: News Production at International Television News Agencies" (paper presented at the annual conference of the International Association for Media and Communication Research, Sydney, Australia, August 1996).

56. David S. Broder, *Behind the Front Page* (New York: Simon & Schuster, 1987), 14.

57. Dianne Rucinski, "Personalized Bias in News, *Communication Research* 19:1 (February 1992): 91–108.

58. Sharon Lynn Sperry, "Television News as Narrative," in *Television as a Cultural Force*, ed. Richard Adler and Douglass Cater (New York: Praeger, 1976), 141.

59. Penn Kimball, *Downsizing the News* (Washington, D.C.: Woodrow Wilson Center Press, 1994).

60. Mort Rosenblum, *Coups and Earthquakes* (New York: Harper Colophon, 1979), 11.

61. The quote is from George A. Gladney's review in the *Journal of Communication* 42:3 (Summer 1992): 195, of Richard V. Ericson et al., *Representing Order: Crime, Law, and Justice in the News Media* (Toronto: University of Toronto Press, 1991).

62. An observation by Jeremy Tunstall in "Europe as World News Leader," *Journal of Communication* 42:3 (Summer 1992): 21.

63. Mentioned in Kay Mills, *A Place in the News* (New York: Dodd, Mead, 1988), 302.

64. Ted J. Smith III, S. Robert Lichter and Louis Harris and Associates, *What the People Want from the Press* (Washington, D.C.: Center for Media and Public Affairs, 1997), 15; also Jolene Kiobassa, "Back to You, Wendy: 'Happy Talk' and Political Discourse," (paper presented at the annual meeting of the American Political Science Association, Chicago, September 1995).

65. For these and other examples, see Howard Rosenberg, "New Channel 2 News Director Sets Off a Storm," *Los Angeles Times,* 4 March 1992, F1.

66. Simon Barber, "The Boss Don't Like Robbery Make It Swindle: Inside the 'National Enquirer,'" *Washington Journalism Review* 4:6 (July-August 1982): 46–49.

67. S. Elizabeth Bird, *For Enquiring Minds: A Cultural Study of Supermarket Tabloids* (Knoxville: University of Tennessee Press, 1992).

68. For a fascinating case study of the news media in action, see Jim Lederman, *Battle Lines: The American Media and the Intifada* (New York: Henry Holt, 1992).

69. For trenchant critiques of the news media, see W. Lance Bennett, *News: The Politics of Illusion,* 2nd ed. (New York: Longman, 1988); Robert M. Entman, *Democracy Without Citizens* (New York: Oxford University Press, 1989); Tom Koch, *The News as Myth* (New York: Greenwood Press, 1990); and James Fallows, *Breaking the News* (New York: Pantheon, 1996).

70. Relevant is John H. McManus, *Market-Driven Journalism* (Newbury Park, Calif.: Sage, 1994).

Chapter 4

Restraints

◆   ◆   ◆

The First Amendment to the U.S. Constitution states that "Congress shall make no law . . . abridging the freedom of speech, or of the press."[1] An absolutist reading of this language precludes any governmental imposed restrictions on media content—no law means no law.[2]

Yet, the amendment was barely ten years old when President John Adams and his Federalist Party members in Congress enacted a sedition law forbidding false, scandalous, and malicious publications against the government, Congress, and the president, and punishing people who urged resistance to federal laws. The penalty was up to two years in prison and a fine of up to $2,000 (a lot of money in those days). The purpose was to stifle opposition newspapers supporting Thomas Jefferson and his party, which were vigorously criticizing the government. Several of the nation's leading newspapers were prosecuted and convicted under the law, which was repealed when Jefferson became president.

In 1918, with the country in the throes of World War I, another sedition act was put into effect. This one made it a crime to utter, print, write, or publish disloyal or profane language intended to cause contempt of, or scorn for, the federal government, the U.S. Constitution, the flag, or the uniform of the armed forces. Penalties were imprisonment for up to twenty years and/or a fine of $10,000. Prosecuted were radicals, people opposing the war, publishers of foreign-language publications, and the like.

Then, in 1940, with the United States' entry into World War II on the horizon, the Smith Act made it a crime to advocate the violent overthrow of the government. Not until seventeen years later did the U.S. Supreme Court rule that advocacy alone was insufficient to sustain a conviction; there had to be evidence of urging actual action.[3]

The sedition examples remind us of A. J. Liebling's observation: politicians "cannot be trusted to regulate the press, because the press deals with politics."[4] They also show that an absolutist interpretation of the First Amendment rarely prevails. Usually, freedom of the press is balanced against competing values.[5] Even so, it often enjoys a preferred position: government has the burden of having to justify any limitation it tries to impose. But not all expression is treated equally: politics and public affairs content enjoy the broadest First Amendment protection, commercial material is less protected, and pornography is on its own.

Paradoxically, while government is seen as liable to repress freedom of speech and of the press, it is also viewed as capable of enhancing it: witness the antitrust laws designed to preserve and promote economic competition and to deter monopoly ownership or control. Governmental regulation of the media has been justified as a means of trying to achieve diversity of ownership and opinion. Because of the scarcity of broadcasting channels in the early 1940s, the U.S. Supreme Court upheld the authority of the Federal Communications Commission (FCC) to regulate some aspects of broadcasting (e.g., licensing stations).[6]

This chapter deals with restraints on the media. It begins with limitations on their acquisition and reporting of information. It then looks specifically at constraints on media content. Next come three types of content subject to particular limitations: advertising, pornography, and coverage of terrorism. The chapter concludes with a discussion of violence against the press.

INFORMATION

The ability of journalists to obtain and report information is variously muddled, obstructed, sometimes facilitated and protected, and often complicated by laws and court decisions. Here's an example. Reporters do not have a constitutional right to obtain documents and reports not publicly available and quite possibly may be open to prosecution if they do so. But they cannot be held liable if they receive and publish information that they have not solicited. Several members of the University of Maryland basketball team found this out when they unsuccessfully sued the *Baltimore Evening Star* for revealing portions of their academic records.[7] However, the reporters receiving the material were possibly vulnerable to a criminal action for possession of stolen property.

Acquisition

This discussion focuses on journalists' acquisition of information from and about governmental administrative and regulatory agencies, judicial proceedings, and individual people. The first involves them with the Freedom of Information Act, the second with trials; and the third with privacy.[8]

Governmental Agencies   The Freedom of Information Act (FOIA), which became effective in 1966, is designed to open up executive branch agencies and independent regulatory commissions' federal records and files previously closed to public inspection. But it lists several exemptions, among them documents protected for national security reasons, law enforcement files, agency working papers, and highly personal information.

Hundreds of thousands of FOI requests are made to the government every year, many of them by journalists and individuals, more by interest groups. FOI data can be very useful to the press; for example, *USA Today* reporters analyzed FBI records to document an enormous increase in the use and dealing of crack by people under age fifteen.[9]

DIRECTORATE OF INTELLIGENCE

20 January 1984

EL SALVADOR: DEALING WITH DEATH SQUADS (U)

Summary

...death threats and other forms of intimidation against national leaders are commonplace, and often are carried out...

Palliative Response

For the past several weeks, government officials have publicly denounced death squads and military leaders have pledged in the local press to punish human rights offenders

Concrete Action

...armed forces...

DIRECTORATE OF INTELLIGENCE

20 January 1984

EL SALVADOR: DEALING WITH DEATH SQUADS

Summary

We believe efforts by the civilian government and the military high command to crack down on rightwing violence have had little progress and have been aimed almost exclusively at placating Washington. Salvadoran officials understandably feel uneasy about openly confronting rightwing extremists; death threats and other forms of intimidation against national leaders are commonplace, and often are carried out. Defense Minister Vides--whose room to maneuver is limited--appear both personally disinclined and politically unable to effect a major cleanup within the armed forces any time soon.

Palliative Response

Since December, the response of the government and military leaders to the problem of rightwing violence has been mainly verbal. For the past several weeks, government officials have publicly denounced death squads, and military leaders have pledged in the local press to punish human rights offenders within the armed forces. Subordinate officers also have received lectures on avoiding involvement with rightwing terrorist organizations.

[redacted] policy meetings [redacted] to discuss were held by senior military officers [redacted] "requirement" presented by Vice President Bush during his visit to San Salvador. Consensus was reached that a few [redacted] would be transferred and that officers identified by US officials [redacted] a military committee would be appointed to investigate abuses within the armed forces.

Concrete Action

Two mid-level police intelligence officers have been [redacted] transferred to diplomatic posts overseas. This gesture is offset, however, by their replacement [redacted] leader of a police death officers, one of whom is [redacted] with ultrarightists. Moreover, in the course of recent general orders, several squad notorious rightwing extremists have been assigned to [redacted] other [redacted] recent Colonels Moran, prestigious commands. These include lieutenant [redacted] close associates of Zepeda, Zacapa, Ponce, and Steben--all D'Aubuisson and his Nationalist Republican Alliance.

The military has reluctantly followed through on US demands to detain Captain Eduardo Avila; suspected of helping to arrange the murders of two US labor advisers in January 1981. Avila is temporarily being held on charges stemming [redacted] months--a vague form of self-imposed inactive duty officers [redacted] believe that of AWOL [redacted] senior military officers [redacted] uncle--a Supreme Court Judge--has manipulated the legal process to protect his nephew, and Salvadoran authorities claim that more serious charges cannot now be legally brought against Avila.

Nevertheless, [redacted] that the government there had [redacted] to El Salvador charging Avila with terrorist activities in 1980, when he served as an attache in San Jose. US officials hope that these new charges [redacted] will enable Salvadoran authorities to hold Avila long enough for the murder case against him to be developed or until he agrees to testify against his accomplices.

Meanwhile, an ad hoc investigative team has been set up by [redacted] Defense Minister Vides to oversee reports of abuses within the armed forces. Nevertheless, the team leader, Captain Arango [redacted] the National Guard, is a cohort of former Major D'Aubuisson. In 1979, Arango [redacted] was a leader of the notorious White Warriors Union--a death squad that specialized in eliminating members of the Catholic clergy.

General Vides has requested US aid to help form a bona fide commission to investigate both rightwing and leftwing terrorist groups. D'Aubuisson's civilian aides to leave the country or face future investigation into their alleged death squad activities. For the moment, however, D'Aubuisson's civilian henchmen have rejected such threats and have made clear that they intend to remain in El Salvador.

This memorandum was requested by Vice-President Bush. It was prepared by [redacted]

Two versions of the same 1984 CIA intelligence memorandum on "Dealing with Death Squads." The first (page 76), released to the National Security Archive in 1987 under the Freedom on Information Act and heavily excised, gives the impression that the Duarte government and the Salvadoran armed forces are taking effective steps to end death squad activities. The second (above), obtained by the Archive in 1993, clearly states that efforts by the government and military have made little progress and have been aimed almost exclusively at placating Washington.

But governmental agencies are reluctant to reveal all to inquiring reporters. Steve Weinberg notes several ways of subverting the FOIA: failing to meet the ten-day time limit because of alleged short staffing; charging high fees for searching for and copying documents; claiming that documents are lost or transferred to another agency; and indiscriminately blacking out information on the document.[10] The effects can be to mislead completely.

There is also the "Government in Sunshine Act" that prevents some executive branch agencies and regulatory commissions from holding secret meetings, which again, can be avoided by meeting certain exemptions.

Many laws actually withhold governmental information (e.g., on national security, espionage, atomic energy, individuals' tax returns). Laws also deny the press access to criminal history records and to students' records and files. Nor do journalists have the right to enter closed executive sessions of public bodies, although where available they can try to invoke laws (e.g., Sunshine laws) to stop such meetings.

Judicial Proceedings   The Sixth Amendment's guarantee of a fair trial to criminal defendants sometimes clashes with, even supersedes, the First Amendment's guarantee of freedom of the press. Judges can close trials or hearings, although they must have reasons other than excluding the public; and reporters can challenge the exclusion.

During a trial, reporters can be denied access to jurors and witnesses and be prevented from identifying juveniles under the court's jurisdiction and victims in rape cases.

Individuals   Journalists can be unrelenting in their pursuit of a story, as evidenced by their reports of the personal (read "sex") lives of public figures. Anyone familiar with the media must wonder if there are any limits to what information can be obtained. In fact, private intimacies are protected by the courts. But that protection does not extend to a right to be left alone, unless there is a legitimate expectation of solitude (in a place where one would expect to be able to exclude the unwanted). Moreover, the newsworthiness of a story, statement, or photograph is relevant to a defense to an invasion-of-privacy claim.[11] Much depends, therefore, on the courts' interpretation of "newsworthy."

Certainly, reporters can be held liable for trespassing, gaining access to someone's home by misrepresentation, stealing, and intruding by electronic means, hidden camera or microphone, or wiretapping. Even using cameras with telephoto lenses is illegal in some states. This doesn't mean that reporters sedulously avoid such tactics: The unscrupulous are inclined to gather information by whatever means possible.

But now, even they had better be careful. In 1992, ABC's "Prime Time Live" showed a segment taken by hidden cameras in which employees of the Food Lion supermarket chain repackaged moldy and out-of-date meat, fish, and poultry for sale. In December 1996, a jury in North Carolina found ABC News guilty of trespass and fraud for getting its reporters hired by deception. Food Lion was awarded over $5 million in punitive damages. The jury did not view the news segment, whose accuracy was not questioned in court.[12] So Food Lion would almost certainly have lost had it sued on the basis of defamation (discussed later in this chapter). In any event, the jury award was ruled excessive by the judge, who reduced it to $315,000.[13]

Prior Restraint

Whether journalists can be prevented from reporting the information they do acquire raises issues of prior restraint.

In *Near v. Minnesota*, the U.S. Supreme Court interpreted the Constitution as requiring a heavy burden of justification before the government can suppress media content prior to publication. The only exceptions permitted were obscenity, incitement to violence, and situations in wartime (now, situations involving national security).[14] Forty years later, the Court reaffirmed *Near* by upholding the right of the *New York Times* and the *Washington Post* to publish excerpts of the purloined classified "Pentagon Papers" chronicling the background and policy decisions of the U.S. government's involvement in the Vietnam War.[15] The government failed to prove that the ban was needed to protect the country.

Note, however, that editors at the *Times* agonized for three months before deciding to publish the excerpts. Then publication of the "Papers" was temporarily stopped by a government restraining order while the case went through the courts.

There are other sorts of prior restraint. Judges can issue court orders restricting what the press may publish or what the trial participants may say about the case, restraints that remain in effect while they are being appealed. However, judges are allowed to prohibit the press from publishing information it has legally obtained about a criminal case only if three conditions are met: intense and pervasive publicity about the case is certain to result if the information is published; no reasonable alternative other than prohibiting publication of the information is likely to mitigate the effects of the pretrial publicity; and prohibiting publication will prevent prejudicial material from reaching the jurors.[16]

It is unclear whether the media can be punished for reporting information that jeopardizes a defendant's right to a fair trial (e.g., a past criminal record, confession, polygraph results), or for inflaming the public mood.

The media can be punished for publishing information in violation of a judge's order. Thus, CNN was convicted of criminal contempt of court for violating a federal judge's order not to broadcast jailhouse recordings of telephone conversations of former Panamanian dictator General Manuel Antonio Noriega. Unbeknownst to him, the recordings were made by federal officials while he was in prison in Miami awaiting trial for drug trafficking. CNN's punishment: broadcasting an apology every hour or so on its two channels for some twenty-four hours and paying the federal government $85,000 to cover legal fees.[17]

Prior restraint can also be imposed on high school newspapers published as part of the school curriculum.[18] College and university newspapers are more protected but not immune.

From Herblock, Through the Looking Glass *(W.W. Norton, 1984)*

Shield Laws

Some of the material journalists have acquired but not reported could be useful to law enforcement officers, grand juries, trial plaintiffs, and defendants and their counsel. These are only a few of the people requesting that reporters reveal information and, more importantly, identify the names of sources, turn over notes, audiotapes and videotapes, news film, photographs, even telephone records.

"Oh, You Wouldn't Be Interested In The Others"

From Herblock, State of the Union *(Simon & Schuster, 1972)*

Reporters often accede to these requests. Refusal can provoke court orders. Several thousand subpoenas are issued annually, most to broadcasters. About half are complied with; the rest are either withdrawn or challenged in court. Roughly 70 percent of the challenged subpoenas are quashed.[19] Submission can dry up essential sources and thereby reduce revelations. Resistance may lead to fines and, on rare occasions, jail.

The U.S. Supreme Court has declined to interpret the First Amendment as protecting journalists from having to testify before grand juries.[20] However, the Justice Department has developed guidelines limiting the use of subpoenas by federal agents against journalists. And a majority of states have passed shield laws. Before members of the press subpoenaed for a legal hearing have to testify, those seeking the information may have to demonstrate that the information is relevant to the hearing, that there is a compelling need for its disclosure, and that there are no alternative sources.[21]

Many public officials in particular abhor leaks of information they want to keep confidential. They seek to stop them and to punish the leakers. Shield laws hardly deter public officials, however. As one example, senators grilled reporters Nina Totenberg of National Public Radio and Timothy Phelps of *Newsday*, trying to find out who informed them of Anita Hill's charges against U.S. Supreme Court nominee Clarence Thomas. The journalists' refusal to identify their source(s) provoked the threat of subpoenas and possible contempt of Congress charges. Eventually, the Senate leadership decided not to pursue the case.

Defamation

Is media content protected? Not if it defames. In essence, defamation (slander when spoken, libel when written) is a false statement of fact that subjects a person to public contempt, injury, or disgrace. Not limited to news stories, defamation can also occur in advertisements, cartoons, film, photos, recordings, and on tape.[22] Ordinary people who are defamed in the media and sue have a fair chance of collecting if they can prove that the comments are untrue and were made negligently (i.e., by failing to exercise reasonable care).[23] Public figures have to show that the damaging remarks were made by the reporter with malicious intent (i.e., knowing they were false or made with reckless disregard as to their truth or falsity).[24] However, statements of opinion are usually immune. Of course, it is not always clear whether someone is a public figure; nor is the fact-opinion distinction always obvious.

Suing is horrendously expensive, and ultimate victory for the suer unlikely. Large media corporations, such as *Time* magazine, contest accusations of libel with vast resources and phalanxes of highly paid lawyers.[25] *Hustler* magazine mounted a spirited defense, as the Reverend Jerry Falwell, then head of the Moral Majority, discovered when he unsuccessfully sued the magazine because of a fake advertisement parody it published portraying him and his mother as drunk and immoral.[26]

Nonetheless, numerous defamation suits are filed every year. Some are entirely justified; others are based on the often valid assumption that simply to file vindicates one's reputation, win or lose. Yet others are filed to harass or punish the press. They can last an eternity. Former Massachusetts Governor Edward King's suit against the *Boston Globe*—claiming defamation in three cartoons, one editorial, an op-ed, and two political columns—took over seven years to litigate before it was dismissed.[27]

The media initially lose between 70 and 80 percent of the cases that reach trial, especially those heard by juries. But 90 percent of these adverse decisions are overturned on appeal or damage awards are substantially reduced.

Even though they usually win eventually, journalists dislike libel suits because they are time-consuming and distracting. Unwillingness to incur libel suits can cause editorial judgment about whether to publish a story to be delegated to lawyers and "has forced many in the press to pull back from aggressive reporting, water down incisive analyses, drop risky projects."[28]

For First Amendment scholar Lucas A. Powe, Jr., libel law neither protects freedom of the press nor individuals' reputations; the main beneficiaries are media attorneys.[29] Because plaintiffs must prove the media were at fault, the focus is not on whether the alleged libel is true or false but on how the media went about putting the story together. To prove fault, plaintiffs must probe into the news-making process. This entails time-consuming and expensive depositions of journalists, examinations of their notes and other documents, and exhaustive delving into newsroom practices. Open to investigation are the reporters' thoroughness of news-gathering, use and reliability of identified and anonymous sources, and use of quotes. And because journalists' motives, such as the existence of malice, are a relevant consideration, they can also be questioned about their state of mind when they did their work.

Right of Reply

There might be fewer defamation suits and complaints about the media if people had a right of reply to its contents, even though this impinges on freedom of the press. In some ways they do. The FCC has the responsibility of enforcing personal attack rules. Stations must notify people whose honesty, character, integrity, and such have been attacked during the presentation of views on controversial issues of public importance and offer them a reasonable opportunity to respond over the licensee's facilities.[30] Excluded are attacks by political candidates and their spokespersons, as well as all kinds of news and the commentary-analysis it includes. But even when personal attacks are clear, many stations fail to contact those attacked. Besides, most people are unfamiliar with the rule, unaware of how to complain to the FCC, and unequipped to broadcast a reply.

At one time, the FCC's "fairness doctrine" required radio and television stations to allow rebuttals to expressions of opinion they broadcast. A stand upheld by the U.S. Supreme Court.[31] But the Court refused to extend the idea to newspapers: It ruled unconstitutional a Florida law requiring the state's newspapers to allow political candidates a right of reply to their attackers. The grounds were that government telling newspapers what to publish violates the First Amendment.[32]

Television and radio stations that endorse or oppose political candidates are still required to notify other candidates for that office, including the one opposed, and offer them a reasonable opportunity to reply. This rule is often blamed for the dearth of candidate endorsements by broadcasters, in contrast to their frequency in newspapers.

These disparities between the treatment of print and broadcasting, combined with the proliferation of television channels via cable, and the free market orientation of FCC members appointed during the Reagan and Bush administrations, led the FCC to drop the fairness doctrine in the late 1980s. This apparently resulted in a reduction in the airing of controversy.[33]

CONSTRAINTS ON CONTENTS

There are always some media contents provoking criticism, offense, outrage, assault, and demands that something be done about them, even outright suppression.

Consider music. In the past, jazz was attacked by clergymen, educators, and parents for its alleged sexual excess, aesthetic incompetence, and the racial inferiority of its makers. Rock, rhythm and blues, and related forms were assaulted on sexual, racial, political, or drug grounds: They were said to stem from Communist efforts to undermine America's political and social systems. Pressure was applied to government to limit public performances and people's access to them.[34] Rap is the most recent target.[35]

Today, children and youth are seen as specially vulnerable to media material. Their nursery rhymes and fairy tales have been criticized as gory and nightmare-inducing; the violent content of their comic books as inuring them from and making them prone to violence. Even worse is the adult content the average child supposedly encounters: 8,000 murders and 100,000 acts of violence on television before finishing grade school.[36]

There are three different, although often overlapping, forces by which content can be and is limited: by pressure, by government, and by media personnel themselves.

Pressure

The first constraint on media content comes from pressure. Examples are people picketing a radio station to stop it from playing songs with controversial lyrics and advertisers withdrawing their sponsorship of a provocative program. But the main exponents of pressure are watchdogs, politicians, and groups.

Watchdogs   Certain organizations publish analyses and assessments of the media and their content from a more or less ideological perspective.[37] Prominent ones are the reactionary Accuracy in Media (*AIM Report*), the conservative Media Research Center (*Media Watch, Notable Quotables*, and *TV, etc.*), the arguably conservative Center for Media and Public Affairs (*Media Monitor*), and the liberal Fairness & Accuracy in Reporting (*EXTRA!*). They all find bias in media content, often justifiably. A cynic would observe that they would probably have to go out of business if they didn't.

They exert pressure on the press by the mere act of scrutiny and by publishing and broadcasting their findings. More importantly, they are endowed with credibility and legitimacy when, as with the Center for Media and Public Affairs in particular, they are used as sources, have their findings reported, and their chiefs publish columns and op-eds in the elite and prestige media.

Politicians   At first glance, appeals for media restraint, even from the highest level of government, seem to have little visible effect. Hours after President Clinton made a highly publicized speech in Hollywood imploring industry leaders to curb depictions of violence in movies and television, studio executives engaged "in a bidding war for a movie script in which 11 people are killed in the first seven pages."[38]

Threats escalate. Testifying about television violence before the U.S. Senate Commerce Committee, Attorney General Janet Reno said, "'The best solutions lie with industry officials, parents, and educators, and I don't relish the prospect of government action. But if immediate voluntary steps are not taken and deadlines established, government should respond, and respond immediately.'"[39]

Then-Senate Majority Leader and Republican presidential candidate Bob Dole joined the fray, mounting a withering attack on the entertainment industry in general and Time Warner in particular for producing "nightmares of depravity." His widely publicized speech was seen as an attempt to exert moral leadership on a politically potent family issue and, not incidentally, curry favor with the hard-line conservatives supposedly dominating his party's primaries. Dole cited the films *Natural Born Killers* and *True Romance,* and the groups Cannibal Corpse, Geto Boys, and (the old standby) 2 Live Crew for their depictions of "mindless violence and loveless sex." He denounced "music extolling the pleasures of raping, torturing, and mutilating women" and "songs about killing policemen and rejecting law." When asked, an aide acknowledged that the senator had not seen the movies or heard the songs, but had read the film reviews and song lyrics.[40]

Critics accused the senator of cynicism and hypocrisy for attacking entertainment violence while opposing gun control and trying to repeal the ban on assault weapons. They remarked upon his opposition to funding for public television and the Arts and Humanities Endowments. They observed that he had picked on material made by Democrats and African-Americans; had avoided the current monster hit *Die Hard With a Vengeance,* starring Republican Bruce Willis; and had praised as a family-friendly film the gorefest *True Lies* in which Republican Arnold Schwarzenegger's character kills with Hollywood high-tech abandon.[41] They had fun identifying the violence, sexual, and antisocial elements of the movies he had endorsed, such as *The Lion King.* They neglected the fact that Dole had demonstrated independence and integrity (and gall) by accepting campaign contributions from and yet attacking Time Warner and other media corporations.

Groups   There is a long history of pressure, both effective and ineffective, from organized and ad hoc groups trying to curtail material they believe to be offensive or unacceptable. As one example, "In 1911, representatives of four western [Indian] tribes journeyed to the national capital to protest their screen treatment to Congress and President William H. Taft."[42]

In the 1930s, the Catholic church organized the National Legion of Decency to police films deemed antithetical to the church's precepts. In response to pressure from the legion and others, hundreds of films during the era of studio production were censored and often edited to promote a conservative political agenda.[43]

More recently, such organizations as the Coalition for Better Television, Morality in Media, and the Telecommunications Research and Action Center have all brought pressure on the television networks to drop shows. In 1997, the

Southern Baptist Convention even voted to boycott the entire Walt Disney empire: movies, ABC network, cable television channels, and other ventures, including theme parks.[44]

Religiously oriented groups are also active at the community level. They "object to the 's' words—sex, suicide, Satanism and swearing."[45] One could add "sensitivity" to culturally disturbing material. Books removed as texts in schools, banned from libraries, and generating complaints to bookstores include *The Catcher in the Rye* by J. D. Salinger; *The Diary of Anne Frank; The Dictionary of American Slang; Huckleberry Finn* by Mark Twain; and William Shakespeare's *The Merchant of Venice.*

Racial and ethnic groups too have brought pressure. The National Association for the Advancement of Colored People (NAACP) campaigned in the early 1950s to get "Amos 'n' Andy" off the air. A decade later, Italian-American groups complained about "The Untouchables." Such organizations as the Gay and Lesbian Alliance Against Defamation (GLAD) have demanded less demeaning and more favorable portrayals of homosexuals.[46]

Sometimes pressure is coordinated. An example is the campaign against Time Warner led by former U.S. Secretary of Education William J. Bennett and C. DeLores Tucker, head of the National Political Congress of Black Women. They apparently coordinated with Senator Dole, who attacked the company, and Rush Limbaugh, who did likewise on his radio show. Their objective: the company "should stop its sponsorship and promotion of lyrics that celebrate rape, torture and murder."[47] The campaign included a television advertisement assailing Time Warner, op-eds, letters containing some of the graphic lyrics sent to the company's board members, a confrontation at the company's annual meeting, and a contentious private session with company executives.[48] The campaign accomplished at least part of its purpose when Time Warner sold off its interest in Interscope Records, producer of gangsta rap.

Without gainsaying Bennett and Tucker's good intentions, it should be noted that the campaign also generated positive publicity for them; kept the former's name in the news as a viable, even desirable, Republican candidate for high office; promoted his political organization Empower America; and maintained morality and the family as a prominent political issue, one that usually favors the Republican party.

Government

Pornography aside, it is not easy for government to exercise direct control over media content. The First Amendment is one reason: the U.S. Supreme Court has ruled, for example, that unless they are obscene, the amendment protects films from state censorship.[49]

Nonetheless, government periodically tries to deal with media content through legislation, regulation, investigations, and prosecution.

Legislation   Legislators are reluctant to offend the powerful media in their districts, media that can influence the ways they are or are not presented to their constituents.

So legislators try to influence content indirectly. In 1990, Congress enacted legislation to encourage officials of the major television networks to develop guidelines on violence in television programming.[50] Predictably, the law contained no sanctions for the industry failing to meet, adopt, or adhere to any guidelines developed.

Members of Congress are somewhat bolder where children are concerned. Inspired by Peggy Charon and her Action for Children's Television (ACT), they passed the Children's Television Act of 1990. It limits commercials on children's programs to twelve minutes per hour on weekdays, and to ten and a half on weekends. In addition, as a condition of license renewal, television stations are required to demonstrate that their overall programming, including shows for youths, meets children's educational needs.[51]

In implementing the law, the FCC defined educational and informational programming as that which furthers children's positive development, including cognitive/intellectual or emotional/social needs, and is produced for those sixteen years old and younger.[52]

In response to the law, some broadcasters added appropriate programs and segments. But as a study of license renewal applications by Kathryn C. Montgomery and her associates at the Center for Media Education revealed, others simply redefined their cartoons and syndicated reruns as educational. They claimed that "Leave It to Beaver" promotes themes of "communication and trust," "Superboy" "presents good as it triumphs over evil," and "Super Mario Brothers" teaches children "self-confidence."[53] Until the FCC demurred, "The Flintstones" was represented as showing kids how life in the past might have been, and the "Jetsons" as teaching them about life in the twenty-first century and future space technology.[54]

The FCC subsequently tightened the definition of "educational programming" to require that it be "'specifically designed' to serve an educational purpose." And it required the networks to broadcast three hours of educational or informational programs for children each week.[55] The initial result was "reruns from PBS or cable, a few innovative shows that appear to have the new mandate at heart, and some entertainment shows with an overlay of educational material slapped on like shellac."[56]

Regulation   Although the FCC has general control over broadcast programming, it currently pays only selective heed to it. Other than children, it is mainly concerned about indecencies: "language or materials that, in context, depicts or describes, in terms patently offensive as measured by contemporary standards for the broadcast medium, sexual or excretory activities or organs." Such programming is prohibited between 6 a.m. and 10 p.m.—a regulation upheld by the U.S. District Court of Appeals for the District of Columbia.[57] Of course, much depends how "patently offensive" is defined. The FCC's sanctions include reprimand letters, fines, and the hardly ever invoked nonrenewal or revocation of broadcast licenses.

Investigations   Quite common are legislative committee investigations of the makers of content that the committee members deem threatening or unacceptable. The most flagrant example was the House of Representatives' Committee on

Un-American Activities, which, aided behind the scenes by the FBI, spent many years, most conspicuously during the late 1940s and early 1950s, ferreting out real and suspected Communists, past and present, in the film and other entertainment businesses.[58] Evidence that these individuals had actually succeeded in inserting political content in the movies to which they contributed was sparse, and whatever they might have done had been entirely legal.

The committee's public hearings were exercises in harassment and exposure. The screenwriters, actors, and other individuals subpoenaed before it were asked: "Are you now or have you ever been a member of the Communist party?" After which they would be told to name other names, no matter whether or how long ago such people had been involved with the party. Given prehearing investigation by the staff, committee members almost always knew the answers to the questions.

Responses by those hauled before the committee ranged from "informing" to flamboyant defiance. Uncooperative witnesses were usually cited for contempt of Congress, often ending up in jail.[59]

Not all investigations are legislative or public. Fueled by files that she disgorged-extracted under the Freedom of Information Act and supplemented by interviews with surviving witnesses, Natalie Robins has chronicled the FBI's extensive surveillance of American writers during the forty-seven-year reign of J. Edgar Hoover.[60] This surveillance activity became known to many of its victims, with concomitant chilling effects. The surveillance and effects extended to political organizations such as the Black Panther Party and the American Indian movement.[61]

Prosecution   Then there is prosecution. 2 Live Crew's sexually explicit album "As Nasty as They Wanna Be" was declared obscene by a Florida state court. The decision was subsequently overturned by a federal court of appeals because no evidence was presented in the trial that it was without serious artistic value. Charged also with giving an obscene performance (at an adults-only nightclub) in the same state, the group was acquitted by the jury. The upside of an obscenity charge can be publicity and profit: the album sold more than two million copies.

Others accused of pornography are less fortunate. Most of the manufacturers, distributors, and retailers (e.g., bookstores, theater owners) so charged prefer to stay in business rather than crusade for the First Amendment. They are therefore inclined to plea bargain, pay a fine, and return to business.

Media Personnel

The third constraint on content comes from media personnel. Media executives deploy an arsenal of tactics to respond to pressures and to try to ward off or thwart governmental restraints. These tactics include outright denials of harm, assertions that there is a complete absence or no compelling evidence of proof of effects (e.g., of violent content), expressions of concern, and meetings with critics.

When these tactics don't work, one way of acknowledging without accepting the validity of the charges is to appoint nominally independent monitors; for example, to measure and report on the amount of violence on television. Another tactic is to refrain from showing certain programs during hours when children are most likely to watch. Agreeing to help develop the technology to allow people to block their television sets' reception of particular kinds of material is another.

The press has also added correction boxes and ombudsmen and ombudswomen to investigate complaints. But the former mainly correct trivial factual errors and are absent from television news, which has no formal response format. As for ombudsmen and ombudswomen, few television stations and only about thirty of the nation's newspapers have them. Rare are reporters, like David Shaw at the *Los Angeles Times,* who write full-time about the journalism profession and its coverage of events.

Under duress and perhaps because of a sense of guilt, media personnel go beyond palliatives: They devise ratings and allow and apply warning labels. But they also censor content, remove, and blacklist people.

Ratings   Ratings, especially for movies, have been a common response to the cries for regulation, restriction, and restraint. Their benefit to the industry is that they avoid outright censorship while providing consumers with some guidance as to violent and sexual content and, for particular ratings, forbidding attendance by those under certain ages.

Currently, the industry classifies movies as G, PG, PG13, R, and NC–17. Although film-makers often argue long and hard with the ratings board and have to agree to cut material to obtain a desirable rating, the code does allow more graphic violence, sexual activities, and explicit language than was permitted in the past.

Meanwhile movies may be edited for television and for showing on airlines, although cable channels can and do show violent and sexually explicit (soft core) films without much fear of regulation. And many videos, no matter how violent, are readily available at the video store for viewing in the home.

In 1997, the television industry produced an age-based, voluntary ratings system similar to that for movies. But many programs were rated G (all ages) or PG (parental guidance suggested) rather than TV–14 (parents cautioned against letting children under age fourteen watch), and TV-MA (for mature audiences only). Advocate groups, such as the Parents and Teachers Association, accused the ratings of being vague so that "few will pay attention to them and shows will not lose viewers, and therefore advertisers."[62] Under pressure, most of the networks subsequently agreed to add content ratings: D for suggestive dialogue, L for coarse language, S for sex, and V for violence.[63]

In 1998, responding to a law passed by Congress requiring the television industry to allow the blocking of objectionable programs, the FCC required that new sets be equipped with a V-chip, enabling people to block programs according to the ratings codes.

Warning Labels   Related to ratings are warning labels. Under pressure from the politically connected Susan Baker (wife of the then-U.S. Treasury Secretary) and Tipper Gore and their Parents' Music Resource Center, representatives of the recording industry agreed in the late 1980s to apply a warning label or print the lyrics on the cover of new releases that are violent, sexually explicit, or promote the use of drugs and alcohol.

Missing was an industry standard demarcating the boundaries of blatantly explicit lyrics. So labeling varied among record companies. Evasion was not unknown: Some companies made their labels too small to be noticed or hid them in the cover's artwork.

Rock musician Frank Zappa was so outraged that he devised a mock "WARN-ING GUARANTEE" on his records. It began:

> This album contains material which a truly free society would neither fear nor suppress. In some socially retarded areas, religious fanatics and ultraconservative political organizations violate your First Amendment Rights by attempting to censor rock & roll albums. We feel this is un-Constitutional and un-American.

The agreed-upon industry label is now a black-and-white sticker containing four words: "Parental Advisory—Explicit Lyrics."[64] But the industry has no standardized method for identifying explicit lyrics, and use of the label is voluntary.

Codes and labels can reduce sales. Blockbuster, responsible for renting around 25 percent of all videos, refuses to stock movies rated NC–17, and insists that some provocative movies be re-edited before stocking them. Chains such as Wal-Mart (the single largest seller of pop music) refuse to sell records with warning labels or lyrics or covers they deem unacceptable. In response, record labels and bands "omit songs from their albums, electronically mask objectionable words and even change lyrics . . . ."[65]

Censorship   Beyond codes and warning labels is the actual censoring of content by media personnel. Throughout the film industry's history, many movies have been subjected to alteration during their production and after completion to ensure that they did not upset social, economic, and political mores.[66]

The three television networks each had departments of broadcast standards and practices (read "censorship"). "They reviewed concepts, storybooks, scripts, raw footage, and sometimes even completed productions to make sure that broadcast content was in accord with network codes which sought to avoid either offense or harm to viewers."[67] While these departments were essentially dismantled in the late 1980s, mainly to save money, guidelines still exist and the networks can communicate their expectations to program and commercial makers. Nor is censorship limited to the networks: human genitals and the sex act are uncommon on cable.

Occasionally, the news media "voluntarily" censor stories at the behest of public officials; the conventional grounds are national security. At the request of President John F. Kennedy, the publisher and editors at the *New York Times* agreed not to publish news stories about the U.S. preparations for the Bay of Pigs invasion of Cuba. Years later, the paper's managing editor at the time of the decision conceded that had the *Times* printed what it knew, the invasion might well have been canceled, preserving the country from enormous embarrassment at the fiasco.

Removal and Blacklisting   The most draconian behavior—removal of the controversial item or the blacklisting of its creator—is imposed by media executives on their industry's creative artists in response to what seems at the time to be unbearable governmental and group pressure. Later, these actions are often seen as cowardly cave-ins in which prudence replaced courage and integrity.

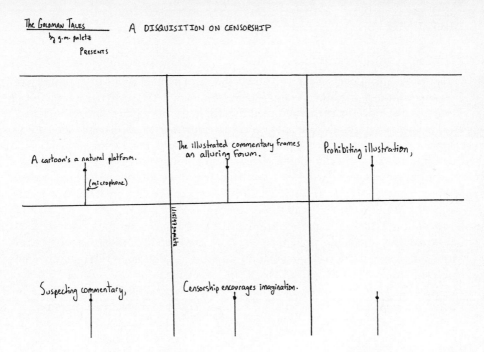

The Goloman Tales
by g.m. paletz
Presents

A DISQUISITION ON CENSORSHIP

A cartoon's a natural platform.

(microphone)

The illustrated commentary frames an alluring forum.

Prohibiting illustration,

Suspecting commentary,

Censorship encourages imagination.

Early in 1992, Time Warner released an album by rapper Ice-T and his heavy metal group Body Count; it included the provocative song "Cop Killer." After a storm of controversy, he "voluntarily" pulled the track, stating his dismay that the police had been (allegedly) threatening Warner Record Company executives.[68] The company subsequently dropped him from its roster, whereupon he signed with another label. Supposedly, some gangsta rappers have also been quietly removed from the Warner label.

Blacklisting is uncommon, but it can be deadly. The most notorious episode occurred from the late 1940s to early 1960s when many actors, writers, directors and others, first in the film industry and then in broadcasting, were denied employment and deprived of their livelihood because of their past alleged or actual leftist perfectly legal political activities. Many had refused to answer questions about their political affiliations ("Are you now or have you ever been a member of the Communist party?") or to name their former associates before the House of Representative's Committee on Un-American Activities. Movie and broadcasting executives blacklisted them because of pressure from the committee, threats of boycotts from interest groups such as the American Legion, and fears of losing audiences.[69]

SPECIAL RESTRAINT CASES

Three types of media content are subject to special restraint: advertising, pornography, and coverage of terrorism.

Advertising

The U.S. Supreme Court has deemed commercial speech less protected than other types. Thus, advertising for unlawful goods and services is subject to regulation. Other advertising is overseen by the Advertising Evaluation Section of the Bureau of Consumer Protection of the Federal Trade Commission (FTC) to determine if it is "unfair or deceptive," and thereby affecting the actual buying decision; or is "false."

This oversight entails examining the substantiation of advertising claims and reviewing complaints from the public. One remedy is voluntary discontinuance of the ad by the advertiser. Otherwise, the main alternative is a hearing before an administrative law judge, who may dismiss some or all the charges, issue a legally binding cease-and-desist order, or require corrective advertising. These decisions can be appealed to the FTC and thereafter to the courts—a process that may take years, during which the contested advertising continues. It took eleven years before Geritol removed its claim to combat "tired blood." Advertisers get away with a lot, especially when antiregulation Republicans dominate Washington, control the commission, and occupy its key staff positions.

Relatedly, Congress and the FCC mandate limits on the amount of time broadcast stations can devote to advertising each hour, especially during children's programs.

Pornography

The conventional justification for freedom of speech and concomitantly of media content is that truth is most likely to emerge from a marketplace of ideas. Pornography can be defended, even justified, as fulfilling some people's erotic fantasies,[70] but whether it contributes to political or intellectual debate is questionable.[71] This explains in part why pornography is denied First Amendment protection, even though laborers in the business are people too, concerned with doing the best work possible often under trying conditions.[72]

According to the U.S. Supreme Court, material is legally obscene when it meets three criteria. First, an average person, applying contemporary local community standards (which can differ by community), finds that the work appeals to prurient interest. Second, it depicts in a patently offensive way sexual conduct specifically defined by applicable state law. But only so-called hard-core pornography is patently offensive. Third, it lacks serious literary, artistic, political, or scientific value.[73] A broader definition may be applied to erotic material aimed at children.

As Kathleen M. Sullivan observes: "The first two parts of this test are incoherent . . . they require the audience to be turned on and grossed out at the same time."[74] The third test is the one that witnesses can try to use to prove the innocence or guilt of work charged with obscenity.

Although a U.S. Supreme Court justice once observed that he knew pornography when he saw it, applying the Court's three criteria turns out to be quite difficult in practice. For pornography poses special and controversial problems of definition, range of contents, measuring effects, and regulation.[75]

Attorney General's Commission   These problems are incarnate in the 1986 report of the U.S. Attorney General's Commission on Pornography.[76]

The commission broke its subject into four not entirely analytically distinct classes. Two were of minor concern: "non-violent and non-degrading materials," and "mere nudity."

What exercised the commission was "sexually violent material." This consists of "sexual activity, actual or simulated, with violence, regardless of what else is present."[77] A majority of the commission's members concluded this material is harmful: "The available evidence strongly supports the hypothesis that substantial exposure to sexually violent materials . . . bears a causal relationship to antisocial acts of sexual violence and, for some subgroups, possibly to unlawful acts of sexual violence." The members unanimously found the "totality of evidence" to show such harmful effects as "acceptance of rape myths," "degradation of status of women," and "societal harm."

A second class constituting "somewhat between the predominant and the overwhelming portion of what is currently standard fare heterosexual pornography, and is a significant theme in a broader range of materials not commonly taken to be sexually explicit enough to be pornographic" involves "nonviolent materials depicting degradation, domination, subordination, or humiliation."

Despite the commission's assertion, it is not clear how behavior falling into this second category can be devoid of any form of violence. Perhaps it is so only in comparison to the overt violence of "sexually violent material." In any event, the commission also found harm in the nonviolent content, including acceptance of rape myths and of violence against women, as well as to the family and society.

How to deal with the supposed harms posed a difficult dilemma for the commission, particularly since several of them were caused by media content that is not defined as pornographic. Indeed, most of the commission's proposals relate to child pornography; few seem connected to the various classes of harm just described, especially graphic sexual violence.

Some recommendations were designed to facilitate enforcement. These included improving resources for combatting pornography (training, funding, establishing a data base on the pornography industry); gathering evidence; assessing pornography's impact; and harsher criminal sentencing, including mandatory terms.

The commission did recommend a few new laws: requiring the forfeiture of proceeds and instruments from offenses violating obscenity laws; making the hiring of individuals to participate in commercial sex performances unfair business and labor practices; prohibiting telephone or other common carrier transmission of obscene material; and using the Racketeer-Influenced Corrupt Organization Act to prosecute major producers and distributors of obscene material. (See also the discussion of the Communications Decency Act in chapter 16.)

In response, the Justice Department created a "National Obscenity Enforcement Unit" and undertook more vigorous anti-obscenity enforcement.

Coverage of Terrorism

Like pornography, the subjects of media coverage of terrorism and what to do about it have provoked a vast literature.[78] Of course, describing an individual or organization as terrorist is a political choice. Many contributors suggest various ways of combating what they believe is the problem of coverage that facilitates terrorists' objectives. For the more thoughtful commentators, this means trying to reconcile the public's right to know, the safety of hostages, the public's need for effective law enforcement responses, respect for the privacy of victims, and the need to deter future acts of terrorism.

Most limit their recommendations to actions the media can take or that can be imposed on the media, such as training and education of journalists, cooperation between media personnel and the authorities, guidelines, codes of ethics, formal controls, and legislation and legal sanctions. Only a few suggest that forces other than the media—such as government, the military, and the police—should share in the burden of rectification by modifying their behavior.

To determine the incidence and effects of demands from governments and other sources for limitations, constraints, and guidelines for media coverage of terrorism, Laura Tawney and I sent out a questionnaire to broadcasting organizations throughout the world. We found most of those in North America use standardized guidelines.[79] They are no doubt responding to the apparent relevance of terrorism in their societies and their governments' placement of the subject high on the agenda of public issues. There is considerable consensus among them about how television should cover terrorism. These include:

Do nothing to make the sensational event more sensational.

Paraphrase demands so as to deny the terrorists a political platform.

Do not provide live coverage of the terrorists unless the head of the news department grants permission.

Reporters are instructed to be attentive to local authorities and experts for useful phraseology and questions and to obey all instructions by the police and other authorities. However, they should report any orders that appear to be intended to manage or suppress the news.

There is clear determination not to legitimize or even provide a platform for terrorists, and to avoid coverage that might endanger hostages or interfere with negotiations for their release.

This helps to explain why so few respondents reported encountering any direct governmental pressure to institute guidelines, or much governmental criticism of their terrorism coverage. Yet it is not certain that the governments are satisfied with coverage of terrorism by television organizations. Public officials and the police forces want coverage (to the extent they want any coverage) that is minimally intrusive and inflammatory, and that lends no credibility to terrorists. Especially in the heat of a terrorist incident, spurred on at times by competition with rival networks and stations, as well as by other media, television coverage can be quite controversial, even incendiary.

VIOLENCE AGAINST THE PRESS

From the reporting of violence by the press, we turn to violence against the press, the most brutal way of trying to silence journalists. Usually neglected, even ignored, it is occasionally thrust into public consciousness by a particularly horrific crime, such as the brutal stoning to death in Somalia in 1993 of the brilliant young photographer Dan Eldon while he was working for Reuters. In fact, attacks and assaults against journalists have been a pervasive feature of the history of the press, continuing today. As the Committee to Protect Journalists (CPJ) documents, all over the world journalists are beaten up and killed, newspapers bombed, television stations occupied and taken over.[80]

The United States is not immune: John Nerone has identified four basic patterns of antipress violence in U.S. history.[81]

Violence against individuals takes editors and reporters as participants and targets. Stemming originally from public quarrels over public affairs, it increasingly stems from alleged invasions of privacy; current targets are reporters and photographers attempting to cover celebrities in the sports and entertainment businesses. At its worst it involves murder (e.g., the killing of liberal talk-show host Alan Berg).

Attacks against the media representing minority social movements and expressing their controversial or dissident ideas in the United States was common during the nineteenth century. Among the movements assaulted, listed by Nerone in historical order, are "loyalism, independence, antifederalism, Jeffersonian Republicanism, Catholicism, anti-Masonry, abolitionism, Mormonism, labor unions, socialism, and civil rights."[82]

Violence against groups is another form of majoritarian antipress activity. It consists of attacks on journalists on the basis of their group identification, usually African-American, foreign-language, or working class.

Finally, nowadays, the media as an institution are subjected to violence as people and organizations struggle to intrude themselves in the news, to induce or force the press to include them in its world. Or at least to present them according to their own valuation and self-definition rather than that of the journalist.[83]

CONCLUSION

The media enjoy broad protection by the First Amendment and from the importance traditionally accorded to a free press. But this media independence has been curtailed at times of (perceived) threat, for example by sedition laws. Journalists' acquisition of information from governmental agencies, judicial proceedings, and individuals is both facilitated and constrained. Their reporting is limited by prior restraint, defamation, and right of reply; and somewhat protected by shield laws.

Pressures on the media come from watchdogs, politicians and groups. Government restrains the media by legislation, regulation, investigation, and prosecution. Media personnel themselves constrain content through codes, warning labels, censorship, and blacklisting, and firing.

Advertising, pornography, and coverage of terrorism are cases of special restraint. The most palpable pressure is violence against the press.

Notes

1. In *Gitlow v. New York*, 268 U.S. 652 (1925), the U.S. Supreme Court extended the First Amendment by defining it as one of the rights protected by the due process clause of the Fourteenth Amendment from impairment by the states.

2. For an attempt to state a comprehensive and effective theory of the First Amendment, see Thomas I. Emerson, *Toward a General Theory of the First Amendment* (New York: Random House, 1963).

3. *Yates v. United States,* 354 U.S. 298 (1957).

4. A. J. Liebling, *The Press* (New York: Ballantine, 1961), 9–10.

5. Rodney A. Smolla, *Free Speech in an Open Society* (New York: Knopf, 1992).

6. *National Broadcasting Co. v. United States,* 319 U.S. 190 (1943). For fresh, conflicting discussions of regulation of the electronic media and freedom of the press, see Lucas A. Powe, Jr., *American Broadcasting and the First Amendment* (Berkeley: University of California Press, 1987); and Cass R. Sunstein, *Democracy and the Problem of Free Speech* (New York: Free Press, 1993); also relevant is Lee C. Bollinger, *Images of a Free Press* (Chicago: University of Chicago Press, 1991).

7. *Bilney v. Evening Star,* 406 A.2d 652 (1979).

8. Comprehensive works on which I have drawn are Don R. Pember, *Mass Media Law,* 6th ed. (Madison, Wis.: WCB Brown & Benchmark, 1993); Donald M. Gillmor et al., *Mass Communication Law,* 5th ed. (St. Paul, Minn.: West, 1990); and Joel M. Gora, *The Rights of Reporters* (New York: Avon, 1974) (an American Civil Liberties Union Handbook).

9. Pember, *Mass Media Law,* 277.

10. Steve Weinberg, "Trashing the FOIA," *Columbia Journalism Review* 23:5 (January-February 1985), 21 (cited in ibid., 278).

11. *Time, Inc. v. Hill,* 385 U.S. 374 (1967).

12. Barry Meier, "Jury Says ABC Owes Damages of $5.5 Million," *New York Times,* 23 January 1997, A1.

13. Lawrie Mifflin, "Judge Slashes $5.5 Million Award to Grocery Chain for ABC Report," *New York Times,* 30 August 1997, A1.

14. *Near v. Minnesota,* 283 U.S. 697 (1931).

15. *New York Times v. United States,* 403 U.S. 718 (1971).

16. *Nebraska Press Association v. Stuart,* 427 U.S. 539 (1976); and Pember, *Mass Media Law,* 386.

17. "CNN Is Sentenced for Tapes and Makes Public Apology," *New York Times,* 20 December 1994, A8.

18. *Hazelwood School District v. Kulhmeier,* 108 S. Ct. 562 (1988).

19. From a study by the Reporters Committee for Freedom of the Press, reported by William Glaberson, "Press," *New York Times,* 27 March 1995, C6.

20. *Branzburg v. Hayes,* 408 U.S. 665 (1972).

21. Pember, *Mass Media Law,* 338.

22. For a study of its legal history and practice, see Richard Labunski, *Libel and the First Amendment* (New Brunswick, N.J.: Transaction Books, 1987).

23. *Philadelphia Newspapers, Inc. v. Hepps,* 475 U.S. 767 (1986).

24. *New York Times v. Sullivan,* 376 U.S. 254 (1964). For a discussion of the background, details, and decision, see Anthony Lewis, *Make No Law* (New York: Random House, 1991).

25. See Renata Adler, *Reckless Disregard* (New York: Knopf, 1986), for a compelling analysis of the libel suits of *General William C. Westmoreland v. CBS* and of Israeli Defense Minister *Ariel Sharon v. Time;* also relevant is Rodney A. Smolla, *Suing the Press* (New York: Oxford University Press, 1986).

26. *Hustler Magazine v. Falwell,* 108 S. Ct. 876 (1988).

27. Gillmor et al., *Mass Communication Law,* 172.

28. Pember, *Mass Media Law,* 116.

29. Lucas A. Powe, Jr., *The Fourth Estate and the Constitution* (Berkeley: University of California Press, 1991); see also Donald M. Gillmor, *Power, Publicity, and the Abuse of Libel Law* (New York: Oxford University Press, 1992). Both books are thoughtfully reviewed, and the main issues outlined by John Soloski in the *Journal of Communication* 43:2 (Spring 1993): 167–71.

30. In *Red Lion Broadcasting Co. v. FCC*, 381 F.2d 908 (1967), *aff'd*, 395 U.S. 367 (1969), the Supreme Court upheld the FCC's personal attack rule.

31. *Red Lion Broadcasting Co. v. FCC*, 395 U.S. 367 (1969).

32. *Miami Herald Publishing Co. v. Tornillo*, 418 U.S. 241 (1974).

33. Patricia Aufderheide, "After the Fairness Doctrine: Controversial Broadcast Programming and the Public Interest," *Journal of Communication* 40:3 (Summer 1990): 47–69.

34. Herman Gray, "Popular Music as a Social Problem: A Social History of Claims Against Popular Music," in *Images of Issues*, ed. Joel Best (New York: Aldine de Gruyter, 1989), 143–58.

35. Tricia Rose, *Black Noise* (Hanover, N.H.: Wesleyan University Press, 1994).

36. David A. Hamburg, *Today's Children* (New York: Times Books, 1992), 192.

37. For background, see Robert Gunsalus, "Media Analysis Organizations" (paper submitted to my seminar entitled "Politics and the Media," December 1991); Mark Jurkowitz, "A House of Canards—Critiquing the Media Critics," *Media Studies Journal* 6:4 (Fall 1992): 31–48; and Ruth Ann Strickland, "Mass Media Criticism in the United States" (paper presented at the annual meeting of the American Political Science Association, Chicago, September 1995).

38. Bernard Weinraub, "Despite Clinton, Hollywood Is Still Trading in Violence," *New York Times*, 28 December 1993, A1. For an earlier, illuminating piece on this topic, see Terry Pristin, "Soul-Searching on Violence by the Industry," *Los Angeles Times*, 18 May 1992, F1, F12.

39. Quoted in Michael Wines, "Reno Chastises TV Executives Over Violence," *New York Times*, 21 October 1993, A1.

40. This account and quotes come from Bernard Weinraub, "Dole Attacks Hollywood Wares as Undermining Social Values," *New York Times*, 1 June 1995, A1, B10.

41. Frank Rich, "Dole's True Lies," *New York Times*, 4 June 1995, E15.

42. Raymond William Stedman, *Shadows of the Indian* (Norman: University of Oklahoma Press, 1982), 157.

43. As detailed by Gregory D. Black in *Hollywood Censored* (New York: Cambridge University Press, 1995); see also Frank Walsh, *Sin and Censorship* (New Haven, Conn.: Yale University Press, 1996).

44. Allen R. Myerson, "Southern Baptist Convention Calls for a Boycott of Disney," *New York Times,* 19 June 1997, A10.

45. Mary B. W. Tabor, "Publishing," *New York Times,* 4 March 1995, D8.

46. For details, see Kathryn C. Montgomery, *Target: Prime Time* (New York: Oxford University Press, 1989).

47. William J. Bennett and C. DeLores Tucker, "Lyrics From the Gutter," *New York Times,* 2 June 1995, A29.

48. Howard Kurtz, "Time Warner, on the Defensive for the Offensive," *Washington Post,* 2 June 1995, A1, A18.

49. *Joseph Burstyn, Inc. v. Wilson,* 343 U.S. 495 (1952). But see Edward de Grazia and Roger K. Newman, *Banned Films* (New York: R. R. Bowker, 1982); Richard S. Randall, *Censorship of the Movies* (Madison: University of Wisconsin Press, 1968); and Cindy Patton, "White Racism/Black Signs: Censorship and Images of Race Relations," *Journal of Communication* 45:2 (Spring 1995): 65–77.

50. Public Law 101-650, title V, The Television Program Improvement Act of 1990.

51. I am indebted to Catherine Jhee and Christopher Nicholas Manning who wrote papers, in spring 1993 and fall 1994 respectively, on Public Law 101–437 for my "Media and Politics" courses at Duke.

52. FCC, *Report and Order,* 9 April 1991.

53. Cited in Edmund L. Andrews, "Broadcasters, to Satisfy Law, Define Cartoons as Education," *New York Times,* 30 September 1992, A13, B8; see also Dale Kunkel and Julie Canepa, "Broadcasters' License Renewal Claims Regarding Children's Educational Programming," *Journal of Broadcasting & Electronic Media* 38:4 (1994): 397–416.

54. Edmund L. Andrews, "'Flintstones' and Programs Like It Aren't 'Educational,' F.C.C. Says," *New York Times,* 4 March 1993, A1.

55. *Federal Register* 61:167, 27 August 1996, at 43981–98, and Lawrie Mifflin, "U.S. Mandates Teaching Time on Television," *New York Times,* 9 August 1996, A1, A9 (for the quote).

56. Lawrie Mifflin, "TV Complies, Barely, With New Rules on Shows for Children," *New York Times,* 11 September 1997, B1.

57. Edmund L. Andrews, "F.C.C. Joining a Move to Curb Violence on TV," *New York Times,* 7 July 1995, A1, A9.

58. Some movies that deal with the Committee on Un-American Activities either explicitly or metaphorically are: *The Front, Guilty by Suspicion, High Noon, My Son John, On the Waterfront, Salt of the Earth,* and *Tell Them Willie Boy Is Here.*

59. Accounts sympathetic to the witnesses are Larry Ceplair and Steven Englund, *The Inquisition in Hollywood* (Berkeley: University of California Press, 1979); and Victor S. Navasky, *Naming Names* (New York: Penguin, 1980). An attempt to defend the committee is William F. Buckley, Jr., ed., *The Committee and Its Critics* (Chicago: Henry Regnery, 1962). The committee hearings themselves are a treasure trove of varieties of human behavior.

60. Natalie Robins, *The FBI's War on Freedom of Expression* (New York: Morrow, 1992).

61. Ward Churchill and Jim Vander Wall, *Agents of Repression* (Boston: South End Press, 1988).

62. Lawrie Mifflin, "Revisions in TV Ratings Called Imminent," *New York Times,* 16 June 1997, B1.

63. Lawrie Mifflin, "Helping or Confusing, TV Labels Are Widening," *New York Times,* 30 September 1997, B1.

64. This information is drawn from Richard Lansky's paper "Censorship in Music" (written for an independent study course with me) in fall 1994.

65. Neil Strauss, "Wal-Mart's CD Standards Are Changing Pop Music," *New York Times,* 12 November 1996, A1, B11.

66. Edward de Grazia and Roger K. Newman, *Banned Films* (New York: R. R. Bowker, 1982), and Murray Schumach, *The Face on the Cutting Room Floor* (New York: Morrow, 1964).

67. George Comstock, *The Evolution of American Television* (Newbury Park, Calif.: Sage, 1989), 88.

68. Jeffrey Ressner, "'Cop Killer' Is Iced," *Rolling Stone* 638 (3 September 1992): 16.

69. For the personal experiences of one of the most fascinating of the individuals blacklisted, see Dalton Trumbo, *Additional Dialogue,* ed. Helen Manfull (New York: M. Evans, 1970).

70. Richard S. Randall, *Freedom and Taboo* (Berkeley: University of California Press, 1989).

71. For various feminist perspectives about pornography, see Catharine A. MacKinnon, *Feminism Unmodified* (Cambridge, Mass.: Harvard University Press, 1987); Varda Burstyn, ed., *Women Against Censorship* (Vancouver, B.C.: Douglas & McIntyre, 1985); Linda Williams, *Hard Core* (Berkeley: University of California Press, 1989); and Pamela Church Gibson and Roma Gibson, eds., *Dirty Looks: Women, Pornography, Power* (Bloomington: Indiana University Press, 1993).

72. See Robert J. Stoller and I. S. Levine, *Coming Attractions* (New Haven, Conn.: Yale University Press, 1993), for a set of interviews with the cast and crew of an X-rated film.

73. *Miller v. California,* 413 U.S. 15 (1973).

74. Kathleen M. Sullivan, "The First Amendment Wars," *The New Republic* 207:14 (28 September 1992): 38.

75. Edward de Grazia, *Girls Lean Back Everywhere* (New York: Random House, 1992).

76. This discussion is based on my "Pornography, Politics, and the Press: The U.S. Attorney General's Commission on Pornography," *Journal of Communication* 38:2 (Spring 1988): 122–36. For a comparison of this commission's findings with those of the 1970 U.S. Commission on Obscenity and Pornography, and the British Home Office 1979 Departmental Committee on Obscenity and Film Censorship, see Gordon Hawkins and Franklin K. Zimring, *Pornography in a Free Society* (Cambridge: Cambridge University Press, 1988).

77. See Paletz, "Pornography, Politics and the Press," 127–28, for this and subsequent quotes.

78. For a survey of this literature, see David L. Paletz and John Boiney, "Researchers' Perspectives," in *Terrorism and the Media,* ed. David L. Paletz and Alex P. Schmid (Newbury Park, Calif.: Sage, 1992), 6–28.

79. David L. Paletz and Laura L. Tawney, "Broadcasting Organizations' Perspectives," in *Terrorism and the Media,* ed. David L. Paletz and Alex P. Schmid (Newbury Park, Calif.: Sage, 1992), 105–10, from which this discussion is taken.

80. See the committee's annual surveys entitled *Attacks on the Press* available from the CPJ at 330 Seventh Avenue, 12th Floor, New York, New York 10001; also relevant is *Media Studies Journal* 10:4 (Fall 1996), devoted to "journalists in peril."

81. What follows is based on John Nerone, *Violence Against the Press* (New York: Oxford University Press, 1994), especially 10–13.

82. Ibid., 11.

83. See K. M. Shrivastava, "Terrorism Related Problems of Indian Media," in David L. Paletz, ed. *Political Communication in Action* (Cresskill, N.J.: Hampton Press, 1996), 225–45.

Part II
The People

◆　◆　◆

Chapter 5

Reception

◆ ◆ ◆

The media are pervasive. Their content is rife with explicit and implicit political meanings. But how people receive and respond to that content is one of the most vexing and bedeviling questions in political communication.[1] To put it in extreme terms: are people supine victims of overpowering media or do they dominate media content, interpreting it in their interests?

There is a lot of conflicting research trying to answer that question, much of it arcane and written in academese. This chapter categorizes, explicates, and assesses the leading theories, trying to make them understandable; inevitably, however, brief summaries cannot convey their subtlety and complexity.[2] This chapter concludes by offering an approach that combines elements from the theories discussed.

POWERFUL MEDIA

We start with theories that conceive the media as powerful.

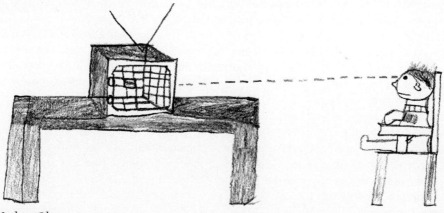

Nathan Olney

Hypodermic Theory

To exaggerate, but not by much, the *hypodermic theory* conceptualizes the audience as an undifferentiated mass unprotected against a mighty media whose content is injected directly into it. This alarmist perspective is particularly prevalent at a time when a new medium or form has recently emerged. It happened with the movies, comic books, video games, and rap music.

Thus, the power of the movies over their audiences was assumed in early communications research, with children and youth deemed most at risk. The Payne Fund studies, conducted between 1929 and 1933, found "massive and irrefutable" evidence of their influence.[3] Producers were admonished to elevate the quality and kinds of movies made, and it was urged that people be educated to improve the ways they watched movies.

Many years later, the same view of the audience as being vulnerable and in need of protection and nurturing is evident in the work of Aletha Huston and her colleagues on the effects of television advertising and programming on women, children, minorities, the elderly, and institutionalized populations; that is, on the most powerless members of society.[4] They claim that television presents these people negatively and leads them to have a poor self-image. Their study does not determine the nature of the relationship between images in the media and self-image or between exposure and influence, but assumes that such a relationship necessarily exists.

Of course, given this perspective, the same powerful media seen by the Payne Fund studies and by Huston and others as harmful can have potentially beneficial effects: Witness the successful attempt to develop content to improve the morale of American soldiers entering World War II.[5] More recently, the assumption that the media can be used to "improve" the attitudes and behaviors of individual audience members is evident in studies of health campaigns and in the range of research on the "prosocial" (e.g., encouraging empathy instead of violence) effects of the media.[6]

All the studies discussed in this section can retrospectively be labeled "hypodermic" because they assume that the media are able to inject or otherwise infect the audience with a message. They take it for granted that the media are powerful and that the audience (particularly children) is vulnerable and subject to being influenced. The general research strategy of these studies, therefore, is to try to measure effects on individual audience members.

Many of these studies are also government-sponsored and thus motivated by the perception of a preexisting need for state intervention of some kind. The exhortations that they make in the interests of the vulnerable audience therefore typically involve state regulation of some aspects of the media industries and/or action to educate the people at risk of manipulation.

The hypodermic approach has long been criticized as mechanistic and simpleminded. Valid in part, such criticisms are often based on selective interpretations of the model, as well as on misuse and misinterpretations of some of the research. It is useful to think of a hypodermic as a metaphor alerting us to the potential power of the media under certain circumstances. It is also still an apt description of the intentions, even the effects, of "many commercial and social communication campaigns."[7] An example is the "Just Say No" antidrug campaign spearheaded by Nancy Reagan during her husband's presidency.

Cultivation Approach

Moving away from the hypodermic idea but still positing the combination of powerful media and vulnerable audience is the *cultivation,* or *cultural indicators,* approach of George Gerbner and his associates. At its most basic, this theory is based on the idea that the more people watch television, the more they will come to believe that the real world is like the television world.[8] People whose everyday environment is congruent with and reinforced by television's messages are cultivated more strongly than others. People belonging to subgroups that hold beliefs that differ greatly from those implied by the television world are pulled toward agreement with it; this is called "mainstreaming."[9] The long-term result is that heavy viewers are supposed to believe that the world is, among other things, more crime-ridden, gender-stereotyped, racist, alienated and anomic, affluent, and above all violent, than do light viewers.

The methodology and findings of this approach have been subjected to caustic challenges. Critics question the measurement of light and heavy viewing. They dispute that heavy television viewing necessarily involves watching programs suffused with particular content (e.g., violence) more than light viewing. They doubt that the world presented on television is in fact uniform across all sorts of programs (and time). Or, even if it is, that watching it is a sufficient condition for a strong cultivation effect.

Besides, measuring the differences between the television and real worlds is only one step. It is far more difficult to establish that the differences translate into attitudes, beliefs, and feelings, such as more generalized fears for heavy viewers, and that these then affect people's behavior.[10]

WEAK MEDIA

In contrast to the hypodermic and cultivation approaches are approaches that depict the media as weak and the audience as little affected by their contents.

Minimal Effects Approach

In the *minimal effects approach,* five mediating conditions are said to come between media content and the audience.

First are predispositions and the related elements of selective exposure, selective perception, and selective retention. *Selective exposure* is the inclination of people to expose themselves mainly to media content that they expect to be congenial to their views. Then, through *selective perception,* they perceive it according to their existing beliefs. *Selective retention* means that they remember the media content in consonance with their views and preferences, even if this takes a certain amount of distortion.

For example, the television show "In Living Color" attracted mainly African-American and young viewers; and while its satirized stereotypes of African-Americans stimulated some viewers to examine their racial prejudices, others misconstrued the images as realistic depictions, thereby confirming their bias.[11]

The second condition limiting the effects of media content is *interpersonal dissemination,* whereby the content of communications is transmitted along, and therefore influenced by, friendship, shared interests, and opinions. This is related to the third mediating condition, which consists of the groups to which the audience members belong and the groups' norms.

Fourth is "the exercise of opinion leadership," meaning the two-step flow process in which messages flow from the media to opinion leaders who disseminate (their) views to others in their community. This is different from the third condition because the leaders are not necessarily friends of or share interests with the people they influence.[12]

The final factor is that for economic reasons, the media don't espouse any view questioned by a large part of their potential audience.

Rather than standing naked before media output, then, the audience is protected by psychological, social, and economic factors. These factors make mass communications "an agent of reinforcement rather than change."[13]

The minimal effects perspective has been powerful, persuasive, and ultimately unsatisfactory. Among its flaws, it ignores advertising, neglects politics and political advertising, and rests on a too-passive concept of the audience. Above all, it is simplistic.

PURPOSIVE AUDIENCE

Further research and the development of more sophisticated and complex approaches to explain media and audience interactions thus became inevitable.

Uses and Gratifications Approach

It came in the form of the *uses and gratifications* (U&G) approach. In this approach, people are conceived of as consciously selecting media content for the ways they can use and find gratifications from it. So they watch television to escape their daily routines and problems, for emotional release (diversion), to keep abreast with what is going on in the world (surveillance), to reinforce their personal identity, and the like.[14]

Extending the approach beyond the personal, and based on observations and interviews, James Lull has added a host of interpersonal and social uses and gratifications that people obtain from watching television in the home. Television provides background noise, companionship, and entertainment (*environmental*). It punctuates time, activity, and talk patterns (*regulative*). It is used to illustrate experience, enter conversations, reduce anxiety, set an agenda for talk, and clarify values (*communication facilitation*). It affects family solidarity and relaxation, conflict, and relationships (*affiliation/avoidance*). It is related to decisionmaking, behavior modeling, problem-solving, value transmission, legitimization, information dissemination, and substitute schooling (*social learning*).[15]

Lull found that individuals from families stressing harmonious social relations used television differently from people in homes where family communication is characterized by the independent expression of ideas. The former watched more television and used it for all the purposes just summarized and more. The latter rejected virtually all the social uses of television.[16]

So, people do not attend to the media for the same reasons. Different gratifications and uses produce different effects. Adolescents studied by Deirdre Johnston reported four motivations for viewing such graphic horror films as *Halloween* and *Nightmare on Elm Street.* They watched to see the ways people die, and blood and guts (gore); to be scared and to freak out (thrills); to feel brave, mature, and different (independence); and because of loneliness, anger, and to avoid problems at home (problems). Their motivations predicted their responses to the films, with gore watchers "most at risk for [engaging in] subsequent violence."[17]

Media Systems Dependency

Beyond uses and gratifications is *media system dependency* (MSD), expounded by Melvin Defleur and Sandra Ball-Rokeach. This theory posits that the primary goals people need to fulfill in their lives are understanding, orientation, and play. Each of these has a personal and social dimension, resulting in six basic media system dependency relations.

First is *self-understanding:* "learning about oneself and growing as a person." Next is *social-understanding*, which entails "knowing about and interpreting the world or community." *Action orientation* includes "deciding what to buy, how to dress, or how to stay slim." *Interaction orientation* involves "getting hints on how to handle new or difficult situations." *Solitary play* consists of "relaxing when alone or having something to do by oneself." And *social play* involves "going to a movie or listening to music with family or friends."[18]

U&G and MSD Comparison and Critique   In both MSD and U&G, the media are used by people to fulfill certain needs and goals. Both are social-psychological approaches in which studying individuals in the aggregate is deemed the best way to understand social processes.

Nonetheless, there are significant differences between the two approaches. U&G theorists focus on psychological and sociodemographic origins of differences in media use, leading them to be impressed with the various ways people can interpret media content. For MSD theorists, psychological, interpersonal, and sociological explanations are the key, with audience members neither in charge of nor controlled by media content.

MSD and U&G, like all the other approaches, are vulnerable to criticisms. They both contain innumerable possible and overlapping needs and goals, uses and gratifications. It is difficult to document why people select one program rather than another given the large amount of media content relevant to their motivations. And the proponents and exponents of both approaches have not yet derived significant political meaning and effects from their research.

ACTIVE AUDIENCE

The purposive behavior in the U&G and MSD approaches consists of selecting and using media content. However, the influence of literary theory on communications research resulted in new conceptualizations of the audience as active interpreters creating unique meanings in the process of apprehending media messages.[19]

This "response" approach focuses on how people comprehend media content. For, to use its phraseology (or jargon), there is no necessary correspondence between the meaning with which makers "encode" the content and what recipients "decode" from it. The reason is that media content is open to interpretation; and interpret it is what people do.

As one example, Tamar Liebes and Elihu Katz studied how different groups in Israel—Arabs, Moroccan Jews, recent arrivals from the Soviet Union, and second-generation Israelis on a kibbutz—plus a set of Japanese viewers in Japan watched and responded to the television program "Dallas." They identified two main types of involvement. *Referential viewers* related the program to reality, especially to their own life situation. *Metalinguistic,* or *critical, viewers* were conscious of the program as a construction, with script and actors, which they could criticize. Most viewers slipped between these different modes quite easily, although some specialized in one rather than another.[20]

Advancing this type of research, Margaret Thompson exposed students to a four-minute music video, "Papa Don't Preach," by Madonna. This video depicts the story of a pregnant teenager who informs her father of her decision to keep the baby and marry her boyfriend, its father. Thompson found that the referentials were more likely to come from families where they were encouraged to obey parental power, had some experience or familiarity with teen pregnancy, were involved in the video's narrative, and identified with its characters. They connected the video with their own lives. In contrast, the metalinguistics distanced themselves from the video, discussing its themes, performances, techniques, camera angles, and such.[21]

Both studies conclude that referential viewers are most vulnerable to and metalinguistics least vulnerable to, media contents.

Response Studies

One of the most celebrated response studies is by Janice Radway.[22] She interviewed women frequenting a bookstore specializing in romance novels. Her purpose was to discover what they liked about this mass-produced, mass-promoted, immensely popular, and critically damned genre.

Such research is in keeping with a tendency in popular culture research to increase appreciation for works that traditionally exist outside the canon of mainstream literature. According respect to an audience (and genre) previously marginalized, Radway ensures that the women are treated seriously and not dismissed because of the kinds of books they enjoy.

At first, the novels appear to take advantage of and exploit women's subservience in a patriarchal (male-dominated), capitalist society. The usual tale is of a woman and man who are attracted to but misunderstand each other. Eventually, the seemingly macho hero displays his nurturant capacities to the independent and feisty heroine, whereupon she realizes the depth of her feelings for him and they marry.

Radway discovered that the novels' characters and plots simultaneously criticize and reproduce the fate of women as wives and mothers. More strikingly, women read the books as protests against their "duty" to nurture others without receiving nurturance themselves. They interpret as strong and positive role models what to many critics would appear to be very negative and repressed female figures. Radway shows the readers to be active creators, not passive recipients: They use the books for empowerment rather than enslavement.

Elayne Rapping wonders whether the effects of the "temporary transformations" that Radway's readers experience may simply lead them to more and more romance reading as a relief from the conditions of their lives rather than to any form of political action. Even though they may feel briefly liberated from their possibly oppressive marriages, they are unlikely to leave their husbands, let alone join a movement for women's liberation.[23]

Nor is people's ability to construct meaning from the media unlimited.[24] There are four main reasons. First, some media contents are more closed to interpretation (less polysemic) than others: their meaning is hard to deny or even to reinterpret.

Second, narrators, anchors, and commentators before, during, or after a program may tell people what to think about it. For example, viewers of televised presidential debates are inclined to change their opinions about who won to conform to the judgments and pronouncements of postdebate analysts.

Third, even though people may be able to subvert some aspects of a "text" (e.g., its narrative), they may still unthinkingly accept its overall ideology (e.g., that of capitalism).

Most important, it is argued that certain meanings, themes, and perspectives (usually ones favoring powerful economic interests) are insistently propounded and promoted in the media. "The power of viewers to reinterpret meanings is hardly equivalent to the discursive power of centralized media institutions to construct the texts that the viewer then interprets."[25]

Thus, three Appalachian families studied by Jim White, instead of rejecting television's stereotypical, demeaning portrayals of people from their region, identified them with segments of the Appalachian community with whom they did not associate: people on welfare, hillbillies, people living in bad situations. This failure to step outside of television's frame of reference "suggests that while families possess considerable power to negotiate with or reject television's images, this process was carried out within the parameters television provides."[26]

The essential conclusion to draw from these response studies is that people can be involved in different ways with media content: "critical or accepting, resisting or validating, casual or concentrated, apathetic or motivated."[27]

PROCESSING MEDIA CONTENT

One explanation for the different involvements people have with media content has to do with how they actually process that content.[28] For Doris Graber, they do so through *schematic thinking*.

Schematic Thinking

"A schema is a cognitive structure consisting of organized knowledge about situations and individuals that has been abstracted from prior experiences."[29] Common schema are a negative view of government and politicians, big business as corrupt, and American democracy as the best form of government for the country.

Their schema enable people to extract and incorporate the information from the media they consider important. Conversely, when people lack schema—for example, about the ways in which governmental institutions operate and important public policies are made—they are unlikely to absorb the information that will enable them to understand these subjects. In such situations, when people are unable to mold incoming information, their views usually reflect media content.

Critics of this approach contend that schema are ill-defined and poorly measured, and that schema research neglects such important factors as why people turn to (motivation) media content and how they feel about it (affect).[30]

Defenders respond that "no one ever has measured or will measure a schema directly . . . only observe the empirical consequences"[31]; and that "some notion of schematic knowledge structure is necessary to understand how people think about and evaluate political issues, candidates, and events."[32]

Constructionist Approach

Going beyond schema theory, three scholars of political communication have proposed what they call a *constructionist approach* to explain how people process media content.[33] They argue that people operate from a core of "common knowledge" that guides their interest in and attention to media fare. This core consists of frames, which "individuals rely on to convey, interpret, and evaluate information."[34]

They show that there is often a disjunction between the dominant media frames for the news and the frames that people use to think about the news. For example, people apply a "human impact" frame to the effects of the event on people twice as often as the frame appears in news stories. Even more striking, the morality frame through which people understand issues was virtually absent from the news; stories are not reported in moral terms of right and wrong.

Overall, the news media personalize and politicize the world as full of conflict. The world people construct through their frames from that media world is similarly personalized; but rather than politicized, it is depoliticized, denuded of its political content.[35]

The constructionist approach is a useful advance, although it is not without its problems. One of these problems is the source of citizens' "common knowledge." As Lance Bennett points out, they acquire this knowledge "(in part) from the same environment of advertising and news that they are actively reconstructing to suit their personal needs."[36]

RECALL

The main politically relevant, empirical research related to the reception of media content involves recall.

People who read the daily newspaper and watch national television news would appear to have a sense of obligation to stay informed about current events.[37] Nonetheless, for television viewers at least, the general finding is dismal: "The average viewer . . . can recall without prompting only about one out of the nineteen news stories covered in a typical news-cast."[38]

Certainly, the ability of people to remember what they have seen differs. Higher socioeconomic status and education mean more recall, as well as greater exposure to news in general.[39] But the learning that does take place is more about people in the news than about why events occurred and their likely repercussions.[40]

There are several explanations offered for the low level of recall, starting with the pace and rapidity of news programs, their relatively low information quotient, and the limited contextual information they provide on the often complicated issues and events being reported.[41] Also implicated are viewers' minimal motivation, their inadequate background knowledge, and their lack of schema into which to fit news items.

Recall may appear to be so dismal for three broader reasons. First, researchers have focused on memory of news topics, narrative information, and surface details in the stories, but these depend on verbal or audio material, not on the visual images central to television news. Visuals, especially those that are personalized because of unusual sites and human figures (e.g., scenes of disease or disaster), enhance recall; but it is a kind of recall that viewers cannot fully communicate in words and that researchers rarely probe for.[42]

Second, recall is inhibited because the ways news is compiled and presented on television (topics, headlines, and reports) do not coincide with the ways viewers process information and their psychology of understanding and remembering.[43]

Third, news is preoccupied with the details of daily events and the pronouncements and activities of public officials. But most people are less interested in the details of politics and government than in the larger issues of economic well-being, war, and peace.[44] Rather than absorb large quantities of information, therefore, people retain broad, lasting impressions from the news.

A few studies have gone beyond the recognition or recall of specific factual knowledge and examined viewers' understandings of news stories and events more broadly; exploring the arguments, time frames, causes, and implications people invoke in discussing news. "Complexity of thinking about public issues appears to be a function both of personal characteristics and [of] patterns of news media use."[45]

CONCLUSION

As this brief survey of the literature documents, there are conflicting theories, each with its strengths and weaknesses, about the relationships between media contents and their recipients. This conclusion tries to make sense out of them with the following overview.[46]

First, people differ in background, gender, ethnicity, age, education, religion, occupation, and socioeconomic status. They also differ in experiences, political interests, and group identification. So people's preferences in media contents vary widely.[47] While some programs attract a heterogeneous audience, there is minimal overlap among others (selective exposure).

Second, many people engage in "selective scanning."[48] That is, they deliberately avoid, ignore, reject, or do not notice most of the proliferation of media content. Certainly, it may be thrust upon them, as with the advertisements accompanying "educational" televised news shown in some schools; or they may let it pass before them as the least offensive program to watch while they are lazing in front of the television. Granted that preferences can be influenced by marketing campaigns for this new record or that new movie. Nonetheless, people control their exposure to media content; they select from the abundance available.[49]

Third, people bring diverse characteristics, knowledge, and predispositions to media content. Thus, depending on how polysemic the content, they may interpret it differently. The same presidential press conference can be praised by the president's supporters and damned by opponents (selective perception). Even if people agree that the conference was doleful, they are inclined unconsciously to modify their reactions over time to conform to their partisan views of the president (selective retention).

Fourth, psychological processes, such as the individual's information processing schema, mediate the communication: "redefine terms, infer meaning, draw parallels, and make connections."[50]

Fifth, understanding does not stop with reception; interpersonal processes intervene. People discuss their media experiences face to face, by telephone, in e-mail and snail-mail correspondence.

These five factors explain how people variously react to media content: They can accept it; use it to reinforce existing opinions or create new ones; resist it, reject it, even subvert it.

Notes

1. For an intriguing discussion of the various meanings and measurements of the term "audience," see Ien Ang, *Desperately Seeking the Audience* (London: Routledge, 1991); see also Justin Lewis, *The Ideological Octopus* (New York: Routledge, 1991).

2. I draw appreciatively from the extensive paper "Conceptualizing the Audience" that Jane Stokes prepared when she was my research assistant at the University of Southern California's Annenberg School for Communication in 1993.

3. Werrett Wallace Charters, *Motion Pictures and Youth: A Summary* (New York: Arno, 1970, first published by Macmillan in 1933); the quote is on p. 60; see also Garth S. Jowett, Ian C. Jarvie, and Kathryn H. Fuller, *Children and the Movies: Media Influence and the Payne Fund Controversy* (Cambridge, England: Cambridge University Press, 1996).

4. Aletha C. Huston et al., *Big World, Small Screen* (Lincoln: University of Nebraska Press, 1992). This work follows up the 1972 Report of the Surgeon General's Advisory Committee on Television and Social Behavior, *Television and Growing Up: The Impact of Televised Violence* (Washington, D.C.: Government Printing Office); and the 1982 National Institute of Mental Health study, *Television and Behavior,* by David Pearl, Lorraine Bouthilet, and Joyce B. Lazar (Washington, D.C.: Government Printing Office). Both studies investigated the relationship between television viewing and the attitudinal and behavioral conditions of the people who watch it, especially children and youth.

5. Carl I. Hovland, Arthur A. Lumsdaine, and Fred D. Sheffield, *Experiments on Mass Communication* (Princeton, N.J.: Princeton University Press, 1949).

6. Valeria O. Lovelace and Aletha C. Huston, "Can Television Teach Prosocial Behavior?" *Prevention in Human Services* 2:1–2 (Fall-Winter 1982): 93–106.

7. Charles T. Salmon, Margaret E. Duffy, and Scott Sorn, "Injecting New Life Into the Hypodermic-Needle Model of Mass Communication" (unpublished paper, 22 September 1992); the quote is on p. 26.

8. George Gerbner, "Towards Cultural Indicators," *AV Communication Review* 17 (1969): 137–48.

9. George Gerbner et al., "The Mainstreaming of America," *Journal of Communication* 30:3 (Summer 1980): 10–29. For an update on the approach, see Nancy Signorielli and Michael Morgan, eds., *Cultivation Analysis* (Newbury Park, Calif.: Sage, 1990).

10. For a summary of these challenges and suggested directions for reconceptualizing and expanding cultivation theory, see W. James Potter, "Cultivation Theory and Research," *Human Communication Research* 19:4 (June 1993): 564–601; John Tapper, "The Ecology of Cultivation," *Communication Theory* 5:1 (February 1995): 36–57; and L. J. Shrum, "Assessing the Social Influence of Television," *Communication Research* 22:4 (August 1995): 402–29.

11. Leda M. Cooks and Mark P. Orbe, "Beyond the Satire" (unpublished paper, School of Interpersonal Communication, Ohio University), 19.

12. See the seminal book by Elihu Katz and Paul F. Lazarsfeld, *Personal Influence* (New York: Free Press, 1955).

13. The minimal effects approach was codified by Joseph T. Klapper, *The Effects of Mass Communication* (Glencoe, Ill.: Free Press, 1960); the quote is on p. 19.

14. Dennis McQuail, Jay G. Blumler, and R. Brown, "The Television Audience: A Revised Perspective," in *Sociology of Mass Communication,* ed. Dennis McQuail (Harmondsworth, England: Penguin Books, 1972), 135–65. For the psychological orientations of media gratification, see Joseph C. Conway and Alan M. Rubin, "Psychological Predictors of Television Viewing Motivation," *Communication Research* 18:4 (August 1991): 443–63.

15. James Lull, *Inside Family Viewing* (London: Routledge, 1990), 36; also relevant is Roger Silverstone, "Television and Everyday Life," in *Public Communication,* ed. Marjorie Ferguson (London: Sage 1990), 173–89.

16. Lull, *Inside Family Viewing,* 57–59.

17. Deirdre D. Johnston, "Adolescents' Motivations for Viewing Graphic Horror," *Human Communication Research* 21:4 (June 1995): 545.

18. Melvin L. DeFleur and Sandra J. Ball-Rokeach, *Theories of Mass Communication,* 8th ed. (New York: Longman, 1989); all quotes on p. 306.

19. The seminal figure in this approach is Stuart Hall. See Stuart Hall et al., eds., *Culture, Media, Language* (London: Hutchinson, 1980). For an overview, see Sonia M. Livingstone, *Making Sense of Television* (Oxford: Pergamon, 1990); see also Henry Jenkins, *Textual Poachers* (New York: Routledge, 1992).

20. Tamar Liebes and Elihu Katz, *The Export of Meaning* (New York: Oxford University Press, 1991).

21. Margaret E. Thompson, "Cognitive Activity and Patterns of Involvement Among Television Viewers," *Mass Communication Review* 21:1 and 2 (1994): 36–48.

22. Janice A. Radway, *Reading the Romance* (Chapel Hill: University of North Carolina Press, 1984). For a development of its ideas and arguments, see Mary Anne Moffitt, "Articulating Meaning," *Communication Theory* 3:3 (August 1993): 231–51. For an earlier seminal study which looked at Harlequin romances, Gothic novels, and television soap operas, see Tania Modleski, *Loving With a Vengeance* (Hamden, Conn.: Archon, 1982).

23. Elayne Rapping, *The Movie of the Week* (Minneapolis: University of Minnesota Press, 1992), xxiv–xxv.

24. For an overview, see Shaun Moores, *Interpreting Audiences* (London: Sage 1993).

25. David Morley, "Active Audience Theory," *Journal of Communication* 43:4 (Autumn 1993): 16. See also Robert Goldman, *Reading Ads Socially* (London: Routledge, 1992), for a discussion of how advertising often manages to restrict, co-opt, even exploit, undesirable interpretations of ads.

26. Jim White, "The Medium in the Mountains" (paper presented at the annual meeting of the Southern Political Science Association, Tampa, Florida, November 1991), 24.

27. Sonia M. Livingstone, "The Rise and Fall of Audience Research," *Journal of Communication* 43:4 (Autumn 1993): 11.

28. Milton Lodge and Kathleen M. McGraw, eds., *Political Judgment* (Ann Arbor: University of Michigan Press, 1995); and Sidney Kraus, ed., *Mass Communication and Political Information Processing* (Hillsdale, N.J.: Lawrence Erlbaum, 1990).

29. Doris A. Graber, *Processing the News,* 2nd ed. (New York: Longman, 1988), 28; the next paragraph is based on pp. 249–65.

30. James H. Kuklinski, Robert C. Luskin, and John Bolland, "Where Is the Schema?" *American Political Science Review* 85:4 (December 1991): 1341–56.

31. Pamela J. Conover and Stanley Feldman, "Where Is the Schema? Critiques," *American Political Science Review* 85:4 (December 1991): 1365.

32. Milton Lodge and Kathleen M. McGraw, "Where Is the Schema? Critiques," *American Political Science Review* 85:4 (December 1991): 1357. See Kathleen M. McGraw and Milton Lodge, "Political Information Processing: A Review Essay," *Political Communication* 13:1 (January-March 1996): 131–38, for a positive discussion of the subject's "controversies, unanswered questions, and future directions" (132).

33. W. Russell Neuman, Marion R. Just, and Ann N. Crigler, *Common Knowledge* (Chicago: University of Chicago Press, 1992).

34. Ibid., 60.

35. For an expansion of the constructionist approach to political communication generally, see Ann N. Crigler, ed., *The Psychology of Political Communication* (Ann Arbor: University of Michigan Press, 1996).

36. Lance Bennett, review of *Common Knowledge, American Political Science Review* 87:3 (September 1993): 796.

37. Maxwell McCombs and Paula Poindexter, "The Duty to Keep Informed: News Exposure and Civic Obligation," *Journal of Communication* 33:2 (Spring 1983): 88–96.

38. Neuman, Just, and Crigler, *Common Knowledge,* 2; see also John E. Newhagen, "The Evening's Bad News," *Journal of Communication* 42:2 (Spring 1992): 30–31, for a chart summarizing the dolorous results from several studies of television news and memory.

39. Barrie Gunter, *Poor Reception* (Hillsdale, N.J.: Lawrence Erlbaum, 1987); see also Vincent Price and Edward J. Czilli, "Modeling Patterns of News Recognition and Recall," *Journal of Communication* 46:2 (Spring 1996): 55–78; and Steven H. Chaffee and Joan Schleuder, "Measurement and Effects of Attention to Media News," *Human Communication Research* 13:1 (Fall 1986): 76–107, for how attention to the news results in knowledge gain.

40. Gunter, *Poor Reception,* 51.

41. Mark R. Levy, "The Audience Experience With Television News," *Journalism Monographs* 55 (April 1978): 25.

42. Doris A. Graber, "Seeing Is Remembering," *Journal of Communication* 40:3 (Summer 1990): 134–55.

43. Gunter, *Poor Reception,* xii.

44. Neuman, Just, and Crigler, *Common Knowledge,* 110–11.

45. Jack M. McLeod, Gerald M. Kosicki, and Douglas M. McLeod, "The Expanding Boundaries of Political Communication Effects," in *Media Effects Advances in Theory and Research,* ed. Jennings Bryant and Dolf Zillmann (Hillsdale N.J.: Lawrence Erlbaum, 1994): 139.

46. For some of the complexities, see Linda Heath and Kevin Gilbert, "Mass Media and Fear of Crime," *American Behavioral Scientist* 39:4 (February 1996): 379–86.

47. For ethnic differences, see Alan B. Albarran and Don Umphey, "Ethnic Diversity: The Uses of Television and Cable Television Services by Hispanics, Blacks, and Whites" (paper presented at the annual conference of the International Communication Association, Miami, Florida, May 1992).

48. The term comes from Gerald M. Kosicki and Jack M. McLeod, "Learning From Political News," in *Mass Communication and Political Information Processing*, ed. Sidney Kraus (Hillsdale, N.J.: Lawrence Erlbaum, 1990), 75.

49. W. Russell Neuman, *The Future of the Mass Audience* (Cambridge, England: Cambridge University Press, 1991), especially 86–97.

50. Neuman, Just, and Crigler, *Common Knowledge,* 119.

Chapter 6
Political Socialization

◆ ◆ ◆

People are not born with political values, beliefs, and knowledge, they acquire them.

There are six main areas of political socialization. The first is *system legitimacy:* the belief that the country's political system and its institutions deserve allegiance, or indifference, or hostility. Second is *political efficacy:* the belief that one's political behavior can be effective, have results, or not. Third is *political participation:* the belief that one should participate in politics, or not. Fourth is *partisan identification:* identifying oneself with one or another political party. Fifth is *group identification:* identifying oneself with various groups in the society. And finally, *policy preferences:* the inclination to adopt or support some policy positions and oppose others.[1]

Socialization has its roots in childhood, develops during adolescence, and is refined, sometimes altered, by adult experiences. So, it changes across the life cycle. Parents, family, schools, peers, religious institutions, and significant events can all influence it. Then there's the media.

Rife with political contents in the four ways specified in chapter one, the media can be powerful agents of political socialization. Despite some notable efforts, however, there is not an abundance of recent research connecting specific media content with the six areas of political socialization.

So, this chapter takes a different approach. It begins with children, arguably the most susceptible to socialization by the media. Then it considers media depictions of women, African-Americans, and homosexuals. These portrayals can influence their self-images and how they are perceived and treated by public officials and the rest of society. The same is true for other ethnic minorities. Unfortunately, space limitations here preclude discussion of Native Americans, Arab-Americans, Asian-Americans, and Hispanics.[2] Nor is there space to explore the media's conflicting depictions of religion.

The chapter concludes with a discussion of violence. For the ability to use violence undergirds the authority of the state and is the weapon of those who try to overthrow it. It is important, therefore, to understand the media's violent content and its consequences.

Throughout this chapter, the conclusions in chapter five about people's reception of media content should be kept in mind.

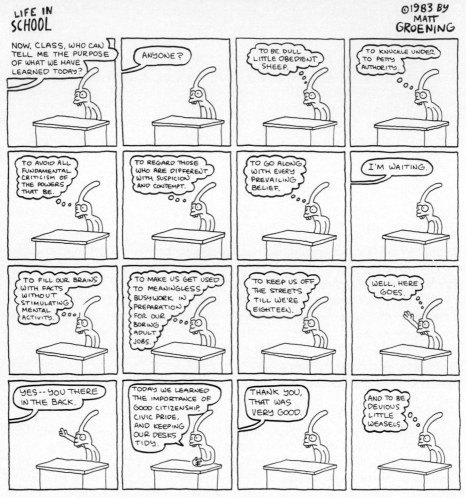

CHILDREN

According to Steven Chaffee and his associates, young people have identified the mass media as their principal source of political information and a significant influence on their political opinions.[3]

Certainly, much of the media material to which children are exposed has political socialization content. Start with the *Weekly Reader,* which currently has 9 million subscribers and was used by two thirds of all the adults in this country when they were in school. This magazine established its political socialization content from the very first issue in 1928 with its encomium to America as the land of opportunity and the presidency as the pinnacle of achievement. "Many of our Presidents have been born very poor. In America, everyone has a chance to become great. It does not matter where we are born, nor what we have. It all depends on what we are."[4]

But much of the socialization content that children encounter is far more negative. One content analysis of television programs shown during times when the audience contained a high percentage of children found the programs full of negative or inaccurate messages about the political system, with the police most likely to be misrepresented and shown as incompetent.[5]

Another study showed that high school students who viewed sports on television had higher levels of national loyalty and acceptance of the legitimacy of those in power than other students. Possible reasons are that sports, especially football, emphasize competition, possession of territory, nationalism, and the strict regulation of behavior by authority (referees).[6]

Awareness and Absorption of Political Media Contents

It is unclear how aware children are of the political socialization ingredients of their media contents and how much they absorb. Marc Taurisano studied sixth graders' understanding of "The X-Men," a Saturday morning futuristic cartoon, featuring a diverse team of mutant heroes who have assembled to protect themselves against the hostility of the outside world, combat their mutant enemies, and use their power for the benefit of all humanity.[7] In this cartoon, normal humans of all social classes and at all levels of authority treat the X-Men and other mutants as outcasts. Many of the X-Men are also members of minority groups historically objects of prejudice in American society: their founder and leader is wheelchair-bound, another leader is of African descent.

The show expresses two themes: (1) the need for tolerance, and (2) liberation (of the mutant race) through peaceful means, although violence is permissible for self-defense. It also implicitly condemns the political system, which is shown variously as incompetent, ineffective, intolerant, subject to manipulation by powerful private interests, responsible for the prejudice the mutants face, and powerless to protect its citizens.

When asked about the show, most of the young viewers in the study were utterly unaware of its basic political and social themes. The only theme they

Calvin and Hobbes   by Bill Watterson

Calvin and Hobbes © Bill Watterson. Distributed by Universal Press Syndicated. Reprinted by Permission. All rights reserved.

recognized, and that by a mere 20 percent, was the need for tolerance. That is because this theme was stated explicitly and repeated often. Otherwise, the youngsters lacked the language skills to comprehend the X-Men's messages in such phrases as "peaceful co-existence" and "people fear what they do not understand." The kids have not been encouraged to expect, or look for, nor be verbally equipped to understand the political and social messages in their (animated) television entertainment.

WOMEN

Oversimplifying outrageously, let us lump women into two broad, opposing camps: traditionalist and feminist. Traditionalists believe the patriarchal family is natural, idealize women as wives and mothers, and welcome or at least condone the existing institutions and practices that maintain male primacy. Their creed could be exemplified by the packaging blurb for the "Romantic Bride Barbie Doll":

> This is the day they've dreamt of so long;
> The magical moment of music and song.
> Candles are flickering with a beautiful light;
> On this day everything must be just right.
> Here comes the bride as the Wedding March sounds
> A vision in white in her glorious gown.
> Her groom looks with love at the light of his life—
> He's waited so long to make her his wife.
> They stand side by side, perfect together,
> Vowing true love till the end of forever.

Attesting to her popularity, Barbie, whose figure defies belief and gravity, in all versions generates roughly $1 billion in sales annually.[8]

In contrast to traditionalists, feminists (of whom there are many different stripes, including postfeminists) oppose the ideas and institutions that establish and implement male domination and female subordination; are discomforted, even outraged, over the inequality and injustices that women suffer as a consequence; and strive individually and through group action to eliminate them all.[9] Capturing their stance is the sign hoisted by a little girl at a rally: "I AM NOT A BARBIE DOLL."[10]

Cautions

The traditionalist-feminist dichotomy is narrowing. Symbolizing it, a new Barbie—with scaled-down chest and long blonde tresses replaced by a power bob—has been phased in. She has her own desktop computer (pink, of course). Meanwhile, "Teen Talk Barbie," after being criticized by a national women's group, no longer says, "Math class is tough."[11]

There is also a diversity of media content about women, ranging from the feminist *MS* to the traditionalism incarnate of *Reader's Digest*. Moreover, content changes over time: compare television's fictional families from the 1950s on. The meaning and effects of the same content changes too: in the 1950s, the eponymous protagonist of the comedy series "I Love Lucy" could be viewed as relatively liberated; but not in the 1990s' reruns. Adding another complication, many programs currently on television (especially on cable) are reruns ("Bewitched," "I Dream of Jeannie") or showings of old movies, whose content reflects attitudes prevalent when they were made.

Much media content about women is polysemic (that is, open to interpretation) or simply ambiguous. There is, for example, an extensive literature on whether Madonna upholds or exposes the patriarchal order.[12]

Consider soap operas in this regard. For several feminist critics, they serve as "a resistant feminine discourse."[13] Many soap operas are centered around a matriarch, while patriarchal male characters are relegated to accessories against which the females define themselves. The soaps feature strong women as chief executive officers, doctors, and lawyers, who distrust the "male" will to power and domination. They portray "feminine" qualities of love and nurturing as strong and desirable. They thus communicate women's subjective experience of the world while simultaneously exposing the contradictions of patriarchy.

When conspicuously feminist, the soap opera "renarrates the conventional patriarch as a kind of criminal, the conventional hero as an agent working for a paternal order that promotes isolation, alienation, and brutality, and the conventional marriage scenario as a sad comedy that mistakes human beings for material possessions."[14]

But not every observer agrees with this argument. Michael Parenti contends that in soap operas the "nuclear family, motherhood, heterosexual monogamy and capitalism are permanent, unquestioned norms."[15] He complains further that the soaps contain no class conflict and ignore the problems of workers: taxes, cost of living, neighborhood destruction, undemocratic corporate power, and environmental destruction.[16]

More subtly, Sonia Livingston and Tamar Liebes argue that soap operas' dominant tendency is "to represent a traditional conception of women's psychological development"; they emphasize its repressive over its liberating aspects.[17]

Past Portrayals of Women in the Media

With these cautions in mind, let us now look at past depictions of women in the media.[18] Our concern is with topics intimately involving women: sexuality and female desire, the female body, marriage, motherhood and family, work and the workplace, violence against and by women, and the women's liberation movement.

Movies and Television Feminist film critics have seen Hollywood as assuming that its women movie characters behave according to their biology and as encouraging the audience to relish or at least accept the "natural" domination of the female by the male.[19] The female is the object of desire by male characters within the film and by male spectators in the audience.[20]

Giving credibility to these views, from the 1940s until the 1970s, the movies were male-dominated. The majority of leading female characters were "young, attractive and motivated by romance."[21] Being married, having children, and running a household were their aims. Sexual activity outside marriage was condemned.

Much of this scenario is captured in the innocent, self-sacrificing, female protagonists portrayed in the Disney full-length, animated movies *Snow*

White, Cinderella, and *Sleeping Beauty.* They are usually controlled by a male power structure. Their female adversaries—the queens, wicked stepmothers, and ugly sisters who possess power—are generally evil. Minor female characters are bad-tempered servants. "Females who show some spirit, intellectual curiosity, or disregard for authority always suffer and inevitably accept the male control."[22] They discard their dreams to become part of the life of their true love.

On television, women have often been confined to traditional and stereotypical roles. Most did not work outside the home. If they did, it was the male characters who made the decisions and ran the organizations.[23] If the women were the subject of the show, it focused on their home life.[24] Sex discrimination, harassment, and poverty were not their lot on television.[25]

Television's ideal feminine type was blonde, beautiful, and young; lesbians and African-American women did not fit. Aging in women was depicted more negatively than in men, and older women were hard to find in television shows, other than on "Golden Girls", where they behaved as if they were much younger.

News Women have often been subordinated in the news.[26] Coverage of the founding of the National Organization for Women (NOW) in 1966 was typical. The *New York Times* reported the story at the bottom of its Food, Fashion, Family, and Furnishings page, under the Thanksgiving menu and photograph of the stuffed turkey; the *Washington Post* ignored it entirely.[27]

In fact, early coverage of the women's movement, when there was any, was unflattering.[28]

When it wasn't relegation, women's fate has been underrepresentation. Men still make up the majority of the anchors, reporters, weathercasters, and sportscasters. To be employed on-air, the females usually have to be much younger and more physically attractive than their male counterparts.

Men also far outnumber women as newsmakers and sources. Women usually appear in news stories "as an anonymous example of uninformed public opinion, as housewife, consumer, neighbor, or as mother, sister, wife of the man in the news, or as victim—of crime, disaster, political policy."[29] They are passive reactors, not participants, in public events. Feminist perspectives are uncommon.[30]

Current Portrayals of Women in the Media

But times change. For women, they have been marked by the activities of the feminist movement and its opponents, the increasing prevalence of women's studies programs in higher education; and a host of social shifts, such as the significant percentage of women now in the workplace, and new patterns of marriage, divorce, and single parenting.

In addition, several issues confronting women, such as sexual harassment, have achieved public awareness. The 1980s were both a continuing struggle for gender equality and a time of increasing antifeminism and nostalgia for traditional family forms. The mass media reflect some of these changes and struggles.

Memorable Television Role Models

I am the girlfriend of either Starsky or Hutch. I will die of Leukemia in the last ten minutes of the show, or, alternatively, my past life as a hooker will be revealed and I will disappear for the good of Starsky and/or Hutch.

I am a psychotic/mute/Indian/Chicana who is restored to normalcy and neatness by a young, attractive, white, middle class doctor from the east. (Lots of flashbacks showing me whipped, raped, and force-fed)

I am the sister/daughter of an unjustly imprisoned man or else the witness to a mafia crime. I am also the client of a blind freelance insurance investigator. I scream often and inopportunely. I always fall and twist my ankle when the investigator and I are fleeing the bad guys.

I am a black/white cop. I have a short snappy name. I am tough but feminine. I like to follow my own instincts about a case. This frequently gets me into trouble; I am inevitably rescued by my male, fellow officers, who are devoted to me . . . I never rescue them.

I am the woman behind the man. I spend a lot of time keeping dinner warm for my crusading policeman/coroner, lover/husband. Sometimes I nag about being left alone so much. Sometimes I am kidnapped by mafia thugs. This makes a welcome break in my routine.

© *Nicole Hollander*

Movies and Television   Women characters in movies now work in nontraditional occupations. Romance is no longer so preeminent in women's lives; it often causes problems when it does occur; and extramarital sex has become acceptable.[31] Even Disney has moved in the feminist direction. Although still a sexpot, the studio's Pocahontas is a child of nature who strives to enlighten the technologically superior but morally inferior English colonists, and (in contrast to her real-life counterpart) declines to stand by her man when he leaves the country.

Nonetheless, the overwhelming tendency of Hollywood films is simultaneously to endorse and confine changes in gender relations. Thus, several Hollywood films of the 1980s appealed to anxiety over women abandoning their traditional place in the home. But rather than return to the patriarchal family, they featured a nontraditional fatherhood as the ideal solution. In such movies as *Three Men and a Baby* and *Mrs. Doubtfire,* men displayed the nurturant femininity that some women have supposedly abandoned.[32]

Depictions of women have also changed on television with such shows as "Cagney and Lacey," "Murphy Brown," "One Day at a Time," and "Roseanne." Quantitatively, the percentages of women as physicians, lawyers, judges, and journalists in television prime time drama more than doubled between 1974 and 1986.[33] Themes and plot lines increasingly advocate women's rights or sexual equality: By 1986, "the proportion of programs advocating that women should be treated equally with men rose . . . to 93.3 percent."[34] In 1998 MTV even spun-off "Daria" (Margendorffer) from "Beavis and Butt-head," giving the intelligent, feminist, straight-talking teenager, with the corporate lawyer mother, an animated series of her own.

This change is visible in the evolution of such television series as "Star Trek."[35] In the show's original 1966–1969 version, women occupied no positions of authority aside from Lieutenant Uhura as communications officer, a role in which she was more of a secretary or switchboard operator than an officer. In the episodes themselves, women appeared in three primary role types: siren and seductress, monster, and love interest.

"Star Trek: The Next Generation" was different right from the opening credits: "Where no man has gone before" became "Where no one has gone before." Though the top two in command remained men, women filled many authority positions: head of security, chief doctor, and counselor. Each of these women was integrally and successfully involved in the operation of the *Enterprise.* Unlike the women of "Star Trek," these women carried weapons. By the time the show progressed through "Star Trek: Deep Space Nine" to "Star Trek: Voyager," even though women were still nurturers, one had become the ship's captain.

Going beyond weekly series, Elayne Rapping observes that movies made for television "offer opportunities for a kind of work not easily done elsewhere in television or film and therefore tend to attract from the start producers, actors, and writers with more politicized agendas."[36] Within limits and despite their contradictions, some of these movies express feminist positions on such subjects as rape, date rape, sexual harassment, incest, abortion, unequal working conditions, and surrogacy.

Most often, however, feminist identity "is defined by appearance, by job, by marital status and by personality, not by political belief or political practice."[37] The shows reduce social issues to personal problems; responsibility for solving them resides on the individual not the government. Issues are also fungible: once featured, they are neglected, replaced by the latest hot topic.[38]

Media Backlash

According to Susan Faludi, the feminist movement provoked a media backlash. Its theme: the struggle for women's rights is over, women are now free and equal, and as a result they have never been more miserable. Displaying this misery has been a horde of media-disseminated myths about burnout, infertility, a shortage of men, depression and confusion, a crisis of confidence, stress-induced disorders, and loneliness.[39] The backlash recharacterized the feminist movement, and women—from heroines into villainesses. Yet the struggle for women's rights is far from over: Most American women have not achieved full economic, social, educational, and political equality with men.[40]

Exacerbating the situation is the fact that when women do predominate in media contents, as in women's magazines and some advertising, the subjects are often appearance, diet, health, and fashion at the expense of women's many other concerns and activities. For, despite exceptions and the occasional focus on substantial issues, the fundamental theme of these magazines is that a woman's ultimate happiness and fulfillment depend on possessing a loving husband and children. For women it's home, personal relations, marriage, and family that matter; for men, it's work, social relations, and action.

Socialization Consequences

The mass media currently purvey ambivalent and contradictory images of women.[41] Their socializing content is a mix of "misogynist atrocities" and "feminist victories."[42] Women are told to assert themselves, pursue careers, enjoy their independence; but also to defer to men and to work hard to look beautiful and thin.

The media's overtly political content, however, continues to represent and reinforce the "political dominance of males over females."[43] The media still tell people that it is the male responsibility and prerogative to be involved in politics and government.

No wonder "that women are less politically interested, informed, and efficacious than men" and participate less in politics.[44]

Thus, women candidates for electoral office often have to face sex-role stereotyping and challenges to their legitimacy and competence not aimed at men.[45] No wonder women are woefully underrepresented in elected and appointed governmental offices at the national and state levels. There are only two women on the U.S. Supreme Court. It took two single women without child care responsibilities to be confirmed as the first female Secretary of State and first U.S. Attorney General.[46] Major issues on the feminist policy agenda, such as the Equal Rights Amendment, have failed to become law.

Political socialization may also contribute to gender-based policy differences among legislators. In one study, female legislators tended to see criminality as originating in childhood experiences, educational deprivation, and lack of adult opportunities, while male legislators viewed criminals as responsible for choosing their life of crime. The women proposed long-term interventionist policies; the men wanted stricter sentencing and more prison space. In general, the bills proposed by men were more likely to be enacted.[47]

AFRICAN-AMERICANS

Even more than women, the fate of African-Americans in the media has been that of marginalization, stereotyping, trivialization, and exploitation.[48]

Portrayals in Movies and Television

During the many years of segregation and racist social policies, African-Americans appeared in the white-controlled media mainly as maids, servants, comic buffoons, and entertainers. With the success of the civil rights movement, they became more visible, even if mainly as tokens, sidekicks, window dressing, and members of raucous families. No black occupied a dramatic starring role in a continuing series on television until 1965 when Bill Cosby appeared in "I Spy." He later starred in the "Cosby Show," which, for several years, was television's most popular program. It promoted black pride and racial tolerance, but it may also have given the misleading impression that racial inequality and discrimination were issues of the past and inadvertently fed the prejudice that success (defined as material comfort and prosperity) depends only on individual talent, ability, and willingness to work hard.[49]

African-Americans, notably Oprah Winfrey, can now be found quite regularly in the mass media. What's more, a cable television channel and several radio stations now cater to the assumed interests of African-Americans. Blacks direct and black actors and actresses appear in movies aimed at mainstream audiences.[50] A controversial movie was even made about Malcolm X and shown widely.[51]

Despite these advances, "television representations of blackness operate squarely within the boundaries of middle-class discourses about 'whiteness.'"[52] That is, African-Americans in entertainment shows on television are presented as basically middle-class whites.

Portrayals in News

News coverage of African-Americans since the 1960s falls into three broad categories. First, it was generally favorable during the civil rights movement, as blacks and their allies strived to end segregation in the South. Then it became negative in the form of reports of black civil disturbances and riots.

Coverage is now mixed. There is little attention to minority communities and issues. Racial stereotyping persists, but blatant racial insensitivity is uncommon.[53] The most negative coverage is of poverty, crime, and drugs: blacks who use crack cocaine are portrayed as "deviants who are beyond rehabilitation."[54]

A revealing study of news on four Chicago television stations by Robert Entman showed that blacks were depicted as more physically threatening in crime coverage and as more demanding in politics than whites. At the same time, employment of blacks as on-air personnel by these stations gave the impression that racial discrimination is no longer a serious social problem. "The mix of these two views of blacks encourages modern racism—hostility, rejection and denial toward black aspirations."[55]

No surprise, then, that survey data indicate that Americans exaggerate the extent to which blacks compose the poor. Whites with the highest misunderstanding are the ones most likely to oppose welfare.

Assuming that the media are the main source for such misinformation, Martin Gilens looked at photographs in stories on poverty in news magazines and on television. Although in absolute numbers most poor people are white, he found that, reversing reality, almost two thirds of the poor people shown were African-American. Even more striking, blacks were disproportionately abundant in pictures of unemployed working-age adults but absent from pictures of the poor with whom people sympathized: the elderly, those working, and people in employment programs. Thus, blacks were identified with poverty at its most unappealing. The impression is that they are mired in poverty and too lazy to work their way out. Gilens concludes that "public support for efforts to redress racial inequality is likely to be diminished."[56]

Socialization Consequences

A major media event can have significant socialization effects. African-Americans who saw the film *Malcolm X* "and received reinforcement from a televised documentary [about him] became more racially conscious, more concerned about race relations, and more knowledgeable about Malcolm X the man."[57]

In general, improvements in the quantity and quality of appearances by and depictions of African-Americans in the entertainment media may be offset by negative news coverage. Probable consequences are lowered or challenged self-esteem of members of the minority group and the persistence of prejudice and racism against them.[58] One policy effect, at least in part, was the enactment in 1996 of a draconian, punitive federal welfare law.

HOMOSEXUALS

Young homosexuals have little help from other people in understanding and defining themselves as gay or lesbian. They are unlikely to be surrounded by homosexual role models. Media images and depictions of homosexuality can thus be important sources of information and models of behavior. It makes a difference then whether homosexuality is shown as normal or perverse, healthy or sick, legal or criminal.[59] However, the basic assumption underlying most mass-media content was and still is that heterosexuality is normal, other sexual behavior deviant, if not abnormal.

Portrayals in Movies and Television

For many years, homosexuals, and especially lesbians, were virtually unseen in the entertainment media. A classic example was the play *Tea and Sympathy* about a homosexual teenager; it became the Hollywood film about a straight teenager who is taunted because he is thought to be gay.

What portrayals existed were homophobic, insulting, and demeaning: "The lesbian was relegated to the role of old spinster, mannish bore, crazed murderess, or lusting vampire."[60] Or the portrayals contained negative subtexts, as in the implied homosexuality that heightened the evilness of some of the villains in Alfred Hitchcock's films.

When actually featured in a program, homosexuality was almost always negatively stereotyped. Mike Wallace concluded a 1967 hour-long show on the subject with: "The average homosexual, if there be such, is promiscuous. He's not interested in, nor capable of, a lasting relationship like that of a heterosexual marriage."[61]

Over time, gays became more common in entertainment shows, and were sometimes depicted sympathetically. For example, an episode of "All in the Family" had a gay character who was a macho ex-football player. Nonetheless, in dramatic programs, homosexuality is a problem that disrupts the lives and expectations of heterosexuals. In comedies, aside from being wittier and more effeminate, gay characters behave essentially straight. Few actors and actresses portraying homosexual characters are openly so themselves, which helps to explain the brouhaha over the actress Ellen DeGeneres and the character she played both "coming out."

Portrayals in News

By the early 1980s, news coverage of homosexuals as homophobic morality tales had diminished. Most news organizations treated homosexuality as a lifestyle issue rather than as related to the civil rights movement or to ethnic or racial communities.

Then came AIDS, a disease that in its early years disproportionally struck male homosexuals. The media initially ignored AIDS: "The *New York Times* ran more stories on toxic shock syndrome in one week than on AIDS in the first three years of the epidemic."[62] Later, the disease was treated in the paper as resulting from promiscuous gay men responsible for their own plight.

But AIDS eventually forced many journalists to take a more realistic view of gay life. They witnessed members of the homosexual community engaged in fundraising, education, patient care, and political action. The change was most noticeable in the news media of large cities, less so elsewhere. AIDS raised the issue of gay male sexual behavior as a media topic.

Nonetheless, adolescent homosexuality and overt displays of homosexual physical behavior remained taboo. "Overall, mainstream network television does not present gays and lesbians in the context of their own identity, desire, community, culture, history or concerns."[63]

This limitation can be seen in press coverage of the issue of gays and lesbians in the military raised by President Clinton at the onset of his first administration and the "don't ask, don't tell" policy that ensued. Although news stories recast homosexuality as a civil rights issue, they asserted a distinction between being and behaving homosexual, thereby refusing to accept homosexual desire as natural. "Just as 'good' blacks in the 1960s civil rights movement were not supposed to be angry or militant, 'good' gay or lesbian soldiers are not supposed to be sexual."[64]

Socialization Consequences

While about half of the public think homosexual relations between consenting adults are immoral and should be illegal, the role of the media in causing, reinforcing, or reducing this number is unclear. And although an overwhelming majority of people polled claim they would discourage their children from watching television programs with gay or lesbian characters, there are no studies of whether they actually do so.[65]

Homosexuals probably cope with an overwhelming heterosexist and still homophobic media contents through avoidance, resistance, or subversion, which entails giving such contents an affirmative gay/lesbian meaning.

They can also turn to their own media. At first, that media consisted of "underground" experimental films, pornography, and newsletters, which were subsequently joined by community media, such as newspapers, magazines, video, books, and computer bulletin boards.[66] These media have been supplemented by leased-access and public-access cable. There are also gay bookstores and film festivals. Women's music labels issue lesbian-oriented music. Few of these media modes rely on advertising. The exceptions are newspapers and magazines catering to an upper-income, urban, white male clientele, which are increasingly receiving the advertising essential to their survival, particularly from the liquor industry.

Many of these media encourage homosexuals to be increasingly active in politics, support particular candidates, oppose others, assert their policy preferences, and demand their rights.

VIOLENCE

Violence is a pervasive element of human existence, going back to biblical times and before.[67] It is expressed in interactions among individuals, relations between groups, and conflicts within and between states.

Violence may be broadly defined as the exercise of physical force, whether or not entailing a weapon, to inflict injury or damage against the person or property of oneself, another, or others. This definition excludes language, although words can often foment behavior leading to violence, even violence itself. Violence can be accidental, but it is usually intentional or at least motivated. It can be random, but it is more often directed at a particular target. It can violate the law or be legally sanctioned. Indeed, sanctioned (institutional) violence is widespread, visible in the actions of the police and the military and in such "sports" as boxing and wrestling.

The ability to inflict violence undergirds authority. As Max Weber observed, the state lays claim to the monopoly of the legitimate use of physical force to enforce its order.[68] Even in the most representative and democratic of states, force is perennially deployed against criminals, rioters, revolutionaries, and terrorists.

Thus, violence is a weapon to protect the political system and its occupants, to discourage what is deemed to be antisocial behavior, to preserve property and class relations, and—in autocratic states—to deter or eliminate opposition.

At the same time, violence can be wielded against those holding authority—the powerful and wealthy. It is deployed to make claims, protest policies, for rebellion, even revolution. Violence pervades the media: it is a staple of fiction programs, a basic ingredient of news. By the time American children graduate from high school, they have witnessed on television thousands of killings and many more verbal threats, fistfights, beatings, muggings, knifings, actual and attempted rapes, robberies, and shootouts.

No wonder the relationship of media and violence has been and remains a perennial subject of controversy and research. This has meant several decades of congressional hearings, assorted studies, and numerous reports by various commissions. The basic issues concern the effects of media violence on the attitudes of children and adults, particularly whether it induces some members of the audience to aggressive, even criminal behavior, or at least makes them more willing to condone it.

Fictional Violence in the Media

Fictiorial violence in the media comes in many diverse genres and forms.[69] On television, these include crime shows, westerns, situation comedies and soap operas, music videos, advertisements (including promotions for violent programs), and animated cartoons aimed mainly at children.

Movies often seem synonymous with violence. Indeed, some of the most memorable moments from movies are violent: the image of an eye being sliced by a razor in Luis Bunuel's *Un Chien Andalou;* the shower murder sequence in Alfred Hitchcock's *Psycho,* so scaringly scored by composer Bernard Herrman.

There are several elements to media fictional violence: the perpetrators, their goals, the amount of force, violence's effects, and moral judgments. Each of these elements contains various possibilities.

The types of people who inflict violence could be, to mention just a few of the possibilities, bureaucratic job fillers (bomber pilots); "ordinary" people, who, given the opportunity, turn sadistic (death camp guards); criminals; or the deranged.

To dichotomize: Goals can be aggressive or defensive, socially approved or disapproved, legitimate or illegitimate, realized or not. The amount of force expended can vary from mild to massive. Consequences can range from deterrence, to destruction, to death.

Equally various are the types of violence: killing, suicide, maiming, assault (including sexual), stabbing, beating, an isolated punch, pushing/dragging, a threat with a weapon, a car chase, and so much more.

Ultimately, the violence can be celebrated, depicted as normal and unexceptional, or condemned. Such judgments may have little to do with the amount of violence shown.

Certainly, media violence content can be quite complicated. In the typical crime drama, for example, "antisocial, criminal, and violent behavior often are rewarded early to establish a challenge to law enforcement. Later on, detection, pursuit, arrest, and other accoutrements of law enforcement are recompensed, antisocial and criminal behavior punished; violence continues to be rewarded, but now as part of law enforcement."[70]

Violence and aggression may be such common features of fictional media content because they cater to people's widespread yearnings that are rarely gratified in reality, such as the yearning to appear self-possessed in dangerous situations, like James Bond or a private detective; or the yearning to disrupt decorum with impunity, like the Marx Brothers do in their movies; or to prove oneself in a supreme test, as in the shoot-outs that often culminate westerns; or to transcend the cumbersome processes of law and order and impose justice oneself, like Rambo does.

Fictional violence and aggression also trade on people's fundamental fears, ones that, perhaps fortunately, are also rarely realized in reality. Among them are the fears of being overwhelmed by internal psychic forces (*Dr. Jekyll and Mr. Hyde*), of being hopelessly corrupted by external forces (the vampire Dracula), and of being implacably hunted (as in the *Terminator* series and Buster Keaton's brilliant *Cops* and *Seven Chances*). Then there are fears of entrapment in a place with a hidden menace, the subject of so many "slasher" movies.[71]

Violent entertainment can also immerse people vicariously in intense physical activity, exemplified by the movies staring Bruce Lee.

At the same time, fictional violence usually conceals the corporeality of the body. While heroes and protagonists may be beaten up, their injuries, when shown, are brief and reparable; they rarely display the damaged sinuses, smashed teeth, amputations, the months of bed-ridden pain that such beatings cause in real life. They invariably survive the villains' attempts to destroy them and end up ritualistically defeating their antagonists.

The villains are clearly identified as such: their evil-doing obvious and vile. Odious, contemptible, and rather unreal, they clearly deserve the violence wreaked upon them by movie heroes incarnated by Clint Eastwood, Arnold Schwarzenegger, and Sylvester Stallone.

As for the villains' victims and the people destroyed during the heroes' derring-do, they are usually anonymous, henchmen, or bystanders deserving of their fate. When individualized—for example, as friends or colleagues of the hero— their deaths function as a justification for the evil-doers' subsequent destruction.

Violence is unappealing to many people when it is unjustified and undeserved, inflicted on characters we have come to know and cherish, particularly graphic and gruesome, or exposes the corporeality of the body.

Socialization Consequences

In theory, fictional violence can have innumerable socialization effects. Benignly, it could be cathartic, relieving people of the urge to be aggressive. Most possibilities, however, appear to be undesirable. Exposure to so much violence could increase tolerance of, desensitize, even inure people to it. It could encourage (susceptible) people to imitate or emulate the violent behavior if the occasion or opportunity to do so arises. It could make people more fearful.

Political awareness and consciousness of violence may be heightened (and exaggerated?) so that people are more willing to abridge or suspend civil liberties, demand or countenance tougher, even draconian, law-and-order measures, such as additional police, more prisons, stiffer sentences served.

Media violence might strengthen authority because criminals often get their comeuppance—or weaken authority because in reality most crimes go unsolved.

There is no limit to speculation. Arthur Asa Berger imaginatively argues that professional wrestling, a form of fictional violence, contains dire political implications. For the format features a hero or heroine who follows the rules, a villain who does not, and a referee who hinders the former and unwittingly aids the latter. The political message is that "evil is rampant, the state is powerless to help us, individuals must look out for themselves and get along as best they can, we must fight fire with fire, the competition is unfair, there are conspiracies that further exacerbate the situation." He concludes that "the values and world view portrayed in wrestling reinforce the fatalistic, apolitical attitudes supposedly possessed by the most disadvantaged in society."[72]

Three effects of exposure to media violence stand out. First is learning or imitation in which people "develop aggressive thoughts, attitudes and behavior."[73] Second is desensitization: Prolonged viewing "can lead to emotional desensitization toward real world violence and the victims of violence." Third is fear: "Viewing violence can increase the fear of becoming a victim of aggression, with a resultant increase in self-protective behaviors and mistrust of others."

With respect to imitation, a meta-analysis of 188 studies embracing more than 240,000 viewers revealed a highly statistically significant association between exposure and aggressive behavior. Most of the studies involved experiments in which one group viewed violent programming and another was shown neutral or none. The subsequent behaviors of the viewers were then compared. One quarter were correlational studies that surveyed people's amount of television viewing, expressed preferences for particular programs, or frequency of viewing actual television shows, then related those exposure measures to differences in antisocial behaviors, including criminal acts and physical violence, verbal aggression, aggressive intent, and willingness to administer electric shocks to others in a laboratory situation.[74]

Correlation is not causation.[75] Other factors may explain the association between violent media content and (increased) aggression. Aggressive children could be attracted to and consume violent programming; perhaps certain personality traits lead people to be aggressive and to watch violence on television. Questions about the experimental studies' methodology and conclusions in particular can be raised. As George Comstock and Haejung Paik observe, the experimental setting "departs from the everyday in the perceptions of the subjects, in the brevity of the television exposure, in the absence of the possibility of retaliation for aggression, in the exclusion of competing and countervailing communications, and in the criterion of immediacy as the measure of effects."[76] Many of the studies, moreover, were conducted in the

Calvin and Hobbes © *Bill Watterson. Distributed by Universal Press Syndicate. Reprinted by permission.*

1960s and 1970s when television was a relative novelty and its contents less graphic.

Nonetheless, the evidence is compelling. Witness a study that tracked a group of children to adulthood:

> The more violent the programs children watched at age 8, the more aggressive they were at age 19 . . . ; the more serious were the crimes for which they were convicted by age 30; the more aggressive was their behavior while under the influence of alcohol; and . . . the harsher was the punishment of their own children.[77]

CONCLUSION

The mass media are a vital agent in the process by which Americans become politically socialized. Political socialization content is inculcated most effectively when it is consistent and persistent. The prevalence of such media content may help to explain why Americans take pride in their country (patriotism), approve of the basics of their political system, prefer (modified) capitalism over other forms of economic organization, and are anti-Communists.

There is a dearth of compelling recent research specifically tracing the cause-and-effect relationship between media content and the various areas of political socialization. Much, however, has been written about media depictions of women, African-Americans, and, to a lesser extent, homosexuals. This literature assumes that these portrayals have a significant impact on these individuals' self-images and the reactions of public officials and the rest of society. Complicating factors are the vast amount, diversity, and changes over time of the relevant media content.

An overview of the high (and low) lights of these depictions shows that women have moved from subordination, relegation, underrepresentation, and traditionalism, to a somewhat feminist perspective, to something of a backlash. The socialization effect appears to be a continuation of male political domination, albeit sightly impaired. African-Americans are now less demeaned and stereotyped, and are more prominent than in the past. But some prejudice and racism persist in their media depictions. Homosexuals, no longer invisible, are still deemed aberrant.

The most studied media subject is violence. In this chapter, the dimensions of violence were detailed, its appeals suggested, and the research critiqued. It was concluded that consuming television violence leads to imitation, desensitization, and fear.

Notes

1. The term "political socialization" was coined by Herbert H. Hyman, *Political Socialization* (Glencoe, Ill.: Free Press, 1959). For an early survey of the literature, see Richard G. Niemi, "Political Socialization," in *Handbook of Political Psychology*, ed. Jeanne N. Knutson (San Francisco: Jossey-Bass, 1973), 117–38. For a critique of the inadequacy of research and proposals to rectify them, see Timothy E. Cook, "The Bear Market in Political Socialization and the Costs of Misunderstood Psychological Theories," *American Political Science Review* 79:4 (1985): 1079–93.

2. For an admirable collection of essays on media depictions of Native Americans, see S. Elizabeth Bird, ed., *Dressing in Feathers* (Boulder, Co.: Westview Press, 1996); and for a lament over the media's stereotyping of people with mental illness, Otto F. Wahl, *Media Madness* (New Brunswick, N.J.: Rutgers University Press, 1995).

3. Steven H. Chaffee et al., "Mass Communication in Political Socialization," in *Handbook of Political Socialization,* ed. Stanley Allen Renshon (New York: Free Press, 1977), 223–58; see also Karl Erik Rosengren and Sven Windahl, *Media Matter: TV Use in Childhood and Adolescence* (Norwood, N.J.: Ablex, 1989).

4. *Weekly Reader: 60 Years of News for Kids, 1928–1988* (New York: World Almanac, 1988), 7 (for circulation data), 9 (for the quote).

5. Karin L. Sandell and David H. Ostroff, "Political Information Content and Children's Political Socialization," *Journal of Broadcasting* 25:1 (Winter 1981): 49–59.

6. Robert H. Prisuta, "Televised Sports and Political Values," *Journal of Communication* 29:1 (Winter 1979): 94–102.

7. The following summary is based on "Recognition and Comprehension of Political Messages in Children's Television" (a paper submitted by Marc Philip Taurisano to my undergraduate "Politics and Media" sequence, Duke University, 30 March 1993).

8. Joshua Mills, "In Toy World '94, Boundaries Are Freely Crossed," *New York Times,* 14 February 1994, C1.

9. For one woman's beguiling evolution into feminism but not without travail, see Mary Kay Blakely, *American Mom* (Chapel Hill, N.C.: Algonquin Books, 1994).

10. Cited in Susan Faludi, *Backlash* (New York: Crown, 1991), xxiii.

11. "Barbie's Remarks Don't Quite Add Up," *New York Times,* 21 October 1992, C3.

12. Cathy Schwichtenberg, ed., *The Madonna Connection* (Boulder, Colo.: Westview, 1993). For contrasting views on MTV, see E. Ann Kaplan, *Rocking Around the Clock* (New York: Routledge, 1987); and Lisa A. Lewis, *Gender Politics and MTV* (Philadelphia: Temple University Press, 1990).

13. E.g., Martha Nochimson, *No End to Her* (Berkeley: University of California Press, 1992), 2.

14. Ibid., 120–21.

15. Michael Parenti, *Make-Believe Media* (New York: St. Martin's Press, 1992), 99.

16. Ibid., 96.

17. Sonia Livingstone and Tamar Liebes, "Where Have All the Mothers Gone?" *Critical Studies in Mass Communication* 12:2 (June 1995): 155; see also Laura Stempel Mumford, *Love and Ideology in the Afternoon* (Bloomington: Indiana University Press, 1995).

18. Key works are Liesbet van Zoonen, *Feminist Media Studies* (Thousand Oaks, Calif.: Sage, 1994); and Susan J. Douglas, *Where the Girls Are* (New York: Times Books, 1994).

19. E.g., Mary Ann Doane, *The Desire to Desire* (Bloomington: University of Indiana Press, 1987).

20. Laura Mulvey, "Visual Pleasure and Narrative Cinema," *Screen* 16:3 (Autumn 1975): 6–18.

21. Stephen P. Powers, David J. Rothman, and Stanley Rothman, "Motion Pictures and the Politics of Gender" (paper presented at the annual meeting of the American Political Science Association, Chicago, September 1992), 10. Their paper provides the material for the rest of the paragraph.

22. Jill Birnie Henke and Dianne Zimmerman Umble, "And She Lived Happily Ever After," in *Mediated Women: Representations in Popular Culture,* ed. Marian Meyers (Cresskill, N.J.: Hampton Press, in press), 19 in manuscript.

23. Leah R. Vande Berg and Diane Streckfuss, "Prime-Time Television's Portrayal of Women and the World of Work," *Journal of Broadcasting & Electronic Media* 36:2 (Spring 1992): 195–208.

24. Nancy Signorielli, "Television, the Portrayal of Women, and Children's Attitudes," in *Children & Television,* ed. Gordon L. Berry and Joy Keiko Asamen (Newbury Park, Calif.: Sage, 1993), 231.

25. Aletha C. Huston et al., *Big World, Small Screen* (Lincoln: University of Nebraska Press, 1992), summarize these research findings on 26–30.

26. For the situation in the late 1970s, see Gaye Tuchman, Arlene Kaplan Daniels, and James Benet, eds., *Hearth and Home* (New York: Oxford University Press, 1978).

27. David S. Broder, *Behind the Front Page* (New York: Simon & Schuster, 1987), 126.

28. Kim Fridkin Kahn and Edie N. Goldenberg, "The Media: Obstacle or Ally of Feminists?" *Annals of the American Academy of Political and Social Science* 515 (1991): 104–13. For news weeklies, see Frauke Schnell and Nayda Terkildsen, "Media Discourse and Public Opinion: The Political Culture of the Women's Movement" (paper presented at the annual meeting of the American Political Science Association, Chicago, September 1995).

29. Patricia Holland, "When a Woman Reads the News," in *Boxed In: Women and Television,* ed. Helen Baehr and Gillian Dyer (New York: Pandora Press, 1987), 133–50.

30. Lana F. Rakow and Kimberlie Kranich, "Woman as Sign in Television News," *Journal of Communication* 41:1 (Winter 1991): 20.

31. Powers, Rothman, and Rothman, "Motion Pictures" paper, 14–15.

32. Elizabeth G. Traube, *Dreaming Identities* (Boulder, Colo.: Westview, 1992).

33. Rothman, Lichter, and Lichter, 262, endnote 14.

34. Ibid., 231.

35. This discussion is based on "'Star Trek' and 'Star Trek: The Next Generation'" (paper submitted by Tim Haddock to my "Politics and the Libido" seminar, Duke University, 16 November 1991).

36. Elayne Rapping, *The Movie of the Week* (Minneapolis: University of Minnesota Press, 1992), xxx.

37. Bonnie J. Dow, *Prime-Time Feminism* (Philadelphia: University of Pennsylvania Press, 1996), 209.

38. Kathryn C. Montgomery, "Promoting Health Through Entertainment Television," in *Mass Communication and Public Health,* ed. Charles Atkin and Lawrence Wallack (Newbury Park, Calif.: Sage 1990), 127.

39. Susan Faludi, *Backlash* (New York: Crown, 1991), ix–x.

40. For a critique of Faludi's argument about the inevitability of backlash as women progress, see Kathleen Hall Jamieson, *Beyond the Double Bind* (New York: Oxford University Press, 1995), 6–8, 19–20, 188–89, and 210–211.

41. For further corroboration, see the Executives Summary, *Reflections of Girls in the Media* of an analysis of media content by Nancy Signorielli, and a national survey of children conducted by Lake Sosin Snell & Associates, for Children Now and the Kaiser Family Foundation (April 1997).

42. The phrases are Elayne Rapping's from her unpublished paper "Gender and Media Theory," (undated), 16.

43. Diana Owen and Jack Dennis, "Sex Differences in Politicization: The Influence of the Mass Media," *Women & Politics* 12:4 (1992): 23.

44. Sidney Verba, Nancy Burns, and Kay Lehman Schlozman, "Knowing and Caring about Politics: Gender and Political Engagement," *Journal of Politics* 59:4 (November 1997): 1051.

45. Kim Fridkin Kahn, *The Political Consequences of Being a Woman* (New York: Columbia University Press, 1996).

46. I am indebted to Professor Lois Lovelace Duke for this observation.

47. Lyn Kathlene, "Alternative Views of Crime," *Journal of Politics* 57:3 (August 1995): 697–723.

48. Venise T. Berry and Carmen L. Manning-Miller, eds., *Mediated Messages and African-American Culture* (Thousand Oaks, Calif.: Sage, 1996); Jannette L. Dates and William Barlow, eds., *Split Image: African Americans in the Mass Media* (Washington, D.C.: Howard University Press, 1990); Jacqueline Bobo, *Black Women as Cultural Readers* (New York: Columbia University Press, 1995).

49. Sut Jhally and Justin Lewis, *Enlightened Racism* (Boulder, Colo.: Westview, 1992).

50. For an historical survey of blacks in movies until World War II, see Thomas Cripps, *Slow Fade to Black* (New York: Oxford University Press, 1977); and from then up to the civil rights era, his *Making Movies Black* (New York: Oxford University Press, 1993). On movies made by African-Americans, see Manthia Diawara, ed., *Black American Cinema* (New York: Routledge, 1993); and for visible evidence if depictions of blacks in American movies, see the Melvin van Peebles' narrated film *Classififed X.*

51. For a thoughtful discussion and review of the film, see Jonathan Rosenbaum, *Movies as Politics* (Berkeley: University of California Press, 1997), 145–53.

52. Herman Gray, *Watching Race* (Minneapolis: University of Minnesota Press, 1995), 9.

53. Christopher P. Campbell, *Race, Myth and the News* (Thousand Oaks, Calif.: Sage 1995).

54. Jimmie L. Reeves and Richard Campbell, "Coloring the Crack Crisis," *Media Studies Journal* 8:3 (Summer 1994): 80.

55. Robert M. Entman, "Blacks in the News," *Journalism Quarterly* 69:2 (Summer 1992): 341.

56. Martin Gilens, "Race and Poverty in America" (paper presented at the annual meeting of the American Political Science Association, Chicago, August 1995).

57. Darren W. Davis and Christian Davenport, "The Political and Social Relevancy of *Malcolm X*," *Journal of Politics* 59:2 (May 1997): 550.

58. Huston et al., *Big World, Small Screen,* 25.

59. For this argument, see Fred Fejes and Kevin Petrich, "Invisibility, Homophobia and Heterosexism," *Critical Studies in Mass Communication* 10:4 (December 1993): 396. This chapter's discussion is based on their article, a magisterial survey of the literature on lesbians and gays in the media.

60. Ged Gemünden, Alice Kuzniar, and Klaus Phillips, "From 'Taboo Parlor' to Porn and Passing," *Film Quarterly* 50:3 (Spring 1997): 2.

61. Cited in Fejes and Petrich, "Invisibility," 400.

62. Paul D. Lerner, "Raising Our Voices" (independent research paper submitted to Professor David Marc, Annenberg School for Communication, University of Southern California, 25 June 1991), 6.

63. Fejes and Petrich, "Invisibility," 402; see also Michelle A. Wolf and Alfred P. Kielwasser, eds. *Gay People, Sex, and the Media* (New York: Haworth Press, 1991).

64. Fejes and Petrich, "Invisibility," 405.

65. Ibid., 409.

66. Lerner, "Raising Our Voices," 12ff.

67. See the imaginative paper by Sari Thomas, "Violence and Sex in the Bible and the Politics of Studying Violence" (presented at the meeting of the International Communication Association, Sydney, Australia, July 1994).

68. Max Weber, *The Theory of Social and Economic Organization,* ed. Talcott Parsons (New York: Free Press, 1964), 154.

69. For differences in media depictions of factual and fictional death, see David L. Paletz and Rocco Femia, "Death in Newsmagazines and Feature Films," *Media Development* 40 (March 1993): 19–21.

70. George Comstock, *The Evolution of American Television* (Newbury Park, Calif.: Sage 1989), 195.

71. I acquired the idea that fictional violence appeals to basic human yearnings and fears from a book or article that I read several years ago. To my distress, I failed to record the citation at the time. I hereby acknowledge my debt to the author and apologize for the absence of a reference.

72. Arthur Asa Berger, *Agitprop* (New Brunswick, N.J.: Transaction Publishers, 1990), 116–19.

73. This and the following quotes are from Barbara J. Wilson et al., "Content Analysis of Entertainment Television" (paper presented at the Duke University Conference on Media Violence and Public Policy, Duke University, Durham, North Carolina, June 1996), 7–8; see also James T. Hamilton, "Violence and the Media: Research Perspectives and Policy Implications" (Conference paper for Working Group on Radio and Television Autonomy and the State, Commission on Radio and Television Policy, The Aspen Institute Communication and Society Program, May 4–7, 1994); see also Barbara J. Wilson et al., *National Television Violence Study,* Vol. 2, *Executive Summary,* ed. Joel Federman (University of California, Santa Barbara: Center for Communication and Social Policy, 1998).

74. George Comstock and Haejung Paik, "The Effects of Television Violence on Aggressive Behavior: A Meta-analysis" (preliminary report to the National Research Council, S. I. Newhouse School of Public Communications, Syracuse University, Syracuse, New York, 1990); see also their "The Effects of Television Violence on Antisocial Behavior: A Meta-Analysis," *Communication Research* 21:4 (August 1994): 516–39; and John Condry, *The Psychology of Television* (Hillsdale, N.J.: Lawrence Erlbaum, 1989), chap. 4.

75. An admonition learned from Susannah Batyah Felicity Paletz.

76. Comstock and Paik, "The Effects of Television Violence on Aggressive Behavior" 241, cited in Hamilton, 6.

77. Leonard D. Eron and L. Rowell Hausman, "Television as a Source of Maltreatment of Children," *School Psychology Review* 16:2 (1987): 198, cited in Hamilton, 9.

Chapter 7

Public Opinion

◆ ◆ ◆

Public opinion consists of the views held by ordinary people, which authority-holders and authority-seekers and other powerful figures can "find it prudent to heed."[1] Obvious subjects of public opinion are the state of the economy, the popularity of the president, and the involvement of U.S. troops in conflicts abroad. Many opinions (e.g., that college athletes should be paid) are unrelated to politics and policy, but they can become relevant, particularly if the media encourage public interest and politicians to become involved.

BACKGROUND

Individual opinions gain political significance when aggregated into public opinion. The important properties of aggregated opinions are their salience, scope, direction, distribution, and segmentation.

Salience concerns the prominence of an issue for the public. At one time or another, drugs, the economy, and crime have each occupied first place. *Scope* refers to the number of people with an opinion on a particular topic. *Direction* recounts what these opinions are and how they are divided (e.g., support of and opposition to capital punishment). *Distribution* specifies the range of opinions; that is, the alternatives held by the public. *Segmentation* refers to differences in opinions between segments of the population on the basis of demographic factors (e.g., 50 percent of Americans who have not graduated from high school but only 18 percent of college graduates would make Christianity the official religion of the United States).

Many public opinions remain relatively stable over time. The overwhelming majority of Americans have long been in favor of gun registration.[2] But public opinion can also change fundamentally; for example, a sizable majority of the public now regards racial prejudice and discrimination as offensive.[3]

Public opinion is often too general and uninformed to apply to the policymaking process and the details of policies. It can be unclear and contradictory. It is prone to alter in response to actions or events.

Nonetheless, public opinion can be powerful. Candidates base many of their campaign positions on the perception of it they derive from focus groups and polls. Policymakers need to appear to respond to the public will and usually calculate the anticipated reactions of the public to their proposed actions. They adapt their justifying rhetoric and sometimes their policies accordingly. Indeed, public opinion "is often a proximate cause of policy."[4]

So naturally, people involved in government and politics strive to influence public opinion on their behalf, to depict it to their advantage, usually through the media.[5]

Media content has significant effects on public opinion.[6] It influences how public opinion is formed; how it is fostered by agenda-setting, priming, and framing; and how it is expressed in bandwagon effects, the spiral of silence, and third-person effects. These are the subjects of the first part of the chapter.

The media sometimes also tell the public and policymakers what public opinion supposedly is. Call-in radio shows, letters to the editor, and op-eds, as well as news stories and columns, are some of the means by which the media can display opinions.[7] But these means can mislead: conservatives are most likely to be regular listeners to call-in shows and to voice their opinions over the airwaves.[8] The media's presentation of polls is the most significant and scientific way of reporting public opinion.[9] A discussion of the media coverage of polls occupies the second part of the chapter.

The RAS Model

But first, the most compelling media-based explanation of the process by which individuals form opinions and answer questions about them comes from John Zaller.[10] He suggests that people employ a variety of considerations, analogous to likes and dislikes, about issues.

Zaller has developed these ideas into a "receive-accept-sample" (RAS) model. It has four axioms. The *reception axiom* states that people with higher levels of factual knowledge about government and politics ("cognitive engagement") are more likely to be exposed to and understand political messages.

According to the *resistance axiom,* people resist arguments that conflict with their political predispositions, but only if they have enough information to understand the relationship of the message to their predispositions. The politically

DOONESBURY   **by Garry Trudeau**

Doonesbury © 1980 G. B. Trudeau. Reprinted with permission of Universal Press Syndicate. All rights reserved.

aware know which messages to resist or to accept; but the less aware accept messages that may be consistent with or contradict their political predispositions. Once accepted, messages become considerations on an issue.

The *accessibility axiom* states that the considerations most easily and quickly brought up from memory for use (e.g., to answer a pollster's question) are those that have been in mind recently. The *response axiom* asserts, problematically in my estimation, that people average their salient considerations if more than one comes to mind when provoked by a question.

"What matters for the formation of mass opinion is the relative balance and overall amount of media attention to contending political positions."[11] The sources of information, arguments, and political messages are the elite discourse contained in the media. It is important, therefore, whether the ruling elite (or which part of it) controls the relevant information necessary to define the terms of discourse for the public. Also important is whether the arguments and interpretations fit images and categories people already find compelling.

When this discourse is evenly mixed among two (but rarely more) sides, the politically unaware will incorporate some of both, but the politically knowledgeable will accept only one side. If media content is disproportionately one-sided, people with low levels of awareness will internalize it but the informed will tend to reject what is inconsistent with their predispositions.[12]

Zaller seems rather sanguine about the reasonableness and rationality of elite discourse and the ability or desire of the media to filter it. A theme of this book is that people in public life understand the potential power of media content; they do what they can to influence it, and therefore public opinion, in their favor. Besides, as documented in previous chapters, media content is often tendentious, polemical, and rabble-rousing. There is no assurance that the public, especially those with limited political awareness is invariably able to distinguish the sane from the silly, the deserving from the disastrous.

However, Benjamin Page and Robert Shapiro argue that although the measured opinions of individuals may be shaky or nonexistent, collective opinion is solid and meaningful.

> First, random measurement errors cancel out across large numbers of respondents, so that surveys yield much more accurate information about the collectivity than about any particular individual. Second, temporary opinion changes by different individuals occur in offsetting directions, so that they, too, cancel out and allow collective measurements to reflect the more enduring tendencies of opinion.[13]

EFFECTS OF THE MEDIA ON PUBLIC OPINION

Emerging from this background, there is evidence, more or less persuasive, of six media effects on public opinion. Agenda-setting, priming, and framing all foster public opinion; bandwagon effects, the spiral of silence, and third-person effects express it. The following sections describe and critique each one.[14]

Agenda-Setting

Agenda-setting is the theory that journalists, selecting and highlighting a few stories each day, determine which issues are treated as important in the news. Given prominent coverage, these subjects become salient to the public.[15] Consequently, the more people are exposed to such news, the greater their susceptibility to media agenda-setting effects.

Supporting evidence comes in three forms: comparisons over time of the national news agenda to issue ratings from opinion polls; panel studies that show how the sequence of changes in the media agenda corresponds with changes in the issue salience of individual respondents; and cross-sectional surveys that compare different media agendas with the issue salience of their respective audiences.[16] The latest evidence is that the five-to-seven issues occupying people's minds at any time, on the whole, reflect their prominence in the media.[17]

Michael MacKuen analyzed responses to the Gallup poll's question asked over many years: "What is the most important issue facing the country?" He found that for most issues, public opinion tracked media attention. On some issues, such as crime, the public's level of concern responded more to the amount of media coverage than to objective circumstances (i.e., media attention to crime predicted public concern about crime better than did the actual crime rate).[18] Similarly, Holli Semetko and colleagues have shown "that there is an important relationship between the visibility of foreign countries in TV news and U.S. public opinion about those countries."[19]

But who sets news agenda and determines the prominence given to some issues over others? In an exhaustive and illuminating study of public opinion during the Gulf War, John Mueller concludes that the war "was put at the top of the agenda far more by the actions and statements of Bush and Hussein than by anything the media did."[20] During the war, the media serviced their consumers' insatiable appetite for news. After the war, sensing that people's interest in foreign events had waned, journalists turned to other issues, conspicuously the disturbing condition of the economy.

Relatedly, Christopher Bosso has shown that the news media were reluctant to cover the Ethiopian famine of the mid-1980s because of the relative frequency of such disasters in Africa. However, NBC's three-day sequence on the story inspired such a huge public response that the network's broadcasting and print competitors subsequently rushed in to report the subject.[21]

So the news agenda is set by some combination of journalists, policymakers, and the public.[22] But journalists are constantly searching for new subjects and discarding old ones. Policymakers often conflict in their preferences for what subjects should be on or lead the agenda. And the public influences the agenda by its own interests or by variously attending to, ignoring, or disdaining topics in the news.

Priming

Shanto Iyengar and Donald Kinder have conducted a series of imaginative experiments designed to determine the effects on viewers of agenda-setting by television news.[23]

Diverse groups of participants, attracted by advertisements and a modest payment, each day for a week viewed a television network's newscasts that they had been instructed to refrain from watching the previous evening. The newscasts had been unobtrusively tampered with by substituting for "innocuous" stories in the middle of the program two to four minutes of "timeless" news broadcast by the same network several months earlier. The purpose: to emphasize a particular subject, such as alleged inadequacies in U.S. defenses, various economic problems, or pollution.

Other viewers saw in one day a supposed cross-section of news stories shown by the major networks during the previous year. These, too, had been subtly organized and structured to emphasize one or another issue. A control group was exposed to unaltered newscasts or to an "assemblage" not emphasizing any particular issue.

All participants were given lengthy pre- and postviewing questionnaires embedded with questions designed to elicit information bearing on the experiments' real purposes.

On the basis of these experiments, Iyengar and Kinder claim that "television news shapes the American public's political priorities."[24] More precisely, it sets the agenda of what Americans believe to be the important issues. It does so by paying attention to some problems and ignoring or paying minimal attention to others. The effect is particularly pronounced in lead stories. The audience's characteristics are important: The agenda-setting effects are most immediately apparent on people directly affected by the problem covered; but political partisans, interested and active in politics, are less willing than politically indifferent viewers to accept television news's agenda.

The authors' most important and intriguing contribution to research is their development of the concept of priming. That is, the influence they claim that television news has on the criteria by which public officials, policies, and candidates are judged. Viewers shown more stories about a particular issue gave more weight to that issue when evaluating the president's performance. The politically involved became just as primed as the politically indifferent.

In general, priming is strongest "when the news frames a problem as if it were the president's business, when viewers are prepared to regard the problem as important, and when they see the problem as entangled in the duties and obligation of the presidency."[25]

Iyengar and Kinder also performed experiments to assess the electoral consequences of priming. Their conclusion: "The priorities that are uppermost in voters' minds as they go to the polls to select a president or a U.S. Representative appear to be powerfully shaped by the last-minute preoccupations of television news."[26]

There are two problems with the research. The first is methodological. Given the use of five-point scales to measure the importance respondents attached to the issues, and how much they talked and cared about them, some increase in the score of respondents exposed to additional news stories about the problems was quite likely. Nor is it clear how long the effects lasted: the latest retest of respondents to measure the retention of the effects took place just one week after the experiment. The number of participants in any one experiment, moreover, was quite low.

The second problem is the research's generalizability. The experiment did not duplicate the news experience and content. No matter how at home the participants felt, the laboratory setting was not the same as watching more or less attentively in one's own abode. Moreover, by adding some stories and deleting others, the researchers gave the news an emphasis it otherwise would not often possess.

Nonetheless, the research established the significance of agenda-setting and the existence of priming.

Framing

After priming comes framing. For, as Maxwell McCombs and Donald Shaw remind us, the "attributes of an issue emphasized in the news coverage can . . . directly influence the direction of public opinion."[27]

Iyengar develops the concept of framing in his follow-up to *News That Matters*. He claims that television news frames issues in two ways: episodic and thematic. Episodic framing, evident in event-based news reports, is more common. But thematic framing provides a broader perspective, presenting the issues in the context of "collective outcomes, public policy debates, or historical trends."[28]

On the basis of the kind of experimental research just described and critiqued, Iyengar concludes that episodic framing on television encourages viewers to blame problems on individuals. Thematic framing, however, has the effect of their blaming social and political institutions (e.g., political parties, Congress).

Because episodic framing predominates on television news, it diverts blame from government to individuals, thus weakening political accountability.

Again, the research is suggestive but open to criticism, not least because of the limitations of the experimental method. As Tom Patterson observes: "It would have been astonishing . . . if Iyengar had not found that his subjects after having just seen an episodically or thematically framed news report on a particular issue, reiterated aspects of the report when asked about the causes and treatment of the issue."[29]

Nonetheless, given the prevalence of frames in news stories, it is understandable that framing can affect public opinion. So, presenting a Ku Klux Klan rally as a matter of free speech produces more tolerance for the Klan among respondents than framing it as an issue of public order.[30]

Framing and emphases can be particularly influential if they are applied consistently and exclude alternatives. In a methodologically intricate study, David Fan and colleagues showed that the decline in public confidence in Social Security over an eighteen-year period was strongly related to the type of information conveyed through the mass media, and exacerbated by economic conditions that people experienced directly *and* learned about through the media. But these changes in confidence may "have been produced by information that was incomplete and that disproportionately focussed on the problems with Social Security rather than on its successes and areas of effectiveness."[31]

Bandwagon

The bandwagon effect posits that many people want to be with the majority, with what is popular. They find this out on the basis of what they are exposed to in the mass media and decide that they will believe it. For example, people will tend to gravitate to candidates whom they are told by the media are ahead in the polls.

Evidence is mixed. On the one hand, voters who decide whom to vote for in the waning days of an election do not disproportionately side with the leading candidate; nor do final preelection polls often underestimate the support of the winner—which they would if many people took their voting cues from the polls.

On the other hand, Albert Cantril writes that voters' preferences are more highly correlated with their assessment of a candidate's likelihood of winning than with their views of his or her personal qualities, ideology, and positions on issues; and when an election outcome is in question and people lack information about the candidates, their preferences can be affected by their assessments of a candidate's likely success.[32]

Spiral of Silence

Relatedly, Elisabeth Noelle-Neumann argues that people's perception of the distribution of public opinion motivates their willingness to express political opinions.[33] In order to avoid isolation on important public issues, many people are guided by what they think are the dominant or declining opinions in their milieu. If they feel that they are a minority, they tend to conceal their views, to keep silent. Conversely, if they think that their views are popular, they express them. This is the spiraling effect.[34] Noelle-Neumann argues that the media are crucial as the most readily accessible sources by which people assess the climate of opinion.

The key components of the spiral of silence are an issue of public interest, divisiveness on the issue, individual perceptions of the climate of opinion, and the belief that a minority or different opinion isolates oneself from others.

The theory was originally based on German data. It assumes that society threatens deviant individuals with isolation, that this fear causes individuals constantly to try to assess the climate of opinion, that the results of this estimate affect people's willingness to express opinions in public, and that people follow the majority opinion.[35]

But does the spiral of silence apply in supposedly ruggedly individualistic America? Not necessarily. For example, the media's propagation of the myth that American public opinion had become conservative on a range of issues was not supported by opinion polls taken over the period in question.[36] But in another study, while Americans who perceived their opinion to be congruent with that of the majority were more willing to speak to a stranger than those whose opinions were shared only by a minority, they did not seem eager to discuss the issue with a stranger holding an opposing viewpoint, or to talk about it with a television reporter.[37]

Looking at the 1988 presidential election, Silvo Lenart found that the spiral of silence applied nationally but not locally: "As opposed to the national climate whose ebbs and flows exert dynamic influences on preferences, the local climate appears to be a steady point of reference that anchors standing opinions."[38]

So, the effect would appear to depend on the issue, its media portrayal, and the ways it is received by different members of the public.

Third-Person

Similar to the spiral of silence in the sense that it anticipates other's reactions, but inspiring quite the opposite response, is the "third-person effect." Coined by W. Phillips Davison, the term describes people's common belief that media content has its greatest effect not on them or those like them but on third persons.[39] Whether this belief stems from underestimating effects on the self or overestimating them on others is unclear.

There is a lot of research documenting and elaborating the third-person effect. In a survey of the literature, Richard Perloff summarizes several conditions that facilitate it. It is likely to occur when the message is perceived to have an objectionable impact and is personally important, "when the source is perceived to be negatively biased, when the respondent is well educated, and when the hypothetical others are defined in broad and global terms."[40]

There is a second part to the theory: the perception of more powerful effects of the media on others can trigger the attitude and even behavioral response by the perceiver that something should be done about the effects.[41] However, there is very little research showing third-person perceptions influencing behavior.[42]

So, the third-person effect enables us to understand why people often complain about the media's (supposed) effects on everyone else while denying that they are affected, indeed priding themselves on their ability to see through "media manipulation." It may also help explain why some people are so eager to restrain the media in the ways described in chapter four.

COVERAGE OF POLLS IN THE MEDIA

The media not only influence public opinion, they also tell people what public opinion is.[43] Almost all the large-circulation papers, about half of other daily newspapers, and more than half of television stations report on their own polls or the ones for which they have contracted with commercial firms or hired outside consultants.[44] But what is actually presented as public opinion by the mass media? How valid and reliable is it? And what are its effects?

Answering these questions is a study examining every poll reported on the NBC and CBS evening news programs and in the *New York Times* during 1973, 1975, and 1977.[45] The study is discussed here to educate readers about the merits and limitations and the uses and abuses of polls and the desirability of having results from more than one poll.

Attraction of Polls

Polls are newsworthy: They are topical, relate directly to issues in the news, are up-to-the-moment. Again and again they were introduced on television news and in the *Times* by such phrases as, "There's a new Harris poll out today," and "According to the latest Gallup poll released today."

Polls also appeal to journalists because they purport to offer hard data and statistical facts that are more reliable than the impressionistic interviews with "typical" Americans. And, as momentary snapshots, polls are hard to criticize: Showing different opinions at different times can be attributed to the volatility of public opinion, not to any inherent defects in polling methodology. And when polls do conflict, pollsters, not journalists, can be blamed.

There is a constant flow of regularly released, predictably recurring polls, many of which emanate from reputable polling organizations.[46] These polls are often dispatched to the media accompanied by press releases that organize the data for easy assimilation and publication. Newspapers and television networks with their own polling units have an added incentive to use the "exclusive" data their pollsters generate, particularly when these polls deal with subjects the news staff have asked the pollsters to investigate.

Pollsters present their survey results at press conferences. They appear at forums where reporters are present and publicity guaranteed. Pollster Louis Harris was especially adept at personalizing his poll data in ways attractive to reporters and conducive to dramatic headlines: "Pollster Tells Mayors That Public Doesn't Trust Them."[47]

Given these elements of attraction, one would expect to find numerous mentions of polls in the *New York Times* and on the CBS and NBC television networks. In 1973, 1975, and 1977, the *Times* published 380 news stories using public opinion polls, averaging slightly more than one every three days.

The figure is substantial, especially when one takes into account that only news stories were coded, not editorials, nor columns mentioning polls, nor stories with only passing references to polls but without data. Also omitted were polls of specific limited groups in American society, such as doctors, and the self-evidently unreliable, misleading, instant, pseudo call-in polls using 800 or 900 telephone numbers.

In the same three years, the NBC evening news offered its viewers data from eighty-three polls; its CBS counterpart, forty.[48] The television figures did not include polls reported during the morning or midday newscasts, or polls used in special reports. Had they been included, the number of television-reported polls would have tripled.

Not only do polls abound in the *Times* and on the networks' news programs, they are often prominently placed and accorded substantial time or space. Half of the poll stories ran longer than thirty seconds. The *Times* initiated 11 percent of its poll items on the front page; and of the 380 poll stories it reported, 42 percent were longer than 100 lines.

Contents

The most frequent news stories involving polls dealt with the presidency: assessments and evaluations of the incumbent president's job performance and of the members of his family. These popularity polls were prominent on television, encompassing almost a quarter of all poll stories, somewhat fewer in the *Times*. At times, the pollsters' desire to measure, and the passion of the press to publish, presidential approval ratings appeared to be fetishistic.

Although presidential election years were carefully excluded from the study, election polls proliferated. There were two kinds: those with at least one undeclared candidate and those with all announced candidates. Roughly 10 percent of stories involving polls were about elections, mainly for the presidency. Indeed, the press seems obsessed with presidential elections, willing to publish polls on the subject no matter how irrelevant and inane.

The next most frequent subject on television was the Watergate scandal. All stories about it appeared during 1973.

In another 15 percent of poll stories, people were asked to rate institutions or public officials, or indicate their attitudes toward or affiliation with the major American political parties.

So, a majority of the poll stories consisted primarily of the public's assessments of and reactions to politicians, who were holding or running or might be running for office. Most of these polls related to the presidency. These data are actually understated, since polls in other subject categories were quite often linked to the president, his policies, and his fate.

In another category of polls that could be more directly related to public policy, members of the public were asked for their opinions on social, economic, energy and environmental, or foreign policy issues. Just over 30 percent of all polls on the CBS and NBC evening news programs and in the *Times* fell into this category. However, as explained later in this chapter, the policy impact of these polls was diminished, if not destroyed.

The main remaining polls concerned "outlook," and "lifestyles and trends." In the outlook stories, Americans were asked to express their fears and hopes for the future. One example was headlined, "Young Women, Blacks Still Have High Hopes."[49] The lifestyles and trends stories were typified by a story headlined, "Tolerance on Sex Is Found Growing."[50]

One way of justifying the inclusion of poll stories is by tying them to stories in the news. Some 70 percent of those on the television evening news were tied to such newspegs as Watergate, energy problems, the 1973 Middle East war, and the Panama Canal treaty. Some connections were forced: In reporting results from the CBS/*New York Times* poll, the television anchor would introduce the reporter, who would link an item from the poll to the previous story, then continue with unrelated data from the poll.

In contrast, 64 percent of the *Times*' stories lacked newspegs; apparently, the newspaper's editors felt less bound to the flow of day-to-day events than the networks did. The *Times* also had more space for poll subjects such as outlook, and lifestyles and trends that had few newspegs.

Reliability and Credibility

Are the media's polls to be believed and trusted? Clearly, they are not without problems and defects.[51] How are these dealt with by the media? Are they openly confessed? Is adequate information provided so that readers and viewers can assess the reliability of the polls presented in the press? Let's look at poll sponsors and methodology.

Sponsors   One way for organizations and individuals to imply public support for their objectives or to insinuate their views into public opinion is to sponsor polls that are then released to and reported in the media. Indeed, in half of the *Times'* stories in which it was possible to identify a sponsor, that sponsor benefitted from the story. Being told who sponsors (i.e., who pays for) the polls might well influence people's assessment of the results. But in only 10 percent of the *Times'* stories, even fewer for the television networks, was that done.

Methodology   Among the many criticisms of pollsters' methodology are the following: defective sampling procedures; interviewers who avoid certain neighborhoods, fill out questionnaires inaccurately, or cheat; questions that are poorly constructed, vague, and tendentious; respondents who refuse to be interviewed by pollsters or lie in answering questions; failure to measure the stability, coherence, and intensity of answers; answers forced into limited alternatives set by the pollster (agree-disagree, favor-oppose); and adjustment by pollsters of the raw data (e.g., by screening out people unlikely to vote).[52]

Leo Bogart has written that "public misunderstanding of opinion surveys can be expected to continue as long as the mass media ignore or belittle their technical intricacies."[53] To what extent, then, are people alerted to the more conspicuous of these methodological concerns in the polls they encounter?

Sample size was given in 67 percent of the *Times'* stories, but only 27 percent of the time on television. The figures for the dates of surveying given were 43 percent in the paper and 30 percent for television. Other methodological information was minimal: below 10 percent for sampling error, intensity, and refusal rate.

Gladys Engel Lang and Kurt Lang have shown how the different wording of various questions about the impeachment of President Richard Nixon in the Watergate coverage elicited different responses from the American public.[54] Knowing how the pollsters' worded the questions allows people to be better equipped to evaluate the answers. But in 95 percent of television stories and some 70 percent of those appearing in the *Times,* none of the polling questions were quoted in their entirety.

This statistic is less dramatic than it seems because words or phrases from some of the questions employed were often quoted in the stories. So, the audience probably had an inkling of the questions respondents were asked.

The order in which questions were asked is not reported. This can be crucial. Consider a Harris poll in which a plurality of Americans was said to favor "some type of agency of the Government for consumer advocacy." Other questions mentioned in the article may have encouraged people to give this response, especially one asking them to react to the statement, "There is a need for more supervision of the quality and reliability of the products people buy."[55]

Reassurance   Generally accurate is Michael Wheeler's accusation that "the reader of opinion polls is given no hint that they may not be trustworthy."[56] Certainly, the ample pages of the *Times,* compared to the briefer time periods allotted to television evening news programs, afford greater possibilities for technical explanations. But with the relative exception of polls conducted by the CBS/*New York Times* unit, the *Times* insufficiently detailed the technical complexities or the possible deficiencies of most of the polls it printed.

More critically, the way methodological information about polling is reported in the media tends more to reassure than to alert the audience about the possible defects of poll data. Journalists have a natural inclination to support rather than undermine the polls they report. As one example, when the NBC anchor told viewers about a Gallup poll showing Ronald Reagan leading incumbent President Gerald R. Ford by 40 to 32 percent among Republicans and Independents, he said: "Statistically, there is an 8 percent error factor in these figures but it does not diminish their political importance."[57]

Interpretation

The problem of when to interpret poll data and what conclusions to derive from them is handled in the *Times* and on the networks' news programs in four different ways. None is entirely satisfactory.

The first way, common in stories of fewer than thirty lines, is simply to provide the raw data and leave it at that. Often, however, neither the language of the poll nor the concomitant data are self-explanatory. For example, when NBC reported a Gallup poll about support for Israel, the meaning and implications of "support" were nowhere given.[58]

A second way journalists handle interpretation is to leave it to the pollsters. This, too, can be questionable. For example, presidential job ratings may be misleading depending on how one defines the term "fair." Pollsters interpret it negatively, but at least some people polled may think of it as meaning acceptable but not great (like getting a B–).

A third mode of interpretation occurs when poll data are integrated into news stories, usually to support or amplify a reporter's main theme. Interpretation of this sort is usually circumspect, but it can be risky. In fact, the poll data did not always support themes.

Among several possible causes, the pollster may impose interpretations beyond the capacity of the data to bear, or the news personnel may truncate the story so severely as to render it incomprehensible. Thus, the *Times,* in reporting a Harris poll, informed its readers that Betty Ford was "one of the most popular" of presidential wives and "a solid asset." But the only data in the story showed a majority agreeing with Mrs. Ford's statement that she "would not be surprised if her daughter had an affair," and slightly more people supporting her statement "that if her daughter were having an affair, she would want to know if the young man were nice or not."[59]

Fourth are the major stories in which reporters expound on and expand the data before them. Such extensive and detailed polls allow for drastic variations in emphasis and interpretation. A lengthy article in the *Times,* based on a CBS/*Times* survey, began with: "Public support of President Carter has broadened in the first 100 days of his Administration because many Americans, especially those who voted against him last November, believe he has turned out to be more conservative than they expected."[60] The CBS evening news story of the preceding night, based on the identical survey data, made no mention of conservatism.

© Nicole Hollander

Political Consequences

Public opinion is a power resource. It possesses the potential of constraining, guiding, even directing public officials, their actions, and policies. Coverage of polls abound on television news and in daily newspapers. They are treated seriously, as if their data were reliable and important—which they often are.

Public Policies   But the reporting of public opinion polls has little effect on specific public policies. For the subjects dealt with in the polls are those of interest to the organizations that sponsor and conduct them. That is why polls constantly ask people to rate presidents and other American officials, to express a preference among candidates in some far-off election (even if many of the "candidates" have indicated no public interest in running), to indicate an allegiance for one or another (or neither) of the two major political parties. Even if the public were absorbed by these subjects, which is doubtful, its opinions would provide little explicit policy guidance.

The public is quizzed about some policy-relevant issues: economic, social, energy and environment, and foreign policy. But the questions and items infrequently deal with policy per se; they rarely ask Americans to respond to the complicated trade-offs that public officials must usually decide; and the forced-choice answer format limits the range of possible responses.

Polls reported in the media do, however, have two sorts of effects: one-shot and cumulative.

One-shot Effect   Under special circumstances, a single poll story can be powerful, especially when its questions and items embody an underlying thematic assumption. An example occurred when more then two minutes of the "NBC Nightly News" was devoted to a poll taken after President Nixon's firing of the special prosecutor and other government officials (events dubbed "The Saturday Night Massacre" by journalists). The poll was introduced by the anchor with words calculated to inspire confidence and credibility in its results: "NBC has been conducting a national poll to get the people's reaction; it was done by the Oliver Quayle organization based on a telephone sample of 947 adults in 300 scientifically selected communities across the country." One need hold no brief for the crimes of Watergate to discern the tendentious and alarmist aspects of this poll. The public's reaction was sought on the following topics:

The firing of the special prosecutor

Impeachment

Whether Nixon should step aside

Whether Nixon was acting in a dictatorial manner

Nixon's job performance

Trust in Nixon

Whether Watergate should be put behind us (as Nixon was asking).[61]

The questions virtually assume illegality and culpability on Nixon's part. But less indicting alternatives could have been posed, such as:

Presidents must act decisively

Presidents must do what they believe is right

The special prosecutor overstepped his authority

Nixon's action was within his authority

Instead, the poll reinforced elite views of public outrage, thereby advancing the prospects of Nixon's departure from office.

Cumulative Effects   The overall impressions and cumulative effects of many of the polls reported in the media may be more important than the specific impact of any one poll. The emphasis in the polls on presidential ratings and the president's electoral prospects may diminish the majesty of the office and the power of the incumbent in two ways: first, by infusing in many Americans the belief that their president should be subjected to frequent, formal public ratings (rather as students are graded); and second, by creating the impression that presidents (and most politicians) are preoccupied with the forthcoming election (no matter how distant) instead of accomplishing policies in the public interest—indeed, that policies are undertaken primarily for electoral reasons.

Poll stories may also have a cumulative political effect if they consistently convey a particular perspective. To examine this possibility, the study categorized their general themes as positive, negative, or mixed/unclear/inapplicable. Positive themes were those that demonstrated faith, affirmation, contentment, willingness to sacrifice, and optimism about the future. Negative themes embodied fear, loss of faith, discontent, and disillusionment.

On television, 70 percent of the story themes were negative and 12 percent positive; the rest were mixed/unclear/inapplicable. Figures for the *Times* were 37, 25, and 38 percent, respectively.

There are several reasons for the excess of negative over positive themes. One is the appeal of bad news. Watergate was news, and most of the themes and polls connected with it were negative. Furthermore, the years analyzed were characterized by negative or declining ratings for American presidents and governmental institutions, reflected in turn in the polls: "Poll Finds Most Residents Believe That State Government Is Corrupt."[62]

In addition, the very questions of interest to the sponsors and conductors of polls often imply negativity. "Which of these groups, if any, do you think are unfairly treated by the Carter Administration?" the Gallup poll once asked Americans, leading to the following headline in the *Times:* "Poll Finds Carter Treats Elderly Most Unfairly."[63] Revealingly, Gallup regularly asks people what in their opinion is the most important problem facing the country: this both frames the question negatively and promotes a negative answer.

Finally, headline writers have a penchant for picking out the doleful aspects of poll data: "Drinking Troubles More Families" headlined the *Times,* even though the percentage "troubled" had increased from 12 to only 18 percent, and 82 percent were apparently untroubled.[64]

The political consequences of the predominance of polls with negative themes may be to reinforce, if not increase, disillusion and dismay with America's incumbent public officials and their asserted incapacity to cope with the nation's difficulties.

CONCLUSION

The media influence the formation of public opinion through agenda-setting, priming, and framing. They influence the expression of public opinion through the bandwagon effect, spiral of silence, and third-person effect. In so doing, they often tell people what topics to think about, sometimes how to think about them, even on occasion what to think. Conversely, by omitting and neglecting stories, the media can indirectly discourage people from thinking about certain topics.

Relatedly, polls covered in the mass media influence public officials and the public by purporting to report what Americans are thinking about. "Purport" because these poll stories focus primarily on politicians holding or potentially seeking office, emphasize the polls' credibility and reliability instead of their methodological and interpretive flaws. Their one-shot and cumulative effects are probably harmful to the political system.

Notes

1. The definition comes from V. O. Key, Jr., *Public Opinion and American Democracy* (New York: Knopf, 1961), 14. For an alternative perspective, see the historical studies of public expression by marginal social groups in Susan Herbst, *Politics at the Margin* (New York: Cambridge University Press, 1994).

2. William G. Mayer, *The Changing American Mind* (Ann Arbor: University of Michigan Press, 1992), 133–34.

3. Ibid., 128.

4. Benjamin I. Page and Robert Y. Shapiro, "Effects of Public Opinion on Policy," *American Political Science Review* 77:1 (March 1983): 175.

5. For a fascinating case study of public opinion and Oliver North in the Iran-Contra hearings, see Amy Fried, *Muffled Echoes* (New York: Columbia University Press, 1997).

6. Michael X. Delli Carpini and Bruce A. Williams, "Constructing Public Opinion: The Uses of Fictional and Nonfictional Television in Conversations About the Environment," in *The Psychology of Political Communication,* ed. Ann N. Crigler (Ann Arbor: University of Michigan Press, 1996), 149–75.

7. For another way of expressing opinions, see Lyman Chaffee, "Public Art as Political Communication" (paper presented at the annual meeting of the American Political Science Association, Washington, D.C., August 1991).

8. Pew Center for the People & the Press, "The Vocal Minority in American Politics" (news release, 16 July 1993), 2.

9. Useful is Michael W. Traugott and Paul J. Lavrakas, *The Voter's Guide to Election Polls* (Chatham, N.J.: Chatham House, 1996). For a discussion of other types of polls (exit, tracking, panels, and focus groups), as well as technological developments, see Kathleen A. Frankovic, "Technology and the Changing Landscape of Media Polls," in *Media Polls in American Politics,* ed. Thomas E. Mann and Gary R. Orren (Washington, D.C.: Brookings Institution, 1992), 32–54.

10. John R. Zaller, *The Nature and Origins of Mass Opinion* (New York: Cambridge University Press, 1992).

11. Ibid., 1.

12. See also Larry M. Bartels, "Messages Received: The Political Impact of Media Exposure," *American Political Science Review* 87:2 (June 1993): 267–76.

13. Benjamin I. Page and Robert Y. Shapiro, *The Rational Public* (Chicago: University of Chicago Press, 1992), 384–85.

14. For thoughtful "reflections on the influence of perceived public opinion" critical of the bandwagon and spiral of silence approaches, see Kurt Lang and Gladys Engel Lang, "Off the Bandwagon," in *Individuality and Social Control,* ed. Kian M. Kwan (Greenwich, Conn.: JAI Press, 1996), 69–90.

15. Agenda-setting research was initiated by Maxwell E. McCombs and Donald L. Shaw, "The Agenda-Setting Function of Mass Media," *Public Opinion Quarterly* 36:2 (Summer 1972): 176–87. For a compilation of research inspired by the concept, see David L. Protess and Maxwell E. McCombs, ed., *Agenda Setting* (Hillsdale, N.J.: Lawrence Erlbaum, 1991); see also the articles in *Journalism Quarterly* 69:4 (Winter 1992): 813–920.

16. Jack M. McLeod, Gerald M. Kosicki, and Douglas M. McLeod, "The Expanding Boundaries of Political Communication Effects," in *Media Effects: Advances in Theory and Research,* ed. Jennings Bryant and Dolf Zillmann (Hillsdale, N.J.: Lawrence Erlbaum, 1994), 137, for citations to the specific studies.

17. Maxwell McCombs, Lucig Danielian, and Wayne Wanta, "Issues in the News and the Public Agenda," in *Public Opinion and the Communication of Consent,* ed. Theodore L. Glasser and Charles T. Salmon (New York: Guilford Press, 1995), 296. Their essay surveys the latest issues and research in agenda-setting; see also Wayne Wanta, *The Public and the National Agenda* (Hillsdale, N.J.: Lawrence Erlbaum, 1997).

18. Michael Bruce MacKuen, "Social Communication and the Mass Policy Agenda," in Michael Bruce MacKuen and Steven Coombs, *More Than News* (Beverly Hills, Calif.: Sage, 1981), 87–88.

19. Holli A. Semetko et al., "TV News and U.S. Public Opinion About Foreign Countries," *International Journal of Public Opinion Research* 4:1 (Spring 1992): 18.

20. John Mueller, *Policy and Opinion in the Gulf War* (Chicago: University of Chicago Press, 1994), 130.

21. Christopher Bosso, "Setting the Agenda," in *Manipulating Public Opinion,* ed. Michael Margolis and Gary A. Mauser (Pacific Grove, Calif.: Brooks/Cole, 1989), 153–74.

22. William J. Gonzenbach, "A Time-Series Analysis of the Drug Issue, 1985–1990," *International Journal of Public Opinion Research* 4:2 (Summer 1992): 126–47.

23. Shanto Iyengar and Donald R. Kinder, *News That Matters* (Chicago: University of Chicago Press, 1987). My comments are taken from my review in the *Journal of Communication* 39:2 (Spring 1989): 134–37.

24. Iyengar and Kinder, *News That Matters,* 33.

25. Ibid., 97.

26. Ibid., 110.

27. Maxwell E. McCombs and Donald L. Shaw, "The Evolution of Agenda-Setting Research," *Journal of Communication* 43:2 (Spring 1993): 63.

28. Shanto Iyengar, *Is Anyone Responsible? How Television Frames Political Issues* (Chicago: University of Chicago Press, 1991), 18.

29. Tom Patterson in his review of Iyengar's book in the *American Political Science Review* 86:4 (December 1992): 1061.

30. Thomas E. Nelson, Rosalee A. Clawson, and Zoe M. Oxley, "Media Framing of a Civil Liberties Conflict and Its Effect on Tolerance," *American Political Science Review* 91:3 (September 1997): 567–83.

31. David P. Fan et al., "The Media's Persuasive Influence on Public Opinion" (paper presented at the annual meeting of the American Political Science Association, Chicago, August 1995), 24.

32. Albert H. Cantril, *The Opinion Connection* (Washington, D.C.: CQ Press, 1991).

33. Elisabeth Noelle-Neumann, *The Spiral of Silence* (Chicago: University of Chicago Press, 1984).

34. See also Irving L. Janis, *Groupthink*, 2nd ed. (Boston: Houghton Mifflin, 1982).

35. For part of this summary, see Denis McQuail, *Mass Communication Theory,* 3rd ed. (London: Sage, 1994), 361.

36. David L. Paletz and Robert M. Entman, *Media Power Politics* (New York: Free Press, 1981), 196–212.

37. Charles T. Salmon and Kurt Neuwirth, "Perceptions of Opinion 'Climates' and Willingness to Discuss the Issue of Abortion," *Journalism Quarterly* 67:3 (Autumn 1990): 567–77.

38. Silvo Lenart, *Shaping Political Attitudes* (Thousand Oaks, Calif.: Sage, 1994), 98.

39. W. Phillips Davison, "The Third-Person Effect in Communication," *Public Opinion Quarterly* 47:1 (Spring 1983): 1–15.

40. Richard M. Perloff, "Perceptions and Conception of Political Media Impact," in *The Psychology of Political Communication,* ed. Ann N. Crigler (Ann Arbor: University of Michigan Press, 1996), 187.

41. Albert Gunther, "Overrating the X-rating: The Third-Person Perception and Support for Censorship of Pornography," *Journal of Communication* 45:1 (Winter 1995): 27–38.

42. For an exception, see Jacqueline C. Hitchon, Chingching Chang, and Rhonda Harris, "Should Women Emote?" *Political Communication* 14:1 (January-March 1997): 49–69.

43. Susan Herbst, *Numbered Voices* (Chicago: University of Chicago Press, 1993), explains how numbers have been used to describe the public mood and why quantitative discourses have gained widespread respect in the United States. Slavko Splichal questions the scientific and democratic validity of public opinion polling in "Political Institutionalisation of Public Opinion Through Polling," *Javnost The Public* 4:2 (1997): 17–38.

44. Everett Carll Ladd and John Benson, "The Growth of News Polls in American Politics," in *Media Polls in American Politics,* ed. Thomas E. Mann and Gary R. Orren (Washington, D.C.: Brookings Institution, 1992), 22, 25.

45. This account comes from David L. Paletz et al., "Polls in the Media," *Public Opinion Quarterly* 44:4 (Winter 1980): 495–513. Used by permission of University of Chicago Press. Copyright © 1980 by the American Association for Public Opinion Research. All rights reserved.

46. For an overview of the commercial, governmental, and academic organizations that produce polls, see Peter V. Miller, "The Industry of Public Opinion," in *Public Opinion and the Communication of Consent,* ed. Theodore L. Glaser and Charles T. Salmon (New York: Guilford Press, 1995): 105–31.

47. John Kifner, *New York Times,* 8 July 1975, 19.

48. These data come from the Vanderbilt Television Archive.

49. Robert Lindsey, *New York Times,* 27 October 1975, 1.

50. *New York Times,* 12 August 1973, 21.

51. Leo Bogart, *Silent Politics* (New York: Wiley Interscience, 1972); and Michael Wheeler, *Lies, Damn Lies, and Statistics* (New York: Liveright, 1976).

52. For a broad and detailed empirical analysis of the effects and implications of nonresponse on survey results, see John Brehm, *The Phantom Respondents* (Ann Arbor: University of Michigan Press, 1993).

53. Leo Bogart, *Silent Politics* (New York: Wiley Interscience, 1972), 23.

54. Gladys Engel Lang and Kurt Lang, *The Battle for Public Opinion* (New York: Columbia University Press, 1983).

55. "U.S. Consumer Protection Unit Approved by House Panel," *New York Times,* 19 July 1975, 28.

56. Michael Wheeler, *Lies, Damn Lies, and Statistics* (New York: Liveright, 1976), xvi–xvii.

57. "NBC Nightly News," 12 December 1975.

58. "NBC Nightly News," 16 October 1973.

59. "Betty Ford Ranks High in Study by Harris Poll," *New York Times,* 11 November 1975, 11.

60. James N. Naughton, "Support for Carter Widens as He Ends First 100 Days," *New York Times,* 29 April 1977, 1.

61. "NBC Nightly News," 22 October 1973.

62. Joseph F. Sullivan, *New York Times,* 25 July 1977, 47.

63. *New York Times,* 18 September 1977, 30.

64. *New York Times,* 13 February 1977, 35.

Chapter 8

Political Participation

◆　◆　◆

By participating in politics, people can try to affect the selection of their rulers, influence governmental actions and policies, and even alter the structure of government itself.[1] Voting (see chapter 10) is the most common form of individual participation. Other conventional modes are contacting officials, contributing (money, time) to a political cause or campaign, and attending political meetings or rallies. Altering signs (see photo), demonstrating and picketing, and disrupting government are forceful ways of participating.[2] Riots and terrorism are the most violent.

This chapter describes how and explains why the media depict the gamut of political participation from conventional to violent, and considers the consequences. It incorporates what theory and relevant empirical studies there are on the subject, but otherwise is original and speculative. So its assertions should be treated as more like hypotheses than certainties.

Susannah B. F. Paletz

The chapter begins by discussing the opportunities and incentives for political participation. It does so by briefly describing the activities of the denizens of Hollywood, people with the resources and media savvy to participate effectively. It then recounts how and why the media discourage individual political participation and encourage pseudo-participation. Next, it looks at media coverage of social movements, tracing how it is variously positive, mixed, or negative. A discussion of violent participation comes last, showing how coverage of riots is incendiary; of terrorism, hostile.

FORMS OF PARTICIPATION

People's socialized beliefs, interests, and identifications influence whether and how they participate in politics.[3] Their participation is then facilitated by the political choices and incentives available: fund-raising letters request donations, social movements recruit members, elections provide opportunities to vote.[4] Thus, people who have disposable income, possess civic skills, and are able to make time available—in other words, the educated and affluent—participate in proportion far more than the impoverished most in need of governmental response.[5]

People in the entertainment industry, loosely dubbed "Hollywood," possess in abundance the ingredients for participation. In addition, their fame gives them visibility and media appeal.[6] Here are three examples of its members, respectively, advocating causes, contributing to campaigns, and running for and obtaining governmental office. (Ronald Reagan, the participant *extraordinaire,* who went from activist to president of the Screen Actors' Guild to governor of California to president of the United States, gets his turn in chapter 12.)

In the 1940s, the intrepid Orson Welles publicly took controversial stands supporting an antilynching bill, the civil rights of blacks and Mexican-Americans, and a union organizing department store employees.[7]

Media mogul David Geffen's interest in politics was sparked by the 1992 Republican National Convention. "'Really, it scared me. . . . They didn't care about anybody but white, Christian, heterosexual males'. . . . Geffen became a major contributor and fund-raiser, helping to fill Democratic Party coffers with millions."[8]

Clint Eastwood was elected mayor of the Californian town of Carmel with 72 percent of the vote. He ran in part because he thought the previous officials were too antidevelopment. After he won, he replaced four of the seven members of the city planning commission. Some said it was a vendetta because the commission had refused to allow him to build a retail office complex. He explained that it was to make the city fairer for business. Among Eastwood's accomplishments: he accelerated construction of stairways to the beaches and sped up completion of a public pathway along the bluffs; he pushed through a plan for a library annex and got rid of ordinances forbidding frisbees in public parks; and he made it legal to sell and consume ice cream cones in the town.[9]

Participation is not confined to famous Hollywood figures. Nor is it limited to giving money and personal involvement in election campaigns. People in show business wear AIDS ribbons at awards ceremonies, sign petitions, testify before congressional committees, appear at the parties' national nominating conventions, and participate in campaigns.[10] They demonstrate against nuclear power plants and are arrested protesting nuclear weapons testing.[11] They are also uniquely able to infuse political messages into films: The daughter in *Lethal Weapon 3* wears a sweatshirt with "Pro-Choice" emblazoned on it in large letters, and the police station displays an antifur poster.

These actions demonstrate that there are several reasons for participating in politics, including the desire to show civic responsibility, to achieve policy objectives, and to enhance self-esteem. Participation also can stem from a sense of outrage.

MEDIA'S EFFECTS ON POLITICAL PARTICIPATION

These reasons should also motivate ordinary people. Yet, in recent years, people's involvement in many forms of political participation, such as attending a rally or speech and working for a political party, has fallen precipitously.[12]

Television

Two scholars who have studied this phenomenon see television as the culprit. Robert Putnam points out that it absorbs Americans' leisure time at the expense of almost every other social activity. Especially for people who view a lot of it, television is related to increased pessimism about human nature and skepticism about the good intentions of other people.[13]

Roderick Hart adds a psychological perspective to the research. "For many citizens, watching governance has become equivalent to engaging governance. Heavy television watching correlates with less political participation. Because of television, even non-voters can now feel politically exhausted."[14] Also, television is ahistorical, atheoretical, and cynical; it makes politics "a display, a curiosity, something to be seen but not engaged in."[15] It provides intimate details about our political leaders, informs us about politics (immerses us if we let it), without involving us.[16] Less political participation seems to be the inevitable outcome.

The exceptions are usually people interested in the media's overtly political content. Those who regularly tune in to network news are "significantly more likely to be involved in all types of political activity, and the relationship between watching public affairs programs on television and civic engagement proved even stronger."[17] C-SPAN viewers report contacting their representatives, contributing to political organizations or campaigns, and volunteering to work in campaigns. Almost all of them who are registered to vote claim to do so.[18]

News

For most people, however, the news appears to discourage participation. A study by William Gamson using focus groups helps to explain why.[19] Gamson shows that people's experiential knowledge plus popular wisdom combine with media content (television and print) to shape how people discuss issues. Whether they then engage in political participation depends on their finding three elements in the mix: injustice (the most important) caused by human actions, a specific adversary, and the possibility of changing the condition through collective action. The presence of these three factors varies from issue to issue.

Gamson found, however, that none of the major frames in the media stories encouraged collective action, although the content was more equivocal on some of the issues than others. People do sometimes contest or ignore the media's framing of issues in the news; and the focus group members occasionally discussed citizen action during their conversations. Nonetheless, the lack of an injustice frame on most subjects in the news (e.g., nuclear power) partly explains why most of the people Gamson interviewed refrain from political participation.

The media can encourage such participation with content that links problems and issues with the suffering or well-being of audience members, associates actual decisionmakers with policy actions and definite outcomes, and suggests political participation as the desirable or appropriate response.

But such content is uncommon in the mainstream press, as coverage of North America's largest oil "spill" (there's a euphemism for you) the *Exxon Valdez* disaster in 1989 in the Alaskan waters of Prince William Sound reveals.

Patrick Daley with Dan O'Neill analyzed coverage in the *Boston Globe,* the *Anchorage Daily News,* and the weekly *Tundra Times* (published by and for Alaska's native population).[20] They found that the two mainstream newspapers initially framed the event as a disaster, with the public and wildlife as victims. This narrative made the "spill" seem natural, thereby foreclosing any discussion of the marine transport system, of ways the oil companies evade national and international regulation, and of alternative energy sources. It "overtly moved the discourse away from the political arena and into the politically inaccessible realm of technological inevitability."[21]

The two daily newspapers subsequently framed the spill in terms of criminality, with the ship's captain blamed for the disaster. This narrative turned the public into spectators. Of course, some people were activated to boycott Exxon. But most victims and spectators resigned themselves to the situation rather than leap into political participation to try to change it.

In contrast, the *Tundra Times'* narratives of the event focused on the effects of the spill on Native Alaskans' subsistence and on Exxon's corporate responsibilities. These narratives encouraged political participation by showing an immediate material effect of the spill on people's lives and giving them a target (Exxon) to pressure for redress and change.

Other Ways of Discouraging Participation

The mass media discourage participation in other ways. For example, they fail to report some of the events that might provoke it. Or do not give the events the prominence and repetition required to make them stand out from the competing morass of news.

Even when actions and occurrences are controversial enough to merit full and continuing news coverage, people are infrequently informed as to where or to whom they should go, and how they should act, to influence the events described. James Lemert and his coauthors call this "mobilizing information" and explain that it is excluded because journalists view it as too dull or biased.[22] Of course, public (civic) journalism (see chapter 16) is designed to provide mobilizing information, but it's the exception.

Bad timing may also deter participation. The people who make policy decisions are the sources reporters primarily rely on for specialized information from government. Officials therefore often try to conceal their conclusions until it is in their interests—or they are legally obligated—to make them public. Thus, policymakers' deliberations and plans may be kept from the news media until they are completed. So news stories are often about governmental decisions already reached, too late to arouse political participation or for it to be effective.

Stimulating Participation

Media content can, of course, stimulate participation. The Senate Judiciary Committee's Clarence Thomas–Anita Hill hearings (discussed in chapter 14), which drew a million calls on just one day, are credited for record numbers of women running for and being elected to Congress in 1992. The hearings are also credited for a surge in campaign contributions to feminist organizations, such as the National Women's Political Caucus, and to Emily's ("Early Money Is Like Yeast") List, which in 1992 "was the largest donor to congressional campaigns."[23] That year the number of women senators trebled to six. Among the victors was Carol Moseley Braun, an African-American woman, who defeated Thomas's supporter Senator Alan Dixon in the Illinois Democratic primary.

Other media content is deliberately intended to stimulate political participation. Three common sources are appeals by government leaders, talk radio, and public service advertisements urging people to vote. An example of the first is when President Clinton appealed to Americans to ask senators to support his budget and Senator Dole urged them to call in opposition. More than 3.6 million calls were routed through the Senate switchboard in four days. Many others were initiated but didn't get through.[24]

Talk radio is a species of participation because it allows callers to express (vent) their opinions.

It can also encourage listeners to take action.[25] Hosts such as Rush Limbaugh have aroused and canalized their listeners' anger and outrage, causing millions of Americans to contact their legislators about such issues as President Clinton's

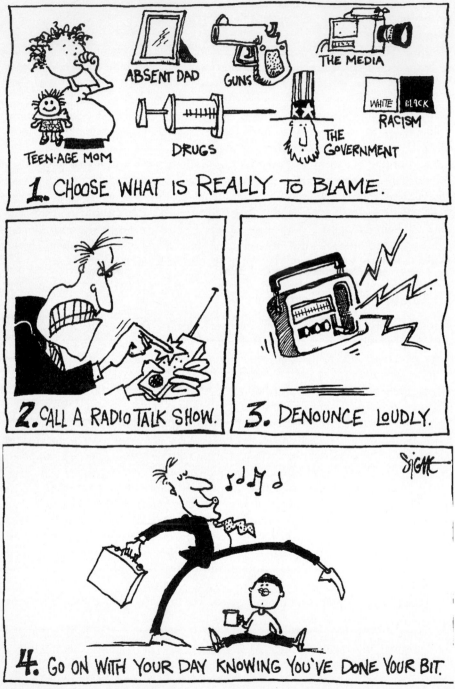

proposals on homosexuals in the military and the nomination of Zoe Baird for U.S. Attorney General. Benjamin Page and Jason Tannenbaum argue that by expressing widespread concern about Baird's hiring of illegal aliens, talk radio overcame elite media indifference to her actions, and thus influenced her decision to withdraw as President Clinton's nominee for Attorney General.[26] During the Baird confirmation hearings, "staff members were coming in, putting little tallies in front of [senators'] desks . . . 160 calls this hour, or 200 or 300 or 800."[27] These tallies ensured the demise of her nomination.

Public service advertisements (PSAs) are sponsored by government and private nonprofit agencies, run about a minute or less each, and are aired without charge by broadcasters. PSAs advocating voting are a familiar sight, especially during presidential elections. In recent years, founts of these PSAs have been the Hollywood Policy Center Foundation and MTV's "Rock the Vote." The latter's thirty-second shorts and clips—featuring all types of musical superstars and aimed at young people—are much jazzier than the staid admonitions of the past.

PSEUDOPARTICIPATION

Public service advertisments (PSAs) are, in fact, the main instrument through which government and private nonprofit agencies undertake public information campaigns.[28] But what kind of participation do they encourage? With the exception of the PSAs urging people to vote, the political activity they propose is so limited it can best be characterized as "pseudo." The following section explains.[29]

PSAs

Public information campaigns use the panoply of tried and persuasive commercial advertising techniques in an explicit and conscious effort to exhort people to engage in certain types of action.[30] Purportedly directed at people's best interests, these advertisements are less liable to evoke the conventional defenses with which people try to protect themselves against product commercials. Consider the slogans:

Give to the College of Your Choice

People Start Pollution, People Can Stop It

Only You Can Prevent Forest Fires

PSAs expose Americans to national and international problems. But the problems selected for public information campaigns almost always reveal an underlying conservative caution. Lana Rakow asks rhetorically why "behaviors such as drug use or teenage pregnancy are portrayed as the country's most important problems and not militarism, violence against women, or homelessness?"[31]

The problems focused on in PSAs are typically revealed through their effects on individuals (actors or nonactors), who are caught in unfortunate circumstances and in need of help—children, foreigners, victims of natural disasters or disease.

Having nothing to do with politics, the causes of their problems are individual carelessness, incapacity, bad luck, affliction, or fate.

So, in PSAs, problems are raised; victims and sufferers are depicted or described; but blame is selectively placed, when it is placed at all. Of all the PSAs in an extensive sample that identified problems, 62 percent assigned no blame, while the remaining 38 percent laid blame on the individual (29 percent), society in general (6 percent), and business (3 percent). Not a single PSA blamed government or any public official.

PSAs offer three kinds of "solutions," either singly or in combination to problems. These are solicitations for support, recruitment, and personal admonitions. Solicitations for support ask viewers for funds or, much less frequently, some other help (e.g., volunteering time for charitable activities). Recruitment PSAs attempt to persuade viewers to volunteer for service in organizations (e.g., the military and the Peace Corps).

Personal admonitions vary from general to specific. There are vague exhortations, such as the Lung Association announcing that alert citizen action can reverse air pollution, or the American Bar Association urging people to support court improvements (which appear to mean more judges and more work for lawyers). There are suggestions that viewers obtain information about certain problems from government or private agencies. There are also specific courses of action (e.g., the Department of Transportation telling people to fasten their seat belts).

Contributing, contacting, and joining are examples of practical political activity. They involve interaction with public officials and issues, the making of claims, assumptions of accountability, and responsiveness. But as defined by PSAs, they are more likely to deflect from, than lead to, greater political participation for most citizens. Charitable organizations may characterize themselves as "your" Lung or Heart Association, but they stand aloof and relatively immune from detailed public scrutiny. PSAs encourage the ordinary viewer to donate but not to join or to play a meaningful part in their affairs. Certainly, donations are not solicited for political parties, candidates, or advocates of policy stands that might be divisive.

Similarly, viewers who respond to PSAs by writing to governmental agencies for information are not expressing policy preferences in a way that will be acted upon by government. They are not establishing meaningful two-way communication that will ensure that policymakers will make decisions consistent with their preferences; nor are they developing the personal skills or resources conducive to future practical participation.

A "Keep America Beautiful" PSA is a typical example. The spot shows a majestic American Indian paddling his canoe down a river that becomes progressively more polluted. Factories and smokestacks are depicted at a considerable distance, virtually unnoticeable. The Indian then comes ashore near a highway littered with refuse. A bag of trash is thrown and lands at the Indian's feet. As the camera focuses on a tear running down his cheek, the slogan appears: "People Start Pollution, People Can Stop It."

The slogan defines the problem as litter and the blame as individual, thereby relieving economic institutions and public officials of responsibility. Criticism of industry's role in causing pollution is deflected by emphasizing the extent to which pollution is the responsibility of individuals. The fight against pollution is equated with antilitter efforts rather than with auto emission controls, smokestack filters, or prohibitions on nonreturnable containers. Keep America Beautiful, Inc., is a privately funded organization, with Pepsi-Cola a major contributor. Other contributors are reportedly Continental Can, Ford Motor Company, American Can Company, United States Brewers Association, and the Glass Containers Manufacturers Institute.

The public information nexus is dominated by the Advertising Council and the governmental departments and advertising agencies with which it works.[32] This nexus denies air time to groups or organizations that could present different perspectives that might introduce political considerations, urge practical or provocative political actions, or define political activity so as to legitimize it in schools and work places.

Meanwhile, the PSAs that are shown beguile the American public on behalf of the siren of pseudoparticipation. They exhort Americans to act in a limited and predetermined manner. Defining both the problems and the solutions, PSAs also define the methods by which the solutions are to be achieved. Implicitly and explicitly, they deny the need for meaningful and active individual and group participation in the institutions that dominate people's everyday lives. They promote the delusion that social and economic problems should be dealt with apolitically— that is, without resort to unbecoming, provocative, or even practical political activity, conflict, and controversy.

MEDIA COVERAGE OF SOCIAL MOVEMENTS

Other than individual activity, political participation stems from social movements. This section looks at why and how the media depict social movements, and with what consequences.

Social movements engage in political participation to gain a hearing and to try to achieve their policy objectives. This entails publicizing their issues and grievances, mobilizing people to join their ranks, and activating more respectable legitimate organizations on their behalf.[33]

Obviously, the media are crucial to these purposes, for the movements need coverage, preferably favorable. So movement leaders' strategy is to try to produce events appealing to the news media (drama, action, photo opportunities) and capitalize on unforeseen occurrences and crises.[34]

Cuteness can be effective. An Associated Press (AP) story about a fifteen-foot replica of a condom inflated on the roof of Senator Jesse Helms's (R.-NC) home by an AIDS activist group protesting his positions on AIDS brought the group a lot of free and positive national publicity.[35]

But mixed coverage is more common. A study of stories about the antinuclear movement of the early 1980s in the *New York Times* and in *Time* magazine showed that they negatively framed the movement's activities but not its objectives. The reasons for the frames was that journalists "are heavily influenced by elite sources and, it appears, by an underlying professional ideology ambivalent toward public participation."[36]

The probable consequences were to discourage people from joining the movement and to enable politicians to respond symbolically rather than substantively to the movement's demands for a nuclear freeze.

If peaceful movements get mixed coverage, movements that conflict with ruling authorities should expect to fare worse. For the tactics of such direct-action movements range from the nonviolent use of civil disobedience to disruption to violence.

But coverage of conflictual social movements need not be negative. It depends on several factors. Gadi Wolfsfeld divides those factors into contextual and media.[39]

The most important contextual factors are the authorities' and protagonists' level of control over the political environment. This means their ability to initiate and control events and regulate the flow of information. Also important are each side's resources, skills, and political power. Public opinion is relevant. And, of course, what actually happens in the conflict can be significant.

The media are framers and interpreters of events, as well as a resource battled over by the competing sides. Thus, the media factors are: the ability of journalists to gain access to the conflict events; how reporters covered this (type of) conflict in the past; what is most newsworthy about it now; and who they deem to be in the right.

Contextual and media factors determine the news frames that reporters apply to the events that occur and how the protagonists are portrayed. An insurgent movement's use of violence is often framed negatively as a threat to law and order, but alternative frames focusing on the "excessive" force used against the challengers—police brutality, military atrocities, torture, and human rights violations—are also possible. Authorities can be portrayed as legitimate, tolerant, and right or as illegitimate, cruel, and wrong.

Wolfsfeld concludes with three possible scenarios. The media can be advocates of a movement—amplifying its views, using injustice and victim frames. The media can be semi-honest brokers—providing challengers with time and space for their views. Most common, the media are faithful servants to the authorities—publicizing official frames, ignoring or discrediting challengers.

With Wolfsfeld's theory in mind, let us look briefly at media depictions of some of the significant conflictual movements in the United States and try to explain why coverage was variously positive, mixed, or negative.

Women's Rights Movement

Elisabeth Israels Perry points out that from the start of the women's rights movement in the mid-nineteenth century, the popular press portrayed women activists negatively: as mannish cigar smokers, as evil temptresses, and even as late as 1910 "as aggressive, overbearing shrews who neglected their children and forced their menfolk into domestic drudgery."[37] The message was that giving the vote to women would undermine America's moral and political structure. Its effect was to delay the movement's success. As one response, women artists created their own cartoons in support of suffrage (see cartoon).[38]

Windsor McKay

Civil Rights Movement

In contrast, the mass media enhanced the legitimacy and power of the civil rights movement of the early 1960s. But the circumstances were special. Segregation was morally wrong; it violated the democratic creed; and it undermined national values. It was opposed in practice by blacks and whites from inside and outside the South, by men and women who risked their lives to confront it nonviolently. Their leader, the Reverend Martin Luther King, Jr., was charismatic. His opponents' responses only clarified the moral conflict between good and evil. Segregation was a regional scar, and the journalists who courageously covered the effort to remove it mainly represented national media.

But Richard Lentz's study of how three news magazines constructed and represented the movement and its leader shows that coverage of the same events differed among them; it also changed over time, becoming more negative as the movement became more radical.[40]

Liberal *Newsweek* consistently celebrated King as a fighter against immorality and injustice but expressed skepticism and ambivalence when he deviated from moderation. *Time* was cautious. It often supported the movement's campaigns against southern racists who could be presented as immoral and unreasonable, but it stressed that inclusion and equality for blacks could be achieved without major changes to American society. The magazine therefore criticized King when he and the movement seemed to question existing social arrangements. *U.S. News & World Report* was usually suspicious of and attacked King.

All three magazines were most sympathetic to and positive about King during his early campaigns and when he died. But his increasing opposition to the Vietnam War; his outspokenness against class inequality, unemployment, and poverty; and his shift in attention from the rural South to the urban North gave them problems. *Newsweek* resolved those problems by reporting on him with caution; *Time*, by ignoring him; and *U.S. News*, by chastizing him.

Resource Poor Movements

Edie Goldenberg studied movements representing the poor and powerless, such as people on welfare and the aged.[41] An outgrowth of the civil rights movement, these movements were less legitimate, more strident, and characterized by inadequate organization, lack of funds, and limited membership.

It was hard for resource-poor movements to attract media attention: They were neither a source for reporters nor on their beats, and they lacked the money and skill to control and package information for the press. Their main route to media coverage was to issue threats, march, sit in, confront. But these tactics produced only intermittent stories and had to be escalated to achieve continuous coverage—an escalation that was impossible to sustain.

Besides, the groups were trying to influence four different audiences—actual and potential members, other organizations, the media, and governmental targets—that required different, even contradictory messages. This task was difficult to accomplish: Disruptive demonstrations attracted media attention and may have increased members' morale, but they alienated other organizations and antagonized targets.

In a similar vein and similarly in vain, the Denominational Ministry Strategy in Pittsburgh used protests to try to convince banks and corporations to respond to unemployment in the city. Its flamboyant, conflictual demonstrations attracted considerable coverage, although the demonstrations became less newsworthy in time as novelty faded into repetition. To sustain members' morale, facts were embellished, strengths and alleged successes exaggerated. But this made the movement an unreliable source for reporters, diminishing its legitimacy with the press. Coverage portrayed it as irresponsible. Partly as a consequence, the movement's policy positions were deemed unviable. It failed to stimulate potentially sympathetic groups, and people (reference publics) to join the battle on its behalf, and made it easier for the banks and corporations to discredit the organization.[42]

New Left

Todd Gitlin studied media coverage of the 1960s' "New Left" student radicals, particularly Students for a Democratic Society (SDS) of which he had been a member. He identifies the initial media frames applied to SDS as "trivialization," "polarization" (in which it was shown as equivalent to right wing extremists), "internal dissension," "marginalization," and "disparagement of numbers and effectiveness." After parts of the antiwar movement moved to more militant tactics, media coverage emphasized the "carrying of 'Viet Cong' flags," "violence in demonstrations," and "right-wing opposition."[43]

Gitlin explains the coverage as stemming in part from traditional news values and routine practices: covering events, emphasizing conflict, using personification, relying on governmental sources, and accepting society's dominant ideological assumptions.

The media were thus partly responsible for isolating the movement politically, changing its leaders into politically irrelevant "public celebrities" and causing the decline of its person-to-person organization and the rise of a moderate alternative.

MEDIA COVERAGE OF VIOLENT PARTICIPATION

If coverage of peaceful social movements is mixed and that of conflictual movements generally negative, what about the violent participation manifested in riots and terrorism?

Riots

Riots in the United States are often racially based.[44] Prior to the 1960s, however, blacks were the victims of white violence, and the press bore considerable blame for the course of events. According to the Chicago Commission on Race Relations, writing in the 1920s, "the policies of newspapers on racial matters have made relations more difficult, at times fostering new antagonism and enmities and even precipitating riots by inflaming the public against Negroes."[45] The *Washington Post* played a major part in provoking the riot of mid-July 1919 in its city with its vastly exaggerated tales of African-American rapists.[46]

The press also tended to misreport the conflicts to the detriment of blacks; then, when trials followed, depicting them as guilty. As Herbert Seligmann wrote bitterly at the time about the effects wreaked on race relations by the majority of American newspapers: "It will be the work of years to undo [their] poisonous and anti-social accomplishments."[47]

Of the civil disorders taking place from the 1960s onward, the most studied was that of Los Angeles in August 1965 in which African-Americans rioted in their Watts and surrounding districts.

The news media were accused of giving excessive publicity to the more intransigent blacks, of reporting inflammatory incidents, and of provoking violence by their very presence. The riots were portrayed as black-white confrontations; law enforcement was emphasized; underlying causes, such as poverty and unemployment, were neglected. In contrast to the earlier period, however, coverage was not overtly racist.

The debate over media riot coverage after the Los Angeles uprising revolved around this tendency of television, newspapers, and radio to inflame and exploit the disturbances. Reports of presidential and gubernatorial commissions, the ministrations of national government agencies and local governmental authorities, and statements by members of the media were designed to discourage flamboyant and exaggerated coverage in the future.

Journalists were encouraged to formally or informally adopt and to follow guidelines for covering civil disorders. One survey identified various voluntary codes in operation, some devised by the police, some by city administrations, and others by the media. These codes required that reporters wait thirty minutes before reporting anything about a disturbance, clear information through a police information center, and embargo all news until the uprising was completely under control.

In the spring of 1992, another riot, much more violent and destructive of people and property, took place in Los Angeles. It followed the acquittal by an all-white jury of the white police officers accused of beating up Rodney King, the African-American motorist whom they had stopped for speeding and other offenses. Because the violence had been captured on videotape and widely shown on news broadcasts throughout the United States, there was widespread anger and fury among African-Americans and many whites at the acquittal. (Conviction came at a later trial.)

Newspapers, notably the *Los Angeles Times,* gave context and explanation to the riot events, which they covered in massive detail. Television coverage, however, was even more inflammatory and incendiary than before, with instant, unedited scenes of looting, buildings being torched, people being assaulted.

Indeed, by showing that the police were not responding and probably would not be able to respond to much of the action, television coverage probably encouraged widespread looting. Looting that, as Larry Dietz pointed out at the time, "reminds us of the power of advertising to teach people the forms of the good life."[48]

There were, however, major differences between the coverage of the networks and that of the local television: the former "contained substantial commentary on social issues while the Los Angeles stations focused almost exclusively on discrete episodes of violence and the restoration of law and order." Local television news depicted blacks "as criminals or victims of crime; on national news, they were most often depicted as victims of society."[49]

Coverage of both of the Los Angeles riots is a reminder that the combination of violence and competitive pressures can produce incendiary local television news coverage, despite governmental pressures for restraint. In the absence of compensating stories about these otherwise relatively peaceful racially segregated minority communities, such coverage causes and reinforces stereotypes about and fosters prejudice towards African-Americans.

Terrorism

The most violent form of political participation is insurgent terrorism, "social-revolutionary, separatist and single issue terrorism aiming at the top of society . . . mainly perpetrated for its effects on others [rather] than the immediate victims."[50]

Insurgent terrorism may not be as deadly as state terrorism, nor its victims as numerous; it has, however, achieved far more visibility. The issues of how terrorism is defined and covered in the media, and what to do about it, have provoked a surfeit of often passionate and polemical literature.[51]

Reprinted with special permission of North America Syndicate

The question dominating the literature is: does media coverage aid and encourage or obstruct and deter terrorism in general and terrorist causes in particular? The resultant works can be divided into the three categories discussed in the following sections.

Terrorists' Strategies and Tactics   The contributors to this category are usually not terrorists, but researchers who seek, more or less dispassionately, to identify terrorists' perspectives and to understand why and how terrorists use or attempt to use the media. Among the objectives of the terrorists that the researchers identified are obtaining publicity about their existence and purposes; achieving legitimacy and status, or at least a boost in morale; getting their objectives on the agendas of policymakers and the public; achieving a contagion effect in which other individuals or groups join the violence; undermining the authority of the state; and having their grievances settled (if possible).

The conventional wisdom is that the success of a terrorist operation, and the concomitant achievement of any of these objectives, depends almost entirely on the amount of publicity it receives.[52] Seeking to advance their causes through the media, terrorists and their surrogates are liable to engage in press relations activities, usually including statements of responsibility and occasionally of apology, and issuing manifestos; they provide press releases and visual materials, hold news conferences, give interviews and even press tours.

Clearly the media can amplify terrorism. Uncommon in the literature, however, are thoughtful analyses and detailed examples of the ways that such amplification can redound adversely on the terrorists and their alleged sponsors.

Indictments of the Media   The vast majority of the literature argues that the media willingly or inadvertently encourage terrorism and/or obstruct attempts to fight it. The media are accused of facilitating many, if not all, of the terrorists' objectives. In addition, their presence at and reporting of particular terrorist episodes are blamed for such damaging effects as prolonging incidents, hindering police operations, providing terrorists with tactical and strategic information, placing the lives of police and hostages in jeopardy, as well as putting inappropriate pressure on the authorities to resolve incidents, to settle with terrorists or meet their demands.[53]

An opposite perspective, espoused by a few writers, indicts the media as antiterrorist. The media are accused of having conspired, although not necessarily consciously, with public and private leaders to constrain mass understanding of the phenomenon of terrorism.[54]

Coverage   A few researchers have attempted to characterize systematically the form and content of media coverage of terrorism. Their work varies widely in originality, methodological reliability, and the validity of its findings. The strongest evidence of a media effect promoting terrorism comes from studies of contagion both within and between states. This is the notion that there is a direct relation between quantity of media coverage and the volume and scale of terrorism.[55]

Contagion aside, most empirical research shows that media coverage is hostile to terrorists. Analyzing the content of the *New York Times*'s and the U.S. television networks' news coverage of three terrorist groups, one study concluded that the stories relied on authority sources and did not legitimate the terrorists' causes. Coverage emphasized violence and destruction and ignored the terrorist groups' motives, objectives, and goals. Moreover, over the period studied, violence had to become more dramatic and extensive to be reported.[56]

The authorities dominate the political environment and control the flow of information. So law-and-order frames rather than injustice and defiance frames dominate media coverage.

CONCLUSION

Ideally, people are political beings who find their highest fulfillment through active participation in public life. Hollywoodites illustrate the opportunities, incentives, and motives for political participation. The media, however, generally discourage such participation or promote a pseudo version of it.

Coverage of peaceable social movements tends to be mixed. Coverage of conflictual movements ranges from positive through mixed to negative, with negative predominating.

The two most violent forms of participation are riots and terrorism. With exceptions, coverage of riots is incendiary; of terrorism, hostile.

Notes

1. M. Margaret Conway, *Political Participation in the United States* (Washington, D.C.: CQ Press, 1985), 2.

2. Katherine Isaac, *Practicing Democracy* (New York: St. Martin's Press, 1995); also relevant is David L. Paletz and William H. Harris, "Four-Letter Threats to Authority," *Journal of Politics* 37:4 (November 1975): 955–79.

3. Steven E. Finkel and Karl-Dieter Opp, "Party Identification and Participation in Collective Political Action," *Journal of Politics* 53:2 (May 1991): 339–71.

4. Steven J. Rosenstone and John Mark Hansen, *Mobilization, Participation, and Democracy in America* (New York: Macmillan, 1993), 5.

5. Henry E. Brady, Sidney Verba, and Kay Lehman Schlozman, "Beyond SES: A Resource Model of Political Participation," *American Political Science Review* 89:2 (June 1995): 271–94; see also Sidney Verba et al., "Citizen Activity: Who Participates? What Do They Say?" *American Political Science Review* 87:2 (June 1993): 303–18.

6. See the comprehensive historical survey by Ronald Brownstein, *The Power and the Glitter* (New York: Pantheon, 1990).

7. Ibid., 96–97.

8. Bernard Weinraub, "David Geffen, Still Hungry," *New York Times Magazine,* 2 May 1993, 40; see also Leslie Wayne, "Hollywood Production: Political Money," *New York Times,* 12 September 1996, A1, A12.

9. Miles Corwin, "Eastwood No 'Dirty Harry' in Last Scene as Mr. Mayor," *Los Angeles Times,* 10 April 1988, I:3; see also Mark A. Stein, "He Buys Out the Problem; Mayor Eastwood Solves Another Thorny Issue," *Los Angeles Times,* 19 December 1986, I:1.

10. Joanna Pitt, "Hollywood and Washington" (paper submitted to my "Politics and Media" course, Duke University, 29 March 1994).

11. Brownstein, *The Power and the Glitter,* 295.

12. Robert D. Putnam, "Tuning In, Tuning Out," *PS* 28:4 (December 1995): 666.

13. See ibid., 678–79, for these explanations.

14. Roderick P. Hart, *Seducing America* (New York: Oxford University Press, 1994), 13.

15. Ibid., 86.

16. Ibid., 154–59.

17. Pippa Norris, "Does Television Erode Social Capital? A Reply to Putnam," *PS* 29:3 (September 1996): 476.

18. Survey cited by Janette Kenner Muir, "Video Verité: C-SPAN Covers the Candidates," in *The 1992 Presidential Campaign,* ed. Robert E. Denton, Jr. (Westport, Conn.: Praeger, 1994), 229.

19. William A. Gamson, *Talking Politics* (New York: Cambridge University Press, 1992).

20. Patrick Daley with Dan O'Neill, "'Sad Is Too Mild a Word': Press Coverage of the *Exxon Valdez* Oil Spill," *Journal of Communication* 41:4 (Autumn 1991): 42–57.

21. Ibid., 53.

22. James B. Lemert, *Does Mass Communication Change Public Opinion After All?* (Chicago: Nelson-Hall, 1981), chap. 6; see also James B. Lemert et al., "Journalism and Mobilizing Information," *Journalism Quarterly* 54:4 (Winter 1977): 725.

23. Marian Lief Palley, "Elections 1992 and the Thomas Appointment," *PS* 26:1 (March 1993), 28.

24. *International Herald Tribune,* 20 August 1993, 3.

25. Zhongdang Pan and Gerald M. Kosicki, "Talk Show Exposure as an Opinion Activity," *Political Communication* 14:3 (July-September, 1997): 371–88.

26. Benjamin Page, *Who Deliberates?* (Chicago: University of Chicago Press, 1996), chap. 4.

27. Senator Alan Simpson (R.-Wyo.), quoted in Sidney Verba, "The Voice of the People," *PS* 26:4 (December 1993): 684.

28. On public information campaigns in general, see Charles T. Salmon, ed., *Information Campaigns* (Newbury Park, Calif.: Sage 1989), esp. chap. 1.

29. This discussion comes from David L. Paletz, Roberta E. Pearson, and Donald L. Willis, *Politics in Public Service Advertising on Television* (New York: Praeger, 1977).

30. For a normative account of the process, see Brian R. Flay and Dee Burton, "Effective Mass Communication Strategies for Health Campaigns," in *Mass Communication and Public Health,* ed. Charles Atkin and Lawrence Wallack (Newbury Park, Calif.: Sage, 1990), 129–46.

31. Lana F. Rakow, "Information and Power," in *Information Campaigns,* ed. Charles T. Salmon (Newbury Park, Calif.: Sage, 1989), 169.

32. The Ad Council's importance may be waning; see Stuart Elliott, "Advertising," *New York Times,* June 10, 1997, C9.

33. Elmer E. Schattschneider, *The Semi-Sovereign People* (New York: Holt, Rinehart & Winston, 1960).

34. Clarice N. Olien, Phillip J. Tichenor, and George A. Donohue, "Media Coverage and Social Movements," in *Information Campaigns,* ed. Charles T. Salmon (Newbury Park, Calif.: Sage 1989): 151–54.

35. "Condom Replica Inflated for Helms," *Raleigh News and Observer,* 6 September 1991, 4B.

36. Robert M. Entman and Andrew Rojecki, "Freezing Out the Public," *Political Communication* 10:2 (April-June 1993): 155.

37. See her "Introduction" in Alice Sheppard, *Cartooning for Suffrage* (Albuquerque: University of New Mexico Press, 1994), 3. This book is devoted to pro-suffrage cartoons and the women who made them.

38. For a later study of the relationships between the media and the women's movement, see Bernadette Barker-Plummer, "News as a Political Resource: Media Strategies and Political Identity in the U.S. Women's Movement, 1966–1975," *Critical Studies in Mass Communication* 12:3 (September 1995): 306–24.

39. Gadi Wolfsfeld, *Media and Political Conflicts* (New York: Cambridge University Press, 1997); see also his "Media, Protest, and Political Violence," *Journalism Monographs* 127 (June 1991).

40. Richard Lentz, *Symbols, the News Magazines, and Martin Luther King* (Baton Rouge: Louisiana State University Press, 1990).

41. Edie N. Goldenberg, *Making the Papers* (Lexington, Mass.: D. C. Heath, 1975).

42. This account comes from Michael Margolis and Robert E. Burtt, "Revolutionaries of the Status Quo," in *Manipulating Public Opinion,* ed. Michael Margolis and Gary A. Mauser (Pacific Grove, Calif.: Brooks/Cole, 1989), 176–204.

43. Todd Gitlin, *The Whole World Is Watching* (Berkeley: University of California Press, 1989), 27–28; also relevant is Theodore Otto Windt, Jr., *Presidents and Protesters* (Tuscaloosa: University of Alabama Press, 1990).

44. This discussion is based on David L. Paletz and Robert Dunn, "Press Coverage of Civil Disorders: A Case Study of Winston-Salem, 1967," *Public Opinion Quarterly* 33:3 (Fall 1969): 328–45.

45. Chicago Commission on Race Relations, *The Negro in Chicago: A Study of Race Relations and a Race Riot* (Chicago: University of Chicago Press, 1922), chap. 10, esp. 523–56.

46. Arthur I. Waskow, *From Race Riot to Sit-In, 1919 and the 1960s* (Garden City, N.Y.: Anchor Books, 1967), 21–38.

47. Herbert J. Seligmann, *The Negro Faces America* (New York: Harper, 1920), 184.

48. Larry Dietz, "What Did the Looters Want? A Piece of the Good Life," *Adweek* (West) 42:18 (4 May 1992): 2.

49. Erna Smith, "Transmitting Race" (The Joan Shorenstein Barone Center, John F. Kennedy School of Government, Harvard University, Research Paper R-11, May 1994), 1.

50. Alex P. Schmid and Janny de Graaf, *Violence as Communication* (Newbury Park, Calif.: Sage, 1982), 1–2; see also James H. Wittebols, "The Politics and Coverage of Terrorism," *Communication Theory* 1:3 (August 1991): 253–66.

51. This section is based on David L. Paletz and Alex P. Schmid, eds., *Terrorism and the Media* (Newbury Park, Calif.: Sage, 1992), esp. chap. 2.

52. Walter Laqueur, *Terrorism* (Boston, Mass.: Little Brown, 1977), 109.

53. E.g., Grant Wardlaw, *Political Terrorism,* 2nd ed. (New York: Cambridge University Press, 1989); and Yonah Alexander and Richard Latter, eds., *Terrorism and the Media* (Washington, D.C.: Brassey's, 1990).

54. Edward S. Herman and Gerry O'Sullivan, *The "Terrorism" Industry* (New York: Pantheon, 1989); also relevant is Steven Livingston, *The Terrorism Spectacle* (Boulder, Colo.: Westview, 1994).

55. Hans-Bernd Brosius and Gabriel Weimann, "The Contagiousness of Mass-Mediated Terrorism," *European Journal of Communication* 6:1 (March 1991): 63–75; and Zoe C. W. Tan, "Media Publicity and Insurgent Terrorism," *Gazette* 42:1 (1988): 3–22.

56. David L. Paletz, Peter A. Fozzard, and John Z. Ayanian, "The I.R.A., the Red Brigades, and the F.A.L.N. in the 'New York Times,'" *Journal of Communication* 32:2 (Spring 1982): 162–71; and "Terrorism on TV News: The IRA, the FALN, and the Red Brigades," in *Television Coverage of International Affairs,* ed. William C. Adams (Norwood, N.J.: Ablex, 1983): 143–65.

Part III
The Intermediaries

◆ ◆ ◆

Chapter 9

Interest Groups and Political Parties

◆ ◆ ◆

Interviewed at the 1996 Republican National Convention, Senator Alan K. Simpson (R.-Wyo.) told a reporter for MTV that young people (18 to 40 as he quaintly defined them) "must get organized as a political lobby. . . . 'Can't just sit around and watch Beavis and Butt-head and scratch yourself.'"[1]

Political lobbies, more commonly known as interest groups, serve as intermediaries between people and government.[2] They cover most conceivable subjects, occupations, and activities.[3] They possess organization, leaders, resources, and some degree of public standing. Their main intent is to influence public policy on behalf of their members through institutionalized methods.[4]

CALLAHAN

"IN AMERICA EVEN A POOR BoY CAN GROW UP TO
WIN THE SUPPORT OF POWERFUL SPECIAL INTEREST GROUPS."

A traditional way of viewing the influence and involvement of interest groups with government has been that of *iron triangles.* Key members of congressional committees, agency administrators, and a few lobbyists essentially decide policy in their subject areas out of the public's sight and mind. Because of the proliferation and diversity of interest groups, decentralization of Congress, and growth of the executive branch, it is argued that iron triangles are being replaced in some policy areas by *issue networks.* This policymaking process is "more open, more decentralized, more conflictual, more dynamic, and more broadly participatory."[5]

THE MEDIA

The media bolster or undermine interest groups, help them to or hinder them from achieving their objectives in two different ways.

First, the media provide much of the information the public possesses about most groups. News about an interest group and its activities can make people aware of, challenge, and even temporarily crack a cozy iron triangle. It can enable them to become part of an issue network. Sparse or nonexistent coverage means public ignorance and unwitting acquiescence to existing group-government relations.

Second, media depictions of groups can affect the willingness of policymakers to interact with them and respond to their demands. Certainly, public officials' knowledge of interest groups is not confined to media coverage. Nonetheless, these depictions combine with their sense of the public's media-derived opinions to influence how they treat groups and group objectives.

Interest group leaders are sensitive to the importance of the media's portrayals of their images and their objectives. So, they deploy whatever techniques they can muster to try to obtain favorable media coverage.

The appealingly named Center for Science in the Public Interest (CSPI) exemplifies how an interest group can achieve its policy objectives by being a valuable source of expertise, information, and news for the press and thereby generate favorable coverage for its views and policy preferences. The Center's primary attributes are quality research, identification as the only consumer organization lobbying on food and nutrition issues, and media savvy. For years, the Grocery Manufacturers of America, the National Food Processors Association, and giants in the food industry have seethed as the Center has been glowingly quoted in the news media and has successfully lobbied Congress and regulatory agencies for warning labels on alcohol, bans on deceptive advertising, and better nutrition labeling.[6]

Unfortunately, there is little definitive research on and analysis of the relationship between the media and interest groups and the contributions of the media to groups' policy successes and failures.

Some groups, such as the CSPI, enjoy positive coverage. Other groups are reported negatively: labor unions have been depicted as greedy and corrupt, protective of unproductive workers, eager to strike, and generally outmoded.[7] Such coverage is abetted by politicians' penchant for publicly denouncing as "special interests" the groups with which they disagree.

Some groups receive both positive and negative coverage. Researchers who analyzed many television news stories on diverse policy issues concluded "that corporations and business groups predominated."[8] One could also conclude from perusing media stories about interest groups that those with economic-material objectives are generally portrayed negatively: as buying access and favors with lavish campaign contributions and other indulgences, wielding undue influence on the policy process, even perverting the American political system.[9]

To go beyond conjecture and impressions, this chapter begins with actual empirical research. It shows how and explains why an interest group successfully managed for several years to advance its objectives through the press. The chapter continues with a survey of the tactics groups currently deploy through the media to influence policymakers before, during, and after the policy process. Group activities on the specific policy issue of health care highlight the latest techniques. The chapter ends with a coda on the media's relationship with political parties.

COMMON CAUSE

For several years, Common Cause was the classic modern example of a group's successful, sophisticated use of the mass media to advance its objectives. A case study of *New York Times* coverage reveals what a group can accomplish and why most fall short. It begins with a brief summary of the data, explains the reasons for the amount and kinds of coverage, and concludes with consequences.

Formed in 1970 primarily at the initiative of John W. Gardner, Common Cause is still prominent among what are known as public interest groups. Gardner described it as a citizens' lobby designed "to revitalize politics and government."[10] He used his initial funding from foundations to send out over 1.5 million direct-mail solicitations and to purchase full-page advertisements in four major American newspapers. Partly because of this extensive publicity and widespread news coverage, by 1976, the organization had a membership of roughly 250,000, an annual income of over $5 million derived from dues and contributions, and an extensive list of claimed victories in Congress and the courts.[11]

Structure of News Analysis

Four categories were devised to analyze the structures of all news stories about Common Cause in the *New York Times* during the early 1970s. "Unilateral" describes the direct transferral of information, ideas, and accusations from Common Cause to the audience. The material is not necessarily transmitted unaltered by the reporter, but no sources other than Common Cause are mentioned in the story. "Elaboration I" means the major source was Common Cause, but one additional source was included to elaborate or verify the organization's material. With "elaboration II," two or more additional such sources were mentioned.

The figures are highly revealing: Of the 149 major stories, approximately 42 percent were unilateral, 17 percent elaboration I, 25 percent elaboration II, and 5 percent not applicable. Only 11 percent could be categorized as "adversary," meaning that the story contained any information, no matter how little, whether derogatory or not, from a source opposed to or conflicting with the Common Cause data or position.

An examination of the actual sources confirms the impression of Common Cause's dominance over the content of *Times'* stories involving the interest group. Sources were separated into major and minor: The former provided the most paragraphs of information in a story; the latter were responsible for secondary material. In 66 percent of the stories, a Common Cause spokesperson was the major source; in an additional 14 percent, it was Gardner. The next highest categories were "other" and "not applicable," at 6 and 5 percent, respectively.

Just because Common Cause official sources dominated *New York Times* news stories involving the organization did not necessarily mean that the stories were favorable. It is possible for reporters to treat information in ways inimical to their sources' interests and objectives. But some 97 percent of the "major" stories were favorable, 3 percent were mixed. Not one was unfavorable. In almost every instance, Common Cause was presented as a champion of citizens' rights, a righter of wrongs, a doer of good. It was also depicted favorably in 79 percent of the "minor" stories, where it appeared in a supporting or peripheral role. The remainder were mixed or neutral. There were no unfavorable minor stories.

Common Cause was further depicted in 98 percent of the major stories as "influential," with the power to influence governmental decisionmaking and decisions. In the minor stories, the percentages were 78 influential, 19 neutral, and 3 not influential. Considering that Common Cause was a mere appendage in some of the stories, these figures are equally striking.

A final way of revealing how reporters and editors at the *Times* perceived and treated Common Cause is by seeing what they called it in their stories. Such phrases as "the civic group," "the good government group," and "the public interest organization" are favorable on their face; others—such as "the very worthwhile people's lobby," "the reformist citizens' lobby," and "the citizens' lobby"—contain the suspect word "lobby" but precede it with exculpatory language. Such terms serve as a "conduit" transmitting the group's self-perception. They composed 54 percent of the sample.

Under "partial conduit" are bland expressions, such as "the new organization," and phrases in which the term "lobby" is not totally redeemed, as in "the public affairs lobby" and "the lobby group." Adding the conduit and partial conduit categories, we find that almost 90 percent of the phrases describing Common Cause were positive and supportive. A mere 9 percent of the characterizations could be called skeptical—"the national organization that calls itself a 'citizens' lobby," "the self-styled citizens' lobby," "the self-described public interest lobby." A paltry 1 percent was "antagonistic"—the so-called citizens' lobby.

Explanation of the Analysis

The *Times* often served as a transmission belt, even a publicity agent, for Common Cause.

In explaining the reasons, one must look first at the group itself—for Common Cause was both credible and legitimate. Founder Gardner had been Secretary of Health, Education, and Welfare in the Johnson administration, president of the Carnegie Foundation, chairman of the National Urban Coalition, and on the board of directors of such corporations as the Shell Oil Company; Time, Inc.; and the New York Telephone Company. He bestowed legitimacy and a patina of non-partisanship upon Common Cause when he founded it. His presence made it worthy of note; his pronouncements brought it attention; his participation gave the organization cachet and cartel with editorial writers and columnists.

Certainly Common Cause possessed legitimacy and credibility through its founder. It reinforced these qualities by the number and social standing of its members, who voluntarily joined, and by its expressed purposes, which were widely viewed as desirable both by journalists and by the public. The result was regularized interaction. Common Cause did not have to struggle desperately to attract the attention of lowly reporters, the appearance of whose stories, if they wrote them, was uncertain. Common Cause had the attention of reporters of repute whose stories, which they were likely to write, would almost certainly be published.

Seeking Press Coverage   This coverage was not automatic. There is a four-stage process involving the relationships of interest groups and the press. There must be an event or occurrence involving the group, brought to the attention of or covered by journalists, who in turn deem it newsworthy and then transform it into a published story. Media-conscious staff members and officers at Common Cause were involved at all stages of the process: creating events, giving them visibility, emphasizing their newsworthy details, and structuring them into a story for the press.

Common Cause's highly developed manipulatory skills were evidenced by the way it did most of the work for the media, thereby responding to their organizational demands. It continuously issued news releases, editorial memoranda, testimonies, and speeches packaged for media consumption and publication. There was detailed information, highlights were summarized, liftable quotes included, and leads virtually composed. Trying to make its coverage convenient, the organization scheduled press conferences far enough in advance of reporters' deadlines and hand-delivered releases to the congressional press galleries. Ready to react immediately for the press, it called "impromptu press conferences," usually in response to a new development in Congress regarding an issue with which the group was concerned.

To ensure adequate coverage, Common Cause maintained extensive press lists. List A, for example, contained the names of approximately thirty key reporters at the wire services, networks, news chains, and largest newspapers. Releases were usually hand-delivered to these reporters. Press List Q contained the names of all the reporters who covered military spending. These extensive compendia reflected the group leaders' knowledge of the "beat" system of newspersons, particularly in Washington.

Obtaining Press Coverage   Common Cause did what it could to obtain extensive and favorable coverage from the press. Why did the *Times* bestow it? The explanations reside in concepts of news, need for information, journalistic norms, and shared values.

Common Cause was covered because it connected with concepts of news. Its targets were "big" names: presidents, campaign finance chairmen, and the members of Congress whose length of tenure is usually commensurate with their arrogance, pomposity, and sense of security. These public targets were approached in the newsworthy terms of their derelictions, duplicity, and malfeasance, their efforts to conceal information that might lead to investigation and, perhaps, exposure. Individuals were attacked, accusations leveled, demands made. There was the tincture of scandal, of corruption. The press did not have to be cajoled; this is the stuff of daily journalism and its headlines.

Besides, Common Cause was adroit at selecting the right target to personalize and dramatize long-standing abuses for press and public, shrewd at identifying symbols of the need for reform. Consider its ultimately successful pressure on Congress to investigate and punish Congressman Robert L. F. Sikes (D.-Fla.) for alleged conflict of interest. The subject contained such news ingredients as unscrupulous or unethical behavior by a powerful but little-known congressman; a struggle between a notoriously dilatory congressional committee and a reform organization sworn to uphold American values; and an orienting question: would the committee act? In one fell swoop, the group received publicity for its specific objective of unseating Sikes, for its general goals of establishing accountability and ending corruption, and for itself.

The press needs information; Common Cause provided it. This was the second reason for its success with the *Times*. It gathered and pried out material using several techniques. Lawsuits were filed, disclosures sought, and data on financial contributions and election expenditures compiled. This was the very information that journalists seek but usually lack the time and resources to obtain. These hard, often statistical data, seemingly objective, accurate, and complete, were provided by an apparently nonpartisan source with an aura of expertise on campaign finance shared by no other organization.

The norm of balance is rarely applied to statistics from authoritative sources. And even if reporters had sought other sources, none of them could expeditiously verify or rebut Common Cause's figures.

It is not only the information provided by Common Cause that was unquestioned. The *Times* usually transmitted the group's views untarnished or merely with additional explanatory material from supporting sources. The journalistic norms of balance and fairness apparently need not be operative on most kinds of stories involving an authoritative, high-status, apparently nonpartisan group espousing widely shared values. Reporters and editors do not appear to regard these stories as controversial or as requiring the inclusion of opposing viewpoints.

Even if journalists did want to be critical, they were inhibited by the norm of objectivity; deterred from including their own views in the stories, they could rarely find anyone to state them on their behalf. Common Cause did have antagonists, but most of them were without credibility, lacked a case, had an impossible one (defending the exclusion of the public from the proceedings of congressional committees or endorsing unethical behavior), or were subsequently discredited.

Shared values is a final explanation for the *Times'* coverage of Common Cause. Both the journalists and the group shared in great part the assumptions that the American political system was basically sound; that there was nothing wrong with it that exposing corruption, reducing the influence of money in campaigns, and reforming some structures and procedures would not put right. Or at least they agreed on the importance of these endeavors. They shared, too, agreement on the desirability of the general goals espoused by Common Cause—a more "accessible," "accountable," "effective," and "responsive" government to "open up the system." They may have agreed on the appropriateness of Common Cause's more specific objectives of public financing of campaigns and lobbying disclosure laws. No doubt they also shared the dismal suspicion that many politicians are self-serving, disingenuous, and hypocritical. Asked to explain his paper's overwhelmingly favorable coverage of Common Cause, a *Times* reporter who had written some of it said, while insisting he not be identified, "We agreed with them."

When values are shared by sources, press, and probably readers too, there is no felt need on the part of reporters to seek countervailing information elsewhere.

Consequences of Press Coverage

The *New York Times* is disproportionately read by public officials, foundation directors, the leaders of Common Cause, and the kinds of people who either join or are potential members of the group. The paper is a guiding light for many people in the media. What, then, were the probable effects of its portrayal of Common Cause and its leaders as active, influential, effective, nonpartisan proponents of good government?

Existing members of the group were given public incentives to continue their allegiance even when their initial enthusiasm dissipated. They received a sense of purpose being fulfilled by an increasingly prestigious organization, and they encountered no damaging news of strain or conflict. Potential members were encouraged to join. No wonder a telephone survey conducted on behalf of the group revealed that more than half of the new members were attracted by stories in the media.[12] The results were organizational maintenance and enhancement and the continued flow of resources.

A related consequence was to affirm and reaffirm Common Cause's autonomy: "a distinctive area of competence, a clearly demarcated and exclusively served clientele or membership, and undisputed jurisdiction over a function, service, goal, or cause."[13] Media coverage in general and that of the *Times* in particular—the way the Common Cause data, claims, attacks, and successes were reported—bestowed national prominence on the group and its issues, and brought pressure on shrouded public officials.

For these reasons, supporters in public life were given additional reasons to believe Common Cause worth supporting. Actual and potential antagonists may have been persuaded to modify or mute opposition and actions that would otherwise expose them to a hostile press. With the *Times* as model, other newspapers, the television networks' news, and the weekly news magazines were reassured that their coverage of the group was responsible. And the leaders of Common Cause may have been emboldened to seek other targets and more difficult objectives.

Most important, the *Times* gave Common Cause the opportunity to imprint upon the public and public officials its definition of and prescriptions for the woes of American politics.

Thus, (chain) links were constructed between money and political favors and corruption and Common Cause's solution—public financing of elections. But the hard data, the figures with which the links began, may not have been as neutral as they were taken to be by the *Times.* David Adamany has pointed out omissions and exclusions in Common Cause's election receipts and expenditure data and wondered "whether these exclusions do not reflect a decision to publish less comprehensive information which somehow better serves the lobbying and litigation strategies of the organization."[14] Nor were the objectives sought by Common Cause invariably or necessarily desirable. Gerald Pomper has argued that campaign finance reform has had bad effects on the stability and viability of American political parties.[15]

Yet, it was primarily through media coverage that these objectives were promulgated as desirable and desired. Other interest groups with quite different definitions and policy solutions were unfavorably depicted, while many went unheard and therefore unheeded.

INTEREST GROUPS' MEDIA TACTICS

Since the heyday of Common Cause, interest groups' tactics toward the media have developed and expanded. Nonetheless, they are still inspired by two basic, overlapping objectives: obtaining the most favorable depictions possible and advancing policy objectives.

Image Portrayal

Well-off groups have been known to hire public relations consultants or firms, at sometimes exorbitant fees, to try to gain them favorable media coverage or at least improve their public images. Members of the firms pitch stories to reporters for the national news media, arrange (often lavishly catered) meetings for their clients with journalists and policymakers, and try to create newsworthy events. If paid enough, they design campaigns to try to influence public opinion.

Such activity is not confined to American interest groups. According to Jarol Manheim, around 160 foreign governments have hired U.S. lobbyists or public relations consultants to represent them in communicating with the U.S. media, policymakers, and the public.[16] They advise the governments' embassy personnel how to deal with the media, facilitate access to reporters, and suggest policies to improve the countries' images. The tactics work.[17]

A notorious example is the so-called Citizens for a Free Kuwait, which spent more than $11 million on American public relations firms, imagemakers, lawyers, and lobbyists.[18] The "Citizens" had two objectives. First was to deflect attention away from Kuwait's autocratic ruling system, its subordinate status of women, and the flamboyant lifestyles of some of its rulers. Second was to arouse and increase Americans' enmity toward Saddam Hussein and Iraq and bolster support for the Gulf War and for Kuwait.

Among the public relations actions were drafting speeches and scheduling speaking tours for the client; providing the only source for U.S. news services and networks of video produced by the Kuwaiti resistance; distributing video and other propaganda, including a book entitled *Rape of Kuwait;* and keeping track of public opinion through focus groups and daily tracking polls.

Consider what might have transpired had Hussein hired a U.S. public relations firm just prior to deciding to invade Kuwait (he did have a U.S. lobbyist on his payroll in earlier years).[19] His hirelings could have portrayed him as America's staunch ally against Iran, chronicled his intimate relationship with the Reagan and Bush administrations, detailed his country's grievances against Kuwait, portrayed Kuwait as an autocratically ruled medieval society in comparison to the more modern and secular Iraq, and shown how his control of Kuwait's oil reserves would benefit the United States by assuring it of an abundant and cheap supply.

Public relations campaigns by foreign countries can be relatively effective because, with conspicuous exceptions, news coverage of events and occurrences abroad is limited and the U.S. public is relatively uninformed. Problems occur, however, when the media report the campaign itself or when the rulers of the country being promoted behave intolerably. But even the most despicable regimes that slaughter dissidents, kill human-rights activists, torture political prisoners, and abuse their people can find someone to represent them. About one lobbyist it was said, "'You can't be a client . . . unless you've killed 10,000 people and stolen $10 billion.'"[20]

Policy Goals

As the Citizens for Kuwait examples reveal, groups' tactics using the media usually go far beyond producing favorable images; they are designed to try to achieve policy goals. These increasingly sophisticated tactics are deployed before, during, and after the policymaking process as the following examples illustrate.

Before Policymaking Process   From an interest group's perspective, having policymakers in office who agree with its views and objectives is ideal. So, when feasible, groups try to use the media to influence the selection of office-holders. They wage campaigns to persuade the public to support or oppose and senators to vote to confirm or reject presidential nominees. At their most intense, as for example with the nominations of Robert Bork and Clarence Thomas to the U.S. Supreme Court (discussed in chapter 14), these efforts entail trying to influence news coverage, columnists, and editorial writers, as well as run political advertisements.

Since the Bork and Thomas episodes, conservatives have established a formidable combination of organizations (foundations, think tanks, legal organizations, direct-mail operations, political action committees) and communication techniques to advance their ideological objectives. The influence of this nexus became apparent when University of Pennsylvania law professor Lani Guinier was nominated by President Clinton to serve as head of the Justice Department's civil rights division.

Guinier was a civil rights lawyer, legal theorist, and friend of the president. She had written lengthy, scholarly articles on how to integrate racial minorities into American government. This involved her in proposing mechanisms by which disadvantaged minority groups might have a fair chance of satisfying their policy preferences.[21]

The depiction and definition of Guinier as the "quota queen" were set the day after her nomination was announced by Clint Bolick of the little-known, conservative-foundation-funded Institute for Justice. Bolick had founded the institute after working in the Justice Department during the Reagan administration.

Bolick's column in the *Wall Street Journal* was headed "Clinton's Quota Queen." This appealingly alliterative appellation was credulously and widely transmitted by the news media. Arguably, the focus should have been on Guinier's qualifications for the job (experiences, skills as a litigator, etc.). But reporters followed Bolick's lead. In so doing, few of them tried to explain her views from her perspective or questioned the relevance of her theories to the position for which she had been nominated.

Defined by her opponents, Guinier was demonized, depicted as an ideological extremist. With the nomination in trouble, news frames moved quickly from "controversy" to "doomed nominee."[22]

The onslaught was particularly effective because the Justice Department's legislative liaison position had not yet been filled, so there was no one officially appointed to take Guinier around to meet the Senate Judiciary Committee members. The White House also forbade her to respond until her Senate confirmation hearings.[23] Since President Clinton withdrew her nomination before the hearings, she never had a serious opportunity to answer the accusations against her.

During Policymaking Process   Groups try to use the media to influence policymakers and opinion leaders, and to mobilize public opinion to put pressure on policymakers as policies are being made.

One way is to make news opportunely. The director of organized labor's Citizens for Tax Justice did a study revealing that during a three-year period, many of the nation's 250 largest corporations paid no taxes. The findings were striking, featuring the barbed bits of information that reduce a complicated subject to easily understood examples. Widely distributed in advance to reporters, the findings enjoyed extensive news coverage, thereby building support in Congress for the corporate tax increases that became part of the 1986 tax reform law.[24]

A second technique is to engage in advocacy campaigns utilizing direct mail, phone banks, focus groups, and polls. The purpose is to show the policy proposal's supposed effects on ordinary people who communicate the group's views to their representatives. But often what appears to be spontaneous grassroot opinion has been manufactured. It is synthetic. Those in the know call it "astroturf."

Given sufficient resources, advocacy campaigns include political advertising in newspapers, magazines, radio, and on local television stations. Ads are run in selected congressional districts with viewers urged to contact their representative, identified by name. Again, the aim is to influence policymakers directly and through public opinion. So the ads are often made provocative enough to generate news coverage.

Interest group involvement in advocacy campaigns is sometimes camouflaged or concealed. Ambiguous names disguise real purposes. Especially on environmental issues, campaigns are sometimes waged under names with more popular appeal than the groups themselves have. Northwesterners for More Fish was the name chosen by big utilities and other companies under attack for depleting the fish population; and "'the Abundant Wildlife Society of North America' . . . advocates for hunters, loggers and miners."[25]

The evisceration of President Clinton's proposed energy tax is an object lesson of advocacy campaigns in action. Lobbyists for the businesses involved used mass mailings and satellite feeds to the hometown people affected, enlisted talk radio, and laid down a blizzard of newspaper advertisements to whip up opposition. So that after making major concessions to aluminum smelters, chemical and glass makers, coal mine owners, electric and gas companies, farmers, grain merchants, and barge operators, the administration essentially gave up on the tax.[26]

After Policymaking Process   When policy actions have been taken, for example a U.S. Supreme Court decision rendered, groups speedily communicate their reactions and analyses to reporters by press conferences, e-mail, and faxes/telephone calls, and get their spokespersons or apparently neutral experts on news and talk shows.

Group leaders also monitor governmental programs affecting their members, keep tabs on regulators and regulations, and then inform the media if they don't like what is going on. News stories of policies gone wrong, of scandal and incompetence, can compel policymakers to revise policies more in line with an interest group's objectives.

Above all, groups often endorse and support selected policymakers for election or reelection, oppose and try to defeat others. These actions are also a way of trying to put people into office who favor the group's views and who will support its policy preferences in the future, but these actions are usually based on candidates' voting records, which is why they come under the "After" category.

One technique is to issue more or less tendentious scorecards and guides telling people how policymakers have voted on issues of concern to the group's members, and sympathizers. Constituents are encouraged to vote for or against candidates accordingly.

The effects of scorecards can be enhanced if they are widely distributed and brought to the attention of the public and policymakers. The Christian Coalition circulates its guides through churches. Gimmicks are useful: The League of Conservation Voters issues its infamous list of the "dirty dozen"—the members of Congress with the supposedly worst records on the environment—and campaigns against them.

Increasingly, interest groups sponsor political advertisements during elections. As long as these ads stop short of explicitly instructing recipients how to vote, they are categorized as educating voters through issue advocacy. This permits unlimited expenditures from any source and precludes federal regulation.

The AFL-CIO took this activity to a new high in 1996 with its $25 million campaign of political advertising attacking Republican members of the House of Representatives, especially first-termers, elected narrowly and therefore deemed vulnerable to defeat. A coalition of business groups reduced the campaign's effects by responding with advertisements supporting some of the Republican incumbents and lambasting their Democratic opponents as supposed tools of labor bosses.

Example of Latest Tactics

The attempt by the Clinton administration to change the health care system spurred interest groups to deploy their latest tactics. For the legislation had enormous potential effects on innumerable interest groups, arousing them to action in support of or in opposition to the parts of the proposal affecting them. As some examples, the American Medical Association was against price controls limiting physicians' salaries; the pharmaceutical industry opposed the government's reviewing of the prices charged for innovative drugs for reasonableness and the proposal for discount or rebate on drugs dispensed to Medicare beneficiaries; therapists sought inclusion of mental health coverage; tobacco companies objected to an increase in the cigarette tax to pay for health care; restauranteurs complained about requiring businesses to pay for health insurance; and leaders of the Christian Coalition opposed what they viewed as extensive government interference into health care.[27]

The resultant advocacy campaigns involved lobbyists, public relations specialists, pollsters (national surveys and focus groups), and direct-mail experts.[28] Some $60 million was spent on political advertising, with opponents outspending supporters 2 to 1.[29]

The purpose of this media offensive was to influence the recommendations of Hillary Clinton's task force and subsequently to have Congress change them after they were proposed. Advertisements were aimed at policymakers, commentators, and pundits who would shape the debate, and at decisionmakers in Washington, D.C., who would decide it. They were therefore placed on local television and in the *Washington Post,* the *Congressional Quarterly Weekly Report,* as well as in national outlets (e.g., CNN, the weekly news magazines, and the *New York Times.*)

Harry and Louise   But it was the Health Insurance Association of America, representing small to medium-sized insurance companies, that waged the most visible campaign. Under the appealing name of the Coalition for Health Insurance Choices, it spent around $14 million on television ads in which a wife (Louise) and her husband (Harry) critically identified alleged defects in the president's health care proposal in consumers' terms: "Having choices we don't like is no choice at all," said Louise in one such ad.[30] No direct reference was made to the health insurance industry behind the ad.

The genesis of "Harry and Louise" was a comment by the president of the insurance group "that the health care debate would be decided by couples sitting around their kitchen tables figuring out how the various proposals would affect them."[31] When tried out on focus groups, this approach resonated more than using celebrities or outlining health care problems. Louise was made the dominant person in the advertisements because women like her were identified as the most vulnerable supporters of the Clinton plan.

The ads were aimed at members of Congress, and were thus aired mostly in Washington, D.C., and New York, and on CNN. This explains why they did not have much measurable influence on public opinion. However, in part because the Clintons made a parody version, they attracted considerable attention from the news media, which amplified awareness about, attributed influence to, and enhanced their effects.

Early polls showed public support for the Clinton health care initiative.[32] Perhaps the administration was overconfident. It certainly underestimated the resources, sophistication (e.g., fax attacks) resources, and impact of the media campaign of its opponents. When powerful Hollywood agent Mike Ovitz offered to lend top executives to devise a counterattack, the White House never got things together.[33]

The opposition campaign had two important effects. First, by framing the health care debate in terms of high cost and big government, it contributed to the proposal's congressional defeat. Second, by portraying the president as a proponent of expensive, enlarged government, and as ineffectual to boot, it contributed to the Democrats' defeats in the 1994 elections.

THE MEDIA AND POLITICAL PARTIES

A second intermediary between the people and government are political parties. American political parties are composed of three overlapping parts: the party organization, the party electorate, and the party members who are elected to fill government positions.

The party organization is made up of national, state, and local committees, leaders, and staff. Party institutions, such as the Republican and Democratic National Committees, and the party organizations in the Senate and House of Representatives are involved in recruiting, helping fund, and training or advising candidates for electoral offices, financing polls and political advertising, and mobilizing voters.

The candidates for whom these services are provided are not controlled by, and may not even feel beholden to, the party organizations and leaders. Coordinated campaigns may, however, be coming more common. Fueled by their nationally publicized Contract With America, many Republican congressional candidates in 1994 advocated similar policies and themes in successfully campaigning against their Democratic opponents.

Also part of the party organization are the people who become members, give money, and/or time. These activists customarily represent the more passionate partisans. Democrats have been characterized (caricatured) as "minorities, gay rights activists, radical feminists, and peaceniks"; Republicans as "fundamentalists, bigots, pro-life activists, and chicken-hawks."[34]

The party in the electorate consists of people who habitually vote for its candidates. High proportions of African-Americans and Jews, pluralities of people with low incomes, union members, city dwellers, and unmarried women vote Democratic. High proportions of white males, high income, Protestant evangelicals, the married, and college graduates vote Republican.[35]

The party in government is composed of people elected under the party banner to legislative and executive offices, and party members appointed to other policymaking positions in government. The parties hold distinct positions on several policies, which their members display with their votes in the subcommittees and committees and on the floor of legislatures.

Media Effects

There is little research on the relationship between the media and political parties. The conventional wisdom is that the media are responsible, at least in part, for the parties supposedly declining in importance in recruiting and grooming candidates, controlling nominations, and managing campaign resources.[36]

The media are accused of encouraging candidates to be entrepreneurial. Because primaries are more or less open to anyone, these candidates can run on their own volition without the imprimatur and sometimes in defiance of party leaders, using a party label more from convenience than commitment. The candidates then wage their campaigns in and through the media. They distance themselves from their party, rarely invoking it in their political advertising.

Further weakening the parties, the media welcome fresh faces unaffiliated with or only superficially connected to the parties. They are open to candidates, such as Ross Perot, who can afford to buy time to advertise themselves and their viewpoints.

The media are also blamed, in part because of their negative coverage of political parties in government, for the apparent dealignment of the two-party system, the decline of party loyalty as a basis for voting for candidates, and the increase in split-ticket voting.

Contradicting the conventional wisdom, the major political parties do benefit from the media: they transmit their views through the news and orchestrate their images through communications' technology.

The parties illuminate issues and fashion policy alternatives; they hold different views about government, business, social welfare, abortion, gay marriage, and many other issues. The news media do report these differences, thereby enabling people to identify and affiliate with the party that best represents their views. This helps to explain why the parties and their candidates continue to be supported by relatively distinct segments of the electorate.

The Democratic and Republican National Committees are allowed to receive unlimited funds from virtually any U.S. sources and are exempt from the limits on campaign expenditures imposed on candidates. They use some of this money on the panoply of media-based modern campaign technologies: computers, data processing, direct mail, electronic mail, focus groups, political advertising, polling, survey research, and television to promote themselves, their accomplishments, and their candidates.[37]

The Republican party in particular has exploited the opportunities afforded by cable television. Its television channel GOP-TV produces its own television shows, sends news clips to local stations, and provides satellite technology through which Republican members of Congress can beam themselves and their messages to their constituents.

Conventions   The ways in which the parties are adapting to and increasingly exploiting the media, especially television, can best be observed in their quadrennial presidential nominating national conventions. This is when and where the parties are most publicly on display and most intensely covered by the press.

Television coverage customarily conveyed the impression that the conventions were rife with conflict, division, confusion, and disorder. In part this was accurate, but it was also a function of the journalistic and production norms and techniques of the networks' television news departments. These included the thematic approach inherent in the statements of anchors and imperative in the questions posed by floor reporters; the tendency of those responsible for the coverage to juxtapose opposing views on the themes and issues with which the convention was concerned; reporters' interviewing techniques; access (what television could and could not or did not show); visual techniques (including image switching, camera angles, brevity of scenes); and the activities, attitudes, and locations of the anchors.[38]

The Republican 1992 convention had over one hundred speakers representing the party's ideological range. But vituperative speeches in prime time by Patrick Buchanan and Pat Robertson generated an aura of negativism and intolerance. Emphasized by press accounts, this gave the impression of the party as extremist. Arguably, it handicapped President George Bush in his unsuccessful bid for reelection.

In reaction, the Republican 1996 convention was designed to be four nights of television infomercials: carefully scripted, scheduled spontaneity, with conflict and controversy excluded. Although 91 percent of the delegates were white and 64 percent male, the screen seemed filled with images of women, blacks, and babies. The Republican-controlled Congress—whose members had been so rigid the previous winter that they had allowed the government twice to shut down—was called at the convention "The Common-Sense Republican Congress."

Some of the television networks' anchors and reporters complained bitterly about the stage-managed convention. But because they covered the convention for only one hour each on most nights, leaving gavel-to-gavel coverage to C-SPAN and others, they had to show the major speeches and events when they were on the air.

The networks were mired, moreover, in the formula of the past; but delegates were primed to avoid the floor reporters' ploys to elicit controversy. The networks were unable to respond creatively, by, for example, devising ways of showing the contradiction between the convention's moderate public face and many of its provocative platform provisions.

CONCLUSION

Interest groups aim to influence public policies. Thus, how (and whether) they are depicted by the media affects their effectiveness. Common Cause exemplifies media-based success. It achieved favorable coverage in the *New York Times* through its legitimacy, credibility, and media-manipulation techniques and because it met the *Times'* concepts of news, need for information, journalistic norms, and shared values.

Since the heyday of Common Cause, interest groups have increasingly engaged in media advocacy campaigns to facilitate their preferences. They are active at all stages of the policy process, from the appointment of decisionmakers to elections. Their objectives are to stimulate public opinion in their favor and influence policymakers in their interests. Defeat of the Clinton health care proposal strikingly illustrates interest group tactics in action.

Political parties consist of three parts: the party's organization, its electorate, and its members elected to fill government positions. The conventional wisdom is that the parties are in decline and the media are partly responsible. This view may be overstated, for the parties are able to use the media to publicize their views and orchestrate their images.

Notes

1. Caryn James, "Coverage That's Most Unconventional," *New York Times,* 15 August 1996, A14.

2. Classic books on interest groups are Arthur F. Bentley, *The Process of Government,* ed. Peter H. Odegard (Cambridge, Mass.: Harvard University Press, 1967); David B. Truman, *The Governmental Process,* 2nd ed. (New York: Knopf, 1971); and James Q. Wilson, *Political Organizations* (New York: Basic Books, 1973).

3. Jack L. Walker, *Mobilizing Interest Groups in America* (Ann Arbor: University of Michigan Press, 1991).

4. See also Jeffrey M. Berry, *The Interest Group Society,* 3rd ed. (New York: Longman, 1997), 4–5.

5. Ibid., 216.

6. Marian Burros, "Heroes of Nutrition or Just Plain Zealots?" *New York Times,* 29 May 1996, B1.

7. William J. Puette, *Through Jaundiced Eyes: How the Media View Organized Labor* (New York: ILR Press, 1992).

8. Lucig H. Danielian and Benjamin Page, "The Heavenly Chorus: Interest Group Voices on TV News," *American Journal of Political Science* 38:4 (November 1994): 1056; see also Danielian, "Interest Groups in the News," in *Public Opinion, The Press, and Public Policy,* ed. J. David Kennamer (Westport, Conn.: Praeger, 1992), 63–79.

9. See the quotes in Berry, *The Interest Group Society,* 17–18. A typical exposé is Neil A. Lewis with Robert Pear, "U.S. Drug Industry Is Battling Image for Price Gouging," *New York Times,* 7 March 1994, A1.

10. John W. Gardner, "America: Toward New Priorities," *Current* 123 (November 1970): 4.

11. "Nader and Common Cause Become Permanent Fixtures," *Congressional Quarterly* 34:20 (15 May 1976): 1197–1205.

12. Telephone survey conducted by Richard Gibson and Jim Chamberlain for Common Cause between November 1972 and January 1973 (pages unnumbered).

13. James Q. Wilson, *Political Organizations* (New York: Basic Books, 1973), 263.

14. David Adamany, "Money, Politics and Democracy," *American Political Science Review* 71:1 (March 1977): 292.

15. Gerald Pomper, "The Decline of the Party in American Elections," *Political Science Quarterly* 92:1 (Spring 1977): 21–41.

16. Jarol B. Manheim, *Strategic Public Diplomacy and American Foreign Policy* (New York: Oxford University Press, 1994), 9.

17. Jarol B. Manheim and Robert B. Albritton, "Changing National Images," *American Political Science Review* 78:3 (September 1984): 641–57; see also Manheim, *Strategic Public Diplomacy,* 147.

18. For the details that follow, see Jarol B. Manheim, "Strategic Public Diplomacy," in *Taken by Storm,* ed. W. Lance Bennett and David L. Paletz (Chicago: University of Chicago Press, 1994), 131–48; see also Gary Lee, "The Selling of Kuwait Moves Into New Phase," *Washington Post,* 17 March 1991, A25.

19. Art Levine, "Publicists of the Damned," *Spy* 6 (February 1992): 57.

20. Quoted in ibid., 52.

21. Randall Kennedy, "Lani Guinier's Constitution," *The American Prospect* 15 (Fall 1993): 43. This article describes and assesses Guinier's views.

22. For these judgments of the media, see Laurel Leff, "From Legal Scholar to Quota Queen," *Columbia Journalism Review* 32:3 (September-October 1993): 36–41.

23. Karen Branan, "Lani Guinier: The Anatomy of a Betrayal," *MS* 4:2 (September-October 1993): 50–57.

24. Berry, *The Interest Group Society,* 122.

25. Jane Fritsch, "Nature Groups Cite Foes' Friendly Names," *New York Times,* 25 March 1996, A8.

26. Michael Wines, "Tax's Demise Illustrates First Rule of Lobbying: Work, Work, Work," *New York Times,* 14 June 1993, A1.

27. Howard Kurtz, "Take Two Ads and Call Me in the Morning," *Washington Post National Weekly Edition,* 10:26 (April 26-May 2, 1993), 13.

28. Robin Toner, "Gold Rush Fever Grips Capital as Health Care Struggle Begins," *New York Times,* 3 March 1994, A1.

29. Darrell M. West and Richard Francis, "Electronic Advocacy: Interest Groups and Public Policy Making," *PS* 29:1 (March 1996): 25.

30. Elizabeth Kolbert, "New Arena for TV Ads: Health Care," *New York Times,* 21 October 1993, A11.

31. Robin Toner, "Harry and Louise and a Guy Named Ben," *New York Times,* 30 September 1994, A9.

32. Darrell M. West and Diane J. Heith, "Harry and Louise Go to Washington: Political Advertising and Health Care Reform" (paper presented at the annual meeting of the American Political Science Association, New York, September 1994), 9.

33. Frank Rich, "Tin Cans and String," *New York Times,* 13 April 1995, A15.

34. Morris P. Fiorina, *Divided Government* (New York: Macmillan, 1992), 74.

35. For this demographic profile, see the Pew Research Center, "Democrats" and "Republicans" (news release, undated but distributed September 1996).

36. William J. Keefe, *Parties, Politics, and Public Policy in America,* 7th ed. (Washington, D.C.: CQ Press, 1994), 28–29, 49–51, 141–53, 289, 305–08, 311, and 318–20.

37. Adam Clymer, "Both Political Parties Wage Medicare Debate on the Air," *New York Times,* 16 August 1995, A13.

38. David L. Paletz and Martha Elson, "Television Coverage of Presidential Conventions: Now You See It, Now You Don't," *Political Science Quarterly* 91:1 (Spring 1976): 109–31.

Chapter 10

Campaigns and Elections

◆ ◆ ◆

This chapter describes the ways the media are involved in elections and analyzes the consequences for candidates, the electorate, and democracy.[1]

Media content is influential well before the formal election campaign begins. Scenes of President George Bush throwing up at a state dinner in Japan, reportedly expressing amazement at a supermarket checkout scanner, stepping off a golf cart in Maine to veto legislation extending unemployment benefits all conduced to giving the impression of him as being passive on domestic issues and out-of-touch with the concerns of ordinary Americans—and all contributed to the defeat of his reelection bid in 1992.

In contrast, President Clinton spent much of 1995 and 1996 presenting himself through the news media and in a barrage of televised political advertising ($30 million worth) as the protector of popular policies against an extremist Republican Congress. At the same time, he co-opted what had been Republican social issues by outlining his views about and sometimes offering proposals to deal with such subjects as affirmative action, a balanced budget, crime, family values, and school prayer. So that by the time formal campaigning began, he was favorably placed for reelection.[2]

CAMPAIGN ELEMENTS

Money, strategies, and voters are key elements of the campaign process for national and statewide contests. The media are intimately involved with all of them.

Money

"Money is the mother's milk of politics," observed Californian politician Jesse Unruh. Candidates seek to raise as much as they can, as early in the campaign as possible. President Clinton's huge war chest in 1996 probably discouraged potential opponents in his party from challenging him in the primaries. Possessing abundant funds is no guarantee of victory, but insufficient funds can ensure defeat.

Many expenditures are media-related. They pay for focus groups and polls to ascertain people's moods, basic concerns, and opinions about the candidates, identify "hot button" issues provoking a strong response from people; test the appeal and catch the effects of political advertisements; and capture voting intentions. They pay for communicating with the press. Above all, the money goes to hire media specialists, sew up advertising time, and produce and air political advertising.

Strategies

The objective of a campaign is to retain or build a winning combination out of the electorate. This entails emphasizing the candidate's positive aspects, gilding or dissembling about those that are problematic, and playing down the negative ones. There are three main subjects: the candidates' party identification, issues, and image.

The value of party identification is limited as party loyalty has been declining among the electorate. Candidates of the minority party have strong reason to play down their party affiliation. Candidates of the majority party in a district may also tend to minimize their party association, probably because they assume voters know it, and because they and their managers believe issue positions and images to be more important.

Issues can be tricky. Candidates do espouse specific policy positions out of personal conviction, to distinguish themselves from their opponents, particularly if their opponents' views are unpopular, or because the candidates have no way of avoiding their record. They particularly like to stake out a popular position (e.g., longer prison sentences for drug dealers) or claim accomplishments. Otherwise, candidates prefer to invoke issues rhetorically (improve health care) without being too specific in their actual proposals (increase taxes to pay for it).

This helps to explain the prevalence of image in campaigns. Images are the impressions conveyed about a candidate's character, competence, style, and personal life. They are not completely malleable: age, gender, service in the military cannot be changed willy-nilly. But they can be modified, even manipulated, by selective accounting and shrewd presentation of the facts. To wit, Bill Clinton's journey from Arkansas to Georgetown then to Oxford then to Yale universities could be depicted as elitism or as "poor boy" making good.

A successful media campaign strategy, then, involves focusing media and public attention on the subjects and themes thought to favor the candidate and hurt the opponent. It requires constant repetition, known in the trade as "staying on message."

In 1996, "'Clinton's strategy was to duplicate Ronald Reagan's successful re-election campaign of 1984. To float above the fray by 'being Presidential and campaigning as President.'"[3] His themes were the relatively sound economy, reduced budget deficit, and creation of new jobs. He tried to depict Bob Dole as an extremist who had always opposed the progressive policies so dear to many Americans on education, the environment, health, and for senior citizens.

As Bob Dole told his staff a few weeks before the end of his campaign: "We've never had a strategy for winning this election."[4] Dole did attack Clinton for "the largest tax increase in history," for derelictions in the war against drugs, for suppos-

edly weakening defense and, mutedly, for corruption and sleeze. More positively, he proposed a substantial tax cut. But his approach, hardly a strategy, seemed to be to run as the "anti-Clinton . . . seeking to turn into assets his liabilities—his age, his inarticulateness, his determinedly undramatic pragmatism, his shyness, his old-fashionnedness—while reminding voters of what they do not like about Clinton: his adolescent self-indulgences, his talkiness, his overpromising, his slickness."[5]

Voters

People decide whether and for whom to vote on some combination of candidates' party identification, issue positions and images, plus their evaluations of how candidates have done in the past and are likely to do in the future.[6]

Much of this information comes from the media. As chapter 5 discussed, people receive media content differently. They bring their predispositions to it. They react to it with selective exposure and selective perception. They variously ignore, embrace, accept, and subvert it.

Nonetheless, in elections, media content can be particularly influential on the decisions of people whose support of a candidate is relatively lukewarm, those who are undecided or uncertain, and the indifferent. It can be crucial for primaries and nonpartisan elections, where the party doesn't cue voters; or in general elections when, as with Ross Perot in 1992, a well-funded candidate tries to disrupt the usual two-party contest.

MEDIA INVOLVEMENT

The media's involvement in campaigns is little regulated. Section 312 of the Federal Communications Act prohibits broadcasters from rejecting all paid and non-paid appearances by candidates for federal (and arguably state and local) offices. Section 315 requires that broadcasters affording access to one candidate must do so for all other legally qualified candidates. However, candidates' appearances in newscasts and spot news, interview programs, and peripherally in news documentaries do not count. And candidates afforded access do not necessarily have the funds to pay for it.

The media are actually involved in American elections in four different although at times overlapping ways, depending on the extent to which the candidates control their contents. The contents in all four forms are explicitly political, placing them in the first two categories specified in chapter one (i.e., explicit and intentional content and explicit and unintentional content).

Candidates lack any control over the first form which is *media-originated* humor and commentary: how they are mocked on Comedy Central, the jokes of Jay Leno and David Letterman, the parodies of "Saturday Night Live." In 1996, these portrayed an ancient and nasty Bob Dole, a slick and duplicitous Bill Clinton.

Nor do the candidates have much influence over the comments of "The McLaughlin Group" and its ilk, columnists, and pundits. Yet commentary can have profound electoral effects, particularly when it emanates from the unabashedly partisan hosts of talk radio. Led by Rush Limbaugh, this predominantly conservative group spurred the Republican congressional victories in 1994 by mobilizing their listeners who "are more conservative and Republican, more negative toward government, and more participatory than nonlisteners."[7]

Newspapers' editorial endorsements of particular candidates for office are a species of commentary. While endorsements are most common for presidential elections, they are more influential when they come from elite media and are for lower level offices, primaries, or nonpartisan elections in which voters have fewer cues to guide them.

Putting media-originated content aside, this chapter concentrates on the three other types of media involvement: mostly mediated, partly mediated, and unmediated.

Mostly mediated coverage consists of news reports of what happens during the campaign. Here, the media ultimately determine the content, although candidates and their campaign advisors naturally strive mightily to influence it.

Interviews, nominating conventions, and debates are *partly mediated* because in these situations candidates have considerable but not complete control over the presentation and content of their pronouncements. While theoretically able to say what they want, they may be limited or affected by the format, questions asked, and the retorts of the other candidates.

Political advertisements and the like are *unmediated* because the media serve merely as their conduits; the candidates' messages reach the public unmarred by comments at the time from the press.[8]

Mostly Mediated Contents

Under the mostly mediated category are the amount of attention, foci, the candidates' media influence tactics, and the news media's early projections of election results. Because the focus is on news in general, the differences in content among elite, prestige, popular, and tabloid forms spelled out in chapter 3 tend to be blurred in this discussion.

Attention to Campaigns   Media coverage of campaigns varies depending on the type of and phase of the election, with discernible effects. For example, the early presidential primaries are given disproportionate importance by the excessive news coverage bestowed upon them (and upon the Iowa caucuses when relevant). This "front-loading" opens the contest to relatively unknown candidates who hope they can do well in an early contest (Jimmy Carter in 1976, Bill Clinton in 1992). But it also closes the nomination more quickly, since aspirants who do not meet the benchmarks for success set by reporters, pundits, and prognosticators (criteria often disputed by the candidates and their managers) in most cases lose their electoral credibility and viability.[9] Yet, "were it not for the media, the Iowa caucus and New Hampshire primary results would be about as relevant to the presidential nomination as opening-day baseball scores are to a pennant race."[10]

Media attention to campaigns for the U.S. House of Representatives varies according to the size of the media markets, the shape of the district, and the competitiveness of the race. Because their media markets often contain a large number of congressional districts, major television stations do not devote much time to any single district race. Congressional districts that snake across several media markets without dominating any of them have to have a competitive race to be covered.

In media-congruent districts, voters are more likely to report contact with and recognize the names of the candidates. Challengers in such districts can "overcome the exposure gap associated with the incumbency advantage."[11] But campaigns with an apparently entrenched incumbent and a weak challenger are unlikely to draw much media notice even in small markets or where the district dominates the market; the challenger's defeat becomes a self-fulfilling prophecy.

Because of such media inattention, incumbents usually have a substantial advantage over their challengers because they acquire coverage through their official duties. In both House and Senate elections, for example, most stories of incumbents deal with their political attributes, those of challengers with campaign events.[12]

Of course, if the voters are in an anti-incumbent mood, as was the case in 1994, incumbents can actually suffer from news media coverage of their official duties and attributes, especially if the news relates their involvement in scandals and outrages, or depicts the institution in which they serve as ineffectual and incompetent.

Foci   In stark contrast to the wide variance in the amount of coverage given to campaigns, the contents of coverage are relatively consistent across the different races and levels of media. Journalists tend to focus on the horse race (who among

the viable candidates is winning and losing), tactics and strategy, conflict and controversy, scandal, and images—and to imbed them in dramatic themes (the front runner faltering, the underdog catching up).

Horse race stories are pervasive. Advances in polling technology have made it easier for the media to report which candidates are ahead and doing better or worse than the reporters and pundits expect.

Indeed, polls are a prominent feature of media election coverage. In the early primaries, the reporting and interpretation of the polls can shape voters' expectations of how candidates should fare. Candidates who meet or exceed predictions can build momentum, often attracting more news coverage. Potential campaign

Doonesbury © 1982, G. B. Trudeau. Reprinted with permission of Universal Press Syndicate. All rights reserved.

contributors, who are more likely to give money to a winner, may be influenced by this type of coverage. General election polls showing a candidate way behind can undermine the campaign, as Bob Dole found out to his frustration in 1996.

Journalists for the elite press increasingly go beyond the horse race to analyze candidates' campaign strategy and tactics. Coverage is often cynical and negative. Studies indicate that negative coverage has increased since 1960, and in 1992 unfavorable stories (excluding horse race reports) made up the majority of coverage for each of the three major presidential candidates.[13]

But categorizing stories as unfavorable-neutral-favorable is far more complicated than commonly appreciated. Moreover, even if the incidence of unfavorability is as high as claimed, it is important to explain why—it may sometimes be more attributable to the candidates' discourse and accusations than to the reporters' intent.

Campaign coverage is also littered with stories of scandal: allegations of misconduct in office, accusations of extramarital affairs, and the like. The media's seemingly insatiable desire for scandal—often of a very personal nature, not always based on substantial evidence, and arguably tangential to a candidate's qualifications for office—has been criticized for distracting candidates and voters from the important issues and problems facing the country. It has been justified as reporters' duty aggressively to scrutinize candidates. It has been explained as stemming from the tabloidization of journalism by which the regular press reports charges once they have appeared in the tabloids.

Candidates' Tactics   Many candidates rely heavily on political consultants to advise them how to obtain coverage (favorable if possible) from the news media; that is, how to accommodate, if not pander to, journalists' news-gathering and reporting needs. Thus, they stage media events and photo opportunities (photo-ops) constructed to attract coverage, dominate the campaign agenda, reinforce their campaign issues, and convey the "right" image.

Some efforts are successful. Pictures of President Clinton surrounded by uniformed policemen as he was endorsed by the nation's largest police union made irresistible television news during the 1996 campaign. Not coincidentally, they also upstaged a major speech and television ads by Senator Bob Dole attacking the president on the very subject of crime.

Other efforts fall flat. A Bob Dole photo-op at a festive waterfront rally was ruined by the appearance of fifteen scantily clad women hanging over a railing watching the rally. Dole was speaking outside a Hooters restaurant.[14]

Candidates' statements are often tailored, especially for television. They have little choice. The networks' evening newscasts have cut down on the amount of air time they allow candidates to express their views. As Kiku Adatto found: "The average 'sound bite,' or bloc of uninterrupted speech, fell from 42.3 seconds for presidential candidates in 1968 to only 9.8 seconds in 1988."[15] While 1992 started out larger, the average sound bite size declined in the last few weeks of the campaign to 8.9 seconds.[16]

So candidates talk in brief sound bites and catchy one-liners, and rely on simple slogans to communicate their messages. In 1980, Ronald Reagan, challenging incumbent President Jimmy Carter, asked the public, "Are you better off now than you were four years ago?" In 1984, as president, he successfully asked the same question about his own record. In 1992, George Bush initially ran on a theme of "family values" that included numerous appearances with families, while the Clinton campaign revolved around the mantra, "It's the economy, stupid," against a backdrop of factories facing layoffs and communities with high unemployment. In 1996, Clinton claimed credit for the improved economy of relatively low unemployment and low inflation.

Bowing to the media's preference for simplicity and clear-cut positions, the need to get their messages through to the electorate, and from their own inclinations, candidates usually avoid discussing detailed solutions to problems. Rather,

BLOOM COUNTY by Berke Breathed

© 1984, Washington Post Writers Group. Reprinted with permission.

they offer broad approaches with little mention of the costs or the feasibility of their proposals.

This tactic contributes to the relative dearth of detailed coverage of substantive issues as candidates often find it easier to distinguish themselves from their opponents in terms of character and competence and tangential topics than on complex or difficult issues about which they hold similar views or lack clear solutions.

News Media's Influence   So candidates and their advisors try to shape news coverage and commentary in their favor, to press the validity of their themes and frames on reporters. Indeed, in a presidential election, the interaction between journalists and the campaign consultants and staff is perpetual and intense.[17] But regardless of how shrewd a candidate's tactics are, the news media still maintain an advantage as observers, reporters, and sometimes critics of campaigns.

Ultimately, it is the reporters and editors not the candidates who decide on the emphases of news coverage of the election, who can even set the agenda of issues dominating public attention.[18]

In so doing they are liable to help or harm particular candidates. Commenting on coverage of the 1992 campaign, former President Bush observed: "'After the election, the media started having seminars on 'Were we fair to George Bush?' I don't think they would have held the seminars if they didn't know the answer.'"[19] In 1996, Bob Dole was even more vociferous about the press, especially the *New York Times*.

Deliberate, intentional reporting bias is uncommon in most prominent elections.[20] Favorability arises, instead, from reporters' choices of which news topics to emphasize. (See discussion of priming and framing in chapter 7.) In 1992, Clinton benefitted by the story appeal of a likely new presidency. Bush suffered from reports of his campaign's disorganization, as well as from the abundance of economy stories, inevitably negative, reminding people of conditions for which he was (perhaps unfairly) being blamed.[21] In 1996, the campaign narrative was "hapless Dole versus the Clinton juggernaut."[22] But when this narrative was partially eclipsed towards the end of the campaign by news of questionable donations to the Clinton campaign, it was the president who suffered and whose lead slipped.

Pack journalism—in which reporters follow the leads of elite journalists on the beat, in this case, the campaign trail, as to what is the newsworthy story—encourages and facilitates such thematic and framing coverage.[23] No wonder Clinton advisor James Carville described the power of the news media as "staggering," reporting that his staff dubbed them "The Beast."[24]

The news media's influence continues through election day. Through exit polls of voters, the television networks are often able to project (actually predict) election results shortly after, sometimes even before, the polls close. This may influence turnout and voting decisions, particularly in the West where, because of the time difference, the polls are still open after they have closed in the East. Outrage is periodically expressed at this state of affairs, especially by losing local and state candidates out West, and caution has sometimes been shown by newscasters, but definitive effects are hard to document, and the situation persists.

Partly Mediated Contents

The partly mediated category encompasses such forums as nominating conventions, debates, talk shows, and town meetings. These forums provide candidates with the opportunity to communicate directly with the public, even if they are somewhat limited in what they can say by the format and by other participants.

The partly mediated forum has considerable appeal to candidates. It enables them temporarily to bypass the press; that is, to avoid having their statements framed or analyzed by journalists before they reach the public. When they respond to questions, their messages may be greeted with less skepticism and suspicion than their advertisements over which they have complete control.

Conventions   As discussed in chapter 9, nominating conventions are one form of partly mediated forum. Depending on how much control candidates and convention managers exercise over the proceedings, conventions can come across on television as coronations at one extreme or barroom brawls at the other. As evidence, compare the Republican unity convention of 1996 with its fractious predecessor. Control can boomerang: The 1996 Democratic convention seemed so regimented and scripted that it lost all semblance of spontaneity.

Debates   Debates have become a staple of primaries and general elections. Challengers and underdogs can be particularly benefitted. Ross Perot gained visibility, legitimacy, even equality, by appearing on the same platform as the incumbent and leading challenger in 1992; his exclusion in 1996 partly accounts for the decline in his vote.[25]

So rather than candidates directly refusing to debate, their representatives joust over format: selection of moderator and questioning journalists, length of answers, height of podium, camera positions, and much more. These are not proforma issues: Candidates are vulnerable to debate depictions, as Richard Nixon discovered in 1960 when camera cutaways showed him sweating profusely and wiping his brow while John Kennedy answered questions.

Debates supposedly consist of candidates' responses to questions about the issues confronting the country, with references to their policy actions and proposals, past behavior, and character. But other elements, such as likability, can be significant. Dale Leathers observed about 1988 Democratic candidate Michael Dukakis, "His body posture was erect, immobile, and seemingly tense. His infrequent gestures were subdued and restrained, his arms were close into his sides, there were no forward leans, and he rarely smiled when a smile would be justified." Emotionally unexpressive, cold and unfriendly, Dukakis spoke with a narrow pitch and range.[26] Compare this to Bill Clinton's practiced ease, physical and vocal expressiveness, and embracing body movement in the 1992 and 1996 debates.

Journalists, abetted by candidates' representatives, frame expectations before the debate. Their postdebate coverage usually revolves around the question, "Who won?" More than the substance of answers, such judgments are a function of the predebate expectations, dramatic moments, candidates' gaffes, and memorable lines (usually practiced although seeming spontaneous), as with the elderly Ronald Reagan quipping in 1984 that he would not hold his opponent's relative youth and inexperience against him.

Even before a debate ends, the candidates' spokespersons are "spinning" the press, giving "reasons" why their candidate did better than the opponent. They realize the importance of journalists' judgments.[27] According to James Lemert and colleagues, postdebate analysis is "the strongest debate-related influence on performance impressions."[28]

Given that viewers differ by predisposition, partisanship, and perspectives, definitive debate victories—in the sense of shifting large numbers of voters from one side to the other—are rare. Slightly more common is for a candidate to reassure the uncertain and undecided that he is presidential or at least an acceptable risk, as Ronald Reagan did in his 1980 debate with President Jimmy Carter. But usually, winning consists of reinforcing the support of tentative supporters and retaining wavering partisans.

Talk Shows   Led by Clinton, the 1992 U.S. presidential election featured an explosion of partly mediated appearances far beyond anything seen in previous campaigns. There were several different, albeit overlapping, types on television. On the morning news/feature shows, such as "Today" on NBC and "Good Morning America" on ABC, questioning by a host is sometimes probing but usually genteel, predictable, and constrained by lack of time. In late-night entertainment shows, the candidate chats and may perform with a supportive host. Interview/call-in shows often treat the candidate as a celebrity.

Clinton and Perot shrewdly entered into the partially mediated format (e.g., on MTV), ultimately followed by Bush, to find and engage the audience they could not reach any other way. Also, faced with the reality of a more adversarial press that wanted to avoid being manipulated as it had been in 1988, they sought direct television exposure and interaction with voters without undue interference from journalists.

Talk shows give candidates a chance to discuss, usually on their terms, issues on people's minds. Less concerned than journalists with appearances of objectivity, and less knowledgeable about the issues, talk show hosts are often willing to let candidates respond to questions without interrupting or contesting each comment. The atmosphere is, on balance, less combative than interviews with journalists or hard news shows—and more controllable: For example, to induce President Bush to appear on the show, an MTV reporter agreed not to ask questions about the Iran-Contra affair. And while journalists tend to ask about horse race issues, strategy, and controversy, talk show hosts and their audiences generally ask more policy and problem-oriented questions.

Unmediated Contents

Media content is unmediated when the candidates and their political consultants control its content and placement, thereby using the media as a conduit for their self-serving messages. Examples are billboards, bumper stickers, and the campaign videos and audios featuring the candidate that are sent to possible contributors and supporters. Computer home pages, discussed in chapter 16, are the latest innovation.

The monarch of unmediated contents is political advertising.[29] Ads usually run thirty seconds, although in 1992 some Clinton ads lasted only fifteen seconds and, in contrast, Ross Perot showed that he could attract a sizable audience to his half-hour infomercials. Protected by the free speech clause of the First Amendment to the U.S. Constitution, the ads face few regulations of their content and accuracy. True, candidates can sue for defamation, but such suits are uncommon, rarely heard by the courts during the election campaign, and usually settled quietly after the election is over.

Advertising expenditures keep going up. In 1992, the three major presidential candidates each spent between $40 million and $50 million—two-thirds to three-fourths of their entire general election budgets—on campaign commercials.[30] In 1996, the Clinton-Gore campaign and the Democratic National Committee spent roughly $85 million on a saturation television advertising campaign that began running in swing states in mid-1995, well before the campaign officially started.[31]

Despite its costs, political advertising is considered essential for national (including congressional) and statewide elections. There are three main reasons.

First, crucially, the candidate's message is not interrupted, interpreted, analyzed, or dissected by journalists at the time it is aired. The candidates and their media consultants have complete discretion over the content of their commercials.

Second, advertising can be targeted. By the strategic choice of station, time, and program placement, ads can be tailored for and directed at particular segments of the public (e.g., retired persons, white voters, women, evangelicals). Ads on cable television and radio cost less and reach even more specific audiences.

Third, many candidates and media consultants believe that effective advertising, especially when done early (even a year before election day) and deployed as part of a media blitz strategy coordinated with news, can make the difference between victory and defeat in most reasonably competitive constituencies. Better to advertise than be sorry; to reach those who lack alternative sources of information about the candidates; to try to sway the uncommitted, comparatively disinterested people.

Adding to their effectiveness, ads are often screened by focus groups and revised as deemed necessary before being aired. Then, nightly tracking polls may be used to monitor how well they are working. New ads can be rapidly devised, tested, and deployed to respond to those of the opponent that are having an effect.

Process   Conventional political advertising campaigns often follow a four-stage process. It starts with the establishment of a foundation: identification, biographical ads favorably characterizing the candidate's background, qualifications, and vision of America. Next come arguments telling people why they should vote for the candidate. These are followed by attack ads telling people why they should not vote for the opponent. Last is a wrap-up, summing up the campaign with positive, feel-good ads.[32]

The most effective ads capitalize on (canalize), rather than create, moods, beliefs, and prejudices already present in the electorate. Thus, while many ads may be made, in the end, "the best presidential campaigns air no more than two dozen spots with about a dozen becoming the prominent core spots."[33]

Formats   There are multifarious possible formats for ads. But even now, when glitzy techniques abound, one of the most common is the talking head in which the candidate speaks directly to viewers. Its object is to demonstrate such desirable qualities as trust and competence as the candidate feelingly addresses an issue. Armed with his self-confident demeanor, familiarity with the television camera, mellifluous voice, and clear position on a few key issues (cut the budget, increase defense spending), Ronald Reagan effectively used such ads in 1980 to reassure voters that he was qualified to be president.

Other formats include testimonial spots from prominent or ordinary people or family (spouse included) and friends enthusiastically supporting the candidate or condemning the opponent; feel-good spots such as the "Morning in America" ones deployed for President Reagan's reelection campaign in 1984; and "compare and contrast" in which the candidate's assuredly popular record on an issue is compared with the assumedly unpopular view or action of his opponent.

Documentary ads utilizing actual footage involving the candidate or those close to him can be quite effective, as in 1992 when pictures of a teenage Clinton shaking President John F. Kennedy's hand linked him with the Kennedy legacy (or myth).

A relatively recent innovation, facilitated by videotape and adroit editing, is self-incrimination of the opponent. The Clinton campaign used the technique in 1992 with ads juxtaposing George Bush making upbeat comments about the improving economy against data showing it worsening. Deviously, "some of the clips were presented out of sequence to the events they were intended to illustrate."[34] Another ad showed the president making his no-new-taxes pledge, while graphics and a voice-over announced that he had reneged on his promise. This self-incrimination technique is likely to become more prevalent in the future, used especially against incumbents.

Techniques   Ads are able to deploy the panoply of cinematic visual and sound techniques. Camera distance (tight close-ups can be unflattering), camera angles (camera looking up makes an individual seem more powerful), camera movement, editing (showing people looking at a candidate with adoration or disgust), and use of color (blue reassures, red threatens) all influence people's reactions. Music and sounds establish moods; appropriately voiced narration (harsh if negative, soft if positive) and voice-overs (Clinton narrated his 60-second biographical documentary called "Hope" featuring the Kennedy sequence) all conduce to ads' effects.

Now, there is also "morphing," a technique for electronically changing and blending photographs and other visuals. One use of morphing is to merge the opponent into an unpopular figure. For example, in 1994 Republican ads, several Democratic candidates were "morphed" into a menacing Bill Clinton; in 1996 Democratic ads, many Republican congressional candidates were morphed into a threatening Newt Gingrich.

Ads often rely heavily on visuals, symbols, slogans, and sometimes innuendo in an attempt to catch and hold viewers' attention and remain in their memories. The more compelling the visual, the more likely the ad is to influence people's voting decisions. In 1996, a Clinton ad "featured an EKG machine monitoring a patient's heartbeat as the announcer describes the premium increases and benefit cuts the Republicans planned for Medicare. Finally, the comforting beeps stop, and we hear the terrifying, continuous monotone and see the flat line on the screen that means Medicare has died."[35] Other examples are a woman in a red dress deploring a candidate's support of abortion; a white male crumpling up a black-marked letter telling him that he lost out on a job to a less-qualified minority applicant, with the dire consequences of family starvation implied by his patently visible wedding ring.

© *1987, Washington Post Writers Group. Reprinted with permission.*

Attack Ads   The previous three examples are attack or negative ads (benignly called "comparative" ads by the candidates issuing them), a prominent feature of many campaigns.[36] They emanate in particular from challengers and from incumbents vulnerable to defeat. In 1992, for example, 63 percent of Clinton's and 56 percent of Bush's most prominent ads were negative.[37] The objective of such ads is to discourage people from voting for the opponent. They thus attempt to publicize and denounce negative aspects (or ones that can be depicted negatively) of the opponent's character, behavior, record, and positions on particular issues.[38]

Among the types of such ads are "flip-flops" that expose apparent contradictions in the opponent's voting record and public statements; "not on the job" denunciations of the opponent's supposedly derelict attendance and voting record; "arrogance" manifested by junkets and pay raises; and "guilt-by-association," in which the opponent is linked to an unpopular organization or individual.

Attack ads are often condemned as mud-slinging (wallowing) or dirty politics. But negativity is not unknown in American political history. Thomas Jefferson was accused of being an atheist radical; Andrew Jackson of being an adulterer, bigamist, and murderer; Grover Cleveland of fathering an illegitimate child.[39] Not all these charges lacked substance. Besides, given the limitations of news coverage of most elections, it is often only the attack ads that bring the derelictions of a candidate's opponent to public attention.

People may dislike and object to, but they also remember, and are influenced by, attack ads.[40] But attacks must be credible or they will backfire, as did the ones accusing an elderly senatorial candidate of being soft on child pornography. Credible is not, of course, the same as truthful.[41]

Some of the most effective attack ads were deployed by Roger Ailes for George Bush in 1988 against Michael Dukakis. Based on focus group research, the ads dealt with topics that resonated with people Bush needed to win over but who favored his opponent. They allied misleading language to powerful and memorable images: for example, a revolving, metal-bars door out of which evil-looking male "criminals" (two of the most conspicuous being black) were freed allegedly through the ineptitude of Dukakis (as the spoken and written language implied) to wreak havoc on unsuspecting Americans. They repeated the same theme: "America can't afford that risk."

Bush's ads were aired for several weeks without response from Dukakis. Unanswered, they gained credibility. They thus *defined* the otherwise little known Dukakis for the voters before he defined himself. The reluctance of Dukakis initially to use negative spots against Bush, and the ineffectiveness of such ads when they were finally deployed, further handicapped the Democratic candidate. In 1992, in contrast, the Clinton campaign responded immediately to attacks against the candidate with rebuttal ads and by fax and e-mail to reporters.

Among the ways candidates try to combat attack ads—aside from denial, explanation, and apology—are "preemption," "reversal," "shame on you," and "rebuttal." Preemption ads entail anticipating an attack, responding in advance, hoping to inoculate voters. So, advertisements for a North Dakota incumbent senator, 80-year-old Quentin Burdick, showed him as physically vigorous and wielding influence on Capitol Hill.

In reversal ads, a candidate's weakness is asserted as a strength. Wisconsin Senate candidate Herb Kohl, who spent almost $9 million, most of it his own money, during his campaign, claimed that such spending made him independent of special interests and campaign contributions.[42]

Shame-on-you ads feature the victim of the initial attack, or a surrogate, sadly denouncing the charge as variously unworthy of the attacker and his or her illustrious forebears, sullying the campaign, and demeaning the voters. Rebuttal ads deny the accuracy of the attack and point out its supposed distortions.

The problem with all four modes of response is that they repeat the original charge, prolonging its visibility. So candidates often respond to an attack ad with attack ads designed to expose the opponent as having committed even worse sins.

News Coverage of Ads   Some television news programs and newspapers provide ad watches that look at candidates' ads in an effort to determine their truthfulness. These analyses sometimes result in the withdrawal of the offending ad. They may also be invoked by the other candidate to denigrate the perpetrator's unscrupulousness.

Ironically, however, ad watches may increase the commercials' visibility and even their influence. Reporters analyze the ads as part of candidates' strategies, adopt the language of the spots, and show the visuals in their news stories. Focus group research indicates that just the images and labels from portions of ads are sufficient to evoke the entire ad.[43]

CONCLUSION

Candidates' election strategy involves focusing media and public attention on the subjects and themes thought to favor them and hurt the opponent. The media are central to this effort. So candidates and their advisors try to control media content as much as possible. This is hard to do with media-originated material.

Candidates are able to deploy an assortment of techniques and tactics (media events, photo-ops, and sound bites) to try to influence mostly mediated content but, in the end journalists decide what makes up the news. This often consists of unfavorable stories about scandals, gaffes, and the like.

Candidates are more comfortable with partly mediated content over which they exercise considerable control.

Unmediated political advertising is candidates' ultimate weapon. It enables them to control their messages and to transmit them directly to the public. Besides, political advertisements have effects: based on a wide-ranging survey and study, Darrell West concludes that unmediated political advertising has a significant impact on political learning, agenda-setting, priming, and defusing (de-emphasizing other issues). In sum, "commercials influence how voters learn about the candidates . . . what they identify as priorities . . . their standards of assessment . . . and attribution of blame."[44] However, exposure to negative ads can decrease intentions to vote. This "demobilizing" effect is accompanied by a weakened sense of political efficacy, meaning an increase in cynicism about the responsiveness to the popular will of public officials and the electoral process.[45]

So, the question is whether the media provide voters with adequate and sufficient information to make their voting decisions. Certainly, many Americans can be woefully ignorant about topics and issues. Even in 1992, a nationwide survey conducted a month before the election showed that only 32 percent could correctly answer any of twenty-one factual questions about the candidates and the issues.[46]

For Samuel Popkin, the media do not deny the public the ability to make informed decisions.[47] Using what he calls low-information rationality, voters can make inferences about candidates' performance and positions based on the personality conveyed and the images and labels used about them. While these inferences are derived from stereotypes, they generally prove accurate enough to permit voters to make rational voting choices. Besides, people who want to use them have ample founts of information. C-SPAN, Public Broadcasting's "The NewsHour with Jim Lehrer," National Public Radio's news programs, and various opinion magazines provide analyses and discussions of candidates' plans and proposals.

On the other side is Thomas Patterson, who has trenchantly albeit polemically critiqued what he views as the degradation of the modern campaign caused in part by the media's emphasis on the negative, trivial, and sensational. He contends that such campaigns are antipolitics and mislead voters about their choices.[48]

Election campaigns are a confluence of the words and actions of candidates, media, and citizens. Under propitious circumstances, as in 1992, they can on balance enhance democracy. In 1996, with the economy stable and the country at peace, with an incumbent president taking no risks and a challenger waging an inept campaign, with the news media appearing to be going through the motions as their polls showed little movement, and with a public apparently disinterested in overly familiar candidates, democracy was not served.

Notes

1. Informative case studies of the media in the 1992 presidential election are Marion R. Just et al., *Crosstalk* (Chicago: University of Chicago Press, 1996); James B. Lemert et al., *The Politics of Disenchantment* (Cresskill, N.J.: Hampton Press, 1996); and Kathleen E. Kendall, ed., *Presidential Campaign Discourse* (Albany: State University of New York Press, 1995).

2. Dick Morris, *Behind the Oval Office* (New York: Random House, 1997), 138–53, 277; see also Michael Kelly, "This Year's Model," *New Yorker* 72:16 (17 June 1996): 45–49.

3. White House Communications Director Donald Baer, quoted in Ken Auletta, "Inside Story," *New Yorker* 72:35 (18 November 1996), 45.

4. Adam Nagourney and Elizabeth Kolbert, "Missteps Doomed Dole From the Start," *New York Times,* 8 November 1996, C18.

5. Michael Kelly, "Accentuate the Negative," *New Yorker* 72:6 (1 April 1996), 46.

6. For a discussion of voting determinants, see John Boiney and David L. Paletz, "In Search of the Model Model: Political Science Versus Political Advertising Perspectives on Voter Decision Making," in *Television and Political Advertising*, vol. 1, ed. Frank Biocca (Hillsdale, N.J.: Lawrence Erlbaum, 1991), 3–25.

7. Louis Bolce, Gerald de Maio, and Douglas Muzzio, "Dial-In Democracy: Talk Radio and the 1994 Election," *Political Science Quarterly* 111:3 (Fall 1996): 477.

8. See Judith S. Trent and Robert V. Friedenberg, *Political Campaign Communication* (New York: Praeger, 1991), for an overview of campaigns. For an assessment of the relative influence on voters of political advertising, television and newspaper news, public opinion polls, and debates, see Diana Owen, *Media Messages in American Presidential Elections* (New York: Greenwood, 1991).

9. Exemplified by the fate of Democratic presidential candidate Larry Agran in 1992, as Joshua Meyrowitz documents in "Visible and Invisible Candidates: A Case Study in 'Competing Logics' of Campaign Coverage," *Political Communication* 11:2 (April-June 1994): 145–64.

10. The phrase is Professor Robert Entman's, see our *Media Power Politics* (New York: Free Press, 1981), 36.

11. Timothy S. Prinz, "Media Markets and Candidate Awareness in House Elections, 1978–1990," *Political Communication* 12:3 (July-September 1995): 305.

12. Peter Clarke and Susan H. Evans, *Covering Campaigns: Journalism in Congressional Elections* (Stanford: Stanford University Press, 1983), 61–62.

13. Thomas E. Patterson, *Out of Order* (New York: Knopf, 1993), 6, 20.

14. Adam Nagourney, "Disorders of All Kinds Plague Dole Campaign," *New York Times,* 25 October 1996, A1, A11.

15. Kiku Adatto, "Sound Bite Democracy: Network Evening News Presidential Campaign Coverage, 1968 and 1988" (Research Paper R-2, Harvard University, The Joan Shorenstein Barone Center, June 1990) 4; see also Daniel C. Hallin, "Sound Bite News: Television Coverage of Elections, 1968–1988," *Journal of Communication* 42:2 (Spring 1992): 5–24.

16. From a study by the Center for Media and Public Affairs, cited in "Sound Bite Nibbled Away," *New York Times*, 31 October 1992, 8A.

17. For a typical example, see Mary Matalin, James Carville, with Peter Knobler, *All's Fair: Love, War, and Running for President* (New York: Random House, 1994), 255–56.

18. For the importance of the U.S. press in setting election agendas, see Holli A. Semetko et al., *The Formation of Campaign Agendas: A Comparative Analysis of Party and Media Roles in Recent American and British Elections* (Hillsdale, N.J.: Lawrence Erlbaum, 1991); and David H. Weaver et al., *Media Agenda-Setting in a Presidential Election* (New York: Praeger, 1981).

19. "Quote/Unquote," *International Herald Tribune*, 25 May 1993, 3.

20. An informative, insightful study of the level of objectivity and fairness in CBS and UPI coverage of the 1980 presidential election is Michael J. Robinson and Margaret A. Sheehan, *Over the Wire and on TV* (New York: Russell Sage Foundation, 1983); see also Guido Stempel and John Windhauser, *The Media in the 1984 and 1988 Presidential Campaigns* (New York: Greenwood 1991).

21. Jeffrey L. Katz, "Tilt," *Washington Journalism Review* 15:1 (January-February 1993), 23–27.

22. Ken Auletta, "Inside Story," *New Yorker* 72:35 (18 November 1996), 56.

23. On television news and the candidates in 1992, see Tom Rosenstiel, *Strange Bedfellows* (New York: Hyperion, 1993).

24. Matalin, Carville, and Knobler, *All's Fair*, 185.

25. For "The History, Impact, and Prospects of American Presidential Debates," see David J. Lanoue and Peter R. Schrott, *The Joint Press Conference* (New York: Greenwood, 1991); see also Sidney Kraus, *Televised Presidential Debates and Public Policy* (Hillsdale, N.J.: Lawrence Erlbaum, 1988); and Robert V. Friedenberg, ed., *Rhetorical Studies of National Political Debates: 1960–1988* (New York: Praeger, 1990).

26. Dale G. Leathers, "George Bush as Impression Manager: Fighting the Wimp Factor" (paper presented at the annual meeting of the International Communication Association, Dublin, Ireland, June 1990), 30, 32.

27. Diana Owen, "The Debate Challenge," in *Presidential Campaign Discourse*, ed. Kathleen E. Kendall (Albany: State University of New York Press, 1995), 135–55.

28. James B. Lemert et al., *News Verdicts, the Debates, and Presidential Campaigns* (New York: Praeger, 1991), 256.

29. For an entertaining overview of political advertising, see Edwin Diamond and Stephen Bates, *The Spot*, 3rd ed. (Cambridge, Mass.: MIT Press, 1992). Kathleen Hall Jamieson offers a detailed history and occasional criticism of presidential campaign advertising in *Packaging the Presidency*, 2nd ed. (New York: Oxford University Press, 1992), and a detailed description of ads' information structures in *Dirty Politics*

(New York: Oxford University Press, 1992). Also very useful is Montague Kern, *30-Second Politics* (New York: Praeger, 1989). A comparative survey of the use of political advertising, broadly defined, is Lynda Lee Kaid and Christina Holtz-Bacha, eds., *Political Advertising in Western Democracies* (Thousand Oaks, Calif.: Sage 1994); also relevant are Lynda Lee Kaid, Dan Nimmo, and Keith R. Sanders, eds., *New Perspectives on Political Advertising* (Carbondale: Southern Illinois University Press, 1986); and Dorothy Davidson Nesbit, *Videostyle* (Knoxville: University of Tennessee Press, 1988).

30. L. Patrick Devlin. "Contrasts in Presidential Campaign Commercials of 1992," *American Behavioral Scientist* 37:2 (November-December 1993): 272–73.

31. Morris, *Behind the Oval Office.*

32. Diamond and Bates, *The Spot;* see also Karen S. Johnson-Cartee and Gary A. Copeland, *Manipulation of the American Voter* (Westport, Conn.: Praeger, 1997).

33. Devlin, in Kaid and Holtz-Bacha, *Political Advertising,* 374.

34. Andrew Rosenthal, "Day of Brawling for Presidential Camps," *New York Times,* 21 September 1992, A12.

35. Morris, *Behind the Oval Office,* 151.

36. Karen S. Johnson-Cartee and Gary A. Copeland, *Negative Political Advertising: Coming of Age* (Hillsdale, N.J.: Lawrence Erlbaum, 1991); see also Lynda Lee Kaid and Anne Johnston, "Negative Versus Positive Television Advertising in U.S. Presidential Campaigns, 1960–1980," *Journal of Communication* 41:3 (Summer 1991): 53–64.

37. L. Patrick Devlin, "Contrasts in Presidential Campaign Commercials of 1992," *American Behavioral Scientist* 37:2 (November-December 1993): 288.

38. Michael Pfau and Henry C. Kenski, *Attack Politics* (New York: Praeger, 1990).

39. Paul F. Boller, Jr., *Presidential Campaigns* (New York: Oxford University Press, 1984), 44–46.

40. Johnson-Cartee and Copeland, *Negative Political Advertising.*

41. For ingenious experimental research showing that some ads are not only misleading, they can actually deceive some viewers into accepting their false conclusions, see John Boiney, "Deception in Political Advertising" (Ph.D. diss., Department of Political Science, Duke University, 1993).

42. For these examples, see Pfau and Kenski, *Attack Politics,* 53.

43. Jamieson, *Dirty Politics,* chap. 5.

44. Darrell M. West, *Air Wars,* 2nd ed. (Washington, D.C.: Congressional Quarterly Press, 1997), 173.

45. Stephen Ansolabehere et al., "Does Attack Advertising Demobilize the Electorate?" *American Political Science Review* 88:4 (December 1994): 829–38; see also Stephen Ansolabehere and Shanto Iyengar, *Going Negative* (New York: Free Press, 1995).

46. Justin Lewis and Michael Morgan, "Issues, Images & Impact," *EXTRA!* 5:8 (December 1992): 8.

47. Samuel Popkin, *The Reasoning Voter* (Chicago: University of Chicago Press, 1991).

48. Patterson, *Out of Order;* see also Bruce Buchanan, *Renewing Presidential Politics* (Lanham, Md.: Rowman & Littlefield, 1996); and W. Lance Bennett, *The Governing Crisis* (New York: St. Martin's Press, 1992).

Part IV
The Government

◆ ◆ ◆

Chapter 11

Congress

◆　◆　◆

Congress is a complicated, industrious institution. Its members annually propose thousands of bills, consider many of them in subcommittees and/or committees, send some to the floor of one or another or both chambers, and vote a few hundred into law.

Members also hold hearings on issues ranging from the mundane to the incendiary and sporadically engage in oversight of governmental agencies.[1] They service their constituents' requests for help and assistance. They interact with their staff, other governmental officials, lobbyists, campaign contributors, and people from their district. They participate in ceremonies from flag-raising to attending the president's State of the Union speech.

All these activities are undertaken in an institution that, despite powerful party leaders and chairs of committees and subcommittees, is less hierarchical than it appears. An institution with a cumbersome structure (bicameralism) and rules and procedures that sometimes facilitate, often obstruct or thwart (the Senate filibuster) decisions. It is a place in which a bevy of staff is indispensable and influential, intraparty loyalty and interparty conflict are the norm, and where competition and cooperation coexist.

Aside from uncommon and brief periods of dispatch, or for special pieces of legislation, Congress, as designed by the U.S. Constitution, is slow, unharmonious, and inefficient. Deliberation and discussion are the norm. Even when a centralized and disciplined party with a dynamic and dominant leader is in control, as with Newt Gingrich and the House Republicans in the mid-1990s, or one party has a large enough majority to overwhelm the minority, as with the House Democrats in the post-Watergate 1970s, compromise and coalitions are often necessary to get bills through the legislative process.

All the while, many members have their reelection or higher office in mind; an objective that entails communicating themselves favorably to their constituents; accomplishing, or at least associating themselves with, projects benefitting their districts, and raising a lot of money for their upcoming campaign (and to pay off the last one).

This chapter focuses on three ways the media intersect with Congress and its members. First, they portray the institution's activities and endeavors, processes and procedures, apparent accomplishments and failures. But the media do this selectively: they emphasize some things, ignore others, depict many in ways legislators consider unfair if not unrecognizable.[2]

Second, some members try to use the media to facilitate and advance their influence and policy objectives within Congress, in the Washington community, and nationally. This chapter describes their techniques, traces their successes and failures, and explains why they occurred.

Third, this chapter chronicles how the local media are intimately involved in most members' communications with their districts, describes the types of coverage that ensue, and explains how they affect members' standing and prospects for reelection.

The media are also a source of information, interpretation, and opinion for members of Congress and their staffs, as they are for all institutions of government. For example, by watching C-SPAN in their offices, representatives can follow debates on the floor of the House. This use of the media for monitoring will be mentioned as relevant throughout the chapter.

MEDIA PORTRAYAL

As illustrated in Appendix B, the movies present an unappealing picture of Congress and its members. This is worsened by the elite, prestige, and popular news media.

Congress, for its part, is little different from other governmental institutions in its relations with the news media. On the one hand, it services reporters. There are seven news media galleries within the Capitol. The House and Senate both have galleries for, respectively, the daily press, radio and television, and the periodical press.[3] Still photographers have the seventh gallery.[4] Reporters detailed to cover events on the Hill also enjoy free parking, use of the Capitol's relatively inexpensive restaurants and barber shops.

On the other hand, congressional leaders try to exclude television cameras and still photographers from scenes and places that might embarrass members. This explains why "there were no authorized pictures of the House Post Office at work—or pictures of the House and Senate barber and beauty shops, the Senate tennis courts or House gym during the 1993 uproar over congressional perks."[5]

What Congress lacks are "the traditions, mechanisms, and mentality for effective public presentation."[6] Moreover, the institution is eminently permeable to the media: most members welcome the chance, or at least are willing, to talk to reporters; committee sessions are usually open; documents available; floor deliberations televised. This makes Congress and its members vulnerable to the news media's decisions of what to cover or not to cover and what approach to take.

Coverage

Television is a prime source of news about Congress for most people. But in recent years the major television networks have more than halved their number of personnel on permanent assignment to Capitol Hill.[7] Correspondingly, the amount of network news coverage declined precipitously from almost 125 stories a month during the 1970s to 41 a month between 1986 and 1992.

Many stories are incomplete, simplistic, and skewed. "There is little attempt any-more to keep track of legislation beyond the major tax and appropriation bills, and cov-erage of congressional hearings is usually limited to headline-grabbing sensations."[8]

"Hey, do you want to be on the news tonight or not? This is a sound bite, not the Gettysburg Address. Just say what you have to say, Senator, and get the hell off."
Drawing by Ziegler, © 1989, The New Yorker Magazine

Mark Rozell surveyed coverage of Congress in elite newspapers and the three leading newsweeklies since the end of World War II. He found that coverage "focuses on scandal, partisan rivalry, and interbranch conflict rather than the more complex subjects such as policy, process, and institutional concerns."[9] He concludes that it "has moved from healthy skepticism to outright cynicism."[10]

Certainly many stories—about gridlock, pork-barrel projects, the untoward influence of lobbyists, and so on—are genuinely newsworthy, but reporters often exaggerate their conflictual and scandalous aspects. Members of Congress are routinely portrayed as driven by political and electoral expediency and as self-indulgently exploiting their positions for personal gain (financial, sexual, etc.) through perquisites, boondoggle benefits, and trips.

Moreover, reporters' approach to stories often consists of a pro-con model in which they limit issues to two sides, for example, Republicans against Democrats, House Speaker Newt Gingrich conflicting with President Bill Clinton, the proponent versus an opponent of a bill.

At the same time, inherent characteristics of the legislative process are defined and presented negatively: politics is reported as selfish power struggles and manipulation inimical to the national interest; compromise as discarding principles and promises.

No wonder two-thirds of all congressional stories on television feature individual or institutional conflicts. And almost every judgment aired about Congress is unfavorable.[11]

Underlying this coverage is the assumption by journalists of the desirability of a "reform-oriented, progressive, policy-activist Congress that works effectively

© 1982, Washington Post Writers Group. Reprinted with permission.

with a strong, ambitious president."[12] But as Rozell observes, this "image of what Congress should be is clearly incompatible with the traditional role of the legislative branch."[13] That role as designed by the framers of the U.S. Constitution is to be infrequently innovative, and to act with neither efficiency nor dispatch.

Thus, C-SPAN, with its unfiltered, contextless, gavel-to-gavel coverage of floor proceedings, shows a Congress seemingly "tortured by intentional inactivity and delay, Byzantine procedures, and anachronistic rules. The monotony is broken by intermittent outbreaks of rancor and rhetoric, leading to protracted votes on incomprehensible motions."[14] This may explain in part why regular C-SPAN viewers are more critical of Congress than nonviewers.[15] According to pollster Mark Mellman, "'People see partisan debate and confuse it with partisan bickering; they see the legislative process and confuse it with inaction.'"[16]

Congress also suffers from the conspicuous, undisguised hostility and acerbity of many radio talk show hosts whose programs have crystallized and mobilized anti-Congress sentiment.[17] They thereby doomed several pieces of legislation, such as the proposed congressional pay raise of 1989.[18]

This caustic attitude did modify a bit after the Republicans took control of both chambers following the 1994 election; a spokesman for the House Republican Conference now serves as a liaison to talk show hosts.[19]

House Bank Scandal   Media coverage of the 1992–1993 House Bank scandal exemplifies the negativity of the news. It started when an uprising among junior Republicans compelled the House leadership to release the names of the more than three hundred members who had overdrawn their accounts at the House's depository for members' salaries, on which the lawmakers could draw by writing checks.

In theory, the overdrafts were covered with funds from the accounts of other members and repaid the following month when the representative's next paycheck was automatically deposited. No public money was involved; no taxpayers' funds were at risk. In fact, several members of Congress eventually ended up pleading guilty to felonies involving check-kiting at the bank or to misdemeanors related to their accounts.

For many weeks, as the scandal unfolded, it was a major story both nationally and in the members' local media. Conducing to coverage, the story was simple, easily understood, resonant with people's lives (most people have bank accounts and are not allowed overdrafts), featured apparently horrific numbers (over 8,000 checks "bounced"), concerned abuse of (another) congressional perk, was relevant in congressional districts nationwide, and seemed to symbolize the legislators' inability to balance the budget.[20]

The House leaders exacerbated the situation by initially refusing to release much, if any, information, then resorting to delay. Both tactics redounded negatively and eventually failed. The leaders did succeed in preventing the media from obtaining or making an authorized videotape of the bank in action: They "allowed only one photo opportunity of the facility, and that was on a day it was closed."[21] In this case, given all the other elements, lack of pictures was no deterrent to coverage.

So, framed by the news media as a scandal, typical of the way members exploited their prerogatives, the bank stories contributed to the retirement or defeat of several representatives, some of them honest and hard working.

Just as the news media highlight congressional scandals and outrages, they often neglect congressional accomplishments. As an example, overwhelming congressional passage in 1995 of legislation overhauling and consolidating numerous worker-training programs was essentially ignored. This bipartisan achievement was the result of years of hard work, negotiation, and compromise by members of Congress, their staffs, representatives of state and local governments, and labor and business. But, as David Broder points out, it was reported fully only in the *Washington Post;* it "rated scant attention in the *Los Angeles Times* and no mention in the *New York Times,* the *Wall Street Journal* or *USA Today.* The big news was O. J. Simpson canceling a television interview."[22]

Causes and Consequences of Coverage

News coverage of Congress and its members is declining, especially on television. What remains highlights conflict, disagreement, controversy, and venality. The legislature's actions are mainly ascribed to members' self-interest, political and electoral expediency, and—for some Republicans—ideological inflexibility. The accomplishments and failures of Congress are implicitly compared by reporters against a mythical standard of efficiency, diligence, and probity hard to attain and sustain.

Partially explaining this coverage are the conflict between reporters' news imperatives (see chapter three) and the tedium and complexity of the legislative process, plus the supposed low public interest in congressional doings. Stephen

"Senator, you have been described as lazy, humorless, uninformed, unscrupulous, lacking in compassion, and totally unfit for public office. How would you respond to that?"

Drawing by Lorenz, © 1982, The New Yorker Magazine

Hess would add other developments: the decisions by the owners of the television networks to scale back news operations (only CNN has full-time correspondents at both the House and Senate), and changing video technologies, which have reduced the networks' reliance on Washington for stories.[23]

Members of Congress are not without some responsibility. Confusing procedures, unethical behavior, abuse of the House post office and bank, excessive perks, ever-accelerating costs of campaigns, the apparent untoward influence of political action committees and lobbyists, gridlock, and partisan bickering, all provide grist for negative coverage.

That is not all. Newsworthy hearings expose problems; expectations are raised, often dashed. The outcome of many congressional hearings is no positive action at all: bills repose in committee are waylaid in the legislative shuffle, vitiated, or defeated. Others are passed as tepid and timid compromises unlikely to resolve what the president and Congress—and people's own experiences—have identified as serious issues.

The frequent result is an impression of congressional ineptitude and irresponsibility. Or, conversely, as with reactions to some of the measures passed by the Republican-dominated House of Representatives of 1995–1996, of Congress as reckless and extremist.

No surprise that the public is dissatisfied with, even hostile to, Congress.[24] Large majorities have a low opinion of the institution's effectiveness. When asked in polls, they usually disapprove of the job Congress is doing. Confidence in the people running the institution fell to 7 percent in 1993.[25] Respondents believe that those elected to Congress "lose touch with the people pretty quickly."[26] They rank members' ethical standards and honesty very low, above only stockbrokers, insurance salesmen, advertising practitioners, and car salesmen. They consider congressional scandals "business as usual."

So news coverage and probably movies exacerbate public dissatisfaction with and downright hostility to Congress and its members. Even researchers who found that people's approval of Congress was not much affected by media exposure (perhaps because it was so low already) show that it clearly influenced people's emotional reactions about Congress, made them angry, afraid, disgusted, uneasy.[27]

Withal, "the public does not hate Congress if by Congress we mean a physical institution with buildings, historical traditions, and constitutionally-defined roles. It is just that the public tends to hate the rabble-rousing collection of members inhabiting Congress at any particular time."[28]

USING THE MEDIA

At the same time, some members of Congress try to use the media to achieve a national reputation or at least visibility; to make their presence known and felt at the White House, in the bureaucracy, and among interest groups; and to promote their policy proposals and preferences.

They seek coverage in the elite and prestige press that influence the content of the other media. Especially welcome is the *Washington Post,* the hometown newspaper for many in all branches of government in the city (the *Washington Times* fulfills this function for many Republicans). They look to appear favorably in such Washington, D.C. influential insider publications as *Congressional Quarterly Weekly Report, National Journal, Roll Call,* and *The Hill;* to be interviewed on "Nightline," the "Lehrer Newshour," and, of course, C-SPAN. They aspire to appear on the Sunday televised discussion shows that have influence because they are watched disproportionately by people in government and politics, and their "news" is often widely reported in the rest of the press.

For some members, particularly party leaders and chairpersons of important committees, national coverage is available when they want it—although it is not guaranteed.[29] Senators interested in running for the presidency seek and often obtain widespread publicity, as do some senators able forcefully to advocate policy positions.[30]

Of course, there are always those who shun the media. For example, a woman answering Senator Lauch Faircloth's (R.-N.C.) Washington office telephone told a reporter: "'He never speaks to the press.'"[31]

House members' degree of activity influences the amount of national news coverage they receive.[32] Those with colorful personalities have an advantage in attracting coverage: "When presented with a funny, smart person who actually has some standing inside the institution, the temptation to use him or her repeatedly is almost irresistible."[33]

One way members of Congress can become media darlings is to pick a recurring issue the press considers important, take a predictable position on it (with polls showing 80 percent on their side), and be adept at memorable quotes about it (or hire someone who can provide them). Thus, Senator Al D'Amato, (R.-N.Y.) on federal banking regulators: "'These guys could screw up a two-car funeral procession.'"[34]

Examples of Media-Influencing Tactics

Phil Gramm's Tactics   Senator Phil Gramm (R.-Tex.) is a prime example of using the media for national self-promotion. He ranked ninety-ninth in seniority out of one hundred senators when he was able to obtain congressional approval of the law to reduce the deficit that bears his name. He had made his refrain "'We've got to balance the budget" resound in the public's ears, rendering opposition "petty at best, profligate at worst." He achieved public recognition, support, and pressure by assiduously and avidly cultivating the media.

> Need to send a crew to Gramm's office? Fine. Like him to come to the Radio and Television Gallery for some questions? How soon? Would a telephone call at home over the weekend be useful? That is fine too. No camera, microphone, or notebook could be too inconveniently located for Phil Gramm, who never seemed to tire of saying the same thing over and over and over again.[35]

This led to the joke, "'Where is the most dangerous place in the Capitol?' 'Between Phil Gramm and a camera.'"[36] And he was quotable: "I do the Lord's work in the Devil's city."[37]

All of Gramm's tactics to cultivate the media contributed to his emergence as a presidential candidate in 1996. But his failure to mount a significant challenge in the Republican caucuses and primaries graphically revealed the vast difference between attracting media attention of reporters and pundits inside the Washington beltway and organizing and running a credible national presidential campaign outside it.

Newt Gingrich's Tactics   The best example of a representative whose tactics display the benefits and pitfalls of using the press was House Representative Newt Gingrich (R.-Ga.). As a virtual unknown member of Congress, he described himself as working "'very hard trying to figure out how can I articulate something in a flashy enough way so the press can pick it up.'"[38] He attracted media attention as a spokesman of the Conservative Opportunity Society, a group of junior House Republicans.[39]

Gingrich and his fellow junior Republicans exploited the presence of C-SPAN's cameras to denounce the Democrats. Locked into a narrow field of vision, the cameras televising the House did not reveal that the Republicans' fulminations were being uttered in an almost empty chamber. So, eventually, then-Speaker of the House Thomas P. (Tip) O'Neill, Jr. (D.-Mass.) ordered the camera operators to show the empty chamber.

Gingrich attacked the most powerful targets, calling the "democratic leadership 'sick' and its past three speakers 'a trio of muggers.'"[40] He was "absolutist, aggressive, hyperbolic, informed, topical, unpredictable and studied in his use of supercharged symbolic language."[41]

Gingrich's C-SPAN attacks attracted widespread attention when the television networks' news shows reported them, sometimes replete with videos.[42] He became, even as a lowly Republican congressman, "by far the most quoted, visible member of Congress."[43]

Gingrich's actions contributed to his becoming minority leader and subsequently Speaker of the House of Representatives when the Republicans obtained a majority in the chamber. In that position, his attempts to use the media continued unabated. He retained his show on National Empowerment Television. He sent the staffs of op-ed pages, TV news shows, and political magazines flattering notes. His pollster had people in focus groups turning dials registering their reactions to the words and delivery of some of his speeches. At first, he allowed television cameras at his daily news briefing, although he had them removed after the conferences became confrontations.[44]

And yet, Gingrich lacked popularity with the public.[45] His combative-partisan rhetoric and the way he came across on television as an arrogant and rude know-it-all were partly responsible. News stories about his bitter divorce from his first wife, his draft deferment during the Vietnam War, and his questionable book deal with HarperCollins did not help. Even worse, the media gave heavy, negative coverage to his petulant comments about being ignored by President Clinton while riding on *Air Force One.* His standing with the public plummeted even further during the budget standoff of late 1995.[46] Appearances with a recalcitrant pig on the "The Tonight Show" and as a substitute host for Larry King did little to redeem his reputation.

So, Gingrich's abundant media coverage bestowed or at least confirmed his preeminence on Capitol Hill but also made him an ideal symbol of Republican extremism for Democrats in the 1996 elections.

Media Entrepreneurs

Given that the media are often the prime source of information for policymakers as well as the public, some members of Congress try to use the media to advance their policy objectives. Especially well positioned to do so are party leaders and the chairs of committees and sometimes subcommittees who often make news. Other members court the media as a way of compensating for their lack of policy power within Congress. They usually have to struggle to solicit media attention.

Of course, much policy still gets made in the old-fashioned way, without any recourse to the media by policymakers or scrutiny of the process by reporters. Nonetheless, members increasingly interact with the media to obtain visibility for their issues, frame the issues to accord with their preferred solutions, and move them through the legislative process.

Karen Kedrowski calls the members who supplement the traditional "insider" strategies of making policy in this way "media entrepreneurs."[47] Their objective is to mobilize some relevant combination of party leadership, partisan colleagues, other legislators, congressional staff, the administration, bureaucrats, outside interest groups, and public opinion behind their policy proposals and desired solutions.

Media entrepreneurs make news through floor statements, press releases and conferences, leaks, and—best of all—op-eds and television and radio interviews. At the least, they keep in contact with reporters who specialize in the subject of their concern. These contacts may well be accomplished socially, at informal gatherings where politicians and journalists encounter each other.

Whether favorable media coverage ensues depends on whether the member is established as a credible, knowledgeable source, the newsworthiness of the issue, and the effectiveness of the media-influencing techniques deployed. At best, the process is interactive but restricted: "Reporters need the news and the insights . . . members can provide; members need coverage to further legislative strategies."[48] But because reporters are beholden to news criteria and need timely, easily described stories, "the relationship also limits the kinds of issues on which legislators focus and shapes the processes by which policies are drafted, debated, and enacted."

Ideally (which is unusual), this can result in their issues getting on the policy agenda, their proposals receiving subcommittee and then committee consideration in both chambers, their designated solutions being preferred, and the legislation enacted. For ordinary members of Congress, getting their views into law is tough because party leaders and committee chairs can often impose their own preferences.[49]

So media-savvy members try to make their issues clear and their solutions reasonably simple or simple to communicate; useful, too, if they are also able to generate widespread editorial and cartoon support, although these may boomerang if there is a conflict between the position espoused by the paper (liberal editorial in the *New York Times*) and the dominant ideology in the legislature (conservative majority in the House of Representatives).

Senators are usually better able than representatives to attract media attention: there are fewer of them; they have longer terms; and they are more likely to chair or be the ranking minority members of subcommittees or committees.

Examples of Entreprenurial Media Tactics Greg Kubiak describes how he helped his boss, Senator David Boren (D.-Okla.), acquire favorable media coverage for the senator's campaign "reform" legislation. It started when ABC's "20/20" featured Boren in a story critical of political action committees, using his sound bite, "'When *special* interests control the financing for campaigns, Congress is verrrry unlikely to act in the *national* interest,'" in promoting the piece.[50]

As Kubiak points out, the story could have undermined Boren by, for example, running a graphic showing oil producers as contributing a large percentage of his individual contributions. It did not. Kubiak subsequently sent a letter and information package on behalf of the senator to selected network anchors, syndicated columnists, editorial writers, and news correspondents. Its purpose was to keep the campaign "reform" bill in the news and put public pressure on senators to support it—or make it difficult for them to oppose it.

It is more difficult but still possible for ordinary House members to interact with the media to mutual benefit. Representative James Inhofe (R.-Okla.), to gain public support for his resolution to identify members of Congress who signed discharge petitions (the devices used to force bills out of committees and onto the floor for a vote), campaigned on the talk show circuit. He demanded an end to secrecy. Opponents argued that making the names public would enable lobbyists and special interest groups to pressure members who refused to sign the petitions. The House approved his measure overwhelmingly.[51] Trading in part on this favorable publicity, Inhofe was subsequently elected to the Senate.

As chair of a subcommittee of the relatively insignificant Small Business Committee in the House, Representative Ron Wyden (D.-Ore.) developed a specialty in consumer and health-related issues. Among his targets: the diet drink Slim-Fast and the quick-fix diet industry, mislabeling of over-the-counter drugs, and junk-food-makers that advertise during Saturday morning cartoons. Aside from the resulting abundant and mostly favorable media coverage, Wyden often achieved substantive results: "Fertility clinics must now make public their success rates; Medicaid now covers senior citizens who wish to receive nursing care at home rather than at an institution . . . and there is a national data bank to track physicians with a history of misconduct or malpractice."[52]

But such media tactics can be a two-edged sword. Wyden's 1995 campaign for the Senate was damaged when he miserably failed a stump-the-candidate test of a local television station: He was unable to answer questions about the price of milk and gasoline, locate Bosnia on a map, or identify the state's major employer. Nonetheless, like Inhofe, he too won the election, although narrowly.

Hearings

Hearings can be of inestimable benefit to members seeking to advance their careers, promote policy, or simply attract media attention.

Hearings are scheduled in advance, take place in convenient locations equipped for reporting, and respectably relieve journalists of some of the burden and expense of investigative reporting.

Widespread coverage occurs when media interest unites with public disquiet, genuine congressional concern, and potential partisan advantage. Such hearings usually contain flamboyant ingredients: some combination of peccadillos, scandals, corruption, crime, exploitation of the public by greedy corporate executives and once-smug now-scared officials, assessments of a presidential policy, and probes of government- (or man-) made disasters.[53] Media-slick members and their staffs do their best to ensure that the subject is presented in its most headline-grabbing form.

Tactics to encourage coverage include eliciting testimony from witnesses who make news because of their prominence (e.g., movie stars) or notoriety; scheduling witnesses who support the legislator's position during the first few days of hearings, when press interest is high; and having these supportive witnesses testify early in the day to facilitate media reporting. Unless it is assumed that they can be discredited, opponents-defendants are relegated to the waning days of the hearings when press interest has probably declined.

Awareness of television as a means of getting a message across both in the daily coverage and in the brief excerpts shown on the evening news is vital. At Representative Henry A. Waxman's (D.-Calif.) hearings on tobacco, his staff placed television cameras so that the only shot of the seven heads of the industry

© 1981, Washington Post Writers Group. Reprinted with permission.

had to include a huge placard. "It read, 'One American dies every 80 seconds from tobacco use,' and was periodically replaced by charts depicting rising nicotine levels in cigarettes and grisly photographs of oral cancer."[54]

But hearings do not always pan out as planned. Democratic members and their committee staff at the Iran-Contra hearings failed to anticipate the visual contrast on television between their intended "victim" Oliver North (in his bemedaled Marine uniform) and the committee's unprepossessing lawyers (one of them balding with long hair reaching the back of his collar) cross-examining him. Nor did they realize that the design of the room, with committee members arrayed in elevated rows facing witnesses seated at floor level, gave the unfortunate impression of pacific Christian witnesses being served up to the congressional lions. Even worse for the committee members, North turned them into sitting ducks at a shooting gallery.[55]

LOCAL MEDIA

Underneath the waves of national coverage received by Congress, its more prominent leaders, and characters; and below the attempts of some members to use the media to advance their personal and policy objectives is the undertow of the local media.

Abetted by their aides, most members of Congress try through these media to communicate to their constituents. They seek to foster support, build trust, and justify their decisions and activities. The main purpose is to ensure reelection. This objective entails claiming credit for accomplishments (sometimes whether or not justified), construing their ambiguous actions favorably, and avoiding blame. It is promoted through the selective release, framing, and withholding of information.

Members use the Capitol Hill television and radio studios, the full-service broadcast bureaus of the Democratic and Republican campaign committees, to communicate to their districts by satellite, to speak live via interactive television with anchors and reporters back home. They send out radio actualities and tapes for cable and local-access channels.

Members' press secretaries or equivalents and other staff send out press releases, advance notification, and texts of speeches and other formal statements; leak information; give off-the-record interviews; and engage in social interaction with and the cultivation of relevant reporters.[56] They know about deadlines and slow news days. They write the releases claiming credit for government largess received (whether or not they were received through the legislator's efforts) by the district.

Members may hold congressional committee hearings in their constituencies. This enables them to reap local media coverage and publicity as they are shown caring about, and sometimes taking a position on, an issue of local concern.

And, of course, members visit their districts, where they make speeches, appear before organizations, deal with constituents, and meet with reporters and editors.

Contents

How do the local media respond to these attempts at management, massage, and manipulation? Danielle Vinson analyzed all content that mentioned Congress or its members in a local daily, a weekly newspaper, and the early and late evening news program of a television station in each of eight media markets for four weeks between September 1993 and January 1994.[57] The markets were chosen to represent variations in local media and differences in their congruence with congressional districts. Congruence means the number of congressional districts that fall at least partially within a media market. Thus, she studied markets low in congruence, with many districts and members in the market (e.g., Los Angeles and Philadelphia), moderate congruence (e.g., Atlanta and Columbia, South Carolina), and high congruence, with essentially one district in the market (e.g., Santa Barbara, California). To explain her results, she interviewed some of the reporters and editors who produced the coverage and the press secretaries and representatives who tried to shape it.[58]

Professor Vinson's research demolishes the conventional wisdom that a symbiotic relationship exists between members and their local media in which representatives and their staff supposedly provide stories and information in implicit exchange for frequent and favorable coverage.[59]

This "wisdom" had already been cast into some doubt for television by Stephen Hess's discovery that members of Congress are rarely mentioned on local television newscasts, particularly in the larger markets, and Timothy Cook's finding that House press secretaries considered local television useful only to the extent its market overlapped the member's district.[60]

Going further, Vinson found, first, that two thirds of congressional content in daily newspapers dealt with national issues, the rest was local or mixed. The figures for weekly newspapers and television was roughly fifty-fifty national-local/mixed.[61] So, much of the coverage was unrelated or peripheral to local members.

More significant, coverage for many members was often nonexistent or sparse. They appeared more often in their daily newspapers than in the weeklies or on television. But even newspaper coverage was infrequent: Seven of the twenty-seven representatives whose districts fell at least in part in the *Los Angeles Times'* circulation area were mentioned just once in the newspaper in the period studied; only eight appeared in five or more articles.[62]

Not only did the amount of coverage vary widely among the members of Congress, so did its favorability. A few of the representatives enjoyed generally uncritical stories, usually focusing on their accomplishments for the district. This is what one would expect from symbiosis. But coverage of 40 percent of the members was either ambiguous or negative. Indeed, "negative stories, if not more numerous, were certainly more prominent and detailed and stayed in the news longer than positive stories."[63]

Limiting the definitiveness of Vinson's research findings was the fact that she looked only at prime time newscasts and excluded radio. Moreover, the television stations in some of the cities that she did not study, such as Phoenix, are reputed to cover their members of Congress extensively.[64] Nonetheless, her findings are important and warrant explanation.

Explanations   Members' relationships with local reporters matter: those "who are accessible to their local media reduce the likelihood that coverage will be unfavorable."[65]

But coverage more often depends on three factors beyond members' control. First are the news organizations' resources: the weeklies often lack and the television stations are unwilling to expend the resources to cover Congress; none in the study had their own correspondents in Washington, D.C. (two stations had access to stringers). Nor did they assign local reporters to cover events and issues involving their legislators.

Second is the level of congruence. Given the number of representatives and the competition for news space, journalists in low-congruence markets cover only members who engage in newsworthy activities, have specialized expertise, or are involved in (or associate themselves with) subjects in the news. Low-congruence members receive little coverage. In contrast, those in high-congruence districts not only receive more coverage but it is more likely to be favorable.

Third is the level of agreement between the policy positions of the newspapers and television stations on the one hand and the member of Congress on the other: "Ideological coherence significantly increased the chances of favorable coverage."[66]

Some representatives use alternative local media to reach their constituents. They provide videos of updates on their activities to cable stations and appear on radio talk shows, on public television and radio, and on access cable.[67] These activities are partial compensations at best. Most members still must rely on their local newspaper and television coverage. Especially for members in low-congruence markets, these local media are an inadequate, uncertain, sporadic, and sometimes hostile way of communicating with their constituents.

CONCLUSION

Congress and its members interact with the media in three overlapping ways. First is the overall impression conveyed by movies and news. As detailed in Appendix B, movies misrepresent and overdramatize the institution's processes, omit its positive and workday side, and portray members as egocentric and expedient. The news highlights conflict, disagreement, controversy, and venality; it ascribes legislators' actions predominantly to political and electoral expediency. The result is a highly negative picture, hostile public opinion, and defeat of some members.

Second are the efforts by a growing number of members to use the media to achieve a national reputation, or at least visibility; to make their presence known and felt at the White House, in the bureaucracy, and among interest groups; and to promote their policy proposals and preferences by getting them featured and favorably framed in the elite and prestige press. Whether beneficial media coverage ensues depends on the member's standing as a credible, knowledgeable source, the newsworthiness of the issue, and the effectiveness of the media-influencing techniques deployed.

Third, most members of Congress seek through their local media to communicate to their constituents. Their essential objective is reelection. Research reveals that, rather than symbiosis, the amount of coverage and its favorability vary widely. A few representatives enjoy generally uncritical stories, usually focusing on their accomplishments for their district. But coverage of many others is either ambiguous or negative. Explanations for the amount and type of coverage relate to the news organizations' resources, the degree of congruence, and, for some members, the extent of agreement between their policy positions and those of the district's newspapers and television stations.

Notes

1. Joel D. Aberbach, *Keeping a Watchful Eye* (Washington, D.C.: Brookings Institution, 1990).

2. The most comprehensive and insightful book on the House of Representatives and the media is Timothy E. Cook, *Making Laws and Making News* (Washington, D.C.: Brookings Institution, 1989); see also Elaine S. Povich, *Partners & Adversaries* (Arlington, Va.: Freedom Forum, 1996).

3. The periodical news gallery is full of correspondents for trade newsletters (and online computer services). They provide the kind of specialized policy-based information about legislation in process that enhances the influence of interest groups, particularly business, and facilitates lobbying.

4. Ronald D. Elving, "Brighter Lights, Wider Windows," in *Congress, the Press, and the Public,* ed. Thomas E. Mann and Norman J. Ornstein (Washington, D.C.: American Enterprise Institute and Brookings Institution, 1994), 186.

5. Gary Griffith, "No Trespassing," *Washington Journalism Review* 15:1 (January–February 1993): 46.

6. Elving, in *Congress,* ed. Mann and Ornstein, 190.

7. Penn Kimball, *Downsizing the News* (Washington, D.C.: Woodrow Wilson Center Press, 1994), 105.

8. Ibid., 109.

9. Mark J. Rozell, "Press Coverage of Congress, 1946–92," in *Congress,* ed. Mann and Ornstein, 110.

10. Ibid., 109; see also his *In Contempt of Congress* (Westport, Conn.: Praeger, 1996).

11. For these data, see S. Robert Lichter and Daniel R. Amundson, "Less News Is Worse News," in *Congress,* ed. Mann and Ornstein, 134–37.

12. Thomas E. Mann and Norman J. Ornstein, "Introduction," in *Congress,* ed. Mann and Ornstein, 4.

13. Rozell, in *Congress,* ed. Mann and Ornstein, 112.

14. Elving, in *Congress,* ed. Mann and Ornstein, 187.

15. Stephen Frantzich and John Sullivan, *The C-SPAN Revolution* (Norman: University of Oklahoma Press, 1996), 249–51, 273.

16. Quoted in Katherine Q. Seelye, "Gingrich Used TV Skills to Be King of the Hill," *New York Times,* 14 December 1994, A3.

17. Kimberly Coursen Parker, "How the Press Views Congress," in *Congress,* ed. Mann and Ornstein, 163–66.

18. Elizabeth Kolbert, "An Open Mike, a Loudmouth Live, and Thou," *New York Times,* 26 September 1993, E2.

19. Steven A. Holmes, "Talk-Radio Crowd Rejoices in Babylon Over New Congress," *New York Times,* 5 January 1994, A1.

20. For the details, see David Shaw, "News With Impact? It's Simple," *Los Angeles Times,* 25 October 1992, A1, 13, 14.

21. Gary Griffith, "No Trespassing," *Washington Journalism Review* 15:1 (January–February 1993): 46.

22. David S. Broder, "Happy Endings on the Hill," *Washington Post,* 18 October 1995, A19, from which this story is taken.

23. Stephen Hess, "The Decline and Fall of Congressional News," in *Congress,* ed. Mann and Ornstein, 141–56.

24. See Karlyn Bowman and Everett Carll Ladd, "Public Opinion Toward Congress," in *Congress,* ed. Mann and Ornstein, 45–59.

25. Ibid., 53.

26. Ibid., 51.

27. Elizabeth Theiss-Morse and John R. Hibbing, "Are the Mass Media to Blame for the Public's Negativity Toward Congress?" (paper presented at the annual meeting of the American Political Science Association, Chicago, August 1995); see also their *Congress as Public Enemy* (New York: Cambridge University Press, 1995).

28. Ibid., 4.

29. Timothy E. Cook, "House Members as Newsmakers: The Effects of Televising Congress," *Legislative Studies Quarterly* 11:2 (May 1986): 203–226.

30. Stephen Hess, *The Ultimate Insiders: U.S. Senators in the National Media* (Washington, D.C.: Brookings Institution, 1986); and James H. Kuklinski and Lee Sigelman, "When Objectivity Is Not Objective," *Journal of Politics* 54:3 (August 1992): 821; see also Martha Joynt Kumar, "Congress: The Best Beat in Town" (paper presented at the annual meeting of the American Political Science Association, Washington, D.C., August 1986), 7–8.

31. Peter T. Kilborn, "Workers at a Pork Processing Plant Find Disease Is One of the Hazards," *New York Times,* 27 September 1993, A7.

32. Charles M. Pearson, "Explaining National News Coverage of Members of the U.S. Congress, 1977–1980" (paper presented at the annual meeting of the American Political Science Association, New York, August 1986), 12.

33. Cokie Roberts, "Leadership and the Media in the 101st Congress," in *Leading Congress,* ed. John J. Kornacki (Washington, D.C.: CQ Press, 1990), 90.

34. Christopher Georges and Katherine Boo, "Capitol Hill 20510," *Washington Monthly* 24:10 (October 1992): 36–43, quote is on 38; see also Judith Olney, "What's Come Over Alan Simpson," *Washington Times,* 5 August 1993, E1.

35. Roberts, in *Leading Congress,* 91.

36. Ibid., 85.

37. Georges and Boo, "Capitol Hill 20510," 43.

38. Lois Romano, "Newt Gingrich, Maverick on the Hill," *Washington Post,* 3 January 1985, B2.

39. Cook, *Making Laws,* 56.

40. Georges and Boo, "Capitol Hill 20510," 40.

41. Seelye, "Gingrich Used TV Skills," A14.

42. Stephen Frantzich and John Sullivan, *The C-SPAN Revolution* (Norman: University of Oklahoma Press, 1996), 275.

43. Georges and Boo, "Capitol Hill 20510," 40.

44. Adam Clymer, "Newt Tests TV and Flunks the Press," *New York Times,* 17 September 1995, E4.

45. Connie Bruck, "The Politics of Perception," *New Yorker* 71:31 (9 October 1995): 52.

46. Robin Toner, "House Republicans Urge Gingrich to Be Less of a Target," *New York Times,* 23 November 1995, A17.

47. This discussion is based on Karen M. Kedrowski, *Media Entrepreneurs and the Media Enterprise in the U.S. Congress* (Cresskill, N.J.: Hampton Press, 1996), and on Timothy E. Cook, "The Fourth Branch and the Other Three" (paper presented at the annual meeting of the American Political Science Association, New York, September 1994).

48. Cook, *Making Laws,* vii for this and the following quote.

49. Cook, "The Fourth Branch," 29.

50. Greg D. Kubiak, *The Gilded Dome* (Norman: University of Oklahoma Press, 1994), 207; emphases and spelling of "verrrry" in the original.

51. "Outflanked by Talk Shows, House Drops Secrecy Rule," *Chicago Tribune,* 29 September 1993, 6; see also Susan Herbst, "On Electronic Public Space," *Political Communication* 12:3 (July-September 1995): 265.

52. Account and quote from Georges and Boo, "Capitol Hill 20510," 42.

53. For an unconventional perspective, see David L. Paletz, "Television Drama: The Appeals of the Senate Watergate Hearings," *Midwest Quarterly* 18:1 (October 1976): 103–09.

54. Michael Wines, "Makers of Laws and Tobacco Joust in Battle for TV Cameras," *New York Times,* 15 April 1994, A10.

55. William S. Cohen and George J. Mitchell, *Men of Zeal* (New York: Viking, 1998), 163–65.

56. For a thoughtful description of the activities of press secretaries, see Cook, *Making News,* 71–86, 199–201.

57. C. Danielle Vinson, "Local Media Coverage of Congress and Its Members" (Ph.D. diss. Duke University, 1996), from which the following discussion is taken. The thesis also discusses two weeks during the election period of September and October 1994.

58. Ibid., see also C. Danielle Vinson, "The Odd Years" (paper presented at the annual meeting of the American Political Science Association, New York, September 1994), and her "In Search of Symbiosis" (paper presented at the annual meeting of the American Political Science Association, Chicago, September 1995).

59. For example, see Susan H. Miller, "Reporters and Congressmen: Living in Symbiosis," *Journalism Monographs* 53 (January 1978); Michael J. Robinson, "Three Faces of Congressional Media," in *The New Congress,* ed. Thomas E. Mann and Norman J. Ornstein (Washington, D.C.: American Enterprise Institute, 1981), 55–98; and Stephanie Greco Larson, *Creating Consent of the Governed: A Member of Congress and the Local Media* (Carbondale: Southern Illinois University Press, 1992).

60. Stephen Hess, *Live From Capitol Hill!* (Washington, D.C.: Brookings Institution, 1991), 68–76; Cook, *Making Laws,* 81–89; see also Charles M. Tidmarch and John J. Pitney, Jr., "Covering Congress," *Polity* 17:3 (Spring 1985): 463–83.

61. Vinson, "The Odd Years," 16.

62. Ibid., 6.

63. Vinson, "In Search of Symbiosis," 22.

64. Appreciation to Paul McCreath for pointing this out.

65. Vinson, "In Search of Symbiosis," 14.

66. Ibid., 11.

67. Ibid., 21.

Chapter 12

Presidency

◆ ◆ ◆

The theme of this chapter is that presidents face numerous expectations, many of which they lack the authority to achieve. With their power to command limited, they often have to rely on persuasion to try to accomplish their objectives. So, they seek favorable media coverage. They have a host of aides, a couple of media-managing institutions, and a set of techniques to help them get it. The media response produces contents that are sometimes favorable, often unfavorable, about the president. The chapter's case studies of Presidents Reagan and Clinton trace presidential successes and failures with the media, explaining why they occurred. The chapter concludes with the consequences of presidential-media interaction for democracy.

PRESIDENTIAL EXPECTATIONS

Presidents are loaded with expectations: to be the chief executive, ensuring faithful execution of the laws; the chief policymaker, proposing and pushing for congressional enactment of legislation; commander in chief, in charge of national security; and the world leader. Presidents are deemed more or less responsible for the state of the nation's economy, for solving societal problems, and for dealing with issues of foreign relations.[1]

The importance of individual presidents is symbolized by the Mount Rushmore memorial and perpetuated by the establishment of presidential libraries around the country (see photo, next page). That importance is a continuing theme in movies such as *Gabriel Over the White House* (1933) and the 1990s' *Dave* and the controversial productions *JFK* and *Nixon*.

In fact, presidential authority to meet these expectations is limited by the U.S. Constitution's checks and balances, overlapping powers, and federalism; by the institutional conflicts inherent in the American political system. It can be and often is contested by other leaders at home and abroad, the opposing political party, members of his own, power-holders in other institutions (e.g., Congress), and interest group leaders. Critics and antagonists abound.[2]

© Monkmeyer & Monkmeyer

The circumstances in which a president takes office are more or less limiting. Whom does he replace? What previous programs is he extending or rejecting? How strong is opposition to items on his policy agenda? What opportunity does he have for leadership?[3]

Inevitably, every president experiences problems. There are debilitating, even intractable, economic and social conditions. There are events that he neither wittingly inspires nor initiates but to which he must react or respond; plus the foolish or disastrous activities he undertakes.

The president, moreover, is surrounded by executive agencies, such as the Office of Management and Budget, and the National Security Council. Lyn Ragsdale calls this "the plural presidency," pointing out how it "makes numerous decisions for presidents without necessarily full-fledged presidential involvement and how [its] ambiguous goals, methods, and participants beset presidential decisions."[4] Moreover, much of the vast bureaucracy of governmental departments (Defense, Health and Human Services, etc.), supposedly under presidential control, operates autonomously on many issues.

True, the president can command, but obedience does not necessarily follow. Indeed, command is often ignored. As Harry Truman observed about handing his presidency over to Dwight Eisenhower: "'He'll sit here . . . and he'll say, "Do this! Do that!' *And nothing will happen.*'"[5]

The president can invoke party loyalty, but members of his own party may be among his most vigorous opponents.[6] He can look to interest groups, but their support is self-interested, therefore often sporadic and uncertain. He can bargain, make promises, offer blandishments and inducements. But his supply of rewards is limited, potential recipients are many. He can threaten, even punish, but these weapons lose their potency if frequently applied and make enemies to boot.

Presidential Persuasion

To try to accomplish their objectives in their dealings with other power-holders, presidents often have little alternative but to rely on persuasion.[7]

In seeking to persuade, presidents go public. As Sam Kernell points out, the objective is to rally public opinion to the president's side, then to use this public support to bring pressure on legislators and sometimes bureaucrats to conform to his views.[8]

Amplifying Kernell's point, Jeffrey Cohen and Ken Collier point out that presidents can go public for several additional reasons: to place items on the policy agenda of other institutions (usually successfully); to persuade people to put direct pressure on other policymakers; and to promote particular solutions to issues. Presidents may also be seeking to build their public prestige overall or to appeal to the populace, or a special segment of it, for support on a particular issue, usually a legislative battle.[9]

To go public, presidents need the media.[10] Indeed, the media may be central to their fate: According to Richard Brody, the "American people form and revise their collective evaluation of the president on the evidence of policy success and failure contained in daily news reports in the mass media."[11]

PRESIDENTS AND THE MEDIA

Presidents like to see media coverage conducive to their personal, policy, and political interests.[12] Such content favorably communicates their beliefs, aspirations, decisions, actions; it shows them in command, thereby improving their standing with the public and their reputation with other policymakers.

The presidential ideal (fantasy) probably goes like this.[13] White House officials lay out the administration's line of the day; which is then amplified by the president using the venue and mode of his choice (a speech, a photo-op, an interview with a journalistic "bigfoot") and by his surrogates' appearances on the media. The line is reinforced by favorable leaks and plants and through nurturing of the press. Journalists transmit the line. Presidential spinners interpret events as favorably as possible for the president. Damage control rectifies mistakes or gaffes that could lead to a frenzy of negative coverage.

Conversely, presidents deplore other people's leaks, reporting that they deem to be inaccurate or distorted, and criticism they believe unwarranted (or even warranted).[14] If unpleasant news must be issued—and they realize its appearance is inevitable—the president and his aides want to structure and interpret it for the media and thus the public.

Presidential Media-Managing Institutions

Most of the White House staff is involved in trying to make the president's media dream come true (that is, when they are not leaking and counterleaking stories to influence his behavior and advance their own interests).[15] There are, however, two basic media-managing institutions—the press office and the Office of Communications.

Headed by the president's press secretary, the press office coordinates presidential news for Washington-based reporters through background sessions, news releases, and related forms. Most important are the daily briefings at which the press secretary presents the president's views and gives the White House's response to events.

In practice, recounts Marlin Fitzwater, long-serving (and -suffering) press secretary of Presidents Reagan and Bush, preparing daily briefings was like preparing for psychological warfare. He and his staff would sit around and talk about individual reporters—the stories they might want to write, their mood, whether they were favorable to the president on the particular issue. Fitzwater would be sure to provide several new comments on different stories so that the reporters had something to write about.[16]

Press secretaries spend much of their time catering to the needs and facilitating the jobs of journalists. In the process, they ascertain and react to reporters' perspectives and views and anticipate their future behavior. They communicate their findings to the president and White House staffers, suggesting proactive initiatives for the administration to take.

The White House Office of Communications was created during the Nixon administration. Presidents Ford and Carter both briefly dispensed with and resurrected the office. It thrived under David Gergen during the Reagan administration and carried on with Presidents Bush and Clinton.[17]

The office coordinates information from the executive branch. It also tries to nullify the Washington press corps by going directly to the friendlier and more malleable local, regional, and specialty media. And it prepares a daily summary of major news stories about the administration culled from various newspapers, magazines, and the leading television networks.

Techniques The White House uses several techniques to achieve its objectives in its relationship with the media, beginning with its ability to bestow upon or deny journalists special access to the president and his aides. When

White House press secretary Mike McCurry is surrounded by reporters in the White House briefing
room Friday, December 15, 1995, after a briefing on the continuing federal budget negotiations.
McCurry refused to comment on proposals presented by White House and Republican negotiators,
saying both parties had agreed to a news blackout.
Joe Marquette, AP/WorldWide

such access is granted, information may be dispensed subject to ground rules
that limit what can be reported (see chapter 3). Reporters sometimes gain inside information at the cost of letting themselves be used for trial balloons (off-
the-record announcements of possible presidential actions to test reactions),
anonymous political attacks, and advantageous and untrue revelations for which
the source is not held publicly responsible. Denial of access is used selectively
to maintain control, preserve power, and prevent untoward information from
reaching the public.

Secrecy is another technique. It can be asserted on the grounds of national
security, executive privilege, and through a complicated and extensive classifica-
tion system; or not justified at all. Secrecy is desirable because, once exposed, policy initiatives can be thwarted by opponents, undone by public scrutiny. *Faits
accomplis,* by contrast, resound with finality and can redound with political triumph—as President Nixon anticipated and realized in his 1972 move toward rapprochement with China.

But secrecy is difficult to maintain. Sooner or later much information
reaches reporters. Presidents perennially complain about leaks. For executive
officials, the question is often not whether to release information, but when and
to whom.

So, the White House tries to control the type and the timing of the information that is released. It feeds reporters positive material and makes negative information difficult for them to acquire. It times releases to achieve maximum or minimum publicity: Friday after 7:00 p.m. is the bad news burial ground, the time when the main newspapers' and television networks' deadlines have passed and the Saturday morning news hole and audience are at their smallest. Then it was that the Reagan White House issued a sudden news release announcing that the long-delayed official portrait of (disgraced) former President Richard M. Nixon had finally been hung in the White House.[18]

In contrast, favorable messages are repeated many times. As President Nixon told aide David Gergen: "'About the time you are writing a line that you have written it so often that you want to throw up, that is the first time the American people will hear it.'"[19]

Striking as their apparent advantages are over the media, some presidents have been tempted to go beyond manipulation to try for intimidation. Only the Nixon administration undertook a concerted, extended effort to punish—to assault—the press. This included lie detector tests and phone taps of officials suspected of giving information to the press; FBI questioning of the neighbors and friends of probing CBS correspondent Daniel Schorr, ostensibly because he was under consideration for a federal job; an Internal Revenue Service audit of the tax records of *Newsday* and its editor after the newspaper ran a series of articles exposing the financial affairs of a Nixon friend and confidante; and investigations of media corporations by the antitrust division of the Justice Department.[20]

Press Conferences

In theory, the televised press conference offers a special opportunity for the president to enhance his power by displaying his leadership, knowledge of issues, charm, and empathy.[21] After all, the president controls the conferences' setting, frequency, and timing, and chooses the questioners. The president usually begins with an uninterrupted statement on one or more topics of his choice. Questions can usually be anticipated, occasionally planted with an accommodating reporter. Follow-up questions are uncommon. Responses are usually prepared and rehearsed. Among the possibilities: direct answers, restatements of policy positions, symbolism, discrediting the opposition, evasion, obfuscation, and refusal.[22]

Many reporters are inhibited, not wanting to appear to the public as malcontents. With conspicuous exceptions, they do not seek to joust with the president—a fight in which his power exceeds theirs and which tumbles them from the heights of objectivity. So they usually temper the toughest of questions with apparent deference and respect.

Yet, presidents tend to avoid televised press conferences. Certainly, when their popularity declines, they hold fewer of them (reflecting a kind of siege or bunker mentality). Even when things are going well, presidents do not hold frequent press conferences. Some presidents are uneasy before the cameras, their personal style unappealing. Others, with things to hide, want to avoid press scrutiny. For press conferences do enable journalists to try to hold the president accountable: to ask him about the issues and events of the day, to ask provocative questions that he may not want or be able to answer, to press follow-up questions. And, when the conferences are televised, to do so in full public view.

PRESIDENTIAL MEDIA COVERAGE

While some 2,000 journalists in Washington have White House credentials, the press corps covering the president ranges from around 60 to 100. The regulars are mainly from the wire services, television and radio networks, major newspapers and chains, and newsmagazines. Assigned seats at the daily briefings and desks in two small rooms, they have been described as "a collection of spoiled and talented individuals pacing a cramped ill-lit corridor, waiting for a hapless government official to vent their frustrations upon."[23] When the president travels, he is accompanied by 100 to 150 journalists on domestic trips and up to 300 on overseas journeys.

Unmediated and Media-Originated Content

The White House is most comfortable with unmediated content, with the media passively transmitting presidential messages in full and without interference.

The media serve as such a conduit when they transmit a president's primetime address, press conference, or other appearance in its entirety, without interference. But this type of coverage may be provided by few outlets—one television network, not the others, leaving the public with lots of alternative media fare.[24]

Broadcasters can also diminish the president's impact by giving voice to the opposition party immediately after his presentation.[25] Following him with a summary-cum-discussion of "instant analysis," which sometimes lays out the president's performance, if not the president, like a cadaver for dissection, can also be destructive.[26]

Media-originated commentary is the opposite of conduit coverage. Ever increasing, it floods out from pundits, columnists, the writers of editorials and op-eds; talk radio and televangelists; and all the other founts listed in Appendix A. Some of it supports the president, but much of it is caustic, critical of and cynical about him politically and personally.

Mostly Mediated Content

The most common content consists of mostly mediated news and feature stories about the president, his family, the administration, and its policies. Such coverage ranges from deferential to hostile.

The White House is a prestige reportorial assignment, carrying with it respect for the president. Journalists' objectives and needs, moreover, sometimes coincide with the interests of the president and his staff. They are expected to file a constant supply of stories about the president, which makes them susceptible to reporting news of the president's devising.

Deference reigns, particularly when the president symbolically embodies the state at times of domestic and especially foreign crises that appear to threaten national security. This supportive coverage is often produced less by media restraint than by a lack of public opposition from members of Congress and other elites waiting to see how the crisis will turn out before criticizing the president.[27]

The press also tends to serve up respectful stories when the president participates in a ceremony that involves his role as symbol of the nation's identity: giving the State of the Union address, welcoming a foreign dignitary, representing the country at an international conference.

But deference violates journalists' professional norms and concepts of news. It substitutes passivity and transmission for initiative and revelation. Journalists see themselves as the public's watchdog, expected to look at the president with a critical, even adversarial, eye, especially when he or his associates' appear to be behaving ineffectually or unethically.

Arguably, this eye on the president has become jaundiced over the years as reporters have moved to more interpretation and comment, and as the bounds of acceptable stories have stretched, even broken, to include White House media-manipulation techniques and the president's personal behavior. Reporters did not tell the public that President Franklin D. Roosevelt was in a wheelchair or about President John Kennedy's affairs. No aspect of President Bill Clinton's life seems immune to media scrutiny.

Dana Summers © 1984, Washington Post Writers Group. Reprinted with permission.

Besides, conflict is a basic ingredient of news. Reporters have an incentive to find and emphasize it. Two familiar conflictual camps are Congress versus the executive branch and Republicans versus Democrats. Both involve the president. So, if there is meaningful opposition to the president, reporters will likely include it in their stories. On the networks' nightly news programs, "a typical White House story is mostly made up of audio and video segments from other sources—members of Congress, Washington experts, file footage, or the journalists themselves."[28]

Media's Depictions

So, reporters and their editors pick the facts to use and decide what to emphasize and how to interpret it. They shape the president's appearances and words, behavior and actions, into news stories replete with quotes, video clips, and sound bites.[29] Crucial is their power to frame: A president's policy compromise can be depicted as a broken promise or as achieving part of his original objective. One need only compare a president's press conference with its media coverage to see this process in action.[30]

Much of this news skeptically interprets presidential actions and emphasizes scandals and blunders, often within a context of political conflict. This can undermine the president. As Richard Cheney, former chief of staff to President Ford and President Bush's Secretary of Defense, observed of the press: "They like to set the agenda. They like to decide what's important and what isn't important. But if you let them do that, they're going to trash your presidency."[31]

Trashed presidencies were the norm from the late 1960s. President Johnson decided not to run for reelection in 1968. President Nixon left office in disgrace two years after his massive reelection victory of 1972. President Ford lost his bid for reelection in 1976, as did President Carter in 1980, and President Bush in 1992. Five presidents of different parties, ideologies, and personalities, with one thing in common: None served two full terms.

Prominent among the reasons adduced to account for this phenomenon have been these presidents' unsuccessful relationships with the media.[32]

Presidents Ford and Carter both failed to appreciate the importance of courting the press. Ford never overcame the media's portrayal of him as "unathletic, slow, dimwitted, bumbling and prone to mishaps."[33] According to his communications advisors, Carter was "inattentive to the press's portrayal of his presidency and did not make enough effort to create a favorable image . . . resisted slogans and simplifying characterizations, making the job of explaining a Carter program or philosophy to the press and public difficult."[34] Once established during the president's first year, this negative image became almost impossible to change as journalists used it to assess Carter's subsequent actions.[35]

President Nixon understood the importance of the media and devised various expedients to try to manage them. His success contributed to his overwhelming reelection victory. But the media-manipulation techniques were undermined by his hatred of the press. Nor could those techniques protect him against the Watergate horrors, revealed in part by two *Washington Post* local (not White House) reporters.[36]

After President Carter failed to gain reelection, it looked as if the media beast was untameable; that President Lyndon Johnson's charge, "'all of politics changed because of you,'" was justified.[37] Then, enter Ronald Reagan.

PRESIDENT REAGAN AND THE MEDIA

After serving two complete terms, Ronald Reagan left office with the highest poll ratings (68 percent approved, 26 percent disapproved of the way he was handling his job) of any modern occupant of the office.

And yet President Reagan violated the norms of presidential behavior prescribed by scholars: He worked only from 9 a.m. to 5 p.m. and took a nap, watched television nightly, and was not a master of detail (to say the least).

A majority of Americans disagreed with Reagan's positions on many major issues, such as aiding the Nicaraguan Contras, cutting federal programs, and opposing abortion. He weathered a major economic recession in 1981–1982, the precipitous withdrawal of U.S. forces from Lebanon, the Iran-Contra debacle, and a huge number of political scandals in his administration.

Moreover, like every other administration, the Reagan White House was a cornucopia of policy and personality conflict. As high-level aide Richard Darman drolly observed: "'There's a great deal of infighting, and we're split into separate warring groups which leak unpleasant things about each other to the amusement and delight of the media, which are not slow in passing it on.'"[38]

Peace and prosperity contributed to President Reagan's success, as did his underestimated political experience and skill, and his ideological flexibility demonstrated by his willingness to reach a rapprochement with the Soviet Union's Mikhail Gorbachev. But above all, the first term of the Reagan presidency was a public relations triumph.[39] It involved three elements: the president himself; his policies and themes; and effective media-manipulation techniques.[40]

The Man

Ronald Reagan was an actor, completely at ease in front of the media's cameras and microphones.[41] His voice was confident and reassuring. "He could read things that couldn't have meant anything to him . . . with the utmost conviction."[42] He brought to the presidency his movie persona of the personable, amiable, nice guy.[43]

Reagan also benefitted from his frequent happy, reassuring facial expressions. He seemed naturally cheerful, or at least buoyant. Intuitively or consciously, he knew that this expression had the best effect on his audience—boosting his supporters and neutralizing his opponents.[44]

Adding to his popularity was Reagan's reported demeanor following the assassination attempt on his life. But his behavior was publicized by his media-savvy aides, who emphasized the appealing elements of the president's response—optimism, humor, courage, and aplomb. They built up expectations to magnify the drama of his first postassassination speech to Congress.[45]

His Policies

During Reagan's first months in office, when the media provided relatively uncritical coverage, the president communicated to the public that he was a strong, uncompromising leader, in command. He stood for a few clear, simple, priorities: tax cuts, military strength, and reduction of federal regulations.

His administration carried out some actions that were also likely to be viewed favorably by the American public, such as the invasion of Grenada. It interpreted ambiguous events to accord with his perspective: the shooting down of a Korean airliner by Soviet forces was effectively defined as an act of aggression rather than of defense.[46] It limited the duration of unfavorable events and thus their media coverage: immediately withdrawing U.S. marines from Lebanon after over two hundred were killed by a suicide bomber. Compare this with the daily reporting of the year-long hostage crisis of U.S. embassy personnel in Iran that so bedeviled the Carter administration but which incurred few casualties.

Reagan may also have been helped by some of the most popular films of the period, such as *Die Hard, Lethal Weapon, Rambo,* and *Robocop.* They disseminated and reinforced the same individualistic, get-tough attitudes and policies that the president seemed to embody and be pursuing.[47] Of course, those movies were critical of those in power, but so was Reagan—even though he occupied the most powerful office in the land.

White House Media Techniques

The president's senior staff, particularly James Baker and Michael Deaver, masterfully managed, manipulated, sometimes even dominated the media. They relied on the standard devices: access to the president, secrecy, and controlled information release. But these techniques were just the start.

Reflecting his inside access to the Reagan presidency, *Time* magazine's then-White House correspondent wrote that "how events had played or would play on the air and in print" dominated every strategy session.[48] A "theme of the day" approach was developed to control the media's agenda and choice of presidential stories, and to enhance the president's purposes and popularity.

White House spokesman Larry Speakes was excluded from the key decision-making meetings so that he would be unable to tell the White House press corps much of significance. Instead, Chief of Staff Baker spent thirty-five hours a week talking to journalists, and David Gergen "'would, day by day, hour by hour, deal with things that came up.'"[49]

The White House also reached over and around the press corps in Washington. The president communicated to the American people by weekly radio broadcasts, parts of which were then reported on the news. His communications office dealt directly with the ethnic press, such as the Chinese dailies in San Francisco.

The president held few televised press conferences because he was not good at unscripted, relatively spontaneous events demanding factual mastery. Consequently, reporters were often reduced to shouting questions while the engines of his helicopter were started to drown them out as he waved to them from its steps.

When the president appeared, nothing was left to chance. According to Donald Regan, chief of staff during the president's second term: "Every moment of every public appearance was scheduled, every word was scripted, every place where Reagan was supposed to stand was chalked with toe marks. The President was always being prepared for a performance."[50]

Television was central. Presidential speech-writer Peggy Noonan called the president's aides "line producers of a show called *White House,* with Ronald Reagan as the President."[51] The objective was to limit what television news could show and exploit its reliance on pictures and sound bites.[52]

So the Reagan managers had the president participate in only one visually newsworthy activity per day. When possible, aides even created "news events" to elicit specific headlines and produce appealing images.[53] To illustrate an increase in home construction starts, for example, the president visited a building site. Wearing a hard hat, standing in front of the homes being developed, he announced the rise and what it meant for the American people and economy.[54]

Compelling television fare, these staged visual vignettes could mislead by giving the impression that they represented actual policy commitments: The president was shown officiating at the Special Olympics and dedicating senior citizens' projects, even though he proposed cutting the budget for the disabled and federal housing subsidies for the elderly.

On display in this media-managing was a sophisticated awareness of the president's ceremonial role, of the importance of (visual) symbols, of the theater and poetry of government, of the president as monarch.[55]

PRESIDENT BUSH AND THE MEDIA

President Reagan and his senior staff showed how to manage the media. Would his successors display the same skills, and would the media remain susceptible to manipulation?

George Bush eschewed a stage-managed presidency. He reduced the public rhetoric, offered few theatrical events, minimized pomp. Slashed was the number of political strategists, official photographers, and traveling entourages. Bush held more news conferences in seventeen months than Ronald Reagan had held in eight years. Bush socialized with reporters, inviting them to his private quarters.

But the absence of a coherent strategy and message hurt Bush's ability to push his policy agenda. His indifference to public relations rendered him vulnerable to journalists' decisions about what should rank highest on the news agenda and how to frame it.

For the last year of the Bush presidency what ranked highest was the economic recession, for which the president was often explicitly or implicitly blamed. In contrast to his decisive Gulf War policy, he seemed to have no solution to the recession. The negative coverage of the economy enabled his opponents to accuse him of being a protector of the rich, uncaring about ordinary Americans.

The Bush media approach did not produce his reelection and may have contributed to his defeat. During their 1992 contest, his victorious opponent and staff displayed considerable media savvy. Would it continue when Bill Clinton became president? The following section describes and explains the media disaster of Clinton's first two years and his subsequent recovery.

PRESIDENT CLINTON AND THE MEDIA

During the 1992 election, Bill Clinton's opponents raised and the media transmitted (sometimes originating) doubts about his experience, competence, proposed policies, and—above all—his character. Although Clinton used the media to try to blunt these doubts (notably by appearing with his wife on "60 Minutes" to discuss their marriage), these concerns persisted when he became president. Important, therefore, for the president to show that he could be effective and trusted.

But elected with only 43 percent of the vote, Clinton was a minority president. During his first two years, he governed with marginal majorities in Congress, his party divided at times into liberal and conservative elements. After the 1994 elections, he faced Republican domination of both chambers.[56]

Republicans, therefore, had little reason to cooperate with him. From the start, they opposed many of his plans and proposals. They and their allies also continued the search for Clinton corruption and womanizing scandals, feeding their findings to the press.[57] Ross Perot also hovered nearby, ready in his media-attention-getting way, to criticize the president.

Clinton, moreover, entered office as an activist with an extensive policy agenda. Rather than a Reagan espousing broad themes on three-by-five-inch cards, he seemed to have a policy-spouting computer in his head. But his position on his party's spectrum was unclear. He could be a liberal or a conservative Democrat, occasionally both. Sensing this, other policymakers, including interest group leaders, competed, often through the media, for the president's ideological soul, pushing him to the right or to the left according to their own preferences.

It was therefore imperative for Clinton to attract public support. This meant commanding a national audience at a time of proliferating, competing attractions on the media, and doing so while simultaneously avoiding overexposure.

Initial White House Media Techniques

Clinton and his media aides chose to follow the Reagan model: few formal presidential press conferences, frequent radio addresses, story of the day, and stage events for television.

But they went much further than Reagan: They initially appeared to disdain the White House press corps.[58] "As much as possible, the president wants his message delivered as he presents it, not filtered, or analyzed by the news media. The catch phrase used by White House officials is that Mr. Clinton intends to speak 'to people' instead of 'through people.'"[59]

This meant televised town meetings, call-ins, and question-and-answer sessions with ordinary citizens. It entailed the deployment of new technologies: a White House web page, e-mail to and from the public, faxes to the press, direct satellite hookups to local television anchors. It involved continued reliance on the partly mediated programs of Larry King, MTV, and the morning news. The president's first exclusive television interview from the White House was with MTV's Tabitha Soren.

The Clinton approach failed. It antagonized a White House press corps described by a distinguished presidency scholar as "'obnoxious, arrogant, pampered and self-important baby-boomers.'"[60] Worse, it hopelessly underestimated the corps' importance. Reporters for the elite and prestige newspapers frame events and issues for much of the rest of the media, including the soft outlets. They disproportionately influence the talk show industry inside the Washington beltway. And the three major networks' nightly newscasts still provide most presidential news for their 30 million viewers.

News Coverage

So the Clinton administration, like its predecessors, had to deal with the White House press corps. The corps members were aware of the Clinton election campaign's sophisticated and effective use of the media. They had been burned by or learned about the manipulation techniques of the Reagan regime. So they waited skeptically, even cynically, to report the actions of the new administration.

What they encountered from the start was a president and staff apparently unaware of the danger of idle journalists. After the election but before Clinton took over the presidency, White House reporters hung around Little Rock, Arkansas. But the Clinton press office failed to fill their days and nights with a continuous flood of press releases, briefings, and interviews featuring fresh and interesting stories about the president-elect, his family, appointments, and policies.

To the White House reporters, this neglect smacked of ineptitude and revealed the disdain of the president and his aides for them. The outrage it generated was compounded over the next two years by a series of presidential actions that could reasonably be framed by the press as misjudgments and policy miscalculations. These were actions that the president's aides did not prevent in advance or finesse after they occurred, and, in fact, often mishandled and then worsened by failing "to provide trustworthy information, whether out of inability, unwillingness or both."[61]

The president proposed and then presided over the withdrawal of several highly visible administration appointments, in part because of inadequate background checks and a lack of a strategy to achieve their public and senatorial approval.[62] He seemed to dither and delay in filling a U.S. Supreme Court seat. There was his $200 haircut in *Air Force One* at a time he was advocating austerity to the American public ("Scalpgate"). It was incorrectly reported that other planes were kept on the runway when the only flight delayed was the chartered press plane.

Firings at the White House travel office illustrate presidential failure to understand the press corps and the latter's excessive antagonism-fueled response.[63] Reaction by the White House press corps was extreme: At one briefing, reporters asked 169 questions about the firings. Several times the story made the front page of the leading newspapers—far more often at the time than the president's deficit-reduction package.

The Clintons were within their rights to change the travel office staff. It was the way the affair was handled that roused reporters' wrath, and the dribbling out of unseemly information that kept the story in the news far longer than initially seemed possible.

Even when a staff change was handled discreetly, negative, albeit humorous, coverage ensued, as with "Chickengate." The White House chef, committed to French cuisine, was replaced by an exponent of American food. Before taking office, the new chef was interviewed by the food editor of the *Washington Times*. Inexperienced in the ways of the press, he incautiously announced that only free-range (uncaged) chickens would be served.[64] The National Broiler Council cried foul; as did Tyson Foods, headquartered in Arkansas, the country's largest producer of chickens, none of them free-range.[65]

Trivial in themselves, these episodes could be taken to symbolize a hypocritical president, whose snooty behavior belied his campaign theme of "Putting People First," and who was running an ineffectual, if not incompetent, presidency.

President Clinton also displayed a penchant for announcing policy positions then reversing himself. And doing so in a way that suggested he had no core beliefs he would not compromise, even abandon. Early on in his administration,

NEW WHITE HOUSE CHEF PLANS TO SERVE **FREE-RANGE** CHICKENS ONLY

Copyright 1994, Christian Science Monitor News Service. Distributed by Los Angeles Times Syndicate.

he prominently raised the divisive issue of gays in the military, the outcome of which showed him as unable to get his way and eventually irresolute. He proposed an energy tax despite a campaign promise not to raise taxes on the middle class. He invested much of his (and his wife's) political capital in a complicated, big-government, health care "reform" proposal that spurred intense opposition from interest groups and ultimately went nowhere. In the process, the president failed to present himself as taking speedy and decisive action to achieve clear, simple, and appealing policies. Instead, he could not resist talking often and at length about his policy opinions and options as he changed his mind over the course of his discussions. This behavior was alien to most White House reporters, who far prefer politics to the intricacies and implications of policy so absorbing to Clinton.

To compete with the president, his opponents also went public. They enjoyed ample access to the media. As one graphic example, Senate Armed Services Committee Chairman Sam Nunn (D.-Ga.) and others solicited public opinion to compel Clinton to retreat from his stand on gays in the military, keeping the issue before the public with committee hearings and photo opportunities, including one in front of the close sleeping quarters on a Navy submarine.

So, reporters tended to report negatively on the president's policy activities. News stories focused on apparent failures. Facilitated by the availability of LEXIS-NEXIS, and videotape, they showed him saying different things at different times, rudderless. After just a few months, journalists characterized the Clinton presidency as an actual or likely failure.[66]

Whitewater   All the while reporters were pursuing and writing about the congeries of alleged fiscal improprieties and conflicts of interest involving the Whitewater land deal and Madison Guaranty Savings and Loan.[67] The issue was kept in the news by apparent evasion and meddling by the Clintons and their associates and their ineffectual effort to engage in damage control; by Republican-dominated congressional hearings; and by the investigation of the independent counsel, whose findings were periodically leaked to the press.[68] As a result, Whitewater received far more coverage than such Clinton-claimed accomplishments as the economic recovery and the crime bill.[69]

Commentators' Coverage

Commentators' views of President Clinton were even more critical than news coverage. True, he had his defenders, although even some sympathizers seemed dismayed by the president's policy fluctuations. His antagonists were widespread and rampant. In increasing intensity, they ranged from conservative columnists, editorial-page writers of such newspapers as the *Wall Street Journal* and *Washington Times,* and the *American Spectator* and similar magazines. Many radio talk show hosts were hostile, notably Rush Limbaugh. Indeed, President Clinton—his character, behavior, and policies—were often talk radio's prime subject; and its audience's opinions about him and his ability to govern were substantially more negative than those of nonlisteners. Talk radio reinforced anti-Clinton sentiments.[70]

Tabloid television probed the president's personal life and past activities in ways never applied to recent presidents. But televangelists launched the most virulent assault on Clinton. With his own station available on cable systems nationwide, Pat Robertson of the Christian Coalition conducted a constant assault. The Reverend Jerry Falwell produced and marketed a videotape containing a broad spectrum of unsubstantiated accusations against the president, ranging from sexual misconduct to murder.

When polled after the president's first six months in office, people felt that he had broken his promises and could not get things done. A majority knew and disapproved of his proposal to ease the ban on gays in the military. Few respondents could identify any of the president's programs or policy accomplishments.[71] His public approval rating as measured by the polls fluctuated according to issues and events, but hovered around 43 percent, his electoral base.

Revised White House Media Techniques

Clinton perceived the source of his problems: "I did not realize the importance of communications and the overriding importance of what is on the evening news."[72] He then hired David Gergen, a veteran of the Nixon and Reagan administrations and a man of such media-manipulating skill that it was said he "'understood how to pick a story, how to get a story that somebody was working on and change it, how to get the reporters to call the people you wanted them to call and make the story come out how you wanted.'"[73] Courting of the White House press corps ensued. Symbolically, the corridor linking the upper and lower press offices was opened, and reporters were no longer barred from the White House press office. Briefings were scheduled earlier so as not to interfere with reporters' lunches.[74]

There was more and better staging of the news for television, especially on presidential trips overseas. The president cultivated particular columnists and reporters. The networks' news anchors were granted sessions with the president at the White House. Ted Koppel of "Nightline" enjoyed special access to and exclusive interviews with the president during a state visit to Prague. Clinton even tried to be less voluble. He humored the White House and radio and television correspondents at their annual dinners.

Gergen departed. The press reported the White House media-manipulation efforts.[75] The president continued to express his frustration:

> I really thought . . . my image would not be twisted, and I would not be able to be turned into a cardboard cutout of myself on talk radio or negative news reports or anything like that. I was wrong about that. I mean, heck, half the time when I see myself on the evening news, I think, "Gosh, if that's all I knew about that guy, I wouldn't be for him either."[76]

The election of a Republican congressional majority in the 1994 election was the president's nadir and opportunity. He took advantage of the Republicans' ideological intransigence and apparent extremism and the governmental shutdowns to establish himself as a reasonable seeker of compromise; but also as a staunch defender of funding for education, the environment, and Medicare against proposed Republican cuts.

Facilitating his recovery and resurgence, the president finally put together a staff, particularly Press Secretary Mike McCurry, able to relate effectively to reporters and news organizations. He exploited the detailed opinion poll data supplied by Dick Morris. He became comfortable with and adept at using his communications tools.

These included a year-long preelection barrage of political advertising, barely noticed or commented on by the press. The president got his message across about his accomplishments, popular proposals, and the Republicans' horrors without interruption and interpretation.[77]

The president's media skill was displayed during the summer of 1996 when he appeared twice weekly before the press, using the White House as a backdrop, each time to highlight one of the appealing issues chosen for his reelection campaign: community policing, uniforms and curfews for school-age children, college tuition rebates, and housing for middle-class families.[78]

The president also exhibited his mastery of the "Skutnik Syndrome." President Reagan had initiated this practice when, during his 1982 State of the Union message, he suddenly pointed up to the House gallery and identified Lenny Skutnik sitting there as the hero who had jumped into the icy Potomac River to rescue survivors of a plane crash. During August of his reelection year, in front of the television cameras, President Clinton signed a welfare "reform" bill in the company of three former welfare mothers and a minimum-wage bill accompanied by working Americans. The widow of a tobacco industry lobbyist, who had died from cigarette addiction, lavished praise on the president at a ceremony celebrating regulations supported by the president controlling tobacco as a drug.

So President Clinton learned from his initial experience of dealing with the press and increasingly and successfully emulated President Reagan's approach to the media. Adroit media management, a buoyant economy and peace, combined with his opponent's inept campaign, lifted President Clinton to a second term.

But that term was dominated for many months by investigations by the special prosecutor and by lubricious media accounts of and speculation about the President's denied then admitted sexual misbehavior and his potentially impeachable conduct so that people became far more familiar with the President's relations with Monica Lewinsky than with his policies.[79]

CONCLUSION

Presidents face numerous expectations, many of which they lack the authority to achieve. Because their power to command is limited, they have to rely on persuasion to try to accomplish their objectives. So, presidents naturally try to obtain favorable media coverage. They have expert aides, specialized institutions, and numerous techniques to persuade, manipulate, and pressure the press into transmitting their statements, decisions, and policies in the best possible light.

In practice, presidents face the media with an ambiguous mixture of strengths and weaknesses. They employ secrecy but are beset by leaks. They control the release of information, but not for long. They can badger, berate, and bully the press, but at the risk of resentful reporting. They offer up good news, but the bad is sure to follow.

The media's response is a combination of media-originated, unmediated, and partly-mediated content. Thus, the media can be accommodating, serving at times as a conduit for the White House's version of events and activities. But reporters' needs and objectives often clash with those of the president. Reporters see themselves as watchdogs, guarding the public interest by uncovering the administration's misbehaviors, blunders, and scandals. They prize news about conflicts above presidential accomplishments. They bring a legitimate but sometimes excessive skepticism to presidential motives.

So the media often oppress the president with a constant scrutiny of his words and actions, by giving voice to his opponents, and by seeking out bad news for which he may be blamed or interpreting ambiguous news negatively.

As the experiences of Reagan, Bush, and Clinton reveal, whether the president has an advantage over the press in the media age depends on the media-manipulation skill of the president and his staff. For although a president is evaluated by his words and actions, it is media coverage that portrays them.

Whether democracy is served and whether the public gets an accurate understanding of the presidency from this combination of presidential manipulation and media response are at best uncertain.

Notes

1. Barbara Hinckley, *The Symbolic Presidency* (New York: Routledge, 1990), stresses the importance of public expectations for presidents' conduct of the office.

2. Aaron Wildavsky, *The Beleaguered Presidency* (New Brunswick, N.J.: Transaction, 1991); see also Mary E. Stuckey, *The Best Laid Plans* (Cresskill, N.J.: Hampton Press, 1997).

3. See the discussion of "regimes" by Stephen Skowronek, *The Politics Presidents Make* (Cambridge, Mass.: Harvard University Press, 1993).

4. Lyn Ragsdale, *Presidential Politics* (Boston: Houghton Mifflin, 1993), ix–x.

5. Cited in Richard E. Neustadt, *Presidential Power* (New York: Wiley, 1980), 9 (emphasis in original).

6. James W. Davis, *The President as Party Leader* (New York: Praeger, 1992).

7. Neustadt, *Presidential Power*.

8. Samuel Kernell, *Going Public*, 3rd ed. (Washington, D.C.: CQ Press, 1997).

9. Jeffrey E. Cohen and Ken Collier, "Reconceptualizing Going Public" (paper presented at the annual meeting of the American Political Science Association, Chicago, August 1995).

10. For an historical survey of the relationship, see John Tebbel and Sarah Miles Watts, *The Press and the Presidency* (New York: Oxford University Press, 1985); also relevant are Richard L. Rubin, *Press, Party, and Presidency* (New York: Norton, l98l); and Colin Seymour Ure, *The American President* (New York: St. Martin's Press, 1982).

11. Richard A. Brody, *Assessing the President* (Stanford, Calif.: Stanford University Press, 1991), 9; also relevant is Jon A. Krosnick and Laura A. Brannon, "The Impact of the Gulf War on the Ingredients of Presidential Evaluations," *American Political Science Review* 87:4 (December 1993): 963–75.

12. The most comprehensive study of the president and the media, deserving updating, is Michael Baruch Grossman and Martha Joynt Kumar, *Portraying the President* (Baltimore: Johns Hopkins University Press, 1981); also relevant are Martha Joynt Kumar, "The President and the News Media," in *Congressional Quarterly's Guide to the Presidency,* 2nd ed., ed. Michael Nelson (Washington, D.C.: Congressional Quarterly, Inc., 1996), 835–80; Robert Locander, "Modern Presidential In-Office Communications," *Presidential Studies Quarterly* 13:2 (Spring 1983): 242–54; and Timothy E. Cook and Lyn Ragsdale, "The President and the Press," in *The Presidency and the Political System,* 4th ed., ed. Michael Nelson (Washington, D.C.: CQ Press, 1994), 297–330.

13. See the synthesis by Michael Kelly, "David Gergen, Master of the Game," *New York Times Magazine,* 31 October 1993, 64–65.

14. Harvey G. Zeidenstein, "White House Perceptions of News Media Bias," *Presidential Studies Quarterly* 13:3 (Summer 1983): 345–56; see also Theodore Windt, "Different Realities: Three Presidential Attacks on the News Media," in *Essays in Presidential Rhetoric,* ed. Theodore Windt and Beth Ingold (Dubuque, Iowa: Kendall/Hunt, 1989), 76–91.

15. See Dick Morris, *Behind the Oval Office* (New York: Random House, 1997), 101–02, 122, and throughout for examples.

16. Fitzwater's observations are in the transcript of Mara Liasson, "White House Briefers Employ Multiple Personalities," *Morning Edition* (National Public Radio), 9 June 1993, 3.

17. For the office's definitive history, see John Maltese, *Spin Control,* 2nd ed. rev. (Chapel Hill: University of North Carolina Press, 1994).

18. Francis X. Clines and Bernard Weinraub, "Washington Talk," *New York Times,* 23 November 1981, A20.

19. Kelly, "David Gergen, Master of the Game," 68.

20. Joseph C. Spear, *Presidents and the Press: The Nixon Legacy* (Cambridge: MIT Press, 1984).

21. An informative study is by Carolyn Smith, *Presidential Press Conferences* (New York: Praeger, 1990).

22. Mary E. Stuckey categorizes and gives examples of the president's answers in "Ronald Reagan as a Not-So-Great Communicator (paper presented at the annual meeting of the Midwest Political Science Association, Chicago, April 1988).

23. Jacob Weisberg, "The White House Beast," *Vanity Fair* 56 (September 1993): 169.

24. Gwen Ifill, "Clinton's Long-Awaited Prime-Time Session Is Spurned by Two Networks," *New York Times,* 18 June 1993, A10.

25. Joe S. Foote, *Television Access and Political Power* (New York: Praeger, 1990).

26. David L. Paletz and Richard J. Vinegar, "Presidents on Television: The Effects of Instant Analysis," *Public Opinion Quarterly* 41:4 (Winter 1977–1978): 488–97.

27. Brigitte Lebens Nacos, *The Press, Presidents, and Crises* (New York: Columbia University Press, 1990).

28. Cook and Ragsdale, "The President and the Press," 308, citing Cook's study, "Staging the News and Covering the News."

29. Mary E. Stuckey, "Media Use in the Contemporary Presidency" (paper presented at the annual meeting of the Southern Political Science Association, Atlanta, November 1994).

30. As Duke undergraduate Kat Allen did of George Bush's press conferences in an independent study paper, December 1992.

31. Cited in Maltese, *Spin Control,* 2.

32. For studies of other presidencies, see Betty Hochin Winfield, *FDR and the News Media* (Urbana: University of Illinois Press, 1990); and Craig Allen, *Eisenhower and the Mass Media* (Chapel Hill: University of North Carolina Press, 1993).

33. John Orman, *American Political Science Review* 87:2 (June 1993): 499. For a detailed survey, see Mark J. Rozell, *The Press and the Ford Presidency* (Ann Arbor: University of Michigan Press, 1992).

34. Mark J. Rozell, *The Press and the Carter Presidency* (Boulder, Colo.: Westview, 1989), 205; see also the memoir by Carter's press secretary, Jody Powell, *The Other Side of the Story* (New York: William Morrow, 1984).

35. Rozell, *The Press and the Carter Presidency,* 231.

36. Joseph C. Spear, *Presidents and the Press* (Cambridge, Mass.: MIT Press, 1984); Carl Bernstein and Bob Woodward, *All The President's Men* (New York: Simon & Schuster, 1974).

37. Quoted in David Halberstam, "CBS: The Power and the Profits," *The Atlantic Monthly* 237 (February 1976): 65.

38. Quoted in Peggy Noonan, *What I Saw at the Revolution* (New York: Ivy Books, 1990), 34. Also see David L. Paletz and K. Kendall Guthrie, "Three Faces of Ronald Reagan," *Journal of Communication* 37:4 (Autumn 1987): 7–23. Used with permission of Oxford University Press.

39. Steven R. Weisman, "The President and the Press: The Art of Controlled Access," *New York Times Magazine,* 14 October, 1984, 36ff. For a different view, see Michael J. Robinson, Maura Clancy, and Lisa Grand, "With Friends Like These . . . ," *Public Opinion* 6:3 (June-July 1983): 2–3, 52–54; and Michael J. Robinson and Maura Clancy, "Teflon Politics," *Public Opinion* 7:2 (April-May 1984): 14–18.

40. For a highly critical view, see Mark Hertsgaard, *On Bended Knee: The Press and the Reagan Presidency* (New York: Farrar, Strauss, Giroux, 1989). More scholarly and analytical is Robert Sahr, "President Reagan's Use of the News Media" (paper presented at the annual meeting of the Western Political Science Association, Eugene, Oregon, March 1986).

41. Bernard Ingham, press secretary to the British Prime Minister, describes Mrs. Thatcher's admiration of the president's skill in *Kill the Messenger* (London: Harper-Collins, 1991), 256.

42. Ben Maddow, explaining his use of Mr. Reagan as a narrator for films made by the Air Force motion picture unit during the World War II, in *Backstory 2,* ed. Pat McGilligan (Berkeley: University of California Press, 1991), 170.

43. For a detailed account of the man and most of his presidency, see Lou Cannon, *President Reagan* (New York: Simon & Schuster, 1991); and for an appealing portrait, see Noonan, *What I Saw,* chap. 8.

44. Dennis G. Sullivan et al., "The Effect of President Reagan's Facial Displays on Observers' Attitudes, Impressions, and Feelings about Him" (paper presented at the annual meeting of the American Political Science Association, Washington, D.C., September 1984).

45. Sahr, "President Reagan's Use of the News Media," 10.

46. David L. Paletz and C. Danielle Vinson, "Constructing Content and Delimiting Choice: International Coverage of KAL Flight 007," *Argumentation* 8 (1994): 357–66.

47. Susan Jeffords, *Hard Bodies* (New Brunswick, N.J.: Rutgers University Press, 1994).

48. Laurence I. Barrett, *Gambling with History* (Garden City, N.Y.: Doubleday, 1983), 442.

49. Michael Kelly, "David Gergen, Master of the Game," 71, quoting Ed Rollins.

50. Donald T. Regan, *For the Record* (San Diego, Calif.: Harcourt Brace Jovanovich, 1988), 277.

51. Noonan, *What I Saw,* 148.

52. See Mary E. Stuckey, *The President as Interpreter-in-Chief* (Chatham, N.J.: Chatham House Publishers, 1991), on television's effects on presidential communication and obtaining of public support.

53. For an insightful analysis of the formats and logic of the news media, especially television, see David L. Altheide and Robert P. Snow, *Media Worlds in the Postjournalism Era* (Hawthorne, N.Y.: Aldine de Gruyter, 1991).

54. Michael Deaver, "Sound-Bite Campaigning: TV Made Us Do It," *Washington Post,* 30 October 1988, C7, cited in ibid., 88.

55. See David L. Paletz, "What If America Had a Monarch?" in *What If?* ed. Nelson W. Polsby (Brattleboro, V.T.: Lewis Publishing, 1982), 17–25.

56. For a critical survey of the first two years, see Colin Campbell and Bert A. Rockman, eds., *The Clinton Presidency* (Chatham, N.J.: Chatham House Publishers, 1995).

57. For the importance of competing political forces on media depictions of a president, see Montague Kern, Patricia W. Levering, and Ralph B. Levering, *The Kennedy Crises* (Chapel Hill: University of North Carolina Press, 1983).

58. For accounts and appraisals of Clinton's interactions with the media, see Martha Joynt Kumar, "President Clinton Meets the Media," in *The Clinton Presidency*, ed. Stanley A. Renshon (Boulder Colo.: Westview, 1995), 167–93; the collection of essays in *Media Studies Journal* 8:2 (Spring 1994); and the three front-page reports by David Shaw, "Not Even Getting a 1st Chance," 15 September 1993, "Dire Judgments on Clinton Started Just Days Into Term," 16 September 1993, and "Did Reporters Let Their Feelings Affect Coverage? 17 September 1993, in the *Los Angeles Times*.

59. Steve Lohr, "White House: A Computer Nerdville," *New York Times,* 20 February 1993, Y13.

60. Richard Neustadt, quoted in H. Brandt Ayers, "The Death of Civility," *New York Times,* 16 July 1994, Y11.

61. Ruth Marcus cites chapter and verse in "Much Disregard for the Truth," *International Herald Tribune,* 23 August 1994, 7.

62. Thomas L. Friedman, "Clinton Concedes He Erred on Baird Nomination," *New York Times,* 23 January 1993, 1.

63. See Peter J. Boyer, "A Fever in the White House," *New Yorker* 72:8 (15 April 1996): 56–73; and David Shaw, "Did Reporters Let Their Feelings Affect Coverage?" *Los Angeles Times,* 17 September 1993, A18–19.

64. Judith Olney, "White House Chef Will Push a Free-Range Chicken in Every Pot," *Washington Times,* 30 March 1994, C4.

65. Judith Olney, "Hillary's PC Chickens Raise Ire of the FOB's," *Washington Times* 11 April 1994, A1; see also Richard Johnson with Kimberley Ryan, "1st Chef Chickens Out in Cockfight," *New York Post,* 13 April 1994, 6.

66. E.g., Thomas L. Friedman, "Will Clinton's Stumbling Ever End?" *International Herald Tribune,* 24 May 1993, 1.

67. Jeff Cohen and Norman Solomon, "Whitewater Under the Bridge," *Extra!* 7:3 (May-June 1994): 9.

68. For the adverse publicity impact of independent counsel investigations, see Suzanne Garment, *Scandal* (New York: Anchor Books, 1992), 97–98.

69. For an analysis essentially exonerating President and Mrs. Clinton of any criminal wrongdoing, see Garry Wills, "The Clinton Scandals," *New York Review* 43:7 (18 April 1966): 59–67.

70. Diana Owen, "Talk Radio and Evaluations of President Clinton," *Political Communication* 14:3 (July-September 1997): 333–53.

71. Times Mirror [now Pew] Center for The People & The Press, "Jury Still Out on Clinton's Success," 5 August 1993, 1–2.

72. Quoted in Bob Woodward, *The Agenda: Inside the Clinton White House* (New York: Simon & Schuster, 1994), 313.

73. Michael Kelly, "David Gergen, Master of the Game," 70–71, quoting Republican political consultant Ed Rollins.

74. Gwen Ifill, "White House Tries Out a Cheerful Face," *New York Times,* 8 June 1993, A10.

75. Douglas Jehl, "All Prague's a Stage for Presidents," *New York Times,* 12 January 1994, A5.

76. Quoted in Peter Maas, "I Think We've Learned a Lot," *Parade Magazine,* 19 February 1995, 6.

77. Morris, *Behind the Oval Office,* 139–53.

78. This paragraph is based on Martha Joynt Kumar, "The White House Beat at the Century Mark" (paper presented at the 1996 annual meeting of the American Political Science Association, San Francisco, September 1996), 29–31.

Chapter 13

Bureaucracy

◆ ◆ ◆

A governmental bureaucracy is a complex organization, with a hierarchical authority structure and job specialization, responsible for administering and enforcing policies. It is usually headed by political appointees and their associates and staffed mainly by ostensibly nonpolitical employees.

At the national governmental level, bureaucracy encompasses the various administrative organs of government from the mammoth Department of Defense to the picayune Iranian Recovery Field Office. The National Aeronautics and Space Administration is a bureaucracy, as are the Federal Bureau of Investigation (FBI), the Bureau of Alcohol, Tobacco and Firearms, and other policing agencies.[1]

Bureaucrats have substantial authority: They issue rules, allocate funds, regulate activity, and enforce compliance. In so doing, they usually exercise considerable discretion because policies passed by the other branches of government often require fleshing out before they can be implemented. Bureaucracies also sometimes originate or propose policies that may receive presidential, congressional, or judicial approval, rejection, or modification.

The policies bureaucrats apply can conflict between departments. For example, given China's problematic record on human rights, the State Department would restrict that country's trade with the United States, whereas the Commerce Department would not. Nor are a department's policies always consistent or compatible: the U.S. Department of Agriculture is charged both with promoting the sale of the meat produced by American cattle growers and with advocating a healthy diet.

The relations governmental departments and agencies have with the presidency, Congress, interest groups, and the public range from favored to benign to beleaguered. Ideal from the bureaucrats' point of view is a chummy, mutually beneficial arrangement with the relevant congressional subcommittees for funding and interest groups for support, under an umbrella of presidential and public approval. Budget-cutting times, however, tend to produce mixed relationships. In recent years, for example, the National Endowment for the Arts has enjoyed a modicum of presidential favor but has suffered from a congressional majority determined to slash its budget, has been supported by some interest groups but opposed by others, and has encountered a public whose diverse opinions have ranged from approval to disinterest to hostility.

Media fictional portrayals of bureaucrats are usually unflattering. Typical is "The X-Files," a popular television program that reflects (and perhaps encourages) deep distrust of officialdom.[2] Regrettably, there is lack of research on the prevalence and effects of fictional depictions of bureaucrats and bureaucracy. In analyzing the governmental bureaucracy-media interaction, therefore, this chapter focuses on news coverage. It examines the relations of politically appointed heads, then of their departments and agencies, with the press. An account of the activities of public information officers follows. Next comes a discussion of media depictions of the police, a bureaucratic organization that trades in and deals with violence.

The heart of this chapter is an extensive case study of the Pentagon's media-manipulating response to false nuclear alerts. This detailed empirical study shows how bureaucrats handled what could have been depicted by the media as very bad news and reveals the very individual responses of specific reporters. This leads on to a brief discussion of the media's relationship with that quintessential bureaucratic organization—the military—at its most stressed, specifically during the Vietnam and Gulf wars.

BUREAUCRACY-MEDIA INTERACTION

For cabinet secretaries and agency heads, cultivating the press can enhance their political influence, further their careers, and benefit the president who appointed them. Certainly, as their department's chief spokesperson, they have the ability to make speeches, hold frequent press conferences, give innumerable individual interviews, engage in informal conversations with journalists, and provide access to departmental officials and documents.[3] Whether these tools lead to glory, disaster, or neglect depends on the officials' willingness to engage journalists, the skills and techniques they apply, and the programs and issues they emphasize.[4]

For example, Nicholas Brady, Treasury Secretary during the Bush administration, disdained the press. He rarely made news, and gave infrequent, invariably uninformative interviews, which he would put off the record or on background, meaning that he could not be quoted. As a result, he received little credit for his accomplishments and was "widely portrayed in the press as a lightweight."[5] In contrast, his predecessor, James Baker, flattered reporters, appeared to take them into his confidence, and fed them information and one-line quotes. Consequently, he received credit for accomplishments not entirely of his making and avoided blame for disasters occurring on his watch.

National Security Advisor, later Secretary of State, Henry Kissinger, during the Nixon and Ford administrations, was famously successful in dealing with the reporters who covered him, especially the three television networks' correspondents, and the influential Washington columnists specializing in foreign affairs. He was able to "disarm them with his wit, intimidate them with his brilliance, flatter them with his confidences and charm them with his attention."[6] His critics were likely to be telephoned, cajoled, stroked, invited to dine, visited at their homes. Contributing to his effectiveness was his ability to persuade many of the journalists of the desirability of his diplomacy succeeding.

Even heads of relatively mundane departments can attract favorable attention and publicity and raise their profile and prestige. Elizabeth Dole, Secretary of Transportation during the Reagan administration, was particularly successful, casting herself as the "'safety Secretary'"—an image that survived worsening airline-safety records and her tepid support for automobile air bags."[7] The light added to the rears of automobiles was even given her name.

Obscure officials can parlay themselves into media darlings or deadbeats. Witness surgeon generals. Some were barely covered by the mass media. But C. Everett Koop enjoyed abundant, positive coverage. In dire contrast, Joycelyn Elders became such a controversial burden to the Clinton administration that she was induced to resign.

Media coverage is not immune to reality. When she first took office as Energy Secretary in the Clinton administration, Hazel R. O'Leary enjoyed favorable, even lavish, coverage, in part because of her decision to investigate her department's human radiation experiments, her call to compensate people who had been harmed, and her declassification of millions of cold war records from departmental archives. She was praised for her "melding of instinct and political acumen," for her "engaging and formidable personality," and for hiring "as her personal aides a brood of restless, well-informed and stubborn men and women who had long been the Department's most influential and vocal critics in Washington."[8] But less than two years later, she was under attack for spending "thousands of dollars in Government money for a consulting firm to monitor the reporters who cover her department and to rank them as to how favorable they were."[9] She was also accused of violating her office by her numerous and expensive entourage-accompanied travels throughout the United States and abroad.

Media Objectives of Departments and Agencies

For the many bureaucrats who prefer to carry out their duties in anonymity, unknown and unobserved, "reporters are considered either frightening or unalloyed nuisances: They are snoopers, troublemakers; publicity is the enemy of sound public administration; reporters do not understand complicated programs or technical jargon; they misquote or quote out of context."[10] Only journalists for trade and specialized publications are relatively exempt from such criticism.

Nonetheless, there are compelling reasons why bureaucrats interact with the media, aside from the fact that they often have no choice. Through favorable press coverage, they can acquire, sustain, or reinforce the legitimacy of their department or agency with the other institutions of government and the public; achieve adequate, even increased, funding for their activities; facilitate their policy goals; and encourage acquiescence to their decisions.[11] Unfavorable stories can have the reverse effects.

Steven Hess identifies and Timothy Cook amplifies on two general objectives that departments can facilitate through media publicity: self-preservation and accomplishing policy goals, especially when lacking other resources to do so.[12]

The Defense Department has a huge budget requiring congressional approval and popular support, or at least acquiescence. It constantly seeks funding for existing and new weapons systems. Pentagon briefings, with their responses to reporters' questions and demands, are exercises in self-preservation. "The Pentagon's strategy is less inclined toward the minutiae of policy than toward educating the public on the need for a big defense, sophisticated (and expensive) weapons systems and a large bureaucracy."[13]

In contrast, the State Department's daily noon briefing can stimulate the need for negotiating foreign policy positions before facing the cameras. The official spokesperson anticipates reporters' questions and solicits answers from within the department and with the Defense Department and the White House. The briefings themselves then set forth the country's official foreign policy, its formal response to events abroad.

Other departments vary considerably in their desire and need for media coverage. Agencies lacking resources to ensure their decisions are enforced—such as the Federal Trade Commission, the Food and Drug Administration (FDA), and the Consumer Product Safety Commission—can try to accomplish their policy objectives "by drawing the news media's attention to unsafe products or unsavory practices, and, by doing so in a public manner, may provoke at low cost the corporations into instituting reforms in order to avoid similarly damaging publicity in the future."[14] So, before the FDA undertook a raid on manufacturers of illegal "look-alike" drugs in several states, a meeting was held to decide which reporters would be called and in what order when the seizure began.[15]

Most bureaucracies, like the Central Intelligence Agency (CIA), seek coverage selectively to report success and minimize failure. Others, the National Security Agency is a conspicuous example, eschew media and public attention for their actions, many of which are clandestine and costly.

Factors Determining Coverage   Some bureaucracies are better insulated against the press than others. Determining criteria are subject matter, partisanship, access, and opposition.[16]

Bureaucracies dealing with significant, visible, controversial, or unpopular issues are likely to attract journalistic attention. In Washington, this means the big four departments: State, Defense, Treasury, and Justice. In contrast, coverage of many other departments is sporadic or nonexistent. The subject also affects coverage: Technical, scientific subjects are protected because investigating them demands knowledge that most reporters are unlikely to possess and bureaucrats can hide behind impenetrable jargon. Thus, Defense Department reporters infrequently undertake detailed investigative reporting on wasteful weapons procurement. The subject is too complicated and too difficult to unravel. Besides, the Pentagon is reluctant to reveal how well a weapon system is working and whether it is worth its cost.[17]

Ostensibly nonpartisan and technical agencies, such as the National Oceanic and Atmospheric Administration, can usually go about their business without reportorial scrutiny; they are regarded with less suspicion than, for example, the oft-political Justice Department.

Journalists thrive on access to bureaucracies for information and revelation. But their access is often restricted, for example to the CIA and FBI. Woe betide any of these agencies' agents who deals independently with the press. The CIA even required its confessed turncoat spy Aldrich Ames to clear with it any public remarks, writings, and interviews with news organizations, and discouraged him from signing book or movie deals by requiring him to turn over any profits to the agency.[18]

A related shield these agencies have is the ability to invoke national security: Reporters believe that they have a responsibility to be careful about intelligence sources and usually consult with the government over potentially sensitive stories.[19]

Some departments are so determined to deny access that they threaten their employees. "Pentagon officials try to terrorize potential news sources into staying away from reporters or into following the official line when they do talk."[20] They have been known to monitor interviews, bug offices, threaten to use lie detectors, and transfer violators to undesirable positions and places.

Conflict within or opposition to a bureaucracy from outside can make it vulnerable to the media. Dissenters reveal disagreements. Whistle-blowers recount incompetence, disasters, and outrages. Vocal, vigorous antagonists in other departments and among interest groups publicize and criticize an agency's actions and inaction. Thus, the Occupational and Safety Health Administration and the Environmental Protection Agency are frequently attacked by the organizations they affect and their actions challenged in court, with concomitant publicity.

Congressional committees or subcommittees can be crucial agents of exposure, holding oversight hearings and investigations into agency operations, compelling testimony, and revelations. Relevant here is the opponents' skill at dramatizing the bureaucrats' supposed sins: witness the widespread media coverage of the Pentagon's $600 toilet seat.

Beyond the four factors of subject, partisanship, access, and opposition, a bureaucracy may be thrust into the spotlight when it willingly or unwillingly expands its scope of activities, thus subjecting its members to unusual demands and strains (e.g., U.S. troops in Somalia). Or when it achieves a notable success or failure.

Public Information Officers

Every department has its assistant secretary for public affairs, every agency its public information officers (PIOs).[21] When Stephen Hess undertook his research, the Pentagon had fourteen press officers engaged in four kinds of activities: "informing themselves and their colleagues, preparing material for the news media, staging events, and responding to reporters' inquiries."[22] The last activity takes more of their time than the other three put together.[23] Thus, they more often respond to rather than manipulate the press and events. Indeed, much of their information about events comes from the media.

The PIOs' work involves many of the weapons listed in chapter 12: secrecy, control or timed release of information, leaks, and occasional deception. They deploy the usual techniques of press conferences, press releases and speech texts, briefings, backgrounders, and personal interviews. Depending on their resources, they can issue publications, films, and videos; set up speaker and conference programs; arrange media engagements.

For Hess, public information officers are most important in connecting journalists and the bureaucracy. They gather information from the bureaucracy, much of it requested by reporters.[24] In so doing, they can be proactive: anticipating questions, cuing reporters on the agency's positive newsworthy activities, spreading and extending the life of the good news. They are also reactive: putting a favorable spin on information that is ambiguous and limiting the visibility and damage of the bad news they cannot keep quiet.

When something happens to put the agency in the public spotlight and blunders are inevitable, PIOs strive to coordinate information, publicize their relief activity, deflect criticism, and ensure positive news. "The minutes of the Nuclear Regulatory Commission show that when the reactor was about to melt down at Three Mile Island, the commissioners were worried less about what to do to fix it than they were about what they were going to say to the press."[25]

Agencies have been known to contrive bad news and encourage its coverage by the media. Facing budget reductions, for example, they will cut popular programs to dramatize the supposedly dire effects. The National Park Service closed the Washington Monument, an action successfully aimed at attracting press stories, public outrage, and the restoration of some of the funds cut from the agency's budget.

Sometimes information officers and other officials engage in deception. Hess lists the types "on a scale of decreasing acceptability to reporters" as "the honest lie, the inadvertent lie, the half-truth, and the lie."[26] Exemplifying the first, President Carter's press secretary Jody Powell lied to protect the Iranian rescue mission. Inadvertent lies occur accidentally in the crush of an event when the press secretary or information officer does not possess all the facts. In half-truths, the question is construed and answered so narrowly as to convey a misleading impression. It is only "the deliberate and consistent pattern of misstatement on a matter of importance" that outrages Washington reporters.[27]

There are also misinformation and disinformation. Reports of Iraqi troops massed at the Saudi border, after Iraq invaded Kuwait in 1990, when, in fact, there were not many at all, exemplifies misinformation. Its intent was to give the American people the impression of an imminent invasion threat. Examples of disinformation were the false stories misleading the Iraqis into believing that the main allied attack would be from the sea. In both cases, the stories were transmitted by the press assumedly unaware of their falsity.

THE POLICE

The police are the most visible of bureaucracies, an all-purpose social agency performing the dirty work of society. They are responsible for enforcing the law, maintaining order, protecting property, reducing threats of violence, and exercising force. They are expected to deal with underage drinking, racial tensions, drug-infested neighborhoods, and a raft of other public dangers and nuisances.

These responsibilities are undertaken selectively, sporadically, and capriciously because the police lack the resources, the inclination, and the public support to do all the jobs asked of them simultaneously, consistently, and continuously. Constitutional boundaries fence the police in. Inevitably, some law enforcement officers are tempted to break the law to uphold it. They tamper with evidence, commit perjury on the witness stand ("testilying"), become involved with drugs, use excessive force, and commit careless killings.[28]

Indeed, massive violations of the law by even the most prestigious law enforcement agencies are not unknown: witness the FBI's long-running, secret COINTELPRO program. Its intent was to expose, disrupt, and neutralize dissident groups: socialist, antiwar, civil rights, black nationalist, and, less extensively, white supremacists.[29] It was directed against people who had committed no crime but held views and were politically active on behalf of causes that Director J. Edgar Hoover and his associates deemed a threat to the nation.

So the agency distributed anonymous and fictitious materials to cause internal dissension, disseminated nonpublic information to the press to develop public opposition to the dissident groups, and pressured employers to fire members and public institutions to deny them meeting places. It had the Internal Revenue Service audit returns; scrutinized bank accounts; coordinated raids on the organizations' headquarters; had local police use minor health code violations as an excuse for political arrests; and used informants as agent provocateurs. All in all, the bureau flagrantly abused its authority, disdaining legal and constitutional prohibitions.[30]

Years later, in the 1990s, the Bureau of Alcohol, Tobacco, and Firearms was involved in the deaths of more than eighty-five men, women, and children in Waco, Texas. Reporters were kept away from the story, some were even refused access to briefings because they asked difficult questions, independent investigations of the story were discouraged, and evidence was lost or destroyed.

So we have good reason to pay attention to the police and the ways the media depict them in fact and in fiction. Complicating analysis, these depictions are far from monolithic. There is a long-standing history of the police as dim-witted buffoons from the Keystone Kops of silent comedies, the incompetent but menacing horde in Buster Keaton's brilliant silent short film *Cops,* the bumbling sheriffs of *Smokey and the Bandit,* and television's "Dukes of Hazzard," on through comedies like the *Police Academy* series. But there is also a tradition of individual officers as action-adventure heroes, usually loners defying the bureaucracy, as in the Dirty Harry character played by Clint Eastwood, the protagonist in the *Lethal Weapon* series, and the like.

Television in particular has presented us with all sorts of police in shows as different as "Columbo," "The Andy Griffith Show," "In the Heat of the Night," "Cagney and Lacey," "Hill Street Blues," "Miami Vice," "N.Y.P.D. Blue," and "Picket Fences."

To identify dominant depictions, let us look at portrayals of the police and their work in the news and in the widely shown and popular television "reality" shows.

News Portrayals

Clashes between the press and police should be inevitable as ideal reporters—inquisitive and probing—challenge the secretive hierarchy and centralized structure of police departments. But this potential for conflict is smothered under a blanket of cooperation.

Crime news is a media staple, and the police have a virtual monopoly on these stories. Police departments are reporters' prime sources of the details of criminal activity and of police responses. Crime beat reporters obtain their stories from police scanners, "hotlines" to police patrol dispatchers, official spokespersons and reports, and interviews with officers. Since most perpetrators are not caught, they are unavailable for questioning by journalists. The accused lack credibility, the convicted have less. Witnesses and victims may be asked for their reactions to the crime, but not to evaluate the performance of the police handling the case.

To increase protection from undesirable media coverage, police departments emulate other governmental bureaucracies by establishing public information offices to formalize and control relations with the press. Press officers may arrange for reporters to accompany selected officers in their grubby, depressing, sometimes dangerous work. They establish personal contact between ranking police officers and reporters, editors, and publishers.

Within this framework of access, the release of information is controlled as much as possible. Police passes are not issued to all reporters; special folders marked "not publishable" are established; in some departments only written questions are answered; and in many towns beat officers are not permitted to respond to reporters' questions unless a superior or public information officer is present. There are even academic courses teaching media relations to law enforcement personnel.[31]

Behind the scenes, meanwhile, other forms of cooperation sometimes insidiously undermine journalists' independence while furthering police-press unity in the fight against actual, alleged, or imaginary evil-doing. At the request of police departments, the mass media relay appeals for information about particular crimes and advertise most-wanted miscreants. But then reporters may informally share with the police information they have gathered from the unwary in pursuit of their stories. Television out-takes (visual material not used on the air) have been secretly given to the police. Despite some resistance and changes, much police-press cooperation persists.

The mass media's news stories about the police emphasize crimes, recounting information the police have uncovered (or stumbled across). They infrequently report the many other activities that dominate police time.[32] Organizational practices, recruitment, training, working conditions, and career patterns are all neglected. There is little mention of procedures, search-and-seizure policies, incentives to issue traffic citations, or other aspects of police administration. Few attempts are made to assess the efficiency of police departments in their myriad activities, let alone in combating crime. Yet, a recounting of crimes committed compared to arrests made and convictions obtained could raise questions about the effectiveness of police departments and their use of power.

Nonetheless, the police do not believe they are indulged by the press. For the scandal, corruption, and violence in which some law enforcement officers occasionally indulge are the stuff of news. Because the police are out on the streets, in the highways and byways, some of their misbehavior becomes visible, occasionally provoking and serving as the grist of an investigative commission's report. The videotaped beating of Rodney King in Los Angeles in 1991 was a sensational example.

© Dan Foote

Before the taping of Rodney King, people whose notions of the Los Angeles police were derived from the positive portrayals of television series "Dragnet," "Adam 12," "S.W.A.T," "T.J. Hooker," and "Hunter" might have found it hard to believe that in five years "the city has had to pay out more than $20 million in judgments, settlements, and jury verdicts in over three hundred lawsuits alleging excessive force."[33]

Ironically, the tape roused public consciousness of police violence after a marked decline in the use of third-degree tactics by many police forces.[34]

Reality Shows

Television features "reality" shows with such names as "FBI: The Untold Stories," "Top Cops," and "Unsolved Mysteries." Accounting for their proliferation are their popularity with some audiences and their low production costs.

A typical example of the genre is "Cops."[35] Its opening montage consists of a memorial for an officer killed in the line of duty, one attempting to extinguish a burning car, two women police wrestling a male suspect to the ground, four officers struggling with a man kicking a police dog, and a policeman crouched with his gun drawn. The police are portrayed as upbeat, happy in their work, and racially unprejudiced. They enjoy admirable community relations: Bystanders are helpful and the police friendly in response. But the community in which they operate is a dangerous place, for most of the arrests they make are for violent crimes; even though, in reality, criminal work is not the main activity of most police.

The most common criminal on "Cops" is male, white, and lower middle class. In contrast to fictional crime shows where the villains are commonly motivated by greed, in "Cops" the miscreants' behavior is usually fueled by alcohol or illegal substances, or the villains are simply crazy. The heroic, humane cops use justified force to apprehend suspects. One way force is justified is by showing the suspects as irrational, engaging in violence, or resisting arrest. Unshown are the preceding events that might vindicate the suspects' outburst, thereby casting doubt on the police's use of force.

Each segment usually culminates with the arrest of the suspects. As in most fiction shows, crime neither succeeds nor pays. Guilt and conviction are implied by the suspects being driven off in a police car or locked up in a cell.

While these shows give the illusion of reality, they are actually carefully edited to favor the police. Debra Seagal worked for one such program, "American Detective," a prime-time reality-based police show that ran on the ABC network in the 1990s.[36] She was one of the story analysts of the vast amount of videotape the show's camera crews shot following detectives around in four cities.

Seagal found that the show's announcement that what the audience sees was filmed as it happened is misleading. Most of the footage is discarded as too mundane or too much like real life: "Hispanic families living in poverty . . . emotionally disturbed, unemployed Vietnam veterans . . . AIDS patients."[37] Dramatic violence is what is wanted.

So reality is skewed and changed to depict the police favorably. Chronologies are reshuffled. Stock visual and sound footage are added as necessary to embellish and enhance stories: close-ups of a suspect's handcuffed wrists, screams, shouts of "Police! Open the door! Now!"

The stories follow the format of introduction, the police raid, the capture, and the placing into the police car of the "bad," and obviously guilty, perpetrator. Downplayed or ignored are "the pathos of the suspect . . . the complexities that cast doubt on the very system that has produced the criminal activity . . . the indiscretions of the lumpen detectives" who are made to "appear as pistol-flailing heroes rushing across the screen" instead of "men whose lives are overburdened with formalities and paperwork."[38]

On balance, the police are depicted in the media as competent and effective. This is particularly the case on television's realistic and reality cop shows that viewers are likely to believe.[39] Some corrupt, racist, violence-prone officers exist on the screen, but the problem is one of individual renegades, not a lax or corrupt system that must be changed.[40] In the shows, most police use good judgment and don't mess with decent law-abiding citizens. They spend the bulk of their time dealing with criminality. Suspects are threatening, often dangerous, and clearly guilty. Civil liberties can impede effective police work: the police have to stop suspects from speaking in order to read them their rights; and they need permission to enter a suspect's home to retrieve evidence they know is present.

The likely effects of such coverage are to undermine respect for civil liberties and justify vastly increased expenditures to put additional officers on the streets and build more prisons. The coverage likely enhances the legitimacy of the police as a bureaucratic institution.

FALSE NUCLEAR ALERTS—A CASE STUDY

With its far greater firepower, the Defense Department is an even more significant bureaucratic institution than the police. It is appropriate, therefore, to devote the rest of this chapter to media coverage of the military and its activities: first a case study of false nuclear alerts, then wars.

As a discrete event with large implications, the false nuclear alerts afford a special opportunity to study news coverage of the Pentagon. The alerts were typical of much Pentagon news: globally significant, potentially detrimental to the public image of the institution, and difficult to dissect because of their secrecy and technology.

This case study is especially important for three reasons. First, it vividly details the ways in which public officials try to manipulate media coverage. Second, it documents and explains their success and failure. Third, it shows the importance of the motives, perspectives, and competence of the individual reporters and editors, and the effects these factors had on the types of coverage they produced.

What Happened

For three minutes and twelve seconds on June 3, 1980, electronic monitoring devices at the Strategic Air Command (SAC) in Omaha, Nebraska, and the National Military Command Center (NMCC) at the Pentagon indicated that numerous Soviet sea-launched ballistic missiles (SLBMs) and inter-continental ballistic missiles (ICBMs) were headed towards the continental United States. Immediately, the SAC duty officer ordered SAC bomber crews to man their aircraft, start their engines, and prepare for takeoff.[41]

The North American Air Defense Command (NORAD) command post in Colorado Springs, Colorado, processes missiles warning information from radar stations and satellites for use by SAC and NMCC. However, SAC and NMCC also receive unprocessed information directly from the radar and satellite sensors. This double routing of information, known as "redundancy" in systems terminology, serves as an internal check on the system. Thus, on June 3, while the information from the NORAD command to SAC and NMCC apparently warned of a major missile attack, the sensors registered no missile launches or flights. This anomaly suggested to officers at the SAC and NMCC posts that the information emanating from NORAD was erroneous. After the first warning of a missile attack, SAC personnel phoned the NORAD command and learned that officers there had no knowledge of any attack.

The NMCC duty officer convened by telephone a missile display conference among the duty officers at NORAD, SAC, NMCC, and the alternate NMCC. They compared warning information being received, or not, by the various commands. This conference is a preliminary action for evaluating sensor data. During the first six months of 1980, there were 2,159 routine conferences and 69 conferences to evaluate possible threats.

As the sensor data were being evaluated, the NMCC duty officer convened by telephone a threat assessment conference. This conference involves more senior figures than the command post duty officers; its purposes are to evaluate the nature of the perceived threat and to direct actions that will enhance the survivability of American forces. There were four such conferences during 1979 and 1980.

As part of the June 3 threat assessment conference, the airborne command post of the Pacific Command went into the air from its base in Hawaii. The NMCC duty officer terminated the conference when the NORAD commander confirmed that there was no threat. The SAC alert was canceled one minute later. SAC bomber crews took about twenty minutes to turn off their engines and return to a normal state of readiness.

The cause of the false warning was thought by military officials to be a malfunctioning NORAD computer. So NORAD personnel applied monitoring equipment to their computers and deliberately left online the computer they suspected of being defective. The NORAD commanders hoped that the specific cause of the malfunction could be determined if it recurred. On June 6, it did. The June 3 sequence was largely reproduced with SAC bombers going on alert for three minutes. But no aircraft were launched, and it appears there was no threat assessment conference.

Subsequently, the offending computer was taken off-line and a backup computer system substituted. The malfunctions were attributed to a faulty $.46 computer chip.

Pentagon's Perspective

Pentagon officials are not likely voluntarily to inform the press or the public of nuclear alerts. Word of the June 3 alarm leaked, however, to a local reporter in Norfolk, Virginia, from the headquarters there of the Atlantic Command. After checking with military bases around the country and receiving a chorus of "No comment" and refusals to confirm or deny, the reporter obtained official Defense Department confirmation. His paper, the *Virginian-Pilot,* a morning newspaper with a daily circulation then of 126,165, published its scoop on June 5 under the headline "Computer Goofs: Military Alerted." This internationally important story appeared on page three.

For the Pentagon spokespersons, the problem now was not how to conceal the alert, but what to say about it. Their function, as they saw it, was to reassure the press and thereby the public at home and abroad that nuclear war was far from imminent during the false alerts. They would portray the events as a success because the safeguards in the American early-warning system had worked and prevented an accidental nuclear war. The severity of the alert would be downplayed.

The Pentagon's argument consisted of three main parts. First, a computerized early-warning system to detect missiles is necessary for the national defense because of the short flight time of missiles from launch. Second, when a missile threat is perceived, the United States must place its nuclear forces on alert to enhance their chances of survival. Third, and most important from the Pentagon's point of view, computers could not launch U.S. nuclear weapons; only humans have the power to make the decision to do so.

This is a plausible framework in which to place the nuclear alerts, and Pentagon officials did their best to ensure that the press would accept and propagate it. Their tactics included such oft-used media-manipulating weapons as secrecy,

obfuscation, and invocation of technical expertise. But the Pentagon's most immediate technique was to funnel its favorable version of events to a preferred
(because sympathetic) reporter.

So, at approximately 10:00 a.m. on June 5, public affairs officials released the
following calm, reassuring, and superficially detailed statement to Associated
Press (AP) Pentagon correspondent Fred Hoffman.

> Early Tuesday morning, June 3, 1980, a technical problem in a computer at the
> North American Air Defense Command caused erroneous data to be transmitted.
> Some displays at the National Military Command Center and Strategic Air
> Command Headquarters indicated multiple missile launches against the United
> States; however, other systems available directly from the warning sensor system con-
> tinued to confirm that no missiles had been launched. As a precaution and in accor-
> dance with standard procedures, certain Strategic Air Command aircraft were
> brought to a higher state of readiness. These aircraft were manned and engines
> started. One Command and Control aircraft in the Pacific took off. There was no
> change in overall US defense posture and, after an evaluation, all systems were re-
> turned to normal. The computer technical problems are now being assessed to deter-
> mine corrective action.

At 11:18 a.m. on June 5, Hoffman's story on the false alert, closely following the
Pentagon release, was flashed across the country over the AP wire.

Eleven minutes later, the Pentagon's press corps gathered in the Pentagon
briefing room. Assistant Secretary of Defense Thomas Ross opened the conference with the inquiry, "Any questions?" Hilary Brown of NBC asked:
"Could you describe the circumstances that led to this false alarm early Tues-
day morning?"

Ross responded to the question with a brief prepared statement that was a
verbatim repetition of the statement that had been released to Hoffman at
10:00 a.m. Ross's statement was followed by fifty-two questions on the false
alert. Most of the Pentagon correspondents first learned of the alert at this
briefing. Their impromptu questions dealt with the specific actions taken, the
time involved, the cause of the false information, the Soviet response, and the
nature of the early-warning system. When a reporter finally stated, "I have a
question on another subject," Ross replied, with a mixture of levity and relief,
"Thank God."

The second alert, that of June 6, was announced on Saturday, June 7. Unable
to prevent a leak after the first alert, Pentagon officials hoped to curtail public
speculation by quietly announcing the second. No briefing was held; Ross simply
prepared a brief statement that was telephoned to the major news organizations
during the afternoon of June 7.

Types of News Coverage

What types of news did reporters produce out of the events? Operating in the
Pentagon, were they subject to institutional and political constraints? Were they
affected by the knowledge that their coverage could make the U.S. government
and its nuclear strategy appear sane and restrained or rash and bellicose not just

to Americans but, perhaps more significantly, to allies, neutrals, and adversaries abroad? Did reporters employ similar frames for handling the alerts? If not, how can we explain the differences?

In fact, media coverage varied widely: from no stories at all in some publications, to docile acceptance of the Pentagon's perspective, through fragmentation, to consideration of the alerts' implications and, ultimately, to sensationalism.

Three sets of factors help to explain this spectrum of media coverage. Naturally, the time and competition constraints the reporters faced are important. So are the reporters' beliefs about the (different) missions of their organizations and, relatedly, the interests of their audiences. But above all are the reporters themselves, especially in their experiences, ambition, and energy (or lack thereof); their understanding of the technical issues involved in the alerts; and their standing and relations both at the Pentagon and with the editors and media executives above them.

No Coverage   Donald Sider had been the national security correspondent for *Time* since September 1978. He described his beat as "geopolitics beyond diplomacy," incorporating issues from the Pentagon, CIA, White House, State Department, and Congress. On the average, he visited the Pentagon three times a week.[42]

The mechanism for assigning stories at *Time* usually begins with a reporter submitting a brief sketch of a potential article to his or her editors. If the editors believe it will make a worthwhile story, they will assign it to the reporter. After Sider learned of the false alerts, he "suggested a story or essay on the whole premise of accidental war," but his editors did not assign the story.

Conduit Reporting   The Associated Press essentially served as a conduit for the Pentagon's perspective. Its correspondent, Fred Hoffman, had a close relationship with Pentagon public affairs officials. Through five presidential administrations, as political appointees and military officers and members of the press corps came and went, he remained, a Pentagon fixture. An official described him as one of the chosen few reporters who had gained the respect of the Pentagon's public affairs officials for their responsible (as defined by the official) coverage of Pentagon stories. Such respect made Hoffman a likely reporter to receive tips from Pentagon officials, and simultaneously jeopardized his ability to question the accuracy, assumptions, and implications of that information. No surprise that Hoffman was the first Pentagon correspondent to be told about and report the false alerts. When he received the official statement, Hoffman was under considerable time pressure to file his story before the news briefing and thus ahead of other news organizations. Even if he had wanted to, he had no time to approach different sources or much ponder the implications of the alerts.

Even though the time pressures subsequently diminished, Hoffman's coverage remained a conduit for the Pentagon. He accepted the Pentagon's explanation. As he said of the alert: "It was the opposite of being on the brink of war. It proved the system works." Moreover, he did not delve into the technical issues of the implications of the alerts because, as he put it, "they say they are taking care of it, and if they explained it to me I probably wouldn't understand and my readers wouldn't read it."[43]

Complacent confidence in Pentagon officials, lack of the requisite understanding to tackle complex issues, and prejudgment of readers' interest and intelligence all combined with Hoffman's self-professed lack of vigor to ensure conduit reporting. (A few years later, Hoffman would retire from the AP and join the Pentagon as the principal deputy assistant secretary of defense for public affairs.)

Fragmented Coverage   The AP did not rely solely on its Pentagon correspondent; stories from other AP reporters contained passing mention of British Labor Party and Soviet comments on the alerts. But it was the AP's rival wire service, United Press International (UPI), that produced the more diverse range of coverage. These disparate reports were united, however, mainly by their common lack of analysis.

The one story from UPI's Pentagon correspondent was essentially a conduit in part because the time pressures prevented the reporter from contacting outside sources. But it and the reporter's failure to follow up were part of a more general philosophy about the purpose and function of the wire services. As the reporter said: "We just reflect everything that happens, and when it's over, we just go on to the next day."[44]

The other UPI stories were reports of statements to the press: by the Pentagon, Union of Concerned Scientists, Senator John Tower (R.-Tex.), the Soviet news agency TASS, and the Senate Armed Services Committee. Apparently UPI sought none of these statements, simply reporting what it was given without much probing. The result was fragmentation, a smorgasbord of reactions. Not provided was perspective, the kind of information that would explain the alerts and their implications.

Cursory Coverage   During June 1980, the *Washington Post* published over forty news stories related to the U.S. military. So defense issues were clearly of interest to the *Post*'s editors. The newspaper's Pentagon correspondent, George Wilson, moreover, spoke of his role as one would expect of a reporter from an elite newspaper: "I'm not here to try and duplicate the wires, I try and develop the stories. . . . What I'm here for is to get behind the facade and get them to open the kimono."[45] Yet only one story on the alerts appeared by Wilson in the *Post*. Entitled "Computer Errs, Warns of Soviet Attack on U.S.," it was mainly a conduit for the official Pentagon statement of June 5, and was relegated to page five.[46]

Three factors help to explain the *Post*'s cursory coverage. First, its Pentagon correspondent did not consider the false alarms particularly significant. As he said, "The fact that it was nipped in the bud made it less of a story."[47] Second, he apparently received no significant pressure from his editors to pursue the story. Third, since some rival media outlets were treating the story as a major issue, Wilson and the *Post* would perhaps have been confessing news judgment errors had they belatedly tried to catch up.

Implicational Coverage   The *New York Times* carried eight stories on the alerts, which relied almost exclusively on U.S. governmental sources and none of them appeared on the paper's front page. However, several of the sources expressed anxiety and concern over the false alarms; the stories maintained questioning attitudes towards the Pentagon's perspective and behavior; and the two reporters who wrote most of the stories took pains to probe the alerts' implications.

One reason for this implicational coverage was Richard Halloran. He had recently begun on the Pentagon beat for the *Times*, and this seemed to spur him to approach each new story as a learning experience. He thus sought more information than Pentagon officials were willing to reveal and raised questions in his coverage they preferred not to deal with publicly.

The *Times'* coverage of the alerts was bolstered by stories from Richard Burt. Not bound by a specific institutional beat, Burt had the subject-oriented responsibilities of military-diplomatic and strategic military issues. In preparing his reports, Burt found anonymous sources at the Pentagon and White House who diverged from the official line. Consequently, he wrote the most thorough discussion of the launch-on-warning strategy found in any mass-media report. His special interest in nuclear strategy gave him the background to relate the false alerts to strategic questions, and his role at the *Times* encouraged him to do so.

So, the combination of two reporters, one knowledgeable and operating at large, the other not bound to the shibboleths of the past; with neither beholden to Pentagon sources; and with both assuming that their newspaper's readers would be concerned and want to learn more about the alerts' causes and implications—all conduced to produce implicational coverage in the *Times*.

Nonetheless, the *Times* never gave the alert articles page-one prominence. According to Halloran, the editors believed these were "good solid stories" but did not consider them weighty enough for the front page.[48] When Halloran's first story broke, the *Times* had two military stories on the front page. The need for balance in front-page subjects kept Halloran's piece off it. Later, the alerts were no longer breaking news. As evolving news, they were relegated to the middle of the paper.

Confused-Sensational Coverage   Hilary Brown became NBC's Pentagon correspondent in December 1979 with an admittedly limited knowledge of defense issues and operations. Commenting on her approach to the Pentagon, she said: "It's your duty not to take what they tell you at face value. . . . Basically it's an adversary relationship."[49]

Pentagon officials prefer a collegial to an adversarial relationship with reporters. To this end, they can be of great assistance to correspondents by suggesting sources and providing background information. The reporter need not be sycophantic, but only cordial personally and "objective" professionally. Brown's attitude made her unlikely to receive the special support that would have rectified her unfamiliarity with the Pentagon. Compounding the situation, Brown's producers at NBC news were apparently uninterested in defense stories: She appeared just seven times on the evening news during the roughly six months she worked at the Pentagon prior to the alerts.

Brown had wanted to do a report on the alerts but her producers were not interested. Then, two weeks later, they learned that ABC news was planning a two-part "Special Assignment" series and was promoting it in advance. NBC news executives then decided to air their own investigative story and to beat ABC by one day. Brown had two days to compile her report. Consequently, time pressures generated by producer indecision, and misplaced perceptions caused by reporter inexperience, culminated in a confused, misleading, and sensational news story.

Many of the visuals used in Brown's story were taken from an air force film of a strategic military exercise. They were graphically edited to reinforce the frightening aspects of the story, thereby demonstrating that Defense Department file film can sometimes be used by the media to the detriment of the military.

Implicational-Sensational Coverage   ABC in its evening news devoted the most air time of the three television networks to covering the false alerts. The first of its three stories primarily reported the official Pentagon announcement; but its second and third reports used diverse sources of information and were extensive and complex. In part, they were sensational: with exciting visuals (crews running to planes; small, red, flashing light; a missile launching as the camera looked down into the silo); quick editing; split screen; and the constant reappearance of correspondent John McWethy as he guided viewers to and at the various locations. ABC even showed its audience an aerial view of the Washington Monument, ominously reminiscent of a missile. But the ABC stories also raised, even if they did not fully explore, such implications of the alerts as poor management, inadequate maintenance, the use of obsolescent computers, and the isolation of decision makers because of their dependence on computers.

ABC Pentagon correspondent John McWethy began working for the network, having previously served as the science and technology and then White House correspondent for *U.S. News and World Report.* Before that, he had worked for *Congressional Quarterly Weekly Report,* where he had written a book on congressional oversight of the Defense Department.

McWethy's prestige at ABC News, combined with his producers' interest in the false alert issue, resulted in a decision to prepare a two-part investigative series which McWethy was given two weeks to prepare. Of all the Pentagon correspondents, he was therefore able to utilize the widest range and greatest number of sources: three political and three technical, three in government and three out of it, four Americans and two foreigners (including Soviet commentator Vladimir Pozner). ABC, moreover, was the only news organization to employ coordinated teamwork in its approach to covering the story.

McWethy raised several important implications of the alerts in his series. Nonetheless, he did not detail them fully. Among the reasons were lack of air time to delve into complexity, and concern that the evening news audience would be bored by technical language. But the most important explanation stems from the dovetailing of ABC's interest in an action-packed, exciting news story and McWethy's determination "to convey the scariness of the incident."[50] Thus, the numerous freeze frames, the editing of film into very brief cuts, and the emphasis on active images all designed to create a mood of tension and tended to sensationalize the alerts.

Analysis of Coverage

Conventional critiques of the Defense Department have focused on its power to impress its perspective on the media and the public, recounting the array of tools it uses to dominate the presentation of military news.[51] Certainly, the Pentagon withholds information, plays favorites with reporters, and attempts to place a positive interpretation on disconcerting military events. This false alerts study, however, demonstrates the ways in which the media mould (and manipulate) military news. Definitions of content newsworthiness, reporters' strengths and weaknesses, and organizational constraints within the press profoundly influenced news from the Pentagon on this issue, resulting in a range of coverage.

The Pentagon presented its interpretation of the events, but could not uniformly enforce it on the press. Some reporters were unperturbed by the alerts, while others were very distressed; both conduit and sensational reports were evident. A primary press question became: "How close were we to accidental nuclear war?" Obviously, this was a necessary question to ask, but by dominating some reporters' concerns, it concealed some very important, but less exciting issues.

This distinction between exciting and important is essential to understanding the Pentagon's press corps. Its members will almost always report extraordinary events and dramatic policy changes if they become aware of them, but the opportunity to use these topics as newspegs for implicational discussions is rarely employed. Pentagon reporters pursue breaking news because these stories are most likely to be published or broadcast. Few incentives exist for reporters to follow issues over time.

The debate in the United States about nuclear weapons has been traditionally quite limited. It is confined to a small community of military, strategic, and technological experts who share many assumptions about the functions and purposes of nuclear weapons. The American public is minimally involved in the debate, partly out of ignorance, and also because nuclear war is a frightening topic. In reporting complex, secret military events such as the false alerts, the news media had the opportunity to ventilate issues that would otherwise have received little sustained public attention.

Yet even the best coverage was incomplete and short-lived. Significant deficiencies occurred in stories of the first alert; in the international, strategic, procedural, and procurement implications of both alerts; and in the corrective measures subsequently taken in the early-warning system.

Many problems in the false alert coverage resulted more from the inadequacies of the news media than from the overwhelming power of the Pentagon. Solutions to these problems required news reporters and managers to be more questioning of the Pentagon, display greater initiative in developing stories, and reflect more on the assumptions that guide their work.

WARS

False nuclear alerts can lead to wars. Governments and their defense establishments have a powerful interest in how the wars they wage are depicted and framed by the media. The defense bureaucracy strives for secrecy, to control the reporting of war events and the informational environment, and to achieve favorable coverage. It restricts reporting, engages in obfuscation and delay, and applies censorship.

The news media are ostensibly dedicated to reporting the truth. Conflict between government and the military on one side and the press on the other would appear to be inevitable.[52] A brief look at the highlights (lowlights) of Defense Department-media relations during the Vietnam and Gulf wars reveals the reality.

The Vietnam War

It is conventional wisdom in the U.S. military and among many commentators that untrammeled media coverage hampered and handicapped the war effort in Vietnam. Serious studies, however, refute this contention. As Daniel Hallin points out: "Day-to-day coverage was closely tied to official information and dominant assumptions about the war and critical coverage didn't become widespread until consensus broke down among political elites and the wider society."[53]

Television news, in particular, was perceived as bringing the war in all its cruelty and futility into Americans' living rooms and kitchens. It is said to have spurred antiwar sentiment, forcing U.S. leaders to limit and then end the war sooner than they might otherwise have done, and to do so in ignominy and defeat.

However, television's contributions to undermining official policy was limited mainly to the first half of 1968.[54] Generally, before and after that, it legitimized presidential actions. Television news helped generate public support for ever-deeper entrapment in the quagmire and then served to mute opposition to the pace of President Nixon's four-year policy of extrication. At the end, it went along with the concerted efforts of American leaders to stifle consideration of the guiding policy assumptions that had led the country into Vietnam in the first place.

The Gulf War

The Bush administration, its Defense Department, and the U.S. military determined that the war against Iraq would be no Vietnam.[55] It would not be protracted. Nor would they make the same "mistakes" of providing journalists with unlimited access to the battlefields and U.S. troops, letting them file their reports without limitation, and permitting candid off-the-record briefings. Indeed, the U.S. invasions of Grenada and Panama were, in some ways, rehearsals for the administration's handling of journalists in the Gulf.

For the Gulf War, the military gave uninformative, or at best guarded, briefings; denied unfettered access to the battlefield; deployed an access-limiting system of reporter pools; used public affairs officers to supervise reporters' interviews; engaged in story-delaying reviews of copy, rendering stories obsolete; and imposed outright censorship.[56]

These tactics, orchestrated and overseen by the Bush administration and implemented by the military, were attacked for providing political protection for policy-makers, precluding challenges to the administration and the military's reports of how well the war was going, and depriving the public of detailed knowledge about and understanding of the war. They were defended on the grounds of

FEIFFER®

reasonableness and necessity, given the size of the press corps and the military's need to preserve the lives and safety of its troops, surprise the enemy, and preclude interference with its logistics.

Given the difficult circumstances and onerous restrictions under which reporters labored, their coverage of the war was inevitably vulnerable to criticism. Television was the primary culprit. Its content was nationalistic if not jingoistic, overwhelmingly relayed the Bush administrations' and Pentagon's perspectives, relied excessively on U.S. sources, adopted the military's sanitized lexicon of war (e.g., "friendly fire"), and transmitted U.S. governmental disinformation.[57]

Coverage of the air war in particular, dependent on the Pentagon and U.S. military, credulously accepted vastly exaggerated reports of the precision and effectiveness of expensive high-tech aircraft.[58] At the same time, it brutally underemphasized the suffering and punishment inflicted on Iraq's civilians and the destruction of nonmilitary targets and the infrastructure of their country.

Numerous explanations were invoked by critics to explain the limitations of media coverage of the war. The acquiescence of media executives to governmental curbs was attributed to weak dedication to the freedom of the press, fear of provoking governmental outrage, shared frames of reference with governing elites, and pursuit of sales and ratings (read "profits"). Reporters were said to be confined by Pentagon rules, dependent on military sources, reliant on technology, and restrained by objectivity.[59]

Both during and after the war, journalists vented their righteous wrath about having been manipulated and censored by the military. For their part, military officials justified their handling of the press by pointing to journalists' irresponsible actions, almost complete inability to agree on any procedures, and downright silliness as complicating their military objectives. Neither side eagerly acknowl-

From How to Go to Hell © *1991 by Matt Groening. All rights reserved. Reprinted by permission of Pantheon, a division of Random House Publishers, N.Y.*

edged its indebtedness to the other. In fact, the press proved (to many reporters' frustration) to be an enormously effective public-relations voice for the military and the military's actions turned out to be a circulation and viewership bonanza (although at considerable financial expense) for the news media.

The Gulf War also revealed the clash between the mythologies of journalists and those of politicians. For journalists, the myth is that of the skeptical adversary of the government and official power. Accordingly, during the war, at least in the national media, an attempt was made (often unsuccessful) to maintain the same nonpartisan, distanced perspective that they claim (hope) characterizes peacetime reporting (a notable example was "CBS Evening News" anchorman Dan Rather repeatedly correcting himself for using phrases like "our tanks," as though such phrases were a role violation).

The government's mythic conception of itself during the war was of being involved in a great enterprise in which engaging in secrecy, limiting access to information, and giving out disinformation (which was rarely admitted) were justified by the objectives sought and the costs of failure.

According to poll data, and to the distress of many journalists and the proponents of a free press, the U.S. public overwhelmingly espoused the wartime government mythology over the mythology of peacetime journalism. This opinion was captured in a "Saturday Night Live" skit portraying journalists asking inane questions at a military briefing.

These data reassured a nervous White House that its restrictions on the press were popular and could be continued safely.[60]

CONCLUSION

Bureaucracies are governmental departments and agencies responsible for administering and enforcing public policies. Their politically appointed leaders usually are self-interested enough to try to cultivate the press. Success depends on their skill and techniques, and the programs and issues they emphasize.

The bureaucracies they govern also interact with the media; for favorable coverage can benefit an organization's legitimacy with other institutions of government and the public; facilitate its funding and policy objectives; and encourage acquiescence to its decisions. Unfavorable stories can have the reverse effects.

Bureaucracies vary in their interest in and need for media coverage. Some crave it, others avoid it. Most have no choice but to deal with the press. Then their preference is to publicize their successes, conceal their failures, and impress a positive frame on their activities that are open to interpretation. In this interaction, some bureaucracies are better insulated and armed against the press than others. It depends on their subject matter, partisanship, access, and opposition.

Public information offices are the bureaucracies' face to the press. They deploy various techniques to be both proactive and reactive; but they do not possess the skills and resources enabling them often and consistently to manipulate the news.

Arguably, the most important governmental bureaucracies are those entitled to use violence on behalf of the state: the police and the military. The probable effects of media depictions of both are to reinforce their legitimacy. A case study of false nuclear alerts reveals that definitions of newsworthiness, reporters' strengths and weaknesses, and organizational constraints within the press profoundly influenced news from the Pentagon on this issue, resulting in a range of coverage. The Pentagon was more successful in influencing media coverage of its wartime activities, as the Gulf War attests.

Notes

1. Hugh Heclo, *A Government of Strangers* (Washington, D.C.: Brookings Institution, 1977), provides an admirable description of the executive branch.
2. I am indebted to a reviewer of this manuscript for this observation.

3. See the recollections of President Jimmy Carter's attorney general, Griffin B. Bell, *Taking Care of the Law* (New York: William Morrow, 1982), esp. 203.

4. Robert B. Reich, Secretary of Labor during President Clinton's first term, was particularly media savvy. See his *Locked in the Cabinet* (New York: Knopf, 1997), 13–16, 72, 120, 210, 231–32, 302, 314–16.

5. David E. Rosenbaum, "Casting a Small Shadow in a City of Large Egos," *New York Times,* 11 April 1991, A17.

6. Walter Isaacson, "The 'Senior Official,'" *Washington Journalism Review* 14:9 (November 1992): 30, for this quote and the rest of the paragraph; see also Walter Isaacson, *Kissinger* (New York: Simon & Schuster, 1992).

7. Jane Mayer, "Blind Trust," *New Yorker* 71:45 (22 January 1996): 64.

8. Keith Schneider, "Disclosing Radiation Tests Puts Official in Limelight," *New York Times,* 6 January 1994, A1, A14.

9. Neil A. Lewis, "Energy Secretary Used Fund to Monitor Reporters," *New York Times,* 10 November 1995, A1, A12.

10. Stephen Hess, *The Government/Press Connection* (Washington, D.C.: Brookings Institution, 1984), 36.

11. Useful studies are Leon V. Sigal, *Reporters and Officials* (Lexington, Mass.: D.C. Heath, 1973); and, at the state level, Delmer D. Dunn, *Public Officials and the Press* (Reading, Mass.: Addison-Wesley, 1969).

12. Hess, *Government/Press,* 61; and Timothy E. Cook, "The Fourth Branch and the Other Three" (paper presented at the annual meeting of the American Political Science Association, Chicago, September 1994), 18–24.

13. Cook, "The Fourth Branch," 23.

14. Ibid., 24, invoking Brent Fisse and John Braithwaite, *The Impact of Publicity on Corporate Offenders* (Albany: State University of New York Press, 1983).

15. Hess, *Governmental/Press,* 95.

16. A thoughtful, detailed study of the relationship between reporters and their sources in governmental institutions is Richard V. Ericson, Patricia M. Baranek, and Janet B. L. Chan, *Negotiating Control* (Toronto: University of Toronto Press, 1989).

17. Morton Mintz, "Stories the Media Miss," *Washington Monthly* 27:3 (March 1995): 11.

18. Walter Pincus and Bill Miller, "Spy Couple Allowed to Retain Some Property," *Washington Post,* 30 April 1994, A12.

19. Jay Petzell, "Can the CIA Spook the Press?" *Columbia Journalism Review* 25:3 (September-October 1986): 29–34; and Bob Woodward, *Veil* (New York: Simon & Schuster, 1987), 174–95, 374–77, 447–63.

20. Richard Fryklund, "Covering the Defense Establishment," in *The Press in Washington,* ed. Ray Eldon Hiebert (New York: Dodd, Mead, 1966), 171–72 for the quote and examples.

21. For informative studies of public information officers, their activities, and relations with the press, see Hess, *Government/Press;* David Morgan, *The Flacks of Washington* (Westport, Conn.: Greenwood Press, 1986); and the pioneering work of Dan D. Nimmo, *Newsgathering in Washington* (New York: Atherton Press, 1964).

22. Hess, *Government/Press,* 38.

23. Ibid., 53.

24. Ibid., 37.

25. Charles Peters, "From Ouagadougou to Cape Canaveral: Why the Bad News Doesn't Travel Up," in *American Politics,* 3rd ed., ed. Allan J. Cigler and Burdett A. Loomis (Boston: Houghton Mifflin, 1995), 414.

26. Hess, *Government/Press,* 24.

27. Ibid., 25.

28. Joe Sexton, "False Arrests and Perjury Are Common Among New York Police, Draft Report Says," *New York Times,* 22 April 1994, A11.

29. Mark Ryter, "COINTELPRO," *First Principles* 3:10 (June 1978): 1–6; and Ward Churchill and Jim Vander Wall, *Agents of Repression* (Boston: South End Press, 1988).

30. Athan G. Theoharis, "The FBI's Stretching of Presidential Directives, 1936–1953," *Political Science Quarterly* 91:4 (Winter 1976–77): 671–72.

31. Offered, for example, by the North Carolina Justice Academy.

32. Ericson, Baranek, and Chan, *Negotiating Control,* 156–71.

33. John Gregory Dunne, "Law and Disorder in LA: Part Two," *New York Review* 38:17 (24 October 1991): 67, reviewing *Report of the Independent Commission on the Los Angeles Police Department* (Christopher Report, 1991).

34. Jerome H. Skolnick and James J. Fyfe, *Above the Law* (New York: Free Press, 1993), 18. This book is a detailed study of the issue of the excessive use of force by the police.

35. I am indebted for my discussion of the show to Jason Sanders, "Cops and Robbers in *Cops*" (paper submitted to my "Politics and Media" course), May 1993.

36. What follows is taken from Debra Seagal, "Tales from the Cutting-Room Floor," *Harper's* 287:1722 (November 1993): 50–57.

37. Ibid., 55.

38. Ibid., 52.

39. James M. Carlson, *Prime Time Law Enforcement* (New York: Praeger, 1985), 25.

40. Regina G. Lawrence, "Policing Brutality" (paper presented at the annual meeting of the American Political Science Association, Chicago, September 1995).

41. This case study is taken from David L. Paletz and John Zaven Ayanian, "Armageddon, the Pentagon and the Press," in *Communicating Politics,* ed. Peter Golding, Graham Murdock, and Philip Schlesinger (New York: Holmes & Meier, 1986), 197–208. Copyright 1986 by Leicester University Press. Used by permission of Leicester University Press, a Cassell Imprint, Wellington House, 125 Strand, London, England and Holmes & Meier Publishers, Inc.

42. Personal interview with John Z. Ayanian, 10 December 1980.

43. All quotes from a personal interview with John Z. Ayanian, 21 August 1980.

44. Personal interview by John Z. Ayanian with Nicholas Daniloff, 19 August 1980.

45. Personal interview with John Z. Ayanian, 19 August 1980.

46. *Washington Post,* 6 June 1980.

47. Personal interview with John Z. Ayanian, 19 August 1980.

48. Personal interview with John Z. Ayanian, 5 January 1981.

49. Personal interview with John Z. Ayanian, 6 August 1980.

50. Personal interview with John Z. Ayanian, 4 August 1980.

51. J. W. Fulbright, *The Pentagon Propaganda Machine* (New York: Liveright, 1970); and Juergen Arthur Heise, *Minimum Disclosure* (New York: Norton, 1979).

52. For a historical survey, see Phillip Knightley, *The First Casualty* (New York: Harcourt Brace Jovanovich, 1975); see also Loren B. Thompson, ed., *Defense Beat* (New York: Lexington Books, 1991); Karen F. Lloyd, "The Nature of Conflict Between the Media and the Military" (doctoral dissertation proposal, Duke University, 1994); and Gadi Wolfsfeld, "The News Media and the Gulf War" (paper presented at the annual meeting of the American Political Science Association, Chicago, September 1992).

53. Daniel C. Hallin, *The Uncensored War* (Berkeley: University of California Press, 1986), x.

54. Robert M. Entman and David L. Paletz, "The War in Southeast Asia: Tunnel Vision on Television," in *Television Coverage of International Affairs,* ed. William C. Adams (Norwood, N.J.: Ablex, 1982): 181–201.

55. This discussion is based on my chapter, "Just Deserts?" in W. Lance Bennett and David L. Paletz, eds., *Taken by Storm: The Media, Public Opinion, and U.S. Foreign Policy in the Gulf War* (Chicago: University of Chicago Press, 1994): 277–92. See the entire book for a comprehensive study of the relationships between the Bush administration, Congress, the public, and the media, before and during the war; also relevant is Philip M. Taylor, *War and the Media* (Manchester, England: Manchester University Press, 1992).

56. See John R. MacArthur, *Second Front* (New York: Hill & Wang, 1992). For a reporter's account, see John J. Fialka, *Hotel Warriors* (Washington, D.C.: Woodrow Wilson Center Press, 1991).

57. For a detailed, polemical assault, see Douglas Kellner, *The Persian Gulf TV War* (Boulder, Colo.: Westview, 1992). For an inside-the-media perspective favorable to the military, see Perry M. Smith, *How CNN Fought the War* (New York: Carol Publishing, 1991).

58. Tim Weiner, "'Smart' Weapons Were Overrated, Study Concludes," *New York Times,* 9 July 1996, A1.

59. Unpublished 1994 paper by David L. Paletz and Morgan David Arant, "Media Criticism of Media Coverage of the Gulf War."

60. Jason DeParle, "Long Series of Military Decisions Led to Gulf War News Censorship," *New York Times,* 5 May 1991, 20.

Chapter 14

The Judiciary

◆ ◆ ◆

This chapter documents that the judicial system is inescapably political, shows how it is intimately involved with the media, and considers the consequences.

Start with appointments to the U.S. Supreme Court. The U.S. Constitution authorizes presidents to nominate judges for the federal courts but gives the Senate the right to confirm them. Often, as with President Clinton's nominations of Stephen Breyer and Ruth Bader Ginsburg to the Supreme Court, the nominees are selected because they are relatively uncontroversial and are then overwhelmingly approved by the Senate. But some apparently innocuous nominees, notoriously law professor Douglas Ginsburg, have withdrawn rather than risk rejection. Others go down to defeat, particularly when they are ideological partisans and the Senate is controlled by the opposition party.[1]

The media are an integral part of the process. Ginsburg's withdrawal was occasioned by news stories of his smoking marijuana in the presence of his Harvard Law School students. Republican senators and Judiciary Committee members Orrin G. Hatch (Utah) and Strom Thurmond (S.C.) have reportedly distributed confidential reports on nominees they opposed to conservative columnists in order to arouse opposition.[2] "In what has become an election-year ritual, Republican and Democratic officials scour the records of their opponents' judicial

© 1987, Washington Post Writers Group. Reprinted with permission.

appointees, looking for rulings that could be politically embarrassing."[3] Thus, during the 1996 presidential election year, the Republicans used speeches and political advertisements to make President Clinton's judicial appointees an issue. The accusations: that they were rewards for successful fund-raising for his campaign and that the judges were liberals soft on criminals.[4]

As John Maltese points out, confirmations are now public affairs involving not just the president, attorney general, Justice Department, and members of Congress, but also interest groups, striving for Senate approval or rejection of a nominee.[5] Tactics can involve the use of focus groups and public opinion polls to design messages, attempts to influence columnists and editorial boards; then lobbying, public appeals, and advertising campaigns. Indeed, political advertisements sponsored by interest groups attacking or supporting nominees have been issued nationally and in the states of key senators.

This process became full-blown and earned the name of "borking" in 1987 when feminist, labor, civil libertarian, and civil rights groups, allied with liberal senators, waged an intense campaign against the White House and conservative senators and organizations to defeat Robert Bork, President Reagan's nominee to the Supreme Court.

In the numbers of interest groups involved, it was an unprecedented mobilization of grass-roots and direct pressure on the Senate. The anti-Bork forces conducted sophisticated research on the nominee's record and extensive writings, then inundated senators and the elite and prestige media with negative "information" and analyses of his ideas. Based on focus groups activities and polling, they conducted a public campaign replete with political ads.

In contrast, the response by the White House and Bork's ostensible supporters was tardy and inadequate. The nominee, who had been touted by his supporters as urbane, witty, and brilliant, contributed to his own demise when he came off unimpressively on national television during five contentious days of responding to statements and answering questions from members of the Senate Judiciary Committee. The professorial, scraggly bearded, wiry-headed Bork was outmaneuvered by his opponents on the committee who came up with such sound bites, featured on the evening television news, as "'You are not a frightening man, but you are a man with frightening views.'"[6]

CLARENCE THOMAS SUPREME COURT NOMINATION

This marshaling of opposition and the use of the media to try to destroy a nomination may have culminated with Clarence Thomas. Because the media were so flamboyantly involved in the fate of this nominee, it is appropriate and instructive to recount the facts, implications, and repercussions of his case.[7]

President Bush nominated Judge Thomas, a Yale-trained lawyer, for the seat of retiring Supreme Court Justice Thurgood Marshall. Marshall and Thomas had several things in common, most obviously they were both African-Americans. But their differences were pronounced: Marshall, the passionate proponent of civil liberties and rights, was to be replaced by the conservative, Republican Thomas, a perceived opponent of affirmative action. The nomination therefore engendered opposition from leaders of feminist and liberal organizations and support from their conservative counterparts; initially divided the civil rights community, which wanted an African-American justice but not one this conservative, and posed a difficult decision for Democratic senators from the South.

Thus, while the Thomas nomination was controversial, it did not at first provoke the same kinds of activities by liberal interest groups that had defeated Robert Bork. Meanwhile, learning from the Bork experience, the White House developed a highly organized public relations campaign in support of Thomas aimed at civil rights organizations, the regional and national press, and thus, indirectly, members of the Senate.

Because the nomination was shrewdly announced on the Monday afternoon of a short work week preceding the long Fourth of July weekend, reporters had time and opportunity to transmit only the favorable story, spoon-fed from the White House, of the nominee's background and rise from poverty (in Pinpoint, Georgia) to prominence, but not riches. Later, they reported some of his more controversial views and decisions during his relatively brief tenure as a federal district and court of appeals judge.

Attention soon dropped, resuming with the Senate Judiciary Committee hearings during which Thomas steadfastly avoided taking clear stands on controversial issues. He had been advised by his White House coaches or handlers (depending on your perspective) to "(1) stress his humble roots; (2) don't engage Senators in ideological debate; and (3) stonewall on abortion."[8] He said that he had never discussed nor had any views about *Roe v. Wade,* even though this controversial and much-debated abortion decision had been handed down by the Supreme Court while he was a student at Yale Law School.

So eager was the judge to placate his questioners that Senator Howell Heflin (D.-Ala.) raised the specter of "confirmation conversation"; that is, the strategic (but temporary) adjustment of views to please, or at least not offend, some members of the committee.[9]

Nonetheless, at what appeared to be the conclusion of the hearings, Senate confirmation seemed narrowly assured. Then Anita Hill's accusations surfaced into the public domain. Media coverage skyrocketed.

Many reasons have been adduced for Anita Hill's decision to testify in grotesquely explicit detail against Thomas, her former boss at the Department of Education and the Equal Employment Opportunity Commission. Many judgments were and still are being rendered about her motives and the truth of her accusations, Thomas's impassioned denials, and the veracity of the other witnesses who confirmed or challenged their positions. The questions, comments, and behavior of the members of the then-all-male, all-white Senate Judiciary Committee—variously hostile, supportive, vicious, devious, condescending, and stridently partisan on the part of some Republican members—were widely and justifiably condemned.

Barely discussed, but almost as significant, were two factors. First, a majority of the Judiciary Committee reluctantly agreed to risk a public hearing of the volatile subject. Second was the decision of those responsible in television and the print media to transmit Hill's accusations without first trying to check them out. Their justification was lack of time and the assumed or anticipated importance and explosiveness of the charges. Still, as Gerald Nachman points out, there was no test, no reasonable suspicion, no probable cause, just someone coming forward and accusing.[10]

Media Coverage and Public Opinion

More than 80 percent of respondents to a CBS News/*New York Times* poll claimed to have watched all or some of the three days and nights of televised coverage of the hearing; many no doubt attracted by the human drama of the clash, the titillating details, and the senators' sporadic and inconclusive search for truth. The daily and weekly press and television news covered and commented on the hearings; tabloid shows treated the topic. There was a lot of humor: On "Saturday Night Live," Chris Rock observed that "if Clarence Thomas looked like Denzel Washington this whole thing would never have happened."

With such abundant coverage, people probably learned about and often discussed with others the specific charges against the nominee; some of the qualifications for Supreme Court justices in general, and those of Thomas in particular; certain aspects of the Senate hearing process and the distinctive personalities of the senators involved; and the diversity of American types on display in the hearings. The hearings may also have influenced public perceptions about affirmative action programs, gender relations, sexual gambits, and Yale Law School.

As we have seen throughout this book, people bring their beliefs and attitudes, their often resilient preconceptions and prejudices to their media experiences. Varying views about race, sexual behavior, and gender relations were all likely to influence reactions to the hearings. Some might have inferred jealousy as Hill's motive and thus discounted the credibility of her charges. For others, Thomas, with everything to lose, would be likely to lie to save his nomination. Yet others would deem him innocent unless proven guilty.

Nonetheless, media coverage of the evocative hearings, the resultant widespread discussion, and the outpouring of comment seemed to firm public opinion, which went from 60 percent undecided on September 5 to nearly 80 percent decided on October 14. Significantly, apparently 75 percent of those decided favored Thomas. This seems an astonishingly high figure since, according to Gregory Caldeira and Charles Smith, who analyzed four CBS News/*New York Times* surveys, opinion "turned on partisan identification, political ideology, and evaluations of the president who had nominated him."[11] Even taking into account that black women were "significantly more likely to support the nomination than white women,"[12] one wonders what had become of all the Democrats, liberals, and those less than enamored with George Bush.

For Timothy Phelps and Helen Winternitz, the polls reflected the fact that Hill was attacked by several of the Republican senators on the committee and effectively defended by none of the Democrats. Accounting for much of their restraint, several of the committee's Democratic senators had been assailed by ads (excerpts of which were later shown on the networks' news shows) from a Conservative Victory Committee decrying their personal conduct, morality, and character as disqualifying them from participating on the committee. Thomas, moreover, was permitted to assert his denial without senatorial challenge and provided with two opportunities to rebut the charges. And committee chairman Joseph Biden (D.-Del.) prohibited any questions about "'the private conduct, out-of-the-workplace relationships, and intimate lives and practices of Judge Thomas, Professor Hill, and any other witness that comes before us.'"[13]

Jane Mansbridge and Katherine Tate point to the failure of the media to clarify why Hill had waited so long and had been so reluctant to air her charges in public; the myth of the strong black woman (who would have reacted and lashed back at the time of the incidents); and the effects on African-Americans of the impassioned charge by Thomas that the proceedings were "a high-tech lynching for uppity blacks." They conclude that race trumped gender for blacks who "supported Thomas because of their desire to maintain representation on the Supreme Court" in the face of unproven charges that he had talked dirty to a black woman many years ago.[14] Besides, in contrast to most Perry Mason-type courtroom dramas on television, there was no last-minute confession of guilt.

Media's Influence on Senate Hearings

The combination of the televised hearings and the impression conveyed by the media of widespread public support for Thomas inspired an unusually vigorous, occasionally eloquent, senatorial debate preceding the full Senate vote. Many senators took pains to spell out the sometimes agonized reasons for their decisions to vote to confirm or reject his nomination.[15]

The media's main effect was to convince most senators to vote as they had originally intended or as they had been leaning prior to Hill's testimony. Before she testified, "Thomas seemed to have the backing of eleven Democrats, enough to put him over the top even if three of the Senate's forty-three Republicans defected."[16] He was narrowly confirmed by a vote of 52 to 48, with 41 of 43 Republicans and 11 Democrats voting for him, including Senator Chuck Robb (D.-Va.), chairman of the Democratic Senatorial Campaign Committee, and Senator Alan Dixon (D.-Ill.), the party's chief deputy whip.[17] "Southern senators who had voted against Robert Bork out of deference to black constituents supported Clarence Thomas because the polls seemed to tell them that was what these constituents wanted now."[18]

There is reason to question the validity of the polls. In one study, unpublicized at the time, Frances Trix and Andrea Sankar and their students conducted in-depth interviews using mostly open-ended questions with one hundred Detroit women, a third of them African-American, the day after Thomas was confirmed. Among their findings: More women favored Hill than Thomas, women's support for Thomas was shallow, some of what appeared to be support for Thomas was probably criticism of Hill, and there were negative feelings toward the hearings among women of all these groups.[19]

BETSY SENSED THAT HER NEWLY-INSTALLED "ANITA HILL COIF-CAM" WOULD BE COMING IN HANDY.

© *John Grimes. Reprinted by permission.*

Such research suggests that more incisive, wide-ranging poll questions and more skeptical reporting of the polls by the news media at the time of the Senate debate might well have reversed the outcome. Indeed, some senators who had voted to confirm Thomas later conceded they might have made a mistake.[20] A change of vote by only three senators would have defeated the nominee. The Judiciary Committee's decision not to ask another former, somewhat mercurial, Thomas employee to appear on television, even though she had provided an affidavit about his alleged sexually offensive behavior toward her, may have been decisive: Her public testimony would have made it harder for senators and the public to discount Hill's charges.

The Thomas-Hill case vividly exemplifies how media coverage of a particular event can reverberate.[21] Hill and her supporters lost the Thomas battle—he is, after all, on the Supreme Court—but they may have won or at least have likely prospects of victory in a larger conflict.

The sexual harassment of women has been stamped on the public's mind and the policy agenda. For many years, as Elayne Rapping points out in an illuminating essay: "feminists–as legal theorists, workplace activists, teachers, journalists, trial lawyers, lobbyists, etc.—had been developing and agitating for the insertion of the . . . concept of 'sexual harassment' as a way of theorizing and acting upon the issue of workplace power relations."[22] Hill was both symbol and catalyst; but it was the media "staffed with so many feminist-influenced workers, and pushed by the collective force of so many political groupings similarly influenced and interested"[23] that took up and pursued the issue of sexual harassment, legitimizing it as a subject of public and governmental concern.

As just one example, in an article headlined "School Hallways as a Gauntlet of Sexual Taunts," the *New York Times* gave extensive and uncritical coverage to a poll taken for the American Association of University Women Educational Foundation showing the hallways of America's high schools and junior high schools to be "daunting, sexually charged terrain where most girls and many boys can routinely expect to be grabbed, poked, pinched or put down in explicitly sexual ways."[24] Interviews with high school teachers and students in Washington, D.C. were used to supplement and support the poll data.

The Judiciary Committee hearings were followed by a surge in the number of sexual harassment complaints filed with the Equal Employment Opportunity Commission. Old laws and regulations bearing on sexual harassment were strengthened and new ones added. A two-year battle between Senate Democrats and the Republican-controlled White House over civil rights legislation was resolved; the resultant law made it easier for women to sue their companies for workplace discrimination and for the victims of sexual discrimination to collect up to $300,000 in damages instead of only back pay.[25]

Then, in November 1993, with Justice Sandra Day O'Connor writing for the majority, the Supreme Court ruled in *Harris v. Forklift Systems, Inc.* that a "discriminatorily abusive work environment, even one that does not seriously affect employees' psychological well-being, can and often will detract from employees' job performance, discourage employees from remaining on the job or keep them from advancing in their careers."[26] That the Court's decision was rendered just a month after oral arguments was attributed to the continuing impact of the Anita Hill-Clarence Thomas controversy.[27]

THE SUPREME COURT

The battle over Clarence Thomas graphically reveals the widespread belief that appointments to the Supreme Court are politically crucial. Yet as soon as nominees become justices, don the robe, and take their place on the bench, they are transformed, invested with the majesty of the office and the law. For the courts are avowedly nonpolitical, indeed above politics: Their decisions are supposedly based on laws enacted, on the precedents of prior cases, and—above all—on the words of the U.S. Constitution.

A Political Judiciary

In fact, the judicial system is inescapably political: judges' beliefs can influence their decisions, which, in turn, affect public policy, sometimes dramatically. For statutes usually require interpretation; precedents bind loosely, can be ignored, reinterpreted, over-ruled; and through the power of judicial review, the Court is the final arbiter of the usually latitudinous or ambiguous meaning of key phrases of the Constitution, thereby giving it the authority to decide on the constitutionality of the decisions of the other branches of government.

Moreover, the Supreme Court wields considerable discretion about which cases it will decide; it is constitutionally required to hear only cases to which either a state or a foreign ambassador is a party, and appeals from state supreme courts that present a substantial "federal question." Most of the Court's cases come when, on the affirmative vote of four or more justices, it grants a *writ of certiorari* accepting a case appealed from a lower federal court.[28] It typically takes around 100 such cases each term from around 5,000 requests.

David Adamany concludes:

> Policy making on the Supreme Court is a reflection of the ideological preferences of the justices, that such attitudes are formed before justices are appointed to the Court, and that justices are highly consistent in casting ideologically oriented votes in most types of cases and from term to term of the Supreme Court.[29]

Given only nine justices, one or two presidential appointments to an ideologically even-balanced Court can produce sudden and dramatic changes in the content, scope, and direction of its decisions.

Even though the courts are inherently political, judges could still disdain the media. Federal judges are appointed, stay in office until they die or leave voluntarily or, rarely, are impeached (and convicted). Many state court judges enjoy long terms and may be reelected without significant opposition. So media coverage would appear to have little effect on judges' longevity and actions in office.

But the judicial system labors under a liability not imposed so extremely on the other branches of government: the implementation of judicial decisions relies on voluntary compliance by the affected parties. When that fails, the courts depend on enforcement and the application of sanctions by other governmental agencies.[30] President Andrew Jackson encapsulated this problem in his perhaps apocryphal words: "[Chief Justice] Marshall has made his decision, let him enforce it."[31]

The Supreme Court has a number of ways of coping with the potential flimsiness of its authority, of maintaining public deference, and of securing widespread compliance with its decisions. Perhaps most important is prudent restraint. The justices are usually reluctant to provoke, to clash with Congress and the presidency, to outrage the public. Certainly, some of the moderate members holding swing positions on the Court have been known to be sensitive to public opinion.[32] And when the justices do issue what they anticipate will be controversial decisions, they often try to do so unanimously, permit reasonable delay in enforcement, and acknowledge social forces with discreet language and verbal formulas designed to placate the contending sides.

But the Court periodically becomes embroiled in contentious social issues: examples are abortion, affirmative action, freedom of speech, racial gerrymandering of congressional districts, religious freedom, school desegregation, and sexual harassment. These and other subjects can generate bickering among the justices, which is occasionally publicly displayed in rancorous split decisions. And whatever the decisions, they are liable to provoke passion among politicians, interest groups, and the public.

It is crucial, then, for the Supreme Court that its legitimacy and moral authority be reinforced rather than undermined. Media depictions of the Court's decisions, the justices, and the judicial system in general can therefore be vital. It matters whether the Court is portrayed as above the fray or as political; as a repository of expertise or of clashing different opinions; and as deriving its decisions from the law alone or from justices' beliefs. This is why televised coverage of Senate confirmation hearings for controversial nominees can denigrate the Court by depicting it as a body of fallible, opinionated, and, above all, political people.

The rest of this chapter considers the strategies the justices can deploy to protect and enhance their legitimacy through the media, examines how reporters cover the Court, and characterizes the coverage that results.[33] Then it looks at the media's relations with and portrayals of other courts, followed by cameras in the courtroom and Court TV. The chapter ends with the consequences of media coverage.

Court-Media Relationship

Members of the Supreme Court seem to be ambivalent about their relationship with the media: they prefer a positive portrayal of their actions but don't appear to do anything to achieve it, except for occasionally anticipating media coverage and modifying their decisions accordingly. Some justices give public speeches but they often exclude television cameras. Individual justices hold off-the-record background sessions "to provide reporters with information that cannot be attributed to them but will affect the shaping of a story or the perception of a reporter."[34] But judicial norms preclude any discussion of current cases. Formal interviews are rare. When held, they are called conversations or chats, and certain subjects, particularly politics, are excluded. Press conferences are unknown. "Aloof" characterizes the justices' public posture towards the press.

Behind the scenes, however, the justices pursue two main tactics designed to achieve a favorable image: accentuate the majesty of the Court, and minimize access to its inner workings.

The justices are usually careful to convey the impression that the judicial process is magisterial and depersonalized, and that the function they perform is to interpret the law with fairness, neutrality, and objectivity. They cite precedents, support their constitutional and statutory rulings with persuasive arguments, and emphasize the logic, the reasonableness, the inevitability of their decisions (even when there are dissenting opinions). Their decisions are written in a specialized, sometimes arcane, legal language.

What reporters see inside the courtroom—all that they see—is designed more to elevate than to expose the judicial process. The ornate setting, the ritual, the ceremony: the justices presiding in their robes and high-backed chairs, physically and metaphorically raised up, occasionally posing and sometimes pressing questions to the lawyers pleading the case below; all sanctify the legitimacy of the

Court and its members.

Unknown to reporters and therefore absent from the news are the justices' "discussion about whether to grant review, the conference following oral arguments where the justices' initial positions are staked out, and the process of forging or keeping a majority through opinion writing."[35] The press is not privy to how decisions are reached, the kinds of informal contacts among the justices, the appeals and persuasion, the negotiation and bargaining, and the sometimes pragmatic compromises.

The justices do select exceptional recent law school graduates to work for them in flagging cases worth deciding and sometimes helping to draft opinions, but these privileged few are excluded from the justices' deliberations in conference. And while sometimes privy to gossip, they have little incentive to leak, compelling reasons to keep silent: Supposedly there is a twenty-second rule that any clerk caught talking to a reporter will be fired within twenty seconds. Secrecy is the norm, revelations uncommon.[36]

Largely by denying access, justices minimize the production of behind-the-scenes stories that might reveal politics and contention and undermine the Court's magisterial image. Imagine their anguish, understand their threat to withhold future donations of papers, when the Library of Congress released the papers (memoranda, working papers, drafts of opinions) of former Justice Thurgood Marshall.[37]

Access denied is reinforced by information controlled. Supreme Court justices—all judges—preside, commune alone, deliberate one with another, and reach their decisions. They address the mass media publicly usually through the staff of the Public Information Office (PIO). The spokespersons, in turn, are mainly a conduit for transmitting decisions and summaries and servicing reporters; they neither expound on the decisions nor describe the process by which they were reached. Thus, the Court makes available transcripts of its oral arguments but the justices asking the questions are not identified by name; it's as if the questions are posed not individually but collectively.

The PIO does provide reporters with an array of documents they can use in preparing or writing their stories. These include the formal requests that the Court hear a case (petitions for *writ of certiorari*) and the written arguments (briefs) of the parties to cases. Of particular importance is the *Orders List* announcing the cases the Court will accept for oral argument, enumerating petitions for hearings granted and rejected, and listing the decisions the Court made without hearing oral arguments.[38]

Reporters   Fewer than a dozen reporters cover the Supreme Court even close to full time.[39] Nowadays, only ABC of the television networks has a correspondent there. The reporters work out of small cubicles in a narrow room. In comparison to other beats, they spend much of their time reading—briefs, legal summaries, and legal publications—and very little time interviewing sources except for legal experts and interest groups.

Upon release of the *Orders List,* they may produce preview stories about some of the cases the Court will be hearing and, less common, cases the justices will not be reviewing. Later, they attend some of the oral arguments in the Court, with the presentations by counsel and the justices' questions.

The bulk of reporting is of the Court's decisions. In a session rarely lasting more than thirty minutes, the justices announce the results, briefly summarizing the opinions and the lineups of concurrences and dissents. Infrequently, a justice will read his or her opinion in full to call attention to it. As Lewis Wolfson put it so cogently: "Supreme Court justices have an official's dream: reporters devote much of their time simply to reporting what they [write]."[40]

Yet reporting decisions is frustrating work. The Court releases most of its decisions in June, toward the end of the term, creating a flood of opinions on some days. Other than on the last day of the term, however, reporters are not told which decisions will be announced on any given day. So several important decisions may be announced all at once, or none of interest to reporters, or some combination. As an added complication, during the latter half of its term, the Court hears arguments on cases and announces decisions on previously argued cases on the same day.

As soon as Supreme Court decisions are issued, reporters covering the Court must quickly decide which ones are most newsworthy and their import; for the Court provides no guidance, accompanies the opinion with no explication or interpretation. Then, reporters must translate into lay language even the most ambiguous decision, no matter how confusing a mixture of partial concurrences and partial dissents accompany it.

Reporters are also bombarded by reactions and analyses from the parties to the case, their attorneys, legal experts, and interest groups. Notable among them are the American Civil Liberties Union (ACLU), the Legal Defense Fund of the National Organization for Women (NOW), the Chamber of Commerce, and such decision-relevant groups as, on abortion, the National Right to Life Committee and Planned Parenthood. Speedy reaction is facilitated by the electronic distribution of the Court's opinions and by the use of faxes and e-mail to respond. Vivid images of demonstrations combined with quick cogent analyses and catchy soundbites are the best ways into news stories. For example, Harvard Law Professor Lawrence Tribe is quoted about the impact of one decision: "'Doctors will be paid to lie.'"[41]

News Coverage

The Associated Press wire service is committed to covering most Supreme Court decisions, at least in summary form. Journalists for elite publications are allocated space to write about more than one case at a time if necessary. But most reporters are limited to one story a day: If several important decisions are issued at the same time, they must pick the one they deem most important.

As a result, many Supreme Court decisions go unreported. Others are recounted briefly. A few cases, unrepresentative of the Court's docket, receive exhaustive coverage, especially those involving the First Amendment, civil rights, and abortion.[42] Despite differences among the television networks in the number of Court-related stories broadcast, their placement and length, there is an overall lack of coverage and what is reported is usually sketchy.[43] The three major newsmagazines focus on only 10 percent of the cases.[44] And even a reader relying on the *New York Times* "would not know what really happened in more than three-fourths of the Court's decisions."[45]

Although most coverage is limited to the decisions themselves, there are differences across media. Expected to report first and fast, the AP emphasizes who is involved in a case, what happened to them, the legal history, and the Court's holding. Major newspapers tend to go beyond wire copy with a more evenly balanced mixture of information on the decision and its ramifications. Television covers the ruling, skimps on the details, and concentrates on reactions and possible policy impact.[46]

All the media label the justices' rulings "decisions" (a practice followed in this book). Decisions are "handed down" as if from on high. Yet often they are also public policies: They allocate scarce economic resources, redistribute political power, and alter social relations as surely as the actions of the president and Congress. By not calling Court decisions "policies," the media acquiesce in the belief and perpetuate the impression that the Court merely ensures that laws enacted through a democratic process are carried out constitutionally and properly.

There are two exceptions to the generally benign and supportive coverage of the Court: personalization and outside perspectives.

To personalize the justices, some reporters have begun to adopt the *People Magazine* approach of more celebrity and less substance. And they have begun to look more closely at individual ones, such as Sandra Day O'Connor, who is considered the key swing vote on abortion and many other issues, and Clarence Thomas on affirmative action cases. Stories have also included more reactions to decisions by representatives of interest groups, law professors, and the like. Such personalization reveals the justices as individuals with peccadillos, predilections, and preferences. The inclusion of outside experts', interest groups', and reportorial perspectives suggests that the Court's decisions are neither inevitable nor immutable.

Yet most coverage still adheres to the myth of judicial exception: the assumption that the Supreme Court is above and beyond politics. In part because of their legal training, many reporters accept, indeed believe in, the Court's role. Rather than adopting an adversary relationship, they tend to be protective of the Court and the justices.

STATE COURTS

States handle more than 97 percent of all litigation. Some 33 million civil and criminal cases are filed annually in state trial courts compared to the 282,000 cases filed in federal district courts.[47] Most civil suits are settled before they get to court. Similarly, the vast majority of criminal court cases are plea-bargained.

Reporters

Reporters who cover state courts are often generalists with many other duties. They are usually untrained in the law and unfamiliar with the intricacies of the judicial process. They are excluded from behind-the-scenes activity, such as prosecutors' decisions about whether to prosecute, when and where, and plea bargaining.

Pursuing the seamy and abnormal, reporters focus on sensational criminal trials. Ignored are important civil "cases on employment discrimination, sexual harassment, product liability, surrogate parents, right to die, prayer in schools, abortion and prison overcrowding."[48]

Even for criminal cases, reporters lack the time and inclination to cover most court actions. Robert Drechsel found that of the sixty-nine criminal cases scheduled on one day in a Minnesota state trial court—appearances, arraignments, trials, pleas or other dispositions, revocations of probation or parole, and sentencings—not one was covered by the reporter he was studying.[49]

Their commitment to criminal cases and lack of time to be in the courtroom leads reporters to rely (aside from perusing documents) on tips and information from sources, mainly law enforcement officers and prosecutors. This reliance makes it difficult for reporters to alienate many of these suppliers lest access be curtailed.[50] It also results in stories favoring the sources or at least presenting their perspectives.

Attorneys Shape the Story

Indeed, cases are increasingly argued outside the courtroom. Even before a trial date is set, plaintiffs and their attorneys, sometimes aided by a publicist, take their cases to the media.[51] Their objective is to influence public opinion and bring pressure on the defendants to settle the case. They appear on televised talk shows and give "human interest" personalized interviews in which they come across as the victims. The absent defendants are usually depicted as the villains.

Related is the attempt to create, or at least reshape and polish, a favorable image for the client before and during the trial. Accused of rape, William Kennedy Smith (of the Kennedy clan) acquired a former *New York Times* reporter as his official spokesperson. Smith cultivated a down-home image in the press: riding in an old family station wagon, attending early morning mass, playing with his puppy, and tossing around a football. In court, his attorney called him by the adult-sounding "Will," not the young and irresponsible "Willie."[52] Simultaneously, his public relations people cleverly redefined the woman involved from "rape victim" to the "accuser."

During prominent trials, to the extent permitted by state regulations on their interaction with the media, attorneys battle to shape the story. So, they feed or leak information and hold press conferences, all aimed at favoring their side with reporters.[53]

Robert L. Shapiro, later to represent O. J. Simpson, wrote a piece advising his fellow lawyers how to use the media. He recommends cultivating relationships with reporters, especially those from the wire services; refusing to cooperate with the tabloids; complimenting reporters who write favorable stories for their objectivity; and providing television with flattering photos of the accused client to replace the ones taken at the time of arrest. He advises speaking low and slow like John Wayne, issuing brief statements to get air time, and calling reporters to have them revise their stories.[54]

Johnnie Cochran, one of O. J. Simpson's lawyers, adeptly used many of these techniques in cultivating reporters during the Simpson trial. He also critiqued reporters' television comments, so that as reporters traveled to the TV studio the next day, "It was hard not to think, What will Johnnie say?"[55]

Not incidentally, media visibility can provide other benefits: advancing the political careers of prosecutors, attracting new clients for defense attorneys, and the signing of huge book contracts for both.

Portrayal in Popular Culture

The combination of news values, inadequate reporting, and the public relations activities of attorneys and their clients produces media coverage of the courts and trials that is "inaccurate, sensational, over-simplified, distorted."[56] The press fails "to give the public the amount and type of information it needs to understand and to evaluate critically the judiciary."[57]

So people find out about the courts from popular culture. This means movies, such as *First Monday in October, The Verdict,* and *A Time to Kill,* and television entertainment shows such as "Perry Mason," "LA Law," "Law and Order," and "Night Court." But also from the networks' magazine-type shows, such as "48 Hours" and "Prime Time Live," and the tabloids "A Current Affair" and "Inside Edition," which use trial footage in their stories.

Then there are prime-time docudrama reenactments of cases, the real versions of which may have already appeared on Court TV. The television versions differ dramatically from the painstaking building of prosecution and defense cases experienced by real jurors. For television stories are framed by the producer, reporter, and editor, not by the attorneys. They are picture and sound-bite driven, the more histrionic the better: "gotcha" attorney, tearful witness, outraged judge.

Above all are the pseudo-real television courtroom shows—"The People's Court," "Superior Court," "Divorce Court," and "Judge Judy." With 2,300 half-hour episodes in the can, "The People's Court" has enough shows to run twice daily, five days a week, all year, for four years.

Purporting to depict real trials, these shows are chosen to be personal and immediate, appeal to the audience's emotions, and exclude juries. Drastically edited, they eliminate procedural elements and all the issues of "jurisdiction, notices to defendants, pleadings, discovery, and choice of a judge or jury trial, all of which can be argued, replied to, and motioned against."[58]

What can people make of this melange of drama and comedy, pseudo-realism and the absurd? Judges are usually portrayed on television as legitimate and judicious, and their decisions almost always correct. Judge Wapner of the "People's Court" is the paragon paradigm (his replacement, former mayor of New York Ed Koch, is more boisterous). Even Judge Harry Stone of "Night Court" is a fair and decent person striving to do the right thing.

Certainly, the judicial process shown on television entertainment is misleadingly brief and uncomplicated.

CAMERAS IN THE COURTROOM

The late, great filmmaker Krzysztof Kieslowski recounts that as soon as he set up his camera in the Polish courts during a time of martial law, "there were either no jail sentences at all, or they were suspended by the judges. . . . The judges were afraid that the reels of film recording their faces at the very moment they delivered unjust prison sentences could one day be used as evidence against them."[59] Unsurprisingly, permission to film was soon withdrawn by the Communist regime.

The use of television cameras has been touted as the way to show people in detail what really goes on in courtrooms; as the cure for the miasma of error and confusion caused by inadequate news coverage and the muddle of popular culture.

Cameras in the courtroom might also reinforce public confidence in the courts. CBS News correspondent Rita Braver argues that people would see how serious and smart Supreme Court justices are. "'When you hear constitutional principles talked about in language that you can understand, it's thrilling.'"[60]

Nonetheless, cameras—still and motion—are prohibited in the Supreme Court during public sessions. Ostensibly, this is to avoid both lawyers (and justices) playing to the cameras and any physical disruption. It would also misleadingly emphasize the brief oral arguments when the essence of appellate advocacy before the Court is in the written briefs.

More important is the fear that the Court's proceedings would be vulnerable to television's editing emphasis on conflict and controversy, vivid pictures, and pithy sound bites. Television stories could juxtapose conflicting positions: one justice against another, a decision against the angry reaction of the president or members of Congress, clashes between interest groups, and ordinary people harmed or benefitted by the decision. The justices would lose their cherished anonymity and privacy; the Court's mystique would be undermined.

The Supreme Court may be a special case in this regard. What about other courts? The Judicial Conference of the United States has voted by 14 to 12 to allow federal appeals courts to televise appellate arguments if they so decide. These proceedings consist of lawyers arguing to a panel of judges; there are no witnesses or jurors. Not much here for television coverage to distort.

The Judicial Conference prohibits cameras in federal district courts. Its authority is not absolute, however, and fourteen of the ninety-four courts do permit judges to authorize cameras in these trial courts. So, on occasion, a federal case is aired.[61]

Television cameras are allowed in the courts of all but three states and the District of Columbia, but under various conditions and restrictions (e.g., the consent of the judge, agreement of the attorneys for both sides, fixed cameras, and no showing of jurors).

Objections

Many arguments are asserted to exclude cameras from these courts.[62] Certain types of trials (e.g., rape) are said to be so personal, so full of shame and embarrassment, that victims would be inhibited from coming forward before a potential audience of millions. Potential witnesses in other cases might be deterred from testifying out of fear of public exposure and embarrassment or mockery.

Once a trial is under way, the presence of a camera could affect all the participants. State court judges soon up for reelection, aware that videos from the trial could be used in political ads for or against them, might rule with voters in mind. Prosecutors with political ambitions for higher office might posture for the camera. Lawyers on both sides could be intimidated or, more likely, turned into self-promoting publicity hounds exploiting the case's (book-writing) income potential. Witnesses knowing that friends and acquaintances are watching might be tempted to adjust

*"Before I read our verdict, I'd like to announce that as soon
as court adjourns, some of us will be appearing on television
to discuss the case, and we hope you'll all tune in."*
Drawing by Fischer, © 1980, The New Yorker Magazine

their words and behavior for the camera. Jurors' decisions in controversial cases
might be influenced by the knowledge that they could sell their stories to the media.

Nor are cameras neutral in their courtroom coverage. Roberta Entner has analyzed the perspectives the television camera takes on trial participants. Close-ups
conveying intimacy are often used for sympathetic witnesses, while lawyers get the
more emotionally detached three-quarters shot. The profile, conveying remoteness,
is for defendants who are typically shown as unsympathetic and culpable.[63] As Paul
Thaler points out: "The presumption of innocence, an integral concept of American
jurisprudence, is not the concern of the camera."[64] Thus, coverage can inflame public opinion, usually against the defendant. It could raise the accused to public figures, condemn them, so that, even if acquitted, it is hard for them to reenter society.

Overall, the argument against cameras in the courtroom is that they "trivialize
legal proceedings and upset fundamental principles of law."[65] Moreover, the high-
profile trials shown in whole or in excerpted highlights are atypical and thus mislead the public.

Court TV

The chief exponent of cameras in the courtroom is Court TV, a $40 million ven-
ture by Time Warner, Liberty Media, Cablevision Systems, and NBC. The channel's financial survival depends on its being on enough cable systems to reach
potential viewers, and then programming to attract them. It fulfills its advertising
slogan of "Great Drama. No Scripts" by showing the proceedings of selected trials from around the United States and, in rare instances, from abroad. Many of

the trials are of people accused of violent crimes, revealing an America of violence and sleaze in which the mentally defective and morally bankrupt commit mayhem and murder. But the channel also shows less lurid and sensational cases: torts, civil rights, sexual harassment, and employment discrimination suits.

Some trials are shown live, usually accompanied by lawyers brought into the studio to explain the proceedings. This play-by-play commentary often extends into judgments and second-guessing about the tactics and skill of the prosecution and defense attorneys and the judge's rulings.

Other trials are recapitulated into taped syntheses of stories mixing courtroom footage with interviews of the attorneys and, if they are willing to speak on camera, judges, jurors, and other participants. Calls from viewers responded to on camera by host and guests are a prominent feature. The channel is not confined to trials and verdicts: it reports on the U.S. Supreme Court, law-making in Washington, the practice of law, and parole hearings. It has a show hosted by O. J. Simpson's former attorney, Johnnie Cochran. To fill the time, it also repeats many of its programs.

Court TV evokes ambivalence. On the one hand, it shows what goes on during certain trials, and it covers many aspects of the judicial system. On the other hand, it gives the false impression that all cases go to trial when, in fact, delays and plea-bargains or out-of-court settlements are the norm. But the biggest criticism is that it seeks to "convert judicial proceedings into a sort of television theater imbued with typical entertainment values."[66]

Arguably, that's what television cameras did when they brought into Americans' homes (and to other parts of the world) the infamous trials of Lorena Bobbitt, Amy Fisher, the Los Angeles policemen accused of beating Rodney King, the Menendez brothers, and William Kennedy Smith. Certainly, these trials captured people's attention: Some 43 percent of Americans said they watched at least four of these five trials.[67] Then, the televised O. J. Simpson trial far surpassed its predecessors in longevity, audience size, and fascination. At its conclusion, a rivetted nation tuned in to any of several television channels for the verdict that acquitted him.[68]

The O. J. Simpson Trial

The Simpson trial was even more atypical than its predecessors. Simpson was a celebrity defendant with sufficient wealth to hire a cast of attorneys able successfully to challenge the criminal justice system: its criminalists, crime labs, the gathering and preservation of evidence, and the veracity of the police on the witness stand. Ordinary trials are far briefer, testimony is rarely so intricate, and lawyers don't berate each other publicly. Los Angeles Superior Court disposed of 51,769 cases between the time of Simpson's arrest and acquittal.[69]

Nonetheless, people probably became more knowledgeable about courtroom rules and procedures, cross-examination, testimony, the validity of evidence, and many more elements of the judicial process as a result of the Simpson case's air time. And one could argue that, rather than causing deficiencies in the judicial system, television coverage exposed them.

The problem was not the live and continuous coverage, but the media circus of tabloid stories elsewhere on television and in print. Indeed, the tabloids would have indulged in reenactments and lurid dramatizations had live and videotaped

CALL 1-800-NO MORE O.J.

- IF YOU'RE NAUSEATED BY THE TABLOID SLEAZE MEDIA, PRESS 1 NOW.
- IF YOU'RE FED UP WITH PREFERENTIAL TREATMENT ALWAYS BEING GIVEN TO CELEBRITIES, PRESS 2 NOW.
- IF YOU FEEL THE RICH HAVE A DIFFERENT SYSTEM OF JUSTICE THAN THE REST OF US, PRESS 3 NOW.
- IF YOU THINK TELEVISION HAS MADE ZOMBIES OF A VAST NUMBER OF AMERICANS, PRESS 4 NOW.
- IF YOU PREDICT A JURY FILLED WITH DUMMIES, PRESS 5 NOW.
- IF YOU CAN'T WAIT FOR THE WHOLE TAWDRY CHARADE TO DISAPPEAR, PRESS 6 NOW.
- IF L.A. WERE TO BREAK OFF AND SAIL AWAY AS A RESULT OF AN EARTHQUAKE, WOULD YOU CHEER? PRESS…

DO IT NOW!

The Miami Herald

Reprinted with special permission of King Features Syndicate

coverage been unavailable. As it was, they hyped the trial and featured often misleading excerpts and snippets from it. They gave employment to "experts," who treated the case as a contest instead of a search for justice, second-guessed the trial participants, and were often misguided or wrong. (Court TV's commentators were less blatant: no anointing of daily winners and losers.)

The Simpson trial made many judges, prosecutors, and defense attorneys warier about permitting cameras in the courtroom to provide live coverage or recording trials for even partical future showing. (Thus, Simpson's civil trial was not televised.)

Simpson's criminal trial may also have eroded the credibility of defense lawyers, raised questions about the competence of prosecutors, diminished respect for judges, and aroused concern about the jury system. It prompted proposals for changes, some desirable, some not, in the judicial process: ease jury selection, make it harder for lawyers to remove prospective jurors with peremptory challenges, avoid sequestration, end the requirement for jury unanimity, limit the number of sidebar conferences, speed up trials, make it easier to convict, and restrict what lawyers can say to reporters outside the courtroom.[70]

The most dramatic aftermath was to reveal a chasm between the races: an overwhelming majority of African-Americans agreed with the verdict of innocence, but 55 percent of whites disapproved of the jury's decision. Both sides did agree that Simpson would have been convicted had he not been rich.[71]

Three factors help to explain the gap. First, from the start a majority of blacks thought Simpson was innocent, whereas a majority of whites thought him guilty. Second, as documented in chapter 5, people from different backgrounds can receive and perceive the same media content in quite diverse ways. Third, while the mainstream press read by whites believed that justice—meaning a guilty verdict—was "likely to be thwarted by a strange mixture of television-obsessed lawyers, book-writing jurors, and sun-addled witnesses," the African-American press defined the case as "a metaphor for the plight of blacks caught in the criminal-justice system."[72] The black view was most forcibly captured by Johnnie Cochran's summation, in part an appeal to the jury for acquittal based on racial solidarity.

CONCLUSION

Starting from confirmation fights on through the policy effects of many of its decisions, the U.S. Supreme Court is inescapably political. To protect its legitimacy and ensure compliance with its decisions, it must appear above politics. In their relations with the media, the justices therefore accentuate the Court's majesty and minimize access to its inner workings. Reporters essentially accept this perspective, focusing on the Court's decisions in their coverage.

Only the decisions receiving saturation media coverage penetrate the public consciousness. Thus, most Americans are uninformed about the Supreme Court. Far fewer people can name any of its justices than can identify Judge Wapner of television's "People's Court."[73] The overall consequence is acquiescent support of the Court's legitimacy based on ignorance of its inner workings.

The lower courts and the judicial system as a whole are less fortunate. Most of the limited media news coverage consists of sensational criminal trials. Fictional shows on television are the public's other main source. In combination, they mislead and confuse. Thus, more Americans have an unfavorable than favorable view of the legal system. These opinions are not informed by much knowledge of how the system works. Almost half of the people believe that a criminal defendant must prove innocence rather than is innocent until proven guilty, and some 40 percent ascribe to the courts sole responsibility for the country's high crime rate.[74]

Cameras in the courtroom, with Court TV in the lead, have the potential to inform viewers through live and videotaped coverage. Two-thirds of the people who claim to watch Court TV say it has given them a greater understanding of how the judicial system works and for half of them it has made the system seem fairer.[75] But the O. J. Simpson criminal trial graphically revealed that these benefits are not unalloyed. After that case, people had less respect for the justice system, and reduced confidence that defense attorneys and, to a lesser degree prosecutors, won't resort to unethical or irresponsible tactics, and that jurors won't let racial attitudes affect their judgment.[76]

Notes

1. Herman Schwartz, *Packing the Courts* (New York: Scribner's, 1988); see also Patrick B. McGuigan and Jeffrey P. O'Connell, eds., *The Judges War* (Washington, D.C.: Free Congress Research and Education Foundation, 1987).

2. David M. O'Brien, "Clinton's Legal Policy and the Courts," in *The Clinton Presidency,* ed. Colin Campbell and Bert A. Rockman (Chatham, N.J.: Chatham House, 1996), 141.

3. Eric Schmitt, "Hatch Renews War of Words Over Judges," *New York Times,* 26 March 1996, A10.

4. James Bennet, "Florida Reproves Clinton on Judgeship," *New York Times,* 28 April 1996, A17.

5. John Maltese's book is an admirable study of the evolution of the nomination process and analysis of its condition, *The Selling of Supreme Court Nominees* (Baltimore, M.D.: Johns Hopkins University Press, 1995).

6. This quote by then-Senator Howard Metzenbaum (D.-Ohio) comes from Mark Gitenstein's revealing insider account of Bork's defeat, *Matters of Principle* (New York: Simon & Schuster, 1992), 239; also insightful is Ethan Bronner, *Battle for Justice* (New York: Norton, 1989). For the perspectives of liberals, conservatives, and the nominee respectively, see Michael Pertschuk and Wendy Schaetzel, *The People Rising* (New York: Thunder's Mouth, 1989); Patrick B. McGuigan and Dawn M. Weyrich, *Ninth Justice* (Washington, D.C.: Free Congress Research and Education Foundation, 1990); and Robert H. Bork, *The Tempting of America* (New York: Free Press, 1989).

7. For relatively academic and dispassionate analyses, see Kathleen Frankovic and Joyce Gelb, "Public Opinion and the Thomas Nomination," *PS* 25:3 (September 1992): 481–84; and Barbara Sinclair, "Senate Process, Congressional Politics, and the Thomas Nomination," *PS* 25:3 (September 1992): 477–80. The definitive journalistic account is by Timothy M. Phelps and Helen Winternitz, *Capitol Games* (New York: Hyperion, 1992); see also Gitenstein, *Matters of Principle,* 335–46. Senator Paul Simon offers an insider's assessment in *Advice and Consent* (Washington, D.C.: National Press Books, 1992). For the diversity of African-American perspectives, see Toni Morrison, ed., *Race-ing Justice, En-Gendering Power* (New York: Pantheon Books, 1992); and Robert Chrisman and Robert L. Allen, eds., *Court of Appeal* (New York: Ballantine Books, 1992). For a discussion of the implications of the case for the Senate confirmation process, see Garry Wills, "Thomas's Confirmation: The True Story," *New York Review* 42:2 (2 February 1995): 36–43.

8. Gitenstein, *Matters of Principle,* 337.

9. For a trenchant critique of this strategy and of the committee for permitting it, see Ronald Dworkin, "Justice for Clarence Thomas," *New York Review* 38:18 (7 November 1991): 41–45.

10. "Talking About the Media Circus," *New York Times Magazine,* 26 June 1994, 31.

11. Gregory A. Caldeira and Charles E. Smith, Jr., "The Dynamics of Public Opinion on the Thomas Nomination" (paper presented at the Annual Meeting of the American Political Science Association, Washington, D.C., September 1993), 29.

12. Ibid., 28.

13. Quoted by Phelps and Winternitz, *Capitol Games,* 393; see also 394–95.

14. Jane Mansbridge and Katherine Tate, "Race Trumps Gender: The Thomas Nomination in the Black Community," *PS* 25:3 (September 1992): 488–92, quote on 488.

15. 102d Congress, First Sess., *Congressional Record,* Vol. 137:147 (October 15, 1991).

16. Phelps and Winternitz, *Capitol Games,* 228–29.

17. L. Marvin Overby et al., "Courting Constituents? An Analysis of the Senate Confirmation Vote on Justice Clarence Thomas," *American Political Science Review* 86:4 (1992): 997–1006.

18. Ronald Dworkin, "One Year Later, the Debate Goes On," *New York Times Book Review,* 25 October 1992, 38.

19. Frances Trix and Andrea Sankar, "Women's Responses to the Hill/Thomas Hearings: Listening for a Change" (1993) (available from Frances Trix, 645 Riverview Drive, Ann Arbor, Michigan 48104).

20. "Sen Boren to Trade His Seat on the Hill for Ivory Tower," *Durham Morning Herald,* 28 April 1994, A3.

21. For a polemical attack on Hill, see David Brock, *The Real Anita Hill* (New York: Free Press, 1993). For a vigorous defense of her veracity, see Jane Mayer and Jill Abramson, "The Surreal Anita Hill," *New Yorker* 69:14 (24 May 1993): 90–96, and their *Strange Justice* (Boston, Mass.: Houghton Mifflin, 1994). Also relevant is the book by Thomas's Senate sponsor Senator John C. Danforth, *Resurrection: The Confirmation of Clarence Thomas* (New York: Viking, 1994). For a judicious discussion, see Kathleen M. Sullivan, "The Hill-Thomas Mystery," *New York Review* 40:14 (12 August 1993): 12–16.

22. Elayne Rapping, "Gender and Media Theory: A Critique of the 'Backlash Model'," *Journal of Social Philosophy* (June 1994): 17.

23. Ibid., 25.

24. Written by Felicity Barringer, *New York Times,* 2 June 1993, A12.

25. Phelps and Winternitz, *Capitol Games,* 422.

26. *Harris v. Forklift Systems, Inc.,* 114 S. Ct. 367 (1993), 2.

27. Barbara Presley Noble, "Little Discord on Harassment Ruling," *New York Times,* 14 November 1993, F25.

28. H. W. Perry, *Deciding to Decide: Agenda Setting in the United States Supreme Court* (Cambridge, Mass.: Harvard University Press, 1991).

29. David Adamany, "The Supreme Court," in *The American Courts,* ed. John B. Gates (Washington, D.C.: CQ Press, 1991), 12.

30. Richard M. Johnson, *The Dynamics of Compliance: Supreme Court Decision-Making from a New Perspective* (Evanston, Ill.: Northwestern University Press, 1967).

31. Cited in Samuel E. Morrison and Henry Steele Commager, *The Growth of the American Republic* (New York: Oxford University Press, 1962), 489.

32. William Mishler and Reginald S. Sheehan, "Public Opinion, the Attitudinal Model, and Supreme Court Decision Making," *Journal of Politics* 58:1 (February 1996): 169–200; David G. Barnum, "The Supreme Court and Public Opinion: Judicial Decision-Making in the Post New Deal Period," *Journal of Politics* 47:2 (1985): 652–66; and Thomas R. Marshall, *Public Opinion and the Supreme Court* (Boston, Mass.: Unwin Hyman, 1989).

33. See Richard Davis, *Decisions and Images* (New York: Prentice Hall, 1994), for a comprehensive, thoughtful study of the Supreme Court and the media.

34. Ibid., 120.

35. Ibid., 144.

36. An exception is Bob Woodward and Scott Armstrong, *The Brethren* (New York: Simon & Schuster, 1979), an account of the Supreme Court based in part on interviews with former law clerks.

37. Linda Greenhouse, "Protecting Its Mystique," *New York Times,* 27 May 1993, A1.

38. Davis, *Decisions and Images,* 49.

39. See ibid., chapter 4, for this and many of the other details in this section.

40. Lewis Wolfson, *The Untapped Power of the Press* (New York: Praeger, 1985), 57.

41. Quoted in Davis, *Decisions and Images,* 139.

42. Jerome O'Callaghan and James O. Dukes, "Media Coverage of the Supreme Court's Caseload," *Journalism Quarterly* 69:1 (Spring 1992): 195–203.

43. Elliot E. Slotnick and Jennifer A. Segal, "Television News and the Supreme Court" (paper presented at the annual meeting of the American Political Science Association, Chicago, September 1992), 26; see also Christopher D. Swann, "The Nightly Network News and the United States Supreme Court" (paper prepared for my Politics and Media seminar, Duke University, December 1991).

44. Dorothy A. Bowles and Rebekah V. Bromley, "Newsmagazine Coverage of the Supreme Court During the Reagan Administration," *Journalism Quarterly* 69:4 (Winter 1992): 948–59.

45. David Ericson, "Newspaper Coverage of the Supreme Court," *Journalism Quarterly* 54:3 (Autumn 1977): 607. For a more sanguine view, see Michael E. Solimine, "Newsmagazine Coverage of the Supreme Court," *Journalism Quarterly* 57:4 (Winter 1980): 661–63.

46. David W. Leslie, "The Supreme Court in the Media" (paper presented at the annual meeting of the International Communication Association, Portland, Oregon, April 1976), 26–29.

47. Judith S. Kaye, "Federalism Gone Wild," *New York Times,* 13 December 1994, A19.

48. Peter A. Levin, "You Want Me to Read a What?" *Media Studies Journal* 6:1 (Winter 1992): 175.

49. Robert E. Drechsel, *News Making in the Trial Courts* (New York: Longman, 1983), 88.

50. Ibid., 89.

51. Carole Gorney, "Litigation Journalism on Trial," *Media Critic* 1:2 (1994): 48–57; and, more generally, Susanne A. Roschwalb and Richard A. Stack, eds., *Litigation Public Relations* (Littleton, Colo.: Rothman, 1995).

52. Val Ellicott and Christine Stapleton, "Manipulating Smith's Image Is Part of Rape Defense," *Raleigh News and Observer,* 12 November 1991, 6E.

53. Jennet Conant, "The Trials of Arthur Liman," *Vanity Fair* 54:6 (June 1991): 40–58.

54. Robert L. Shapiro, "Using the Media to Your Advantage," *The Champion* 17 (January–February 1993): 7–12.

55. Jeffrey Toobin, "A Horrible Human Event," *New Yorker* 71:33 (23 October 1995): 44.

56. Thomas S. Hodson, "The Judge: Justice in Prime Time," *Media Studies Journal* 6:1 (Winter 1992): 87.

57. Drechsel, *News Makings*, 4.

58. Wende Vyborney Dumble, "And Justice for All," in *Television Studies*, ed. Gary Burns and Robert J. Thompson (Westport, Conn.: Praeger, 1989), 106.

59. Krzysztof Kieslowski, *Decalogue* (London: Faber & Faber, 1991), x.

60. Quoted in Davis, *Decisions and Images*, 151.

61. Linda Greenhouse, "Reversing Course, Judicial Panel Allows Televising Appeals Courts," *New York Times*, 13 March 1996, A1.

62. See Paul Thaler, *The Watchful Eye* (Westport, Conn.: Praeger, 1994), for many of these arguments.

63. Roberta Entner, "Encoding the Image of the American Judiciary Institution" (Ph.D. diss., New York University, 1993), 73–75; see also Bethami A. Dobkin, "Video Verdicts," in *Theory and Practice of Political Communication Research*, ed. Mary E. Stuckey (Albany: State University of New York Press, 1996), 84–94.

64. Thaler, *The Watchful Eye*, 10.

65. Ibid., 14.

66. Ibid., 5.

67. Times Mirror (now Pew) Center for the People & the Press, "The Year in Figures," (Washington, D.C.: 1995), 2.

68. David Margolick, "Jury Clears Simpson in Double Murder," *New York Times*, 4 October 1995, A1.

69. "Simpson Trial and Trivia," *U.S. News & World Report* 119:15 (16 October 1995): 43.

70. Stephen Labaton, "Lessons of Simpson Case Are Reshaping the Law," *New York Times*, 6 October 1995, A1.

71. These data come from Richard Morin, "Poll Reflects Division Over Simpson Case," *Washington Post*, 8 October 1995, A31.

72. Jeffrey Toobin, "Putting it in Black and White," *New Yorker* 71:20 (17 July 1995): 32.

73. Richard Morin, "Wapner v. Rehnquist: No Contest," *Washington Post*, 23 June 1989, A21.

74. Cited in Thomas S. Hodson, "The Judge: Justice in Prime Time," *Media Studies Journal* 6:1 (Winter 1992): 92.

75. Times Mirror (now Pew) Center for the People & the Press, "The Year in Figures," (Washington, D.C.: 1995), 2.

76. Joe Urschel, "Poll: A Nation More Divided," *USA Today*, 9 October 1995, 5A.

Chapter 15

Public Policy

◆ ◆ ◆

In the end, much of politics comes down to public policy: the polity's responses to what are perceived to be public problems. After a brief overview of policymaking, this chapter discusses the types of media content most relevant to policy. It then shows how and with what consequences the media are involved at each stage of the policy process. Next, it considers differences in the media's relations with foreign policy. Two contrasting case studies of the media and policy follow. The first looks at the media's contribution to the savings and loan debacle. The second shows how the media were instrumental in the decision to regulate the chemical industry. The chapter ends with consequences and conclusion.

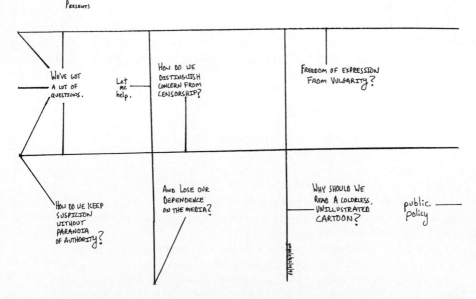

The Coleman Tales
by g.m. paletz

Presents

A FORUM FOR READERS

We've got a lot of questions.

Let me help.

How do we distinguish concern from censorship?

Freedom of expression from vulgarity?

How do we keep suspicion without paranoia of authority?

And lose our dependence on the media?

Why should we read a colorless, unillustrated cartoon?

public policy

POLICYMAKING

Policies are usually aimed at solving or at least alleviating public problems. They consist mainly of governmental decisions and actions, such as enacting laws, issuing regulations, allocating funds, and undertaking military action. Governmental responses can also be symbolic, meaning that they do not materially change a situation but indicate concern about and attention to it, as exemplified by a visit to a disaster-hit town by the president. Decisions not to take action about a problem are also a species of public policy.

Governments make most public policies, but government is far from monolithic. In the U.S. system, the desirability and substance of policies and the best ways to achieve them are decided by and between the Congress, the presidency, the bureaucracy, and the judiciary—the institutions discussed in the last four chapters.

Interest groups at home and abroad are often involved. Usually the groups lobby government (see chapter 9). But, if they have the resources, they can also try to circumvent the policymaking process through state ballot initiatives, on which people can vote directly, and then waging media campaigns full of political ads, to get the measures approved.

Interest groups also include the so-called think tanks that advocate and promote policies.[1] Think tanks cover the ideological spectrum, but the ones with the most resources, influence, and media attention are the centrist Brookings Institution and the conservative Heritage Foundation, American Enterprise Institute, and Cato Institute.[2] They aggressively market their "research" to policymakers and the public through public relations and media outreach strategies. The combination of claimed policy expertise, media visibility, and the failure of the press frequently to identify their ideological leanings reinforces the legitimacy of think tanks and their not-always-justified credibility.[3]

Policymakers also respond to the range and intensity of public opinion, often as reported in the press. Indeed, Lawrence Jacobs and Robert Shapiro summarize a decade of research on the relationship between public opinion and policy as finding "that the collective decisions of government institutions have been strongly related to public opinion."[4]

Policy Stability and Change

For some subjects, there exist policy subsystems or communities, consisting of members and staff of congressional committees or subcommittees, bureaucrats in the administrative branch, interest groups, and policy experts, as well as specialist reporters. Many of these communities are ideologically homogeneous and resistant to challenge.[5] They are characterized by consensus and control of information, a low profile, media disinterest in their activities, and minimal possibility of public mobilization for or against them. These policy subsystems are disrupted only by struggle or disagreement or increased diversity among their members.

Much policymaking consists, therefore, of continuing existing policy or of marginal changes to it. For long periods, such policies attract little attention.

But vast policy changes and innovations do take place. Ideas and arguments, often based on partisan conflict, provoke them. Deliberation and discourse matter. Policies can be reevaluated on the basis of their substantive merits.[6] New policymakers with different ideas take office.

For Frank Baumgartner and Bryan Jones, issue definition in, and control over, the policy agenda are central to policy change.[7] Mobilization is the key. Policy entrepreneurs, both individuals and organizations, want to put some social situation or condition on the policy agenda as deserving of a policy response. So they exploit opportunities to define issues, activate the public, and gain access to policymakers.

The mobilization of new voices and formerly excluded interests occurs in two ways. The first is the creation of a wholly new policy subsystem during a wave of enthusiasm for a particular policy. The authors call this a cycle of "alarmed discovery" and "euphoria" about a policy solution. A positive policy image is purveyed by the media (e.g., "peaceful uses of nuclear power") and often results in the creation of government agencies likely to support policy subsystem hegemony (e.g., the Atomic Energy Commission).

The second type of mobilization comes from opponents' criticism of and attack on an existing policy subsystem. Some of these opponents may come from within the policy subsystem. Their attacks capitalize on and add to already occurring negative policy images in the media (e.g., the health dangers of nuclear energy) and increase the policy role of institutions (e.g., congressional oversight committees) less likely to offer unconditional support for the policy subsystem's status quo. If successful, this type of mobilization leads to the subsystem's destruction.

THE MEDIA

Media content can reinforce or undermine policy subsystems and affect policies. So, to repeat one of this book's themes, public officials and those trying to influence them strive to advance their policy perspectives and preferences through the media.[8]

To reiterate another of this book's themes, the media are rife with explicit and implicit political content. Much of it is policy related. Consider "Beverly Hills, 90210," a show considered by many as shamelessly, mindlessly trivial. Its makers list a plethora of social issues featured on the series, including racism, teen pregnancy and abortion, drug and alcohol addiction, rape, AIDS, drunk driving, violence at school, and sexual harassment.[9] Many of these issues are policy-relevant.

News Coverage

The policy contents of news usually focus on a limited number of topics and shift over time. They range from prominent and continuous for several months (Americans held hostage in Iran) to nonexistent (rebellion in Madagascar). The amount and duration of coverage depend on such factors as whether the subject is accessible to the press, is foreign or domestic, or is technical or emotionally charged; whether interest groups are involved; whether there is elite policy consensus or disagreement and the range of policy debate; and the extent of public interest.[10]

Whether government takes action is also important in stimulating media attention. Media coverage of child abuse has been long-lived, in part because of frequent governmental action to deal with the issue. "Every state passed a child abuse reporting law between 1963 and 1967, and all amended and reamended their law several times, with each legislative action renewing newspaper interest in the problem."[11]

Issue-Attention Cycle   Normally, however, media policy content falls into what Anthony Downs calls an "issue-attention cycle," in which media attention to a topic goes from popularity to eclipse, or at least wanes over time. One reason this happens is because the ever-restless public becomes bored by the coverage.[12]

Two important sources of such coverage are icons and investigative reporting.

News Icons   The media highlight certain events, particularly scandals and outrages, that often embody or exemplify policy inadequacies or failures. Lance Bennett and his co-authors call these "news icons," arguing that they "provide dramatic news material and bring popular fears, cultural tensions, or politically marginal ideas into the news narrative. . . . The result is that the news can become a cultural broker, defining the problem, and hence *re*defining the policy situation, in often surprising ways."[13] The extensive media coverage of the garbage barge that for three months unsuccessfully sought a port on the east coast to unload its cargo "provided an occasion for both journalists and their sources to refigure cultural scripts about garbage and recycling."[14]

Investigative Reporting   Probing situations in depth, exposing scandals and corruption, investigative reporting is a second important source of the media's policy coverage. In the traditional view, such journalism leads to outrage from the public or from organizations with a stake in the controversy, and demands for reform, which in turn inspire governmental action.

According to David Protess and his coauthors, investigative reporting is best understood as a transaction between journalists and policymakers. Most of the investigative cases they studied had been taken up and addressed by policymakers with relative speed, had effects on the content of the policy initiative, and had achieved policy outcomes. These outcomes ranged from deliberative (hearings) and individualistic (firings) to, in most cases, substantive (legislative, regulatory, or administrative) change. "These policy developments . . . clearly occurred independently of either manifest changes in public opinion or interest group pressures."[15] Indeed, reform proposals were often announced by policymakers before complete publication of the investigations in the press. Public officials were neither reactive to nor defensive about the accusations of wrongdoing, treating them rather as policy opportunities stemming from their collaborative media strategies.

POLICY STAGES

In theory, the policy process proceeds through six stages. These are problem formation, agenda setting, policy formulation, legitimation and adoption, implementation and administration, and policy evaluation. Reality, however, is more chaotic. In practice, the stages overlap, do not always follow in the order indicated, and are not fulfilled for every policy.

FEIFFER®

Feiffer © 1991 *Jules Fieffer. Reprinted with permission of Universal Press Syndicate. All rights reserved.*

Nonetheless, the stages give us a way to approach the effects of media content on the policy process.[16]

Problem Formation

The media can be quite influential at the problem formation stage. By routine reporting and commentary, they bring events and issues to the public's and policymakers' attention as they occur. For most subjects, however, coverage is fitful: lots at one time, little at another when journalists lose interest or decide there is nothing more to report. Consequently, many events and issues, conceivably quite important, are unlikely to reach policymakers through the press unless they become icons or the subjects of investigative reporting.

Moreover, many onerous occurrences, deplorable situations, and unfortunate conditions covered by the media are not taken to be problems about which the American government should try to do something. For years, many of the difficulties women faced at home and at work were regarded as private affairs, not part of larger societal problems.

So, when the media influence the problem formation stage it is by depicting events in a policy-relevant way, as expecting, deserving, even requiring a governmental response. Labeling treatment of women as sexual harassment or wife abuse had the effect of transforming private misfortunes into failures of public policy. At its most detailed, such media coverage can include the problems' causes, severity, and longevity; relevance to various segments of the population; responsibility and blame; and possible solutions.[17]

Not all subjects that are irresistible to the press and receive widespread policy-relevant media coverage are in fact major social problems. On the basis of their examination of the official data, Craig Reinarman and Harry Levine found no evidence of an epidemic of crack cocaine. Indeed, "cocaine use by young adults peaked 4 years before the current [1989] scare began and it has declined since then."[18] But the media stories, combined with politicians' use of the issue in their rhetoric and campaigns, elevated drugs to the "most important problem facing the country" in public opinion polls.[19]

Agenda-Setting

The policy agenda consists of issues commonly perceived by public officials as meriting governmental attention and those actively being considered by them for action.[20]

The interplay between politicians and the press produces this agenda. But cause and effect are difficult to untangle. On the basis of ingenious research into the amount of attention devoted to four major policy issues by the *New York Times,* ABC News, and three local newspapers, Larry Bartels has shown that during the first three years of the Clinton administration, the executive branch led on the foreign policy subjects of Bosnia and the North American Free Trade Agreement (NAFTA); Congress led on the domestic issues of Medicare and Whitewater.

> However, *New York Times'* coverage led political activities even more than it followed them, with especially strong agenda-setting effects for NAFTA and Whitewater. The independent agenda-setting power of ABC News was substantially less than that of the *Times,* but still considerable, while local newspapers tended . . . to follow the lead of politicians and the national news media."[21]

He concludes that "each side's activities play an important role in setting the other side's policy agenda."[22]

President Carter's policy of linking U.S. aid to progress in human rights, especially in South America, exemplifies this interaction. Carter increased the number of governmental officials dealing with the issue and available to talk to reporters on the record. So, as Catherine Cassara points out, "reporters had sources for their stories, editors believed those stories were newsworthy, and human rights sources in and out of government became 'routinized.'"[23]

When the media set agendas for officials, it is often by portraying an event as a crisis or by imposing deadlines.[24] The media gave so much coverage to Iran's takeover of the American embassy and its refusal to release embassy officials that the Carter administration had no choice but to put the event high on its policy agenda.

The transmission of news via satellites and computers as the events happen means that the public and policymakers know about them at the same time, thereby forcing subjects on the policy agenda that policymakers might otherwise prefer to ignore. This situation places demands on policymakers for a quick response when their inclination is to wait and see how the situation develops. So, the media coverage speeds up the decision process.[25]

The media can also move issues off the policy agenda by not covering them any longer; or by giving the impression, rightly or wrongly, that they are not serious social problems; or by indicating that they do not require resolution through the policy process.

Formulation

Once an issue is on the agenda, policymakers have to decide what to do about it. Arguably, policymakers most commonly respond to media coverage symbolically. These responses are usually easier to make and publicize more favorably than substantive policy decisions that tangibly benefit or burden segments of society and reallocate resources.[26] But often symbolism won't suffice. Policymakers are expected and required to propose substantive solutions.

They usually have several alternatives. If the problem is low student achievement in public schools, they could propose setting national standards, giving grants to local districts, equalizing school funding, encouraging teacher training, and much more. Traffic safety can be facilitated by "building more highways (the solution of the 1950s), requiring safer cars (the solution of the 1960s), or putting drunk drivers behind bars (that of the 1980s and 1990s)."[27] As well as changing speed limits, beefing up enforcement, making radar detectors illegal, and so on.

Journalists have the time and resources to cover the often complex and detailed formulation of policy on only a few major issues. They particularly eschew the intricacies of technical, specialized, or arcane topics, such as arms control. Often unobserved by the press, policymakers therefore enjoy considerable discretion at this policy stage.

Limiting Choice   But decisionmakers, especially those elected to office, usually try to respond to policy issues in ways that appeal to the public.[28] So, they are often influenced by their sense of how their proposals will play in the press.

Besides, even in the netherworld of defense policy, the media can have a policy effect: By characterizing President Reagan's proposal for a space defense system as "Star Wars," the press made it more vulnerable to attack and difficult to accomplish. And certainly some defense issues, such as nuclear testing, can be simplified as "for" or "against."

How an issue is defined at various stages of the policy process can be crucial. Often, the frames used to structure and organize the contents of policy-relevant news stories support one policy position over other alternatives. An article about pesticides headlined "'New Double Duty Insecticide'" conveys a quite different impression and understanding from one headlined "'Nerve Gas in the Orchards.'"[29] Homelessness can be framed as a societal problem or as a public-safety problem. Whether one supports a policy to provide jobs and welfare to the poor can depend on whether the persistent poverty of many African-Americans and the crime in their communities are blamed on racial and class exclusion or on improper personal values, and lack of initiative and the desire to succeed.

So, it is crucial whether in media coverage one frame dominates or whether several alternatives are provided. Policymakers know this. President Clinton framed the issue of gays in the military as a question of status: "'Should people who have served their country with distinction—many of them with battlefield ribbons—and who have never had any kind of question about their conduct, be booted out of the military?'"[30] He proposed lifting the ban. But his antagonists

© Tom Tomorrow

framed the issue in terms of disrupting military discipline and morale, undermining combat readiness, and negative images of immoral predatory homosexual behavior.[31] The media framed it as interest-group conflict with the military on one side and gays on the other.[32]

Legitimation and Adoption

At the legitimation and adoption stage, which takes place predominately in the legislature, formulated policy proposals meet their fate. Often that fate depends on the amount and type of coverage the policy proposals receive in the press. There are several different possibilities.

Many proposals disappear and die. In the aftermath of a massive oil spill in Santa Barbara, California, local and national media coverage intensely aroused people, leading to hearings and the introduction of legislation. But, in part because of a lack of media attention at this stage, no substantial changes in federal off-shore policies ensued.[33]

On prominent policy issues, the media can be a forum for debate and discussion in which various sides argue their cases. NAFTA was a prominent example. Relatedly, the press can influence a proposed policy by assessing its status and prospects, by predicting its likely fate. One way news organizations do this is by polling members of Congress about their preferences on important pieces of legislation. The data can work in opposite ways, emboldening opponents but also spurring supporters.[34]

But coverage is sometimes one-sided. When favorable, it enhances a policy's likelihood of adoption; the reverse if unfavorable. Or coverage can result in policy proposals being revised and reshaped.

Indeed, media content can kill a proposed policy. This is most common when hostile interest groups mobilize press and public opinion predominately against it, as occurred with the Clinton health care proposals.[35] But such campaigns—in which vast sums were spent on tendentious ads that enjoyed relatively uncritical coverage in the press—are uncommon.[36]

What is common for such a complicated subject as health care, in the words of Tom Hamburger, Ted Marmor, and Jon Meacham, is "that the American press, by and large, is culturally incapable of confronting an issue, explaining it, exploring possible solutions, and sorting fact from fiction."[37] Marmor and Meacham chronicle a slew of ads made by interest groups containing fear-mongering distortions of the Clinton health care plan about loss of choice, bureaucracy, quality, and cost that the press transmitted uncritically. They castigate the media for hyping the politics and for focusing on conflict at the expense of explanation of the plan and analysis of its details, and for failing to compare the proposals to health coverage programs in other countries.

© 1997, Mark Alan Stamaty. Reprinted with permission.

In contrast, reporters sometimes kill by exposing a dubious provision favoring a "special interest" that a legislator is trying quietly to sneak through without public attention.

Implementation and Administration

The media's effects on policy implementation can be complicated. By giving widespread coverage to president Clinton's signing of the Brady bill requiring gun registration, they added to the bill's legitimacy. But by later reporting that many people were not registering their guns, the media may have encouraged widespread defiance of the law.

Most policy decisions, however, are not self-executing; they require implementation and administration, usually by bureaucrats. Messy reality can make the job difficult for even the most conscientious and dedicated bureaucrat. Incompetence is not unknown. Nor is resistance and refusal to execute a policy. In 1986, President Reagan directed that any company found abusing a governmental program be prohibited from all governmental work. Despite demands by the Agriculture Department's inspector general, top officials of the department persisted in giving many millions of dollars in contracts to large dairies and other agricultural companies that had defrauded federal programs.

So the media can be a significant force at this stage in the policy process by reporting whether and how policies are being administered and implemented. Certainly, there are derelictions, ineptitude, and scandals enough for reporters to unearth. But there is so much implementation and administration, usually out of the media's view, and it is time-consuming to expose. So press coverage is inevitably sporadic, intermittently focused on a few policies.

When it occurs, such coverage can have effects. After the *New York Times*, using documents obtained under the Freedom of Information Act, exposed the Agriculture Department's resistance to Reagan's directive, the department quickly announced that it would now abide by the directive. But the stall had lasted for several years, and the department would most likely apply the policy only to new contracts.[38]

Media investigations can also spur members of Congress to review programs they have delegated to the bureaucracy by exposing flaws in how they are implemented. These stories are often about or stem from the complaints by people or groups about the conduct of administration.

Evaluation

In theory, policy evaluation involves identifying the goals, devising a means for measurement, targeting a population for feedback, and measuring policy goal attainment, efficiency, and effectiveness. This is then followed by decisions to maintain or terminate or modify the policy under examination. But because public officials put their efforts into other stages of the policy process, evaluation is relatively uncommon. There is no premium in undertaking it except for politically partisan reasons or if there are outrages and scandals to be exposed.

But policies often fail. The 1995 Telecommunications Act was supposed to unleash the powers of competition, reduce cable rates, and spur technological development. At the end of its first year, it had the opposite effects. One reason was the unjustified assumption that the cable business would become a full-fledged, nationwide competitor to the telephone industry.[39]

Policies may be counterproductive, having unanticipated and undesired consequences. The federal student loan program enabled students to enroll at fly-by-night trade schools. The training they received was inadequate, if not useless. After dropping out or even graduating, most were unable to find jobs. They ended up defaulting on their loans, thereby ruining their credit ratings and diminishing their hope of escaping poverty. Taxpayers footed the bill for these federally guaranteed loans.

The press can be important at the evaluation stage by holding government accountable for its actions. One way is by showing what is going on. Another is through reporters' research. Others are by reporting studies and transmitting the complaints of whistle-blowers, the findings of interest groups, and the like.[40] The press also reports and therefore publicizes some of the assessments the government does, for example by covering congressional hearings of campaign finance abuses.

Media coverage can cause policies to be reappraised, changed, even abandoned. According to David Gergen, who was working in the Reagan White House at the time, "'Television had an enormous impact on our policy in Lebanon. We withdrew those marines from Lebanon in part because of television. We asked the Israelis to stop bombing in part because of the television pictures that were coming back from Beirut.'"[41] Similarly, television cameras in Manila showing crowds stopping tanks revealed the failing repression of the Marcos regime, thereby adding to the pressure on the Reagan administration to withdraw its support and contributing to the overthrow of the Philippine president.

Of course, media content may be partial, one-sided, and inaccurate. It can mislead policymakers and the public by reporting positive policy outcomes when a less encouraging conclusion is warranted; or by suggesting a policy has failed when it is more or less working.[42]

FOREIGN POLICY

The media's coverage of and intriguing effects on foreign policies deserve special mention.

Start with the fact that an administration's foreign policymakers usually convey an impression of consensus. Of course, acrimony and conflict are rife behind the scenes. The memoirs of George Shultz, Secretary of State during the Reagan presidency, graphically reveal the intense infighting sometimes characterizing the apparently most united and coherent foreign policy. Shultz had a bitter personal feud with Secretary of Defense Caspar Weinberger as well as serious problems with the president's national security advisors and their staff, with the CIA, and with other governmental agencies, such as the Justice Department.[43] Nonetheless, as Peter Feaver puts it: "Policy coordination shows a public face of discipline, resolve, and tenacity . . . [even though] it is the product of feverish behind-the-scenes deal-cutting, compromises, and uncertainty."[44]

This appearance of agreement connects with Lance Bennett's indexing theory discussed in chapter 3: that American journalists "'index' the range of voices and viewpoints in both news and editorials according to the range of views expressed in mainstream government debate about a given topic."[45] Disagreement and debate reign on many domestic policies. With foreign policies, the index of voices is correspondingly narrower. The press infrequently reports the views of concerned people outside Washington, let alone those who dissent from or reject the policies. Thus, the news rarely disputes America's foreign policies.[46]

Moreover, in reporting the world, America's newspapers and television networks overwhelmingly focus on the United States' relationship with other countries. Stories about foreign countries per se, their institutions, and policies are uncommon.[47] Local television is even more limited, all but ignoring the world.

Consequently, under normal circumstances, the public is usually inclined to go along with America's foreign policies or at least give policymakers the benefit of the doubt. That is, unless things go visibly wrong.

But when the news media do cover foreign countries, it is often with vivid, dramatic news of disasters. Such stories are partial. They emphasize starvation, human rights abuses, relief agency bungling of needs. They ignore causes of the conflict, the credibility of relief agencies, the self-help ability of local communities, and the long-term problems. They oversimplify complex issues, reducing them to victims, villains, and heroes.[48]

Such coverage is facilitated by the combination of new communications technologies and global media systems that can instantly transmit overseas events and the effects of foreign policies to American policymakers and the public alike. When Saddam Hussein brutally repressed the Kurds' attempt to assert their independence after the Gulf War, television showed pictures of the cold and hungry, sick and dying refugees; framing the Kurds as victims.

Many Americans, ignorant about situations overseas, can be powerfully affected by such coverage. Thus, public outrage compelled an initially reluctant President Bush to establish a safety zone in northern Iraq. When he announced at a news conference that the refugee camps would be set up, CNN divided the screen: "to the lower right was the President; upper left was a larger picture of the refugees. Mr. Bush seemed to be responding to the pressure from above."[49]

Similarly, television pictures of people, especially children, starving in Somalia mobilized Americans to demand humanitarian intervention by their government. Then, months later, television images of battle scenes and dead American servicemen caused President Clinton to withdraw the troops.

Media coverage thus goes far to explain the American government's response to the Kurds' situation and starvation in Somalia. The absence of media coverage from equally horrifying events in Azerbaijan, Sudan, Angola, and Liberia in part explains governmental inaction. And the anticipation of Somalia-type negative coverage contributed to the Clinton administration's decision not to do anything to stop the genocide in Rwanda in 1994.

Public acquiescence transformed into public outrage by the media has another significant effect on policymakers. They feel required to respond with alacrity to foreign events and situations depicted by the media as crises or emergencies (e.g., CNN covered the Clinton administration's disagreement with Iraq in November 1997 as "Showdown with Iraq" and introduced its stories with ominous music).

But quick reactions by policymakers are not always desirable. "In retrospect, several key members of the Carter administration thought they were wrong to respond within hours to the Soviet invasion of Afghanistan, a decision based in part on a perceived need to make the evening news."[50]

TWO CASE STUDIES

This section illustrates the intricacies and effects of the media-policy relationship with contrasting case studies of the savings and loan business and the chemical industry. The former reveals the deleterious consequences of inadequate media coverage. The latter, more briefly, shows the beneficial consequences for public policy of more intense, although sporadic, media coverage.

The Media and the S&L Debacle

The pillaging and subsequent bankruptcy of many savings and loan associations (S&Ls) during the 1980s was barely reported by the news media. Yet, because many of the S&Ls were federally insured, the cost to the taxpayers amounts to hundreds of billions of dollars, and still continues. This woeful tale has two parts: inadequate media coverage of the enactment of the law that essentially freed the S&Ls from regulatory restraint and the neglect in coverage of the debacle that ensued.[51]

The 1980 Depository Institutions Deregulation and Monetary Control law deregulated or at least loosened governmental supervision and control of S&Ls. Limits were removed on the amount of interest that the S&Ls could pay, and they were permitted to lend in areas traditionally limited to commercial banks. Most telling, the amount of passbook accounts insured by the federal government was raised from $40,000 to $100,000. This meant that the federal government would reimburse any depositor up to that amount if the S&L holding the funds became insolvent.

Freed from regulatory restraint, competing with each other for deposits by raising interest rates, many of the owners and executives of S&Ls made risky loans, spent profligately, and committed other legal and illegal sins. The result, spurred by the economic recession of the late 1980s, was a financial disaster. Numerous S&Ls went bankrupt, requiring a federal governmental bailout of the insured depositors.

Whether that scenario was at all predictable is questionable. Nonetheless, shrewd observers and analysts might have sensed that some of the S&L provisions of the act were dubious and could lead to financial problems for the S&Ls and for the government. After all, the legislation had been wending its way through the congressional process for some time. Final passage and presidential approval were not unexpected. Journalists had time to study the bill's provisions. With this in mind, let us see how passage of the banking bill and its subsequent signing into law by the president were reported by the press.

Limited Media Coverage   The *Wall Street Journal* reported the story in one column on page 2 of its March 6, 1980, edition under the headline "Banking Bill Is Approved by Conferees." Datelined Washington and written by a *Journal* staff reporter, the story leads with the news that the conference committee has agreed to phase out interest-rate controls on deposits within six years. The next paragraph cautiously ventures that the legislation will produce major changes in the U.S. banking system: "increase interest rates on deposits, heighten competition between different types of banking institutions, and substantially strengthen the ability of the Fed to conduct monetary policy."

The bulk of the story is devoted to the ways in which the bill strengthens the authority of the Federal Reserve Board. Only in the last paragraph does the story report the bill's provision to increase to $100,000 the amount of bank deposits insured by the Federal Deposit Insurance Corporation.

The *New York Times* reported the conferees' action in a one-column story on its March 6, 1980, front page under the heading "Conferees Move to Let Interest on Savings Rise." The subhead reads: "Bill Would Also Override State Mortgage Ceilings."

The report comes from the AP wire service rather than a *Times'* staffer, indicating that the newspaper had not formally assigned a reporter from its Washington Bureau to cover the bill.

The story describes the action as "sweeping" and emphasizes, as the headline suggests, the interest rate decision. The House-Senate compromise is described as "a sensitive balancing act pitting the interests of thrift institutions, commercial banks and the credit unions against those of labor unions, consumer groups and senior citizen organizations that complain of interest rate discrimination."

The rest of the account is relegated to page D15 of the Business Section. It primarily details the increase in the authority of the Federal Reserve Bank. Only the New York State Superintendent of Banks is identified as being interviewed about the legislation. She comments on the mortgage rate effects for her state.

The *Times* returns to the subject on April 1, after President Carter has signed the bill at a White House ceremony. The front-page story, headlined "Far-Reaching Banking Legislation Signed by President," is written by *Times* reporter Clyde Farnsworth. Again, the key provisions are identified as the gradual raising of the ceiling on interest paid to small savers, the increased authority given to the Federal Reserve, and the override of state-imposed ceilings on mortgage rates. President Carter is quoted as saying that the law will "'help control inflation, strengthen our financial institutions and help small savers.'"

U.S. News & World Report of April 7, 1980, devotes three pages to the new law under the heading, "A Banking Bill With Good News for Savers." On page 77, the article claims to spell out how the legislation "will affect individuals in months and years to come." The changes are listed as affecting savings, checking accounts, deposit insurance, credit unions, mortgage rates, savings and loan institutions, and the Federal Reserve Board. On page 78, the magazine explains that the "idea behind these changes is to put thrift institutions on a more equal footing with banks so that they will be able to attract deposits and afford to pay the highest rates of interest that are bound to result from removing the present ceilings."

Comparisons of Media Coverage   Coverage by the *New York Times*, the *Wall Street Journal*, and *U.S. News and World Report* was quite similar. They all provided, to various extent, the legislation's main provisions. No sources were cited or quoted aside from President Carter's praise and, in the *Times*, the New York State Superintendent of Banks. The story was framed as a major change. Either explicitly or implicitly, the newspapers and newsweekly viewed the changes favorably. One reason is that revisions of the banking laws were overdue. They occurred, moreover, at a time when deregulation was a policy increasingly in favor as a way of spurring competition in the U.S. economy. Besides, the law had a democratic component: it would help those Americans whose finances confined them to relatively low interest rates paid by S&Ls and who were unable to acquire the higher-paying interest rate money-market mutual funds and certificates. The language used to describe the law's provisions was neutral or favorable.

The key finding for us, however, is that none of the newspapers or the magazine probed in any detail the extensive involvement of interest groups nor, even more significantly, communicated the slightest inkling of the national disaster ahead. One reason is that all of them—including the *Journal*, which specializes in covering business and commerce—focused their stories on the act's passage and provisions. That was the news. Reporters seem to have waited for enactment of the law before examining its details. They had not studied it beforehand. They apparently left themselves little time to assess the legislation's merits or consider its possible effects.

Reporters, moreover, tend to avoid making judgments and predictions about the effects of a just-passed law that engenders no conflict among policymakers. They stick with the factual details rather than enter the uncertain realm of speculation. Their caution is reinforced when the legislation is complex and multifaceted. In such cases, analysis requires the kind of in-depth subject matter expertise that most journalists covering Congress do not possess.

There is one other way in which doubt about the legislation's effects on the S&L business might have found its way into the stories: if some individuals who or organizations that were respected enough to have contacts with or attract the attention of journalists (well-known S&L executives or bankers, prominent politicians, leaders of relevant interest groups such as the American Bankers Association) had made newsworthy predictions of disaster or expressed concern about the legislation. This seems not to have occurred.

Reasons for Lack of Coverage   The 1980s unfolded with scant news coverage, little of it prominently placed, of the bankruptcies in the S&L scandal that was to become the most costly public finance disaster in U.S. history. Ellen Hume and David Shaw provide several reasons for the mainstream media's overwhelming failure to realize the full magnitude of the story or tell it memorably.[52] These can be broken down into news and sources.

Journalists deemed the subject complicated, technical, and boring, a story about numbers not people, that did not lend itself to television visuals. And, although the effects of the scandal were being felt in many communities, the journalists saw it as a local not a national story. Besides, serious investigative reporting is expensive, time-consuming, and more and more a luxury in contemporary cost-conscious, corporate-controlled media.

Possible sources of information for reporters consisted of politicians, regulators, S&L operators, and ordinary people. With members of both political parties complicit, neither party had a major interest in pushing or pursuing the embarrassing subject, and every reason to keep it quiet. Nor was it an attractive campaign issue, since no politician knew how to fix the debacle without increasing taxes. Regulators were reluctant to disclose the facts from fear of triggering withdrawals from financially vulnerable thrifts.[53] Many pertinent documents were kept secret by law.

Those responsible for and those involved in the S&L debacle assiduously avoided media coverage. Some S&L operators occasionally abetted by their lawyers and accountants, were manipulating their records to conceal their losses. As for ordinary people, the immediate victims, with their funds insured by the federal government, they did not complain; and the ultimate victims (U.S. taxpayers) were unaware of what was happening.

As a consequence, according to Robert Kaiser, managing editor of the *Washington Post,* "it took 'an enormously long time'" for the press to understand that "this very conservative, small-bore, local American institution had been transformed into something very speculative, a high-flying, risk-taking, business."[54] Public attention might have been aroused, as Narda Zacchino, associate editor of the *Los Angeles Times,* pointed out, "'If Bush had gone on television and said, 'I am adding $100 to each . . . family's tax bill this year to pay for the S&L scandal,' then people would've reacted to it a little more.'"[55] But he never did. Only when the scandal touched the president's son, involved some senators, and generated widely reported Senate committee hearings did it begin to penetrate public consciousness.

So, the story largely failed to achieve prominence. Consequently, the public was neither informed nor activated, and policymakers were not forced to take action to deal with the debacle until late in the day. Similar fates would appear to have befallen such other significant but unglamorous subjects as "scandals involving President Ronald Reagan's Department of Housing and Urban Development, the Bank of Credit & Commerce International, and the Bush Administration's dealings with Saddam Hussein before the Gulf War."[56]

The Media and Regulation of the Chemical Industry

Regulation of the chemical industry shows what media coverage can achieve.

In December 1984, the city of Bhopal, India, was overwhelmed by toxic fumes leaking from its Union Carbide pesticide plant. Hundreds died, many others were hospitalized.[57] Media coverage was intense. At the behest of its executive editor, A. M. Rosenthal, the *New York Times* used four reporters, including a science specialist, and published more than sixty articles in two weeks.

Such coverage of the incident changed public and governmental attitudes toward the chemical industry, revealed the possibility for disaster from similar plants in the United States, placed the issue on the policy agenda, and alerted decisionmakers to take action. Congress held hearings at which leaders of the environmental movement testified. They framed the issue as the design, siting, operating, and monitoring of hazardous facilities to prevent a repetition of Bhopal in the United States. The media extensively transmitted their testimony and perspective.

Formulation, legitimation, and adoption of the policy dealing with the chemical industry was the province of Congress.

> The road through Congress bristled with obstacles and delays at every stage: from lawmakers supportive of business or protective of jobs, from technical snags in the wording of legislation, from environmentalists who thought the rules did not go far enough and from an industry and an administration which thought they went too far.[58]

But in contrast to coverage of the hearings, coverage of this law-making process, even in major newspapers, was sparse. Only the specialist and trade press reported the legislative embroglio.

Then, gas leaked out of a Union Carbide plant and into Institute, West Virginia. Although no deaths occurred, 135 people were hospitalized and hundreds evacuated. This leak occurred despite a $5 million plant safety upgrade, and belied the earlier claims of the corporation's director for health that such a leak could not happen in the United States. In the next few days, the *Times* reported several small spills and fires at chemical plants and, in a detailed piece, claimed that "about 50,000 processing units at chemical plants 'were not designed to prevent leaking hazardous substances.'"[59]

The Toxic Waste Campaign organized a well-publicized, nationwide public relations campaign, catchily entitled, "Super Drive for Super Fund." It collected 2 million signatures in support of the legislation and presented them to Congress.

The combination of emotionally powerful events, widely covered by the media, and the publicity-inspiring activities of public interest groups ensured enactment of the legislation. It bolstered sympathetic lawmakers sensitive to assuaging public anxieties as well as desirous for public attention, and attuned to the issues of the day. It helped convince undecided legislators who were swayed by the evidence and arguments and, more important, aware of constituent pressure. And it discouraged opposition.

CONCLUSION

Public policy is composed of governmental decisions and actions, such as enacting laws, issuing regulations, allocating funds, and undertaking military action against other countries. Much policymaking consists of continuing existing policy or of making marginal changes to it. For long periods of time, such policies attract little attention. But vast policy changes and innovations do take place.

The media can be a crucial influence on the process and content of policies. Aware of this, public officials and those trying to influence them strive, with more or less success, to infuse their perspectives into the news or at least respond to press stories and depictions.

Media influence on policy is a function of what is covered, how often, and how it is framed. News icons and investigative reporting are particularly important.

In practice, the media are more or less involved at each policy-making stage: problem formation, agenda setting, policy formulation, legitimation and adoption, implementation and administration, and evaluation.

Foreign policy is a special case. The impression of elite consensus, allied to indexing and the media's U.S. focus, encourage public acquiescence to U.S. governmental policies. But vivid, dramatic media coverage can put pressure on policymakers to intervene, e.g., by sending troops. Absent such coverage, or when they anticipate negative media depictions, e.g., of dead troops, policymakers can avoid foreign interventions, unless called for by the national interest (as they define it, e.g., the Gulf War).

Two case studies, the savings and loan debacle and enactment of a law to regulate the chemical industry, illustrate and explain the media's different types of involvement with and effects on domestic policy.

Notes

1. See Donald E. Abelson, *American Think-Tanks and Their Role in U.S. Foreign Policy* (New York: St. Martin's Press, 1996), esp. 68–71 81–89; see also Jeffrey M. Berry, *The Interest Group Society,* 3rd ed. (New York: Longman, 1997), 126. An earlier version of this chapter was published in Doris A. Graber, Denis McQuail, and Pippa Norris, ed., *The Politics of News: The News of Politics* (Washington, DC: CQ Press, 1998).

2. See list of media citations in Michael Dolny, "Think Tank Monitor," *EXTRA!* 11:3 (May-June 1998): 9.

3. Michael Dolny, "The Think Tank Spectrum," *EXTRA!* 9:3 (May-June 1996): 21.

4. Lawrence R. Jacobs and Robert Y. Shapiro, "Studying Substantive Democracy," *PS* 27:1 (March 1994): 9–17.

5. Robert M. Stein and Kenneth N. Bickers, *Perpetuating the Pork Barrel* (New York: Cambridge University Press, 1995); see also Paul A. Sabatier, "Toward Better Theo-

ries of the Policy Process," *PS* 24:2 (June 1991): 147–56. For a perspective that places greater emphasis on experts, see John Zaller, *The Nature and Origins of Mass Opinion* (New York: Cambridge University Press, 1992), 319–32; also relevant is David Whiteman, *Communication in Congress* (Lawrence: University Press of Kansas, 1995).

6. Marc K. Landy and Martin Levin, ed., *The New Politics of Public Policy* (Baltimore, Md.: Johns Hopkins University Press, 1995).

7. The following discussion is based on Frank R. Baumgartner and Bryan D. Jones, *Agenda and Instability in American Politics* (Chicago: University of Chicago Press, 1993).

8. On the relationship between the media and public policy, see Martin Linsky, *Impact* (New York: Norton, 1986); Patrick O'Heffernan, *Mass Media and American Foreign Policy* (Norwood, N.J.: Ablex, 1991); and Robert Spitzer, ed., *Media and Public Policy* (Westport, Conn.: Praeger, 1993).

9. List provided by Katie Botel, assistant to the executive producer Aaron Spelling, in a fax to me dated February 18, 1997. It was requested by Gabriel Michael Paletz, who heard some of the items at a lecture given by Aaron Spelling at the University of Southern California. My secretary, Marisa Law drolly places all the items in one episode.

10. W. Lance Bennett, "A Policy Research Paradigm for the News Media and Democracy," *Journal of Communication* 43:3 (Summer 1993): 180–89; see also Nayda Terkildsen, Frauke Schnell, and Cristina Ling, "Interest Groups, the Media and Policy Debate Formation" (paper presented at the 1996 American Political Science Association Meeting, San Francisco, September 1996).

11. Barbara J. Nelson, *Making an Issue of Child Abuse* (Chicago: University of Chicago Press, 1984), 72; see also John M. Johnson, "Horror Stories and the Construction of Child Abuse," in *Images of Issues,* ed. Joel Best (New York: Aldine de Gruyter, 1989), 5–19.

12. Anthony Downs, "Up and Down with Ecology—'The Issue Attention Cycle,'" *Public Interest* 28 (Summer 1972): 38–50.

13. Megan K. Dahl and W. Lance Bennett, "Media Agency and the Use of Icons in the Agenda-Setting Process" (paper presented at the annual meeting of the American Political Science Association, Chicago, August 1995), 1 (emphasis in the original).

14. W. Lance Bennett and Regina G. Lawrence, "News Icons and the Mainstreaming of Social Change," *Journal of Communication* 45:3 (Summer 1995): 20.

15. David L. Protess et al., *The Journalism of Outrage* (New York: Guilford Press, 1991), 244–45.

16. I am indebted to Deneen Nethercutt. In 1993, when she was a graduate student in the Annenberg School of the University of Southern California, she collected some of the relevant policy literature and worked closely with me in analyzing whether and how it fits into each stage.

17. David A. Rochefort and Roger W. Cobb, ed., *The Politics of Problem Definition* (Lawrence: University of Kansas Press, 1994).

18. Craig Reinarman and Harry G. Levine, "The Crack Attack," in *Images of Issues,* ed. Joel Best (New York: Aldine de Gruyter, 1989), 120.

19. Reinarman and Levine, 129.

20. Roger W. Cobb and Charles D. Elder, *Participation in American Politics; The Dynamics of Agenda-Building,* 2nd ed. (Boston: Allyn & Bacon, 1983).

21. Larry M. Bartels, "Politicians and the Press: Who Leads, Who Follows" (paper presented at the annual meeting of the American Political Science Association, San Francisco, September 1996), 1.

22. Ibid., 24.

23. Catherine Cassara, "Presidential Initiatives and Foreign News," in *News Media and Foreign Relations,* ed. Abbas Malek (Norwood, N.J.: Ablex, 1997), 174.

24. Leon V. Sigal, *Reporters and Officials* (Lexington, Mass.: D. C. Heath, 1973), 185.

25. Patrick O'Heffernan, "A Mutual Exploitation Model of Media Influence in U.S. Foreign Policy," in *Taken by Storm,* ed. W. Lance Bennett and David L. Paletz (Chicago: University of Chicago Press, 1994), 240.

26. David Pritchard, "The News Media and Public Policy Agendas," in *Public Opinion, the Press, and Public Policy,* ed. J. David Kennamer (Westport, Conn.: Praeger, 1992), 110–11.

27. Frank R. Baumgartner and Bryan D. Jones, *Agenda and Instability in American Politics* (Chicago: University of Chicago Press, 1993), 124.

28. John Zaller, "Strategic Politicians, Public Opinion, and the Gulf Crisis," in *Taken by Storm,* ed. Bennett and Paletz, 270–72.

29. Actual headlines cited in Baumgartner and Jones, *Agenda and Instability,* 51.

30. Quoted in Carl M. Cannon, "The Story in the Closet," *Forbes Media Critic* 1:1 (1993): 46.

31. Alan S. Yang, "Mass Opinion Change With and Without Elites" (paper presented at the annual meeting of the American Political Science Association, San Francisco, September 1996), 1–8.

32. Janet E. Steele, "Don't Ask, Don't Tell, Don't Explain," *Political Communication* 14:1 (January-March 1997): 83–96.

33. Harvey L. Molotch, "Oil in Santa Barbara and Power in America," *Sociological Inquiry* 40:1 (Winter 1970): 131–44.

34. Martha Joynt Kumar and Michael Baruch Grossman, "Congress: The Best Beat in Town" (paper presented at the annual meeting of the American Political Science Association, Washington D.C., August 1986), 10–11.

35. Lynda Lee Kaid, John C. Tedesco, and Julia A. Spiker, "Media Conflicts over Clinton Policies," in *The Clinton Presidency,* ed. Robert E. Denton, Jr., and Rachel L. Holloway (Westport, Conn.: Praeger, 1996), 103–21.

36. Darrell M. West and Diane J. Heith, "Harry and Louise Go to Washington" (paper presented at the annual meeting of the American Political Science Association, September 1994), 13.

37. Tom Hamburger, Ted Marmor, and Jon Meacham, "What the Death of Health Reform Teaches Us About the Press," *The Washington Monthly* 26:11 (November 1994): 37.

38. Dean Baquet, "Agriculture Department, in Shift, Will Punish Corrupt Contractors," *New York Times,* 23 November 1993, A1.

39. Mark Landler, "Instead of Flood of Competition, the Communications Act Brought a Trickle," *New York Times,* 10 February 1997, C7.

40. Fox Butterfield, "Most Efforts to Stop Crime Fall Far Short, Study Finds," *New York Times,* 16 April 1997, A16.

41. Quoted by Richard Valeriani, "Talking Back to the Tube," in *The Media and the Gulf War,* ed. Hedrick Smith (Washington, D.C.: Seven Locks Press, 1992), 237.

42. Jerry F. Medler and Michael J. Medler, "Media Images as Environmental Policy," in *Media and Public Policy,* ed. Robert J. Spitzer (Westport, Conn.: Praeger, 1993), 131.

43. George P. Shultz, *Turmoil and Triumph* (New York: Scribner's, 1993).

44. Peter Feaver, "Domestication of Foreign Policy" (unpublished manuscript, Duke University Department of Political Science, 1997), 11.

45. W. Lance Bennett, "Toward a Theory of Press-State Relations in the United States," *Journal of Communication* 40:3 (Spring 1990), 106.

46. Nicholas O. Berry, *Foreign Policy and the Press* (New York: Greenwood Press, 1990).

47. Times Mirror (now Pew) Center for the People & the Press, "A Content Analysis: International News Coverage Fits Public's Ameri-Centric Mood" (undated news release on polls conducted from March 1 through June 30, 1995), 1–2.

48. See Robert I. Rotberg and Thomas G. Weiss, ed., *From Massacres to Genocide* (Washington, D.C.: Brookings Institution, 1996).

49. Walter Goodman, "The Images That Haunt Washington," *New York Times,* 5 May 1991, H33.

50. David R. Gergen, "Diplomacy in a Television Age," in *The Media and Foreign Policy,* ed. Simon Serfaty (New York: St. Martin's Press, 1990), 54.

51. A thoughtful study is Lawrence J. White, *The S&L Debacle* (New York: Oxford University Press, 1991); see also L. William Seidman, *Full Faith and Credit* (New York: Times Books, 1993); Kitty Calavita, Henry N. Pontell, and Robert H. Tillman, *Big Money Crime* (Berkeley: University of California Press, 1997); and Mark Carl Rom, *Public Spirit in the Thrift Tragedy* (Pittsburgh, Pa.: University of Pittsburgh Press, 1996).

52. Ellen Hume, "Why the Press Blew The S&L Scandal," *New York Times,* 24 May 1990, A25; and David Shaw, "Coverage: Why S&L Story Was Slow to Ignite," *Los Angeles Times,* 26 October 1992, A17.

53. For mainly anecdotal evidence, see Kathleen Day, *S&L Hell* (New York: Norton, 1993).

54. Quoted in Shaw, "Coverage," A17.

55. Ibid.

56. Ibid.

57. This discussion is taken from Sanjoy Hazarika *From Bhopal To Superfund,* Discussion Paper D–17, The Joan Shorenstein Center for Press, Politics, Public Policy, Harvard University, September 1994.

58. Ibid., 2.

59. Ibid., 9.

Chapter 16

Conclusions and Change

◆ ◆ ◆

The findings from the preceding chapters about the contents and consequences of the mass media's involvement with politics and government can be summarized as follows.[1]

Media content is pervasive and rife with explicit and implicit political meaning. This content comes in various modes, most of them corporate controlled and advertiser supported. It is provided as popular culture by people in the entertainment industry and as news by journalists.

The mass media's explicit political content tends to emphasize conflict over consensus and derelictions over accomplishments.

Elected and appointed public officials, interest groups leaders, and political activists understand the importance of this media content and try to control or at least influence it in their favor. They are sometimes successful, sometimes not.

The mass media offer a relatively narrow ideological range of content, mainly from liberal to ultraconservative, neglecting unconventional voices and marginalized groups.

The public are recipients, willing or unwilling, passive or active, of this media content, over whose making they have little direct influence.

There are specialized sources of information for those interested but most people are given little incentive to search them out.

So, many Americans, particularly the economically disadvantaged, are poorly informed about, even unaware of, the details of many governmental decisions and actions. They have a limited awareness and understanding of the range of policy perspectives and policy alternatives.[2] Common is a simplified, one-dimensional understanding of politicians as pursuing their selfish, sometimes corrupt, objectives instead of the public interest. Many people are cynical about government and politics.

CHANGE

Seeking to change this situation, some academics (notably Jay Rosen) and journalists (e.g., Davis Merritt) have opted for a different kind of reporting. They call it public or civic journalism.[3] In brief, it is based on the assumption that the press should connect with its audience to facilitate political participation. During the 1992 election, for example, the *Charlotte Observer* "sought to ground its coverage in what it called a 'citizens' agenda', meaning a list of discussion priorities identified by area residents through the paper's own research."[4] Other public journalism practices include reporting about people who make a difference by getting involved, giving residents the information and incentives they need to improve their neighborhoods, and searching for solutions to public problems.[5]

Despite disdain and dismissal from many practicing journalists and some academics, public journalism is making inroads. But it has far to go.[6]

So, many of those seeking changes in media content and political consequences put their faith in new technology.

Certainly changes in information technology affect our lives.[7] Consider the fates of postage stamps discussed in chapter one and of editorial cartoonists. Stamps are becoming obsolete as e-mail replaces snail-mail; cartoonists have been dismissed as technology has increased the number of media outlets, newspapers' readership has declined, and staffs have been downsized.[8]

More directly political, television is given responsibility for the rise of candidate-centered campaigns and the decline of voting based on party affiliation.[9]

© Rob Rogers

THIS MODERN WORLD by TOM TOMORROW

© Tom Tomorrow

Unraveling all the possible and likely effects of diverse and changing technologies on American government and politics is daunting.[10] There is a lot of optimistic speculation and some nay-saying.[11] Empirical research, although burgeoning, is limited.[12] Nonetheless, intriguing possibilities are discernible, even though most of them must at this stage be hedged with caveats and cautions.

The new technology is likely to have political effects for six reasons.[13] First, it gives people access to masses of information, interpretations, and opinions from diverse sources never before so available. Second, because people can store, copy, comment on, change, and forward this material to others, as well as generate and transmit material of their own devising, the new technology creates a forum for and enhances the opportunity for expression and discussion. Third, it increases the capacity of interest groups and social movements to organize and mobilize their members as well as people belonging to no common membership group.[14] Fourth, it facilitates the ability of political candidates, elected and appointed officials, to communicate their views and actions to the public. Fifth, it vastly expands communication between government and the public. Sixth, because it enables people to express their preferences directly to policymakers, new technology can influence the making and content of public policy, even allow for the possibility of plebiscitary democracy.

The bulk of this chapter examines each of these possibilities. Corresponding to the order of this book, it starts with the elements of new technology; continues with the public, discussing the availability and expression of information; follows with the intermediary functions of mobilization and elections; and finishes the section with government and public policy. All of which lead ineluctably to the final section of this chapter, which discusses issues.

Elements of New Technology

The new technology includes cable and satellite television, videocassette recorders, and camcorders. Their effects are obvious. The availability of news throughout the day on computer and cable makes people less willing to abide by the scheduling of networks and local stations. Zappers enable people to be speedily selective watching television, to switch from one channel to another, to skip past advertisements. Videocassette recorders free people to watch programs at their own volition, unbound by the media's schedules.[15] Camcorders can be used to record the actions of authority figures (e.g., police treatment of Rodney King).

Computers can serve as "combined typewriter, memory bank, mailing device, debate tool, publishing instrument, modeling and forecasting agent."[16]

They bring us the Internet, with its World Wide Web communication system. Prominent features are electronic mail, through which people send messages to others on the system, and listserves, which automatically transmit people's e-mail messages to everyone on the mailing lists. One result is a proliferation of newsgroups discussing specific subjects: messages are posted to the group for all participants to read, forward, and respond to as desired.

Even more significant, anyone and everyone can establish a home page on the net and link it to other sites. Advanced sites can even incorporate sound and video (e.g., of the bombing and of events at and around the federal building in Oklahoma).

Availability of Information

So, new technology vastly expands the amount and diversity of political material available to the public. Cable and satellite television bring CNN (and CNN's "Headline News"), C-SPAN, and Court TV. Given the prospect of hundreds of specialized "narrowcasting" stations, even Bruce Springsteen would no longer have to get mad about "57 Channels and Nothin' On," and blow his television to bits.

It is the Internet and the web, however, that provide access to a hitherto unimaginable range of instant information and opinions from around the world.

The mass media are there, in the form of the Associated Press and other wire services, some foreign, national, and many local newspapers, magazines, broadcasting networks and individual stations, as well as CNN, C-SPAN, and so on. Mostly they provide their regular material, with the occasional addition of audio and video clips. Some newspapers, notably the *San Jose Mercury News,* offer raw

Reprinted with special permission of King Features Syndicate

(unedited) information, material that does not get into print.[17] Some media outlets, such as Africa News Service, whose print version closed in 1993 after thirty-three years of publication, have even been resurrected and thrive on line (http://www.africanews.org).[18]

There are nonpartisan organizations, such as Policy.com, which provides information about the policy positions of government, think tanks, advocacy groups, and business; and "Project Vote Smart," which circulates biographical information, campaign finance data, issue positions, voting records, ratings by interest groups, and other information on elected public officials and candidates. Organizations and individuals repackage governmental data (e.g., from the Federal Election Commission) to make it user-friendly and revealing (e.g., to tell who in people's hometown gave more than $200 to a candidate or party or which candidates have the most cash available to them during an election).[19]

There are information clearinghouses. Ones by and for women include Femina, Guerrilla Girls, and Geekgirl.[20]

Interest groups of all types are there, too, from the well-known American Bar Association and American Medical Association, to the American Indian Movement, and the National Coalition for the Homeless. There are ideological groups, such as the American Conservative Union; social movements, such as the Christian Coalition; and think tanks of all stripes.

Political parties from the most prominent to the most obscure, from the national, state, and local levels, are all there. The Green, Libertarian, and Socialist parties have sites, as do the College Republican War Room and Democrats at the University of Washington.

The government and politicians supply a horde of speeches and pronounce-ments, public documents, and records. All this material is available to journalists to enhance their researching and reporting capabilities, often as soon as they are available: notably the complete text of the report by the Independent Counsel Kenneth W. Starr.

At the same time, the availability and flexibility afforded by new technology liberate people from having to rely on the news, information, and opinions sup-plied by the press. For they can select what they want from the Internet, access the same (and alternative) sources as reporters, bypass the frames imposed by journalists, and thus form their own views.

The criminal trial of O. J. Simpson is a graphic example. Innumerable sites appeared full of news, theories, and gossip. Among them were alt.fan.oj-simpson, alt.fan.oj-simpson.die.die.die, alt.fan.oj-simpson.drive.faster, and alt.fan.ojsimp-son.gaschamber. Their contents included the complete texts of the grand jury transcript, the judge's rulings, and the actual trial testimony, questions to and answers from legal experts, collections of Simpson and lawyer jokes; and discussion of such arcane items as why Judge Lance Ito changed from using a Toshiba laptop to an I.B.M. Thinkpad (perhaps to tap into the Internet for information about the trial). People worldwide could "retrieve hourly news feeds, follow daily court tran-scripts, dissect the American legal system, study and debate the finer points of DNA analysis, and propose and attack various theories about the crime."[21]

Expression of Information

Having views is one thing, expressing them widely quite another. Technology is perennially seen as the means to facilitate expression. Thus, cable access was expected to create a democratic forum, to allow unconventional voices on televi-sion. "Yet, the greater democratic potential of access television is stymied by its insecure legal and regulatory status, its partial provision of the resources necessary to produce and distribute programming, its predominantly local orientation, and its marginalization as a sphere of public debate."[22]

The Internet is expected to do better. In theory, most anyone can have a home page and use e-mail to send and exchange messages inexpensively, almost instantaneously, and simultaneously to sizable audiences. People can participate in dialogue, posting to thousands of people, through the spontaneity of uncen-sored, usually uncontrolled, listserve newsgroups. These thematic groups pro-vide a venue for almost any posting no matter how peripheral, idiosyncratic, or bizarre.

In a study of USENET political newsgroups—such as alt.activism.d, alt.politics.clinton, alt.law-enforcement, alt.politics.nationalism.white, alt.poli-tics.usa.constitution, talk.politics.guns, and talk.politics.misc—Kevin Hill and John Hughes found over 470,000 messages posted to them in just one month. These include *threads* (responses to the original message or to something in someone else's reply), but not *cross-posting* (the same message is sent to more than one newsgroup simultaneously).[23]

Mobilization Efforts

New technology also facilitates mobilization by reducing the costs of organizing and building political coalitions. Activists are able to link with and mobilize other people, the unlike- as well as the like-minded. Technologically sophisticated organizations, such as the Christian Coalition, deploy a host of "contacting" techniques, including computer bulletin boards, telephone trees, faxes, and talk radio outlets.

Through e-mail and web sites, interest groups in particular can maintain contact with their members, recruit new ones (membership applications online), and encourage political action. One study found that almost two-thirds of a sample of people using the Internet "had been asked to petition or otherwise contact a public official about an issue or public policy, and one-third reported having used e-mail to contact a public official."[24]

The Internet makes it relatively easy to circulate information about meetings and protests, to sign and circulate (electronic) petitions, even to organize marches.[25] As just one example, Internet-based communication enabled advocates of home schooling, people widely dispersed throughout the country, to mobilize to defeat a proposal in Congress in 1994 that would have erected barriers against the practice.[26]

Nonpartisan organizations also use the Internet to facilitate political participation. The American Voter Coalition, whose avowed purpose is to educate and empower people, offered access to online voter registration. Voters could register by completing the form online. But they still had to receive the completed form in the mail, sign, and mail it to state election officials in an envelope provided.

Elections

During the 1992 election, politicians finally began to catch up with corporate America in the use of technology. Before that, their main innovation was to send out biographical videotapes to groups of interested voters, video news releases to the press, and display video endorsements and messages at campaign functions.

It was the Clinton campaign that most effectively exploited the technology of computer modems, faxes, e-mail, and interactive satellites. Constantly monitoring breaking news and pulling the television networks' news feeds from satellites before they were broadcast, the Clinton campaigners rapidly responded to attacks; even tracking down sometimes grateful reporters by beeper to feed them quotable, instant rebuttals to President Bush's latest statements even before he uttered them in public.

Clinton's advisors also used satellites to beam the candidate and surrogate speakers into interviews, meetings, and gatherings throughout the country. They electronically transmitted his speeches and press releases, making them available through online computer services.[27] One benefit, abetted by the candidate's bus tours with their photo ops, was fulsome news coverage from accommodating anchors and unchallenging reporters at local television stations.[28]

In 1996, technology was incorporated into the parties' nominating conventions. Web sites featured delegate's diaries, vote counts in real time, speech texts, state rosters, and news releases.[29] Republican politicians answered digital questions in online chats. A media monitoring organization posted "Convention Watch," reporting supposed biases in media coverage.

The 1996 election also featured the advent of candidates' home pages.[30] Logical designations for the Clinton and Dole 1996 sites would have been "www .clinton96.org" and "www.dole96.org," but an imaginative individual obtained the rights to these addresses and created spoof sites.[31]

The genuine sites for Clinton and Dole gave sanitized versions of their records, and not always candid descriptions of their positions on some issues: "President Dole will reinstate the long-standing military policy regarding homosexuals in the military" meant that he would forbid them from serving.[32] The home pages also described the candidates' campaigning activities, offered some of their commercials, recruited volunteers, and solicited contributions.

New technology was especially useful for minor party candidates for national offices and for all candidates running for state and local positions. They could communicate their backgrounds and records, platforms, and texts of their speeches to the electorate, thus elevating ideas and arguments over appearances and ads. Some were able to express their views and rebut their opponents in online debates.

Michael Margolis points out, however, that the major parties, their candidates, and office-holders "have an increasingly dominant presence on the Internet." In part, this is because they can afford to develop, maintain, and update the sites; equip them with greater visual appeal and interactive multimedia; and establish links to related web sites.[33] But even the major candidates' election sites, consisting mainly of pages of text, failed to capitalize on the Internet's potential.

Nonetheless, Internet users had access to reams of campaign material from diverse sources. The MS-NBC website even had a "Truth in Advertising" feature that showed questionable political advertisements, noted their inaccuracies, then reran altered versions designed to correct them.[34] So people could equip themselves to discuss the candidates and their records, the campaign's news coverage and political advertising, and anything else that caught their fancy.

Election night brought a bountiful harvest of information to the Internet. Grazers could obtain early and instant dissemination of election results as well as select returns from the contests that interested them.

Government

Public officials variously use electronic means of communication for three purposes: to promote and publicize themselves and their policy objectives, to educate and inform, and to encourage participation in public affairs.

Local governments, especially those controlled by liberal Democrats, have been at the technology forefront.[35] The system devised for the city of Santa Monica, California, provides publicly available computer terminals. These connect people to large databases of local information about city events and policies, make city services more accessible, offer electronic forums, and increase residents' knowledge of computers and new communication technology. Reportedly, the system has been a success due, in part, "to the socioeconomic status, technological literacy, and political activism of Santa Monica residents."[36] As one example, middle-class homeowners and the homeless worked together to influence the city's housing policy.

At the national level, the White House home page is big on promotion and publicity, extolling the president and vice president and their families, lauding their accomplishments, advocating their policies. But it also tells people how to obtain presidential announcements, transcripts of daily press briefings, and texts of major documents.[37] And by providing e-mail addresses for the president and vice president, it gives people another way to communicate with them (actually with members of their staffs).

Most members of Congress have home pages giving their backgrounds, committee assignments, legislation they have sponsored and cosponsored, and other information. Many members send and receive e-mail, although fewer than 25 percent answered a message within two weeks.[38] The House of Representatives' web site puts online the text of all bills, resolutions, and amendments introduced in the chamber. House committees have sites reporting their actions, including hearings and markups, summarizing the contents and fates of recent bills. For both House and Senate, current floor proceedings and the *Congressional Record* are online. "Thomas," the Library of Congress site named after Thomas Jefferson, also provides information about the institution, its members, and their legislative activities.

Governmental departments and agencies, from the prosaic General Service Administration to the relatively arcane Central Intelligence Agency, have home pages. They supply full texts of documents and publications. The State Department provides the Secretary's speeches and testimony before Congress, the Department's daily press briefings, and background notes, as well as the status of U.S. policies toward most nations in the world.

As usual, the U.S. Supreme Court is (deliberately) laggard. Full texts of the Court's decisions and majority opinions and concurring and dissenting opinions can be found on bulletin boards. But only a few of its major rulings before 1989 are currently available on the web. The Court does not have its own web site; fewer than half of the federal courts of appeal put their decision on the web; and the decisions released are not explained in everyday language.

In progress, however, is "Oyez Oyez Oyez," a web archive of more than five hundred cases and seven hundred hours of audio of the Court's oral arguments and judgments/opinions that raise important constitutional issues.[39]

Public Policy

The Internet provides an abundance of information and arguments, facilitates the mobilization of political participation, and enhances communication between government and the people. We might assume, therefore, that it encourages public involvement in policymaking; but evidence is skimpy.

Christopher Arterton looked at demonstration projects in the 1980s that used new communications technologies to facilitate public participation in policymaking. Two-way cable brought community groups together; electronic town meetings included polls, debates, even plebiscites; computer conferences linked members of Congress with their constituents. But in every case save one, completion of the demonstration project marked the end of the initiative. The one that survived involved the use by a mayor and community groups of community cable television for public discussion. It continued because the mayor believed she derived political benefits from it. Politics, not technology, explained the project's perpetuation.[40] Arterton's cases, however, are all short-run campaigns, pre-dating the growth of the Internet.

In a more recent example, in 1995 the Federal Nuclear Regulatory Commission created a "virtual hearing room" on the web in which it can gather comments and ideas from electric utilities, safety groups, reactor manufacturers, and anyone else. Its purpose is to help the commission write rules as well as comment on rules already drafted. But, full of legal and technical jargon, the site is not easy for laypersons to use. Nor does it replace traditional hearings.[41]

One way the web can contribute to public involvement in policymaking is through interactivity. As a simple example, the White House's web site allows people to express agreement or disagreement with the president's policy positions.

There could be electronic town meetings with push-button voting. Or even the possibility of direct, plebiscitary democracy in which governmental decisions can be decided, after discussion and debate, by the electronically tabulated views of the relevant populace. Of course, how interactive the process is depends on the range and openness of the questions asked and answers allowed.

A species of interactivity is also possible between the public and the press. Bulletin boards connected with online publications and general discussion groups are venues for direct and immediate online responses, usually critical, to media stories or developments. They offer a forum for journalists' peer review, foster dialogue between readers/viewers and reporters, and can subject reporters to questioning by experts and others.[42]

ISSUES

It is premature to conclude that new media technologies can dramatically change American politics for the better (or worse). It is possible, for example, that they could destroy individual privacy by allowing the processing and transmission of personal data by profit-seeking marketing and entertainment interests. Even worse, government agencies could use them for surveillance: monitoring messages, drawing up profiles of, and targeting people with unorthodox opinions.[43]

Putting such dire speculation aside, let us consider the issues of information gap, control, regulation, frustration, and contents.

Information Gap

Start with the fact that the expense and exclusivity of the Internet will increase the gap between the information rich and the information poor.[44] For use of the Internet is essentially limited to people connected with educational institutions, government, research organizations, and business. Many other people, even if

© *Brian Duffy. Reprinted with special permission of North America Syndicate.*

they have access to a computer, lack the funds, training, and technical knowledge to go online. Thus, current users are predominantly white males, "younger, more affluent and better educated."[45] Users of the Internet for political purposes are from the same high-status demographic categories as those involved in conventional political participation.

Without funding for widespread access to the use of and literacy in computers, the Internet is unlikely to compensate for political and social inequality and economic deprivation, and may exacerbate technological inequality.

Control

Currently, no one seems to control the Internet. Whether and for how long this situation will continue are unclear. Two factors likely to influence it are costs and the profit motive.

Costs are mainly born by institutions connected to the Internet—the organizations with home pages and sites, governmental subsidies, advertisers, and audience payments. Since many individual users balk at paying for online material, aside from pornography, advertising is increasing in importance as corporations run and advertise on their own sites. Even web pages about politics include advertising and offer services for "advocate organizations" and interest groups. Town Hall, the umbrella group for conservative public policy organizations, "sells advertising, links to relevant Web sites, and 'other promotional opportunities.'"[46]

But advertising is not increasing fast enough. So sites with insufficient advertising or no products to sell, and which are costly to run, fall into jeopardy. Politics Now was a joint venture of ABC News, the *National Journal,* and the *Washington Post.* It was one of the Internet's busiest sites during the 1996 election, but it no longer exists after the *Post* pulled out.

What this all seems to portend is increasing influence, if not control, of the Internet by business. More and more companies are trying to use it for profit through sales and marketing. Other corporations, notoriously Microsoft, and conglomerates such as NBC and Time Warner, with deep pockets, are willing temporarily to lose money on the Internet while they profit in related areas. Meanwhile, they seek, sometimes in alliance with each other, to dominate access and become significant providers of content to the Internet. As a consequence, the Internet's common carrier status, in which its facilities are available to everyone equipped to go online on a first-come, first-served basis, may be at risk.[47]

Regulation

For the time being, anarchy appears to rule on the Internet, with people posting whatever they want. Laws on data protection, copyright, and libel, even if applicable to cyberspace, seem to be violated with impunity. Deception is not unknown. A site devoted to conservative Republican candidate Pat Buchanan appeared authentic except that the American flag in the background featured a Nazi swastika instead of fifty white stars. The Bob Dole for President page turned out to be a parody linking the candidate with Dole pineapples and other fruits and vegetables. Sincere inquiries about the senator's position received e-mail replies such as, "We're sorry, but your position on this issue directly contradicts one of our major campaign contributors. Therefore we have no interest in your suggestion."

In practice, however, institutional administrators, providers, and the government all try to regulate Internet content.

Regulation attempts by institutional administrators, particularly at schools, are the most sporadic and ineffectual. Administrators at Stanford University barred student access to a national electronic jokebook after complaints about ethnic slurs. After complaints about denial of free speech, the file was restored on the recommendation of a faculty-appointed panel. Below the college level, free speech is less protected, "a high school student was suspended . . . for creating a Web site that listed his school's 'most hated' teachers."[48]

Providers attempt to regulate the Internet more systematically. American On-line warns its members that it may terminate them if they "'transmit any unlawful, harmful, threatening, abusive, harassing, defamatory, vulgar, obscene, hateful, racially, ethnically or otherwise objectionable content.'"[49] Many newsgroups and mailing lists have moderators who can and do exclude material they deem inappropriate. People who insist on posting irrelevant or untoward material may be banned. Sometimes an entire USENET newsgroup, such as alt.sex, is excluded.

Whether such regulation is widely and consistently applied is unclear. Certainly, with the proliferation of distribution points, it is increasingly easy to evade the regulator, for example by using a different provider to transmit a rejected piece.

Pornography   The regulation issue has crystallized around pornography. Parents complain that it is easily available to their children on the Internet. Accounts periodically surface of adults and minors using computers to transmit explicit sexual images and adults seeking out minors for sexual encounters.[50]

In response, Congress passed and the president signed the Communications Decency Act of 1996. It imposes hefty fines or criminal penalties for posting not only "obscene" content, but also the vaguer "indecent" and "patently offensive" content on the Internet. A three-judge federal appeals court subsequently upheld the government's right to outlaw unprotected speech, such as obscenity and child pornography, but called the attempt to curtail other types of communication a "profoundly repugnant" affront to the First Amendment's guarantee of free speech.[51]

Central to the decision was the finding that technology did not yet exist to shield even well-intentioned providers from criminal liability because there was no way to ensure that children would not see the indecent content. Symbolizing the importance the court placed on the Internet, "the decision was distributed on computer diskettes and published on the court's computer bulletin board system."[52]

In *Reno v. American Civil Liberties Union* (No. 96-511), the Supreme Court upheld the decision, declaring that speech on the Internet is entitled to the same First Amendment protection accorded to books and newspapers.[53] The decision sent the Clinton administration back to the drawing boards.

Frustration

The pornography debate gives the impression that using the Internet is easy. In practice, however, it can be a frustrating, even nightmarish, experience.[54] Instead of reaching sites that should exist according to a search engine or a site-to-site link, one often encounters the following phrases: "System cannot connect to the web site"; or "Server did not respond"; or "The requested object does not exist on this server. The link you followed is either outdated, inaccurate, or the server has been instructed not to let you have it." The story may not have been put on the Internet or put on but removed shortly thereafter. Many newspapers keep primarily the current day's news online; earlier articles are unavailable and no archive service provided.

Also frustrating is the propensity of search engines to turn up overwhelming numbers of citations tangential and even totally unrelated to a topic. For they are crude instruments that operate by taking the searcher's keyword entry or search string and then scanning web sites or archived newsgroup posting for word matches in the title and text of sites. Thus, entering "Pamela Harriman," the name of the recently deceased U.S. ambassador to France, produced approximately 71,000 matches on one search engine and 11,650 on another. Many were irrelevant: "Harriman State Park Site Map" in Idaho, home pages for various people with the surname Harriman. Others were conspiratorial: an essay entitled "The Woman Behind Clinton is Not Hillary!!!" Precision doesn't necessarily work either: specifying "Harriman, Pamela, Ambassador, obituary," turned up very few sites, probably because the word "obituary" did not appear in the articles.

Contents

Someone once quipped that there are two issues concerning the contents of the Internet: what is not on it and what is.

People in government in particular keep confidential and certainly damaging material off it. So the president's speeches are there, but not the drafts revealing the disagreements and decisions made as the speeches were being written. Congressmen and—women's Web pages rarely include their voting records. The sessions in which congressional subcommittee and committee members argue about the details of what to include and exclude from bills are not on the Internet. Nor, unsurprisingly, are the deliberations of U.S. Supreme Court justices.

Public officials vigorously oppose releasing their private Internet communications to each other. It took a costly six-year lawsuit by the National Security Archive and its allied public interest lawyers, historians, and librarians to save from destruction and preserve the candid, unedited e-mail messages of the Reagan and Bush White Houses and the Bush National Security staff. The compilation the archive was able to publish of five hundred messages is a treasure trove of policymaking, descriptions of and comments on people, and even an occasional office flirtation.[55] Especially interesting are memos about how to deal with (manipulate and spin) the media. Whether White House personnel will continue to write candid e-mails and, even if they do, whether these will be made available in the future is uncertain.

Most observers are concerned less about what is not on the Internet than what is. Political speech has often been uninformed, inane, erroneous, and intolerant. But Internet discourse seems particularly prone to expressions of discontent, anti-government views, conspiracy theories, extremism, and hate.[56] All of them can be widely disseminated in a credible form even by crackpots and sociopaths. Nor is there much balance among ideological groups on the Internet: Right-wing ones substantially outnumber and appear to be more cohesive than those on the left.[57]

Compounding concern, the way the Internet is organized can conduce to social and political fragmentation. People are able to select material that conforms to and reinforces their views and to communicate only with the like-minded. White racist groups, for example, may have limited resources, but they can combine desktop publishing, shortwave radio, magazines, citizen access television, a record label, video documentaries, fax networks, and above all computer billboards and Internet sites to spread their beliefs, keep in contact with existing adherents, and attract new ones.[58]

CONCLUSION

New technology gives people unrivaled opportunities to obtain information and to encounter a diversity of views. It can reduce their dependence on the mass media and increase their ability to reach their own conclusions about politics and governmental decisions and actions. It can facilitate political mobilization by interest groups and social movements. It can spur communication between policymakers and the public.

But new technology can also be used for demagoguery, to mislead and deceive, to reinforce intolerance and hatred. It can be used to promote fringe ideologies, giving the impression that they are widely accepted.

Which leads us to a paradoxical conclusion. New technology can retard or encourage democracy. In this way, it is just like the mass media we have studied throughout this book.

"I KNEW IT WAS JUST A MATTER OF TIME BEFORE THE ULTIMATE MERGER AND TAKEOVER"

© 1995 by Herblock in the Washington Post

Notes

1. What follows also uses Jack M. McLeod, Gerald M. Kosicki, and Douglas M. McLeod, "The Expanding Boundaries of Political Communication Effects," in *Media Effects Advances in Theory and Research*, ed. Jennings Bryant and Dolf Zillmann

(Hillsdale, N.J.: Lawrence Erlbaum, 1994), 128–29, which in part is an adaptation of the eight normative standards adumbrated by Michael Gurevitch and Jay G. Blumler, "Political Communication Systems and Democratic Values," in *Democracy and the Mass Media,* ed. Judith Lichtenberg (Cambridge: Cambridge University Press, 1990), 270.

2. Michael X. Delli Carpini and Scott Keeter, *What Americans Know About Politics and Why It Matters* (New Haven: Yale University Press, 1996), 265.

3. Jay Rosen and Davis Merritt, Jr., *Public Journalism: Theory and Practice* (Dayton, Ohio: Kettering Foundation, 1994); for an overview see Jay Black, ed., *Mixed News* (Mahwah, N.J.: Lawrence Erlbaum, 1997); and for a thoughtful discussion, see Hanno Hardt, "The Quest for Public Journalism," *Journal of Communication* 47:3 (Summer 1997): 102–09.

4. Jay Rosen, "Public Journalism," *Change* 27:3 (May-June 1995): 35.

5. Ibid., 36.

6. Michael Schudson, "The Public Journalism Movement and Its Problems," in *The Politics of News, The News of Politics,* ed. Doris Graber, Denis McQuail, and Pippa Norris (Washington, D.C.: CQ Press), 132–49.

7. For a brilliant essay on the impact of technology, see Walter Benjamin, "The Work of Art in the Age of Mechanical Reproduction," in his *Illuminations,* ed. Hannah Arendt (New York: Harcourt, Brace & World, 1968), 217–51.

8. Doug Marlette, "Editorial Cartoonists—An Endangered Species?" *Media Studies Journal* 11:2 (Spring 1997): 113–26.

9. See Sandra Moog, "The Impact of Media Technologies on American Politics, 1960–1996," *Javnost The Public* 4:2 (1997): 39–55.

10. For a pioneering effort, see Jeffrey B. Abramson, F. Christopher Arterton, and Gary R. Orren, *The Electronic Commonwealth* (New York: Basic Books, 1988).

11. Quintessentially optimistic are Nicholas Negroponte, *Being Digital* (New York: Knopf, 1995), and Howard Rheingold, *The Virtual Community* (Reading, Mass.: Addison Wesley, 1993); negative are Clifford Stoll, *Silicon Snake Oil* (New York: Doubleday, 1995), and Timothy W. Luke, "The Politics of Digital Inequality" (paper presented at the annual meeting of the American Political Science Association, San Francisco, September 1996); and relatively balanced is William H. Dutton, ed., *Information and Communication Technologies—Visions and Realities* (New York: Oxford University Press, 1996).

12. For examples of thoughtful research, see Bonnie Fisher, Michael Margolis, and David Resnick, "Breaking Ground on the Virtual Frontier," *American Sociologist* 27:1 (Spring 1996): 11–29, and Kevin A. Hill and John E. Hughes, "Computer-Mediated Political Communication," *Political Communication* 14:1 (January-March 1997): 3–27.

13. Richard Davis, on whose work I have drawn, identifies four functions; see his "Political Communication on the Internet" (paper presented at the annual meeting of the American Political Science Association, San Francisco, September 1996).

14. Bruce Bimber, "Politics on the Net" (paper presented at the annual meeting of the American Political Science Association, San Francisco, August 1996).

15. Julia R. Dobrow, ed., *Social and Cultural Aspects of VCR Use* (Hillsdale, N.J.: Lawrence Erlbaum, 1990).

16. John D. H. Downing, "Computers for Political Change . . ." *Journal of Communication* 39:3 (Summer 1989): 154.

17. William Glaberson, "In San Jose, Knight-Ridder Tests a Newspaper Frontier," *New York Times,* 7 February 1994, C6.

18. Gregory Jordan, "Publications Focusing on Africa Disappear," *New York Times,* 18 November 1996, C8.

19. Michael Taub, "Government Data at Your Fingertips," *New York Times,* 17 February 1997, Y29.

20. Anna Sampaio and Janni Aragon, "To Boldly Go (Where No Man Has Gone Before)" (paper presented at the annual meeting of the American Political Science Association, San Francisco, September 1996), 20.

21. Peter Lewis, "Discussion of the O.J. Simpson Murder Trial Is On-Line as Well as on the Air," *New York Times,* 14 February 1995, A9.

22. Laura Stein, "Access Television and Grassroots Political Communication in the United States" (paper presented to the Political Communication Section at the annual meeting of the International Association for Media and Communication Research, Sydney, Australia, August 1996), 28.

23. Kevin A. Hill and John E. Hughes, "Computer-Mediated Political Communication," *Political Communication* 14:1 (January-March 1997): 8.

24. Bonnie Fisher, Michael Margolis, and David Resnick, "Breaking Ground on the Virtual Frontier," *American Sociologist* 27:1 (Spring 1996): 22.

25. Mary S. Furlong, "An Electronic Community for Older Adults," *Journal of Communication* 39:3 (Summer 1989): 145–62.

26. Bruce Bimber, "Politics on the Net" (paper presented at the annual meeting of the American Political Science Association, San Francisco, September 1996), 7.

27. Dee Dee Meyers, "New Technology and the 1992 Clinton Presidential Campaign," *American Behavioral Scientist* 37:2 (November-December 1993): 181–84.

28. See the op-ed by Phyllis Kaniss, "A Victory for Local News," *New York Times,* 5 December 1992, A15.

29. Mike Allen, "On-Line Access to G.O.P. Convention," *New York Times,* 12 August 1996, C4.

30. Robert Klotz, "Positive Spin: Senate Campaigning on the Web," *PS* 30:3 (September 1997): 482–86.

31. This discussion stems from John Carvalho, "Old Wine, New Wineskins" (paper written for my seminar on Politics and the Media, December 1996). The "rogue" site reference is on p. 6.

32. Michael Margolis, "Electioneering in Cyberspace" (paper presented at the annual meeting of the American Political Science Association, San Francisco, September 1996), 7 note 12.

33. Ibid., 1.

34. Professor John Boiney brought this to my attention.

35. K. Kendall Guthrie and William H. Dutton, "The Politics of Citizen Access Technology . . ." *Policy Studies Journal* 20:4 (Winter 1992): 574-97.

36. K. Kendall Guthrie et al., "Communication Technology and Democratic Participation . . ." (paper presented at the annual meeting of the Association for Computing Machinery, Washington, DC, September 13-16, 1990), 24.

37. Kenneth L. Hacker, "Virtual Democracy," in *The Clinton Presidency,* ed. Robert E. Denton, Jr. and Rachel L. Holloway (Westport, CT: Praeger, 1996), 73.

38. Eric Schmitt, "Congress Remains in Touch on the Web," *New York Times,* 24 November 1997, C8.

39. Jerry Goldman and Joe Germuska, "The Supreme Court Oral Argument Archive" (paper presented at the annual meeting of the American Political Science Association, San Francisco, September 1996).

40. F. Christopher Arterton, *Teledemocracy* (Newbury Park: Sage Publications, 1987).

41. Matthew L. Wald, "Nuclear Agency Goes on Line for Ideas on Rules," *New York Times,* 24 November 1995, A16.

42. Thomas S. Valovic, "Encounters On-line," *Media Studies Journal* 9:2 (Spring 1995): 115–16.

43. Charles D. Raab, "Privacy, democracy, information." In *The Governance of Cyberspace,* ed. Brian D. Loader (London: Routledge, 1997), 155–74.

44. Robert S. Fortner, "Excommunication in the Information Society," *Critical Studies in Mass Communication* 12:2 (June 1995): 133–54.

45. Pew Center for the People and the Press, "One-in-Ten Voters Online For Campaign '96," news release, 16 December 1996, 5.

46. Michael Margolis, "Electioneering in Cyberspace" (paper presented at the annual meeting of the American Political Science Association, San Francisco, September 1996), 2.

47. Robert W. McChesney, "The Internet and U.S. Communication Policy-Making in Historical and Critical Perspective," *Journal of Communication* 46:1 (Winter 1996): 118.

48. Abby Goodnough, "Free Access to Internet Puts Burden on Schools," *New York Times,* 19 April 1997, Y9.

49. David Cay Johnston, "The Fine Print in Cyberspace," *New York Times,* 11 August 1996, E5.

50. David Johnston, "Use of Computer Network for Child Sex Sets Off Raids," *New York Times,* 14 September 1995, A1.

51. Peter H. Lewis, "Judges Turn Back Law to Regulate Internet Decency," *New York Times,* 13 June 1996, A1, 18.

52. Ibid., A18.

53. Linda Greenhouse, "Court, 9-0, Upholds State Laws Prohibiting Assisted Suicide; Protects Speech on Internet," *New York Times,* 27 June 1997, A1.

54. This summary of some of the difficulties involved in using the Net is based on Lyndon Allin et al., "Between the Sheets" (paper submitted to my research seminar on International Communication, Duke University, May 1997).

55. Tom Blanton, ed., *White House E-Mail* (New York: New Press, 1995). This book was brought to my attention by Susannah B. F. Paletz.

56. Michael Janofsky, "Anti-Defamation League Tells of Rise in Web Hate Sites," *New York Times,* 22 October 1997, A17.

57. Kevin A. Hill and John E. Hughes, "Computer-Mediated Political Communication," *Political Communication* 14:1 (January-March 1997): 11–12.

58. Michael Whine, "The Far Right on the Internet," in *The Governance of Cyberspace,* ed. Brian D. Loader (London: Routledge, 1997), 209–27; see also Keith Schneider, "Hate Groups Use Tools of the Electronic Trade," *New York Times,* 13 March, 1995, A8.

Appendix A
Commentary

◆ ◆ ◆

As a readers' guide, this appendix identifies the values, perspectives, and political ideologies, or at least preferences, of the most prominent commentators and opinion publications and shows.[1]

IDEOLOGY

This undertaking is not easy. Terms such as "radical," "liberal," "moderate," "conservative," and "reactionary" can be quite nebulous. Nor is there any guarantee that most expressions of opinion will fit easily into their mold. Many issues, moreover, defy easy categorization because of worldwide political, military, and economic changes; as well as evolving beliefs and attitudes in the United States.

Nonetheless, there are general distinctions. For, as comedian Mort Sahl said: "A liberal is someone who believes in busing but is repelled by school prayer. A conservative is someone who is repelled by busing and believes in school prayer. And a moderate would like to compromise between these two extremes and perhaps have prayer on the bus."

Placement

Our criteria for categorizing commentators are less droll but more elaborate: They are based on economic-fiscal, social, and foreign policy issues.

Economic-Fiscal Issues   Liberals are for greater governmental intervention in the economy and regulation of business; they are also pro-union. They endorse some redistribution of wealth through the tax structure, take a somewhat protectionist view of trade, and are for active social welfare programs.

Conservatives are pro-business and anti-union; they favor less government involvement in the economy, and lower taxes for corporations and individuals. They usually support free trade and endorse only a minimal welfare state.

Social Issues   Liberals are tolerant of nontraditional lifestyles and attitudes, committed to civil rights and civil liberties. More specifically, they support the assertion of rights by racial minorities, feminists, and homosexuals, are pro-choice on abortion, anticensorship, and favor gun control. Because liberals view such problems as crime and drug abuse more in terms of social causes than individual responsibility, they are inclined to endorse such government-mandated responses as affirmative action and oppose the death penalty.

Conservatives revere traditional lifestyles and morality and assert that government must function as a moral force for society. As a result, they oppose homosexual rights, are pro-life on abortion, and support the censorship of materials they consider obscene or pornographic. Since they also believe in individual responsibility, they object to equal opportunity legislation, are tough on crime, support the death penalty, and oppose gun control.

Foreign Policy Issues   With the removal of the cold war, foreign policy views are in flux, making categorization of political writers difficult.

Nonetheless, there seem to be identifiable differences. Liberals tend to be globally oriented internationalists, evaluate foreign governments in terms of their commitments to and practice of democracy and civil liberties, and are desirous of seeking and achieving international agreements. They are dubious about the necessity of the United States going to war or even engaging in military actions, although this can conflict with their support of intervention to deter aggression or stop the domination of reactionary autocratic regimes. They are for mutual disarmament with America's adversaries and for cuts in what they usually take to be a bloated and wasteful defense budget. Global environmental issues are of particular concern.

Conservatives espouse peace through strength, and so they want a mighty defense. They are sometimes willing to deploy American force around the world, although doing so conflicts with their tendency to favor isolationism. Global economic concerns take precedence over environmental issues.

Moderates   Ideologically, moderates come between liberals and conservatives. They may express liberal sentiments on some issues, conservative views on other subjects, but hew to no side consistently. They may take no clear positions whatsoever, being more inclined to describe events and situations than express strongly held opinions about them. Since commentators and columnists are often paid to have opinions and be provocative, few of them are categorized as moderates.

Radicals and Reactionaries   Radicals are more ideologically extreme and intense than liberals. Reactionaries have the same relationship to conservatives. Both contribute to the marketplace of ideas by espousing beliefs that challenge, even outrage, conventional opinion.

Because the press is not often in the business of provoking and disturbing its readers, expressions of radical and reactionary beliefs are relatively uncommon. The syndicates that collect and sell opinion columns to newspapers do not recruit more than a few radical and reactionary writers. For those it does employ, the daily grind of writing columns tends to take the edge off their extreme views. Because of some combination of these and other reasons, most of the commentators and columnists with identifiable views are either conservative or liberal.

This is one among many reasons to lament the death of I. F. Stone, the legendary journalist who, after becoming unemployable in the early 1950s because of his radical background, successfully created his own paper, *I. F. Stone's Weekly* (later biweekly) as a voice for his reporting and analyses of the news.[2]

NEWSPAPERS

Certain newspapers may incline to one or another side of the political spectrum in the subjects, headlines, prominence, framing, emphases, and language of some of their news stories. For example, the *Washington Post* referred to the president's wife as "Hillary Clinton" or "the First Lady," the *Washington Times* called her "Hillary").[3] But their ideological opinions are most visible in their editorials. Among the prominent newspapers, the *New York Times* and *Washington Post* are liberal; the *Los Angeles Times, Miami Herald, Philadelphia Inquirer,* and *San Francisco Chronicle* are moderate; conservative are the *Chicago Tribune, USA Today,* and the *Wall Street Journal.* The *Washington Times* is reactionary.

A few newspapers, most significantly the *New York Times,* extend their editorial pages with op-ed sections. At their best, op-eds afford access to distinctive points of view unlikely otherwise to appear in the paper. Too often, though, the op-eds are by well-known people, representing a narrow ideological range, with little original thought to contribute to discussion and debate.

Columnists

Commentary and opinion appear most prominently in newspapers in the little essays of nationally syndicated columnists. To be categorized, they have to write at least two columns each week, dealing with public affairs and social problems, that are published in newspapers throughout the country. Humorists whose targets are politically relevant are included.

Excluded are feature writers, columnists who write only for their local newspapers, or whose work (like that of Hal Crowther, one of the best columnists in the country) is not widely distributed.[4] Also omitted are columnists whose subject matter is primarily personal (even though, as with counselor to the lovelorn Ann Landers, their advice sometimes touches on the political).

There are no syndicated columnists who can be categorized as radical or reactionary. We are limited to liberals, moderates, and conservatives. The selections are alphabetized, by ideology, with comments as appropriate, and with the caveat that none of the individuals named is necessarily always ideologically consistent; on occasion some of them can surprise us.

Start with the liberals. Jack Anderson still occasionally muckrakes (searches out and reveals outrages). Russell Baker offers wry and insightful social commentary. Dave Barry is a humorist offering more ridicule than scorn. Ellen Goodman often expresses a feminist perspective. Molly Ivins is tough-mindedly unpredictable. Jesse Jackson is a leader of the social activist side of the Democratic party. Anthony Lewis retains a capacity for outrage. Mary McGrory is the doyenne of distinguished liberal observers, bringing a capacious memory to bear on the politics of the day. Ralph Nader is the long-time crusader for consumer rights. Richard Reeves represents traditional liberalism. Carl Rowan provides a distinctly African-American perspective. Mark Shields is full of impish humor and a vast store of political lore.

Moderates include the thoughtful and judicious David Broder; the arguably liberal Art Buchwald, whose proximity to power has blunted his spear; the ubiquitous former conservative Kevin Phillips; William Raspberry specializing on inner-city and civil rights issues; CNN's William Schneider; and Edwin Yoder.

The conservatives begin with occasional presidential candidate Patrick J. Buchanan and long-time conservative spokesman William F. Buckley, Jr., mellowing of late. Mona Charen is tough-minded. There is the omnipresent Robert Novak, plus his writing partner Rowland Evans. Suzanne Fields is a rising star with a conservative feminist view. James J. Kilpatrick is an ever-curmudgeonly, traditional conservative, modified by a sentimental streak. Jeanne Kirkpatrick is a former academic and U.S. ambassador to the United Nations. William Safire is the former Nixon speech writer, lover of language, and dogged pursuer of issues. Phyllis Schlafly is traditionalist and antifeminist, yet a most successful careerist in her own right; Thomas Sowell is an African-American who applies free-market ideas to economic and social issues. Cal Thomas focuses on social, cultural, and moral issues. Political theorist *manqué* George Will tempers a traditional conservative perspective with idiosyncratic exceptions. Walter Williams is an African-American, free-market economist.

RADIO

The two main founts of opinion on radio are call-in shows and some noncommercial programs.

Call-In Shows

Talk has always been cheap and common on radio, but never so much as now, with over a thousand stations employing a news-talk format. Talk hosts, mostly white, middle-aged males, stalk the airwaves, ventilating and venting their opinions; variously cultivating, cajoling, castigating their callers and listeners.[5]

Because they permit callers to express themselves in their own words, sometimes quite emotionally, and to address a sizable audience, call-in programs offer more of an outlet for public discourse and opinion than public opinion polls, letters to the editor in newspapers, and the like.[6] Of course, talk radio's producers screen callers, only permit some of them on the air, and use a brief transmission time delay to insulate the show against untoward material.

Calvin and Hobbes   by Bill Watterson

Even the most apparently apolitical talk show figures, such as the sexually obsessed Howard Stern, get into the political act. Stern entered then exited the 1994 New York gubernatorial election, endorsed and promoted the Republican candidate on his show, and was seated in a prominent place on the dais at that victor's inauguration.[7]

Indeed, most prominent talk show personalities express conservative opinions and are pro-Republican and hostile to Democrats. They have been credited with contributing mightily to the Republican 1994 election takeover of the House of Representatives and the Senate, as well as to that party's victories in the states.

Most talk show practitioners operate on the city or regional level, but those with the greatest influence are presented via satellite transmission on stations nationwide, addressing a national audience.[8]

The most conspicuous (notorious) of these is the bumptiously caustic or genially combative (depending on your perspective) Rush Limbaugh, heard on roughly six hundred and fifty stations with an estimated audience of 20 million. He also has a widely syndicated television show and is credited with at least two best-selling books. Overtly partisan, he espouses the Republican cause and is stridently antiliberal.[9] His show has been called the "Revenge of the Conservative Nerds."[10]

Among talk radio's other well-known practitioners are the uncategorizable Don Imus (see chapter one), the conservatives Paul Harvey, who is widely heard and distinguished by his longevity; Cliff Kincaid; G. Gordon Liddy of the Watergate burglary fame; and Michael Reagan, son of the former president. Leading liberals are Gloria Allred and Michael Jackson in Southern California. The nationally syndicated, droll Texas populist, Jim Hightower, was removed from the air on the grounds of low ratings when Disney acquired ABC.[11]

Late arrivals are prominent, defeated office-holders and candidates. They have included the liberal former Governors Jerry Brown, Jr. (California), Mario Cuomo (New York), Lowell P. Weicker, Jr. (Connecticut), and L. Douglas Wilder (Virginia), as well as former senator and presidential candidate Gary Hart. A prominent conservative is Oliver L. North, narrowly defeated for Senate in Virginia and before that publicly known for his appearance before the Senate committee investigating the Iran-Contra affair. Their survival in the medium is uncertain.

Noncommercial Radio

Listeners can hear a range of views on National Public Radio's (NPR) "All Things Considered" and "Morning Edition," as well as on its weekend morning news programs. NPR's most distinguished commentator may well be the judiciously liberal Daniel Schorr.

Of particular distinction is NPR's "Fresh Air," a magazine of contemporary culture and public affairs, aired each weekday afternoon or evening, in which host Terry Gross's gently probing and informed questions produce revealing interviews. Originating from WHYY in Philadelphia, the program is broadcast on public radio stations nationwide.

Radical perspectives can be heard on the four Pacifica stations in Berkeley (California), Los Angeles, New York, and Washington, D.C. In her discussion of these stations, Nina Eliasoph shows that there is nothing "to prevent the propagation of oppositional interpretations of the world if news organizations could exist which were not so beholden to corporate *and* commercial interests, *and* which had different relations both to their audience and the social movements on which they reported."[12]

TELEVISION

The most significant but still unsung contributors to U.S. democracy may well be cable's two C-SPAN channels. C-SPAN was set up to transmit the daily sessions of the U.S. House of Representatives and then, through its second channel, the U.S. Senate. Its channels air an array of public affairs events, including congressional hearings, elections' debates and political advertising, press conferences, discussion forums, interviews with newsmakers and journalists and authors, and viewer call-ins. Although the bulk of its programs hew to the middle of the road and perpetuate the conventional wisdom, C-SPAN quite often ventures out to the ideological byways.

Less venturesome but similarly laudable, the "Newshour with Jim Lehrer" on PBS and "Nightline" moderated by Ted Koppel on ABC usually focus on one subject per program. This gives them the opportunity to explore an issue in more detail, if not depth, than is usually found on television. These news programs are moderate because their formats (aside from occasional investigative reports) consist of the moderators posing questions to guests who represent different political persuasions and perspectives, and who usually, but not always, balance each other out. Even here, the range of opinions is relatively narrow, appearances by reactionaries and radicals are rare.[13]

Political Interview Shows

Similarly moderate are the Sunday morning political interview shows in which a prominent government official or well-known politician (some are both) is interviewed by the moderator and a regular, but not unvarying, guest panel. Worth watching, "Face the Nation" (CBS), "Meet the Press" (NBC), and CNN's weekend "Newsmaker" programs can be quite challenging to their guests. This may explain why presidential candidates prefer the softer interviews of the networks'

© *Tom Tomorrow*

morning shows and the softball questions of CNN's Larry King. For there are major differences between interviewers: contrast on CNN the sycophantic King with the tough-minded and knowledgeable Judy Woodruff.[14]

News Magazines

Their formats complicate categorizing news magazines: A single program may include an interview with a celebrity or name in the news, an investigative report exposing some institutional outrage or abuse usually perpetrated by government or business, and a feature on an upright adolescent female math prodigy. So, through different stories, a show can display, if not condone, extramarital relations while celebrating traditional American values.

Some prominent programs are "Dateline" on NBC, "Prime Time Live" and "20/20" on ABC, and "60 Minutes" on CBS, the most venerable, highly rated, and influential of them all.[15] Related, but less prestigious, mainly because they lack highly visible and lavishly paid star anchor personalities such as Diane Sawyer, are the tabloid shows discussed in chapter 3.

Arguably, the general thrust of news magazines is liberal because of their penchant for exposing the rip-off, the disreputable behavior, the seamy sides of American political, economic, and social life.

Partisan Programs

A few television programs are avowedly partisan. One type has a host vigorously asserting opinions about the issues of the day. Or there can be a regular moderator, invited guests, and a studio audience discussing a particular subject or problem. The host is the central figure and force, his or her perspective usually dominates. Leading examples are the liberal "The Jesse Jackson Show," the conservative "Tony Brown's Journal," William F. Buckley's "Firing Line," and, of course, Rush Limbaugh's show.

National Empowerment Television   NET is a cable channel that broadcasts avowedly conservative programs, including "On Target With the NRA," "The Accuracy in Media Hour," and "The Progress Report With Newt Gingrich," its best-known personality. Starting in December 1993 on only one cable system, in a few years it supposedly reached 11 million households (some with satellite dishes). Viewership was expected to grow with Tele-Communications Inc., conservative John Malone's cable giant, planning to carry it on more of its systems.[16]

Religious Broadcasters   So-called televangelists offer worship, music, and salvation; proselytize and recruit; strive to heal through invocations of faith; and appeal for funds with a mixture of promises, predictions, and threats, delivered with passion, lachrymosely, and a judicious modicum of desperation. They discuss moral issues and promote their usually conservative, if not reactionary, political and policy views.[17] Particularly prominent in purveying a conservative point of view are the Reverend Pat Robertson, with his Christian Broadcasting Network (CBN) and the cable Family Channel.[18]

Public Access   Cable operators are required to provide a public access channel over which they exercise no editorial control. In theory, therefore, such channels can show government in action via meetings of city councils, school boards, and so on. They can also provide a panoply of opinions. Some do: Raleigh, North Carolina, has Louis Farakhan, "Universe of Yahweh," "Super Natural," "God's Truth for Today," "Dan Savage and the Sex Kittens," "Girls Are Not Just Long-Haired Boys," and much more. Most public access channels, however, are stunted by their corporate owners who, eschewing controversial programs, minimally equip the studio, give rudimentary training, and transmit blurry pictures with poor sound.

Pundits

Pundits are an ever-proliferating addition to the opinion-expressers and opinion-makers of television.[19] They are usually journalists who self-confidently assert views, pronounce judgments, and offer predictions in a discussion format that is more ("The McLaughlin Group") or less ("Washington Week in Review") combative.

In theory, each pack of pundits covers a range of opinions so that all sides are heard. This is not always the practice. And even when it is, particular pundits, usually the conservatives, bellicose John McLaughlin on his show, or the sometimes sophistical George Will on "This Week" dominate the group. These programs can be quite entertaining but, given the number of topics raised, the brief time for each one, the ferocity of the exchanges, far more heat than illumination is generated. Characterizations and descriptions follow.

On "The Capitol Gang" (CNN), argument and disagreement are leavened by humor as the conservatives Robert Novak ("a schoolyard bully in a banker's vest"[20]) and various cohorts mix it up with the likable, albeit more pragmatic than liberal Al Hunt (Mr. Judy Woodruff) of the *Wall Street Journal,* and droll Mark Shields.

CNN's "Crossfire" features the belligerent conservatives Pat Buchanan and (ubiquitous) Robert Novak engaged in almost mortal combat with mild liberal Bill Press. The show's guests often serve as fodder for the combatants.

On "The McLaughlin Group" (PBS), under the whip of the dominating and domineering conservative host, a bunch of journalists offer their brief opinions (vehement) and make predictions (more often wrong than not). Among those making regular appearances are the conservative Pat Buchanan and the relatively liberal Eleanor Clift and Clarence Page.

Featuring several journalists discussing the news events of the past week is "Washington Week in Review" (PBS). Analysis takes precedence over opinion, although judgments are rendered. The ideologically "moderate" Washington, D.C., perspective prevails.

A combination news of the week and guest program, "This Week" ends with a discussion among the articulately conservative George Will, the more combative than liberal Sam Donaldson, the centrist Cokie Roberts, and former Clinton aide George Stephanopoulos. As a columnist and commentator, Will is advantaged over Donaldson and Roberts, who seem somewhat inhibited by their reportorial roles from commenting too freely.

Talk Shows

Television also abounds with shows, some more sensational than others, that purport to deal with social and psychological issues. They can be identified by their prominent hosts (Jenny Jones, Ricki Lake, Maury Povich, Sally Jessy Raphael, Jerry Springer, Montel Williams, and, biggest of them all, Oprah Winfrey).

They are typified by audience involvement, often outrageous topics, confessions of sins, and the frequency with which therapists appear. Although usually treating peculiar or quirky individual behavior, they sometimes range out to society and politics.

At first blush, television talk shows appear politically liberal: "They make public many problems that once were deemed private—especially women's concerns . . . they give voice to people who have historically been silenced (women, people of color, the working class); and they dramatize the embodiment of selected public issues in personal experience."[21] Their topics break the bounds and bonds of conventionality.

But the shows are also socially conservative. The attitudes of the hosts and the reactions of many studio audience members are often judgmental, critical, even condemnatory of the words and actions of the "guests." As Janice Peck points out, "The programs discourage critical engagement with and reflection on those problems in favor of immediate identification and catharsis, and undermine the ability to take these problems seriously in the service of making them entertaining."[22] They substitute therapy and individual solutions for analyses of underlying social, economic, and political causes.[23]

Yet, by giving airtime and space to the bizarre and odd, the shows acknowledge their existence, begin to legitimize, and—implicitly at least—encourage tolerance of such behavior among some people.

Late Night   Of particular distinction is the show hosted by Charlie Rose on PBS. Government and politics are often the subjects. The guests are a more unusual lot than commonly found on television. Some topics are probed in relative depth. The mildly liberal Rose can pose thoughtful questions, although he tends to rush to the next one rather than react to the answers.

One does not conventionally think of the late night talk shows hosted by David Letterman, Jay Leno, and others as political, but they occasionally become so. This happens when guests are avowedly partisan or promote social causes and when hosts and guests express views or take positions on political issues.

But the most common expression of political opinion comes through humor in the hosts' monologues that introduce the shows and in the appearances of comedians as guests. Since these comments are often critical of public officials and the status quo, but not extremely so (benign in the terminology of chapter 1), the late night chat shows can be categorized as liberal. Uncategorizable is Geraldo's show, with its focus on the salacious conduct and legal imbroglios of public figure, especially President Clinton.

MAGAZINES

Aside from books, of all the media, magazines provide the most nourishment for opinions. They offer the widest spectrum and the most reflective analysis. Stretching the definition a bit, one can even place an occasional magazine in the radical and reactionary categories. Of course, not every article or essay in a magazine deals with public affairs or politics, and those that do may not adhere to the magazine's political perspective. With that in mind, the following categorizations are offered.

In These Times, Mother Jones, and arguably the *Nation* are radical. *The American Prospect, Harper's Magazine, Mad Magazine, Ms, The Progressive, Rolling Stone, Tikkun*, the *Utne Reader*, and *The Washington Monthly* are liberal. Moderate are *The Atlantic*, the celebrity-oriented, glossy, sometimes fawning, occasionally illuminating *George, The New Republic* (moving conservative), *The New Yorker* (moving liberal), and *Vanity Fair*.

Prominent conservative magazines (and far better funded than their ideological rivals) are *The American Spectator, Commentary, The National Review, Reader's Digest*, and the newly created *The Weekly Standard* supported by Rupert Murdoch. *Human Events* and *The New Criterion* are reactionary.

Revealing the caution of the mainstream media, few of the writers for and editors of these magazines, especially the radical and liberal ones, appear on television or are heard on radio.

CALLAHAN

CONCLUSION

Clearly, there is a lot of opining in the media. Much of it is superficial and uninformative. Views are asserted and reiterated rather than considered and revised. Too many topics are broached too briefly in too little time. Historical perspective is slighted, in-depth analysis infrequent, complex arguments and nuance uncommon. There is an excess of disagreement for the sake of what is believed to be lively television. Belligerence is common, often disguising ignorance and vacuity. Conservatives and moderates dominate the broadcast media. And yet, amidst the cacophony, ideas, thoughtful discussions, insights and illuminations can be found.

Notes

1. Some of this material stems from David L. Paletz, *Guide for Interpreting the Media*, 2nd ed. (New York: Longman, 1995). Gratitude to Susannah Batia Felicity Paletz, at the time an undergraduate student at Wesleyan University, and to John Rattliff, a graduate student in Political Science at Duke University, for the thoughtful ideas, categorizations, and diligent research they contributed. Suggestions from readers for additions, deletions, and recategorization are invited and welcome.

2. For a selection of his writings, see I. F. Stone, *In a Time of Torment* (New York: Vintage Books, 1968).

3. As Jana Novak reported in "The *Washington Post* and the *Washington Times*" 4–5, (paper written for my "Politics and Media" course" for the Fall, 1993 semester).

4. Fortunately, his columns have been collected in book form. See Hal Crowther, *Unarmed But Dangerous* (Atlanta, Ga.: Longstreet Press, 1995).

5. Annie M. Brewer, *Talk Shows & Hosts on Radio,* 2nd ed. (Dearborn, Mich.: Whitefoord Press, 1993).

6. This insight is from Susan Herbst, "On Electronic Public Space," *Political Communication* 12:3 (July-September 1995): 271; see also David A. Jones, "Political Talk Radio as a Forum for Intra-Party Debate (paper presented at the annual meeting of the Southern Political Science Association, Norfolk, Virginia, November 1997).

7. Ian Fisher, "A New Dawn in Albany," *New York Times,* 2 January 1995, 29L.

8. For details, see Peter Viles, "Talk Radio Riding High," *Broadcasting & Cable,* 15 June 1992, 24.

9. See Rush Limbaugh, "Why Liberals Fear Me," *Policy Review* 70 (Fall 1994): 4–10.

10. Thomas Byrne Edsall, "America's Sweetheart," *New York Review* 41:16 (6 October 1994), 9.

11. Edmund L. Andrews, "ABC Pulls the Plug on a Texas Populist," *New York Times,* 9 October 1995, C4.

12. Nina Eliasoph, "Routines and the Making of Oppositional News," *Critical Studies in Mass Communication* 5 (1988): 330.

13. See Stephen D. Reese, August Grant, and Lucig H. Danielian, "The Structure of News Sources on Television: A Network Analysis of 'CBS News,' 'Nightline,' 'MacNeil/Lehrer,' and 'This Week with David Brinkley,'" *Journal of Communication* 44:2 (Spring 1994): 84–107; see also Elizabeth Kolbert, "Nightline Wakes Itself Up," *New York Times,* 20 June 1993, H35.

14. Woodruff was a Duke undergraduate a few years ago.

15. For analyses of the show's techniques and explanations of its success, see Richard Campbell, *60 Minutes and the News* (Urbana: University of Illinois Press, 1991); see also Axel Madsen, *60 Minutes* (New York: Dodd, Mead, 1984).

16. "You Want Your Newt TV? Whether You Do or You Don't, It's Here," *New York Times,* 8 January 1995, E7.

17. See Steve Bruce, *Pray TV* (New York: Routledge, 1990). For a comparison with the situation on British television, see Barrie Gunter and Rachel Viney, *Seeing Is Believing* (London: John Libbey, 1994).

18. David M. Timmerman and Larry David Smith, "The World According to Pat: The Telepolitical Celebrity as Purveyor of Political Medicine," *Political Communication* 11:3 (1994): 233–48.

19. Worthwhile books on the pundit phenomenon are Eric Alterman's, *Sound and Fury* (New York: HarperCollins, 1992); Alan Hirsch, *Talking Heads* (New York: St. Martin's Press, 1991); and Dan Nimmo and James E. Combs, *The Political Pundits* (New York: Praeger, 1992).

20. James Wolcott, "Mighty Mouths," *New Yorker* 70:43 (26 December 1994–2 January 1995), 132.

21. Janice Peck, "TV Talk Shows as Therapeutic Discourse: The Ideological Labor of the Televised Talking Cure," *Communication Theory* 5:1 (February 1995), 76. For an illuminating, empirical analysis of why people appear on the shows, see Patricia Joyner Priest, *Public Intimacies* (Cresskill, N.J.: Hampton Press, 1995).

22. Peck, "TV Talk Shows," 76.

23. Elayne Rapping, *The Culture of Recovery* (Boston: Beacon Press, 1996).

Appendix B

Movies on Congress

◆ ◆ ◆

Many people lack basic knowledge and understanding of Congress, its procedures, practices and processes, and members. What they know comes mainly from news and movies. Since one of the prime purposes of this book is to reveal the relationship between popular culture and politics, this appendix describes how Congress and its members have been portrayed in the movies.

There is an axiom in Hollywood that politics is box office poison. As the notable director and writer Billy Wilder told George Axelrod early in the latter's screen-writing career: "'My dear boy, you and I will leave political satire to others. You and I will write about screwing and become very rich.'"[1]

Defying such cynically realistic logic, fictional portrayals of Congress and its members in feature films are more common than one would imagine.[2] As will be discussed, the congressional election campaign, political ambition within Washington, the legislative process, and congressional committees in action, especially the House Committee on Un-American Activities (HCUA), have all made their cinematic appearances.

THE CAMPAIGN

Early films, such as *Washington Merry-Go-Round* (1932) and *The Farmer's Daughter* (1947), portrayed elections as controlled by party political machines. The most realistic movie about political campaigns in the media age is *The Candidate* (1972). Written by Jeremy Larner, a speech writer for Senator Eugene McCarthy in the 1968 presidential campaign, it stars Robert Redford as an altruistic legal aid attorney who is asked to run for the Senate against an entrenched incumbent. He wins by modifying his principles and giving up control of the campaign to his handlers who concentrate on style and image. A related film, *Power* (1986), traces the activities of a political campaign strategist (Richard Gere) in his work for various candidates.

In 1992, *Bob Roberts,* directed by and starring Tim Robbins, depicted an extreme right-wing senatorial candidate devoted to greed and power, who wages a slick campaign against an upright liberal opponent played by the writer Gore Vidal. What Roberts lacks in sincerity he more than makes up in expert packaging, wealth, and his career as an entertainer. Roberts wins a close race after he fakes a shooting he claims has partially paralyzed him.

The movie is a virulent attack on conservatives, insubstantial candidates who wage campaigns based on people's fears and the invocation of patriotism and drug-fighting, and a system that enables them to win election to the Senate. But it undermines its credibility and effects by exaggerating Roberts to the point of unbelievability.

POLITICAL AMBITION

A recurring movie character is a senator who wants to become president. These include the dimwit in the 1947 farce *The Senator Was Indiscreet* (he is "against inflation, against deflation, for flation"); the unscrupulous conservative senator vying for the nomination at the presidential convention in *The Best Man* (1964, adapted by Gore Vidal from his stage play); and the stop-at-nothing senator in *A Fever in the Blood* (1961).

The Seduction of Joe Tynan (1979), written by and starring Alan Alda, offers the most sympathetic portrait, focusing on the conflicts between the senator's personal and political lives. Even this film, however, shows senators as variously lecherous, immoral, or senile, and the legislative process as characterized by manipulation and frustration.

This treatment is mild compared to the portrayals of senators in the extraordinary political thriller *The Manchurian Candidate* (1962). The conservative is an ignorant buffoon (loosely modeled on the late senator Joseph McCarthy) controlled by his evil wife; the liberal is hopelessly ineffectual. Both end up dead.

CONGRESSIONAL PROCESSES

The best known movie on Congress is *Mr. Smith Goes to Washington* (1939). James Stewart stars as the idealistic Jefferson Smith, appointed to complete the term of a recently deceased senator. Naturally, his first action on arriving in Washington, D.C., is to visit its monuments, notably the Lincoln Memorial. Inevitably, he is spiritually lost in a Senate of practical politicians. His one legislative effort, to establish a boys' camp in his state, falls prey to the scheme of the boss of his state, abetted somewhat unwillingly by the state's senior senator, Joseph Paine, for a personally beneficial and machine-enriching federal dam project. Framed by the schemers, Smith is about to flee Washington in despair but is inspired to return to the Senate by his once cynical, now redeemed (by Smith) loving secretary, played by Jean Arthur. To fight his impending expulsion, Smith stages a one-man filibuster on the Senate floor (the chamber was meticulously recreated for the film). Although the state boss uses his control of the media to inflame the public against

Smith, the senator's sincerity, grit, and natural eloquence begin to persuade the senators, particularly the presiding officer. After twenty-three hours Smith collapses, his cause apparently lost. But the conscience-stricken Senator Paine, failing in a suicide attempt, declares his own guilt and Smith's innocence.

With its paean to American ideals, its theme of a Christ-like Smith redeeming a Senate whose members have forgotten their heritage, memorable performances from its stars and supporting players, and fast-paced direction by Frank Capra, *Mr. Smith* was a financial and critical success. But it outraged many members of Congress, for its portrayal of the Senate is ambiguous at best. As Senator Paine tells Smith, the Senate is "a man's world and you've got to check your ideals outside the door like you do your rubbers."

Based on the best-selling novel by Allen Drury, *Advise and Consent* (1962) follows the congressional process as the Senate majority leader tries to achieve confirmation of the president's controversial nominee for Secretary of State Robert Leffingwell, played by Henry Fonda. Opposition comes from within the party in the person of a conservative southern senator (incarnated with relish by the English actor Charles Laughton), who uses the testimony of a mentally unbalanced clerk to brand the nominee a communist. Leffingwell denies the accusation to the committee but confesses its partial truth to the president, who dismisses it as a youthful indiscretion. The subcommittee chairman learns about the perjury, but the president rejects his demand that the nomination be withdrawn. The chairman, blackmailed by a liberal peace activist senator (the film's most obnoxious character) over a past homosexual indiscretion, commits suicide. The nomination is brought to the Senate without the perjury being revealed, and the vote ends in a tie. Before it can be broken, news arrives of the president's death. The formerly docile, now assertive, vice president announces that he will appoint his own Secretary. This is a film full of archetypes, sometimes degenerating into stereotypes, and of plausible individual events that become incredible in combination.

In 1992, the comedian Eddie Murphy appeared in and as *The Distinguished Gentleman,* directed by Jonathan Lynn (of *Yes Minister* fame) from a screenplay by experienced Washington hand Marty Kaplan. Thomas Jefferson Johnson is a con artist who is elected to Congress because he shares the name of the recently deceased member. Johnson (Murphy) finds Congress to be a con man's cornucopia, with lobbyists and corporate interest groups eager to bestow largesse upon him. But his conscience is stirred by the electric-power-line-caused cancer of a girl constituent and the appeal-attraction of a female public interest advocate. So he exposes a powerful and corrupt committee chairman (persuasively portrayed by Lane Smith). Whereas Jefferson Smith was honest and naive, Jefferson Johnson, befitting the 1990s, is streetwise and savvy, qualities that facilitate his victory.

The movie is visually and aurally authentic in some details (aspects of staff influence, of lobbying, of committee processes), while caricaturing others (election campaigns, members' motives, and the power of lobbyists). Overall, it depicts Congress, despite the presence of a few good public-spirited members, as a corrupt and cynical forum for farce.

CONGRESSIONAL COMMITTEES

Much of the congressional workload is undertaken by committees. Most committee work—slow, complicated, and undramatic—makes unpromising material for fiction films. The major exception are committee hearings, with their potential for confrontation and conflict. No wonder that fictional movies on Congress often feature dramatic hearings as effective devices, witness *Mr. Smith* and *Advise and Consent.*

In *First Monday in October* (1981), a tense moment comes with the testimony before the Senate committee of the first woman U.S. Supreme Court nominee (Jill Clayburgh). *Seven Days in May* (1964) depicts a committee hearing involving a confrontation with the chairman of the Joint Chiefs of Staff. In *Protocol* (1984), a congressional hearing enables the heroine (Goldie Hawn) to root out corruption and deliver a patriotic speech.

More often than not the hearings are unrealistic, the senators portrayed negatively. *The Happy Hooker Goes to Washington* (1977) revolves around the title character's testimony upstaging the hypocritically prudish member of a Senate committee investigating the supposed danger and damage of sex to America. The Senate investigating committee in *The Godfather, Part II* (1974), containing one member beholden to the godfather and its counsel controlled by a mob boss, is shown as ineffectual against organized crime.

House Committee on Un-American Activities

During the late 1940s and early 1950s, the HCUA investigated alleged Communist activities in Hollywood. Individuals who refused to testify before or to cooperate with the committee, or who were named as Communists, usually lost their jobs and were blacklisted, thus rendered unemployable under their own names in the movie industry.

The committee soon began appearing in feature films. Praise came first, as in the inadvertently hilarious *Big Jim McClain (1952),* starring John Wayne, which opens with a simulated hearing of the committee, replete with some actual members.

Allegorical treatments followed. In *On the Waterfront* (1954), a movie directed and written by men who had cooperated with the committee, the protagonist chooses to testify before a state investigative committee concerning corrupt union activities (implicitly equated with naming names before the HCUA). Above all for superb acting, most notably by Marlon Brando and Rod Steiger, and Boris Kaufman's cinematography (in glorious black and white), this is an outstanding American movie despite its problematic theme.

Similarly allegorical, and almost as compelling, is *High Noon* (1952), starring Gary Cooper as a sheriff who ends up essentially alone, having to defend a western town against the villains (the committee).

Movies later took on the HCUA more directly. Charlie Chaplin literally hoses down its members in *A King in New York* (1957). *The Way We Were* (1973) condemns the committee's methods and effects, but less so than originally intended by its screenwriter, Arthur Laurents. Deleted at the last moment was a scene in which the character played by Robert Redford tells his wife, played by Barbra Streisand: "The studio says I have a subversive wife and they'll fire me unless you inform." She replies, "We get a divorce. Then you don't have a subversive wife."[3] An emphasis on romance at the expense of civil liberties and politics no doubt contributed to the film's enormous commercial success.

Next came *The Front* (1976) starring Woody Allen as a front man who submits the work of blacklisted writers in his own name and shares the proceeds. Its director, writer, and several cast members had been blacklisted. The film's point of view is best expressed by Allen's character, who when called to name names states that he does not recognize the committee's right to "ask those kinds of questions and furthermore you can all go fuck yourselves."

In *Guilty by Suspicion* (1991), the main character played by Robert DeNiro, has his directing career ruined by false rumors that he is a Communist. Given the opportunity to save himself by testifying about others, he too preserves his integrity by defying the committee.

MEMBERS OUTSIDE THE INSTITUTION

Members of Congress occasionally appear outside the institution other than as candidates for office. Some portrayals are favorable, others negative. An Iowa congresswoman is humanized while in Berlin to investigate corrupting moral influences on American occupation troops in Billy Wilder's droll *A Foreign Affair* (1948). In *Fail Safe* (1964), an apocalyptic military drama, a congressman in the central military control center presciently voices his concern about the dangers of U.S. nuclear policy. Two senators, one honest and the other corrupt, appear in *State of the Union* (1948). In *Seven Days in May* (1964), one senator participates in an attempted military coup, another helps rescue the country. In *Tucker* (1988), Francis Ford Coppola's film about the man who in 1948 challenged the Detroit automakers by producing his own innovative car, a Michigan senator causes Tucker's plant to be taken away from him.

Sometimes plots and portrayals go to extremes. In the sexploitation film known as *Party Girls for the Candidate* (1964), senators are involved with women of dubious reputation; in *Wild in the Streets* (1968), they consume hallucinogenic drugs.

CONCLUSION

Depictions of Congress and its members from the 1930s through the early 1950s were relatively benign (*Washington Merry-Go-Round, The Farmer's Daughter*, and *Washington Story*). Even *Mr. Smith Goes to Washington* is ambiguous. The 1960s brought cynicism (*The Best Man, A Fever in the Blood, The Manchurian Candidate*). The movies of the 1970s depicted character, election campaigns, and legislative processes with greater complexity and a more critical eye (*The Candidate, Power, The Seduction of Joe Tynan*). After that, Congress was virtually absent from, and congressional characters peripheral to, American movies. Members who do appear usually come off badly as in *The Godfather Part II* and *Tucker.* Meanwhile, portrayals of the House Committee on Un-American Activities have gone from attempts to curry favor to condemnation, the latter culminating with *Guilty by Suspicion.*

Congress as seen on the screen is not a pleasant place, especially in recent times. Its processes are misrepresented and overdramatized, its members portrayed as egocentric and expedient. Films of the late 1990s, such as *Striptease* and *The Birdcage,* each featuring a hypocritical and corrupt senator, perpetuate the negative images. Overall, Hollywood's depiction of Congress has occasional valid elements, but is mostly wildly exaggerated. Almost entirely missing is the institution's positive and workaday side.

Notes

1. Cited by George Axelrod in Tom Milne, "The Difference of George Axelrod," *Sight and Sound* 37:4 (Autumn 1968): 165.

2. This discussion comes from "Movies on Congress" by David L. Paletz and Daniel Lipinski. Reprinted with permission of Macmillan Library Reference USA, a Division of Simon & Schuster Inc., from *The Encyclopedia of the United States Congress,* edited by Donald C. Bacon, Roger H. Davidson, and Morton Keller, Vol. 3, pp. 1420–1426. Copyright © 1995 by The Fund for the Study of Congress.

3. Pat McGilligan, *Backstory 2* (Berkeley: University of California Press, 1991), 152.

Photo Credits

◆ ◆ ◆

369

Index

◆ ◆ ◆

Note: Pages referring to authors in endnotes are followed by an "n," and are listed twice: the page on which the note is called out and the page on which the text of the endnote appears.